WOMEN
and
PUBLIC POLICY IN IRELAND

WOMEN
and
PUBLIC POLICY IN IRELAND

A Documentary History 1922–1997

Richard B. Finnegan
and
James L. Wiles

Stonehill College, Massachusetts

IRISH ACADEMIC PRESS
DUBLIN • PORTLAND, OR

First published in 2005 by
IRISH ACADEMIC PRESS
44, Northumberland Road, Dublin 4, Ireland

and in the United States of America by
IRISH ACADEMIC PRESS
c/o ISBS, 5824 N.E. Hassalo Street,
Portland Oregon 97213-3644

Website: www.iap.ie

© Richard B. Finnegan and James L. Wiles 2005

British Library Cataloguing in Publication Data
A catalogue entry for this title is available on application

ISBN 0-7165-2778-2

Library of Congress Cataloging-in-Publication Data
A catalogue entry for this title is available on application

Typeset by FiSH Books, London
Printed by CPI Bath

Contents

Preface

WE ARE GRATEFUL for the help we have received in putting together this documentary history. The initial scanning and preparation were done by Donna Benoit, who also worked to bring the manuscript into its final form. This is not the first time that we have relied on Donna Benoit's invaluable assistance. The Academic Vice President of Stonehill College, Katie Conboy, provided support for the research and the preparation of the manuscript, and we are grateful for her assistance. We also want to thank Francis X. Dillon, Vice President for Advancement at Stonehill College, for additional institutional support. Finally, our thanks go to the Irish Academic Press for its efforts in bringing the idea to fruition.

Richard Finnegan would also like to thank the Women's Studies Program at Harvard University for welcoming him as a Visiting Scholar in 1995–96. The preliminary work on public policy with respect to women was undertaken on that sabbatical leave. The research contributed, not only to this book, but also to papers on women's rights given in 1996 and 2001, and to the chapter 'Veneration versus Rights: the Role of Irish Women' in Richard B. Finnegan and Edward McCarron, *Ireland: Historical Echoes, Contemporary Politics*, (Boulder, CO: Westview Press, 2000).

We also want to thank the Office of Public Works in Dublin for giving permission to use the materials from the official publications of the Stationery Office that form the core of this book.

This volume represents the results of another in a series of collaborative projects, which began when we created the Archive of Irish Government Official Publications at Stonehill College. This Archive is the only comprehensive collection of Irish official publications, from 1922 to the present, in the United States. The initial collection of these materials was facilitated by the cooperation and generosity of Donal Nevin, of the Irish Congress of Trade Unions, and Tony Eklof, Documents Librarian at University

College, Dublin. An earlier work, *Aspirations and Realities: A Documentary History of Economic Development Policy in Ireland Since 1922* (Westport, CT: Greenwood Press, 1993), and a reference book, *Irish Government Publications 1972–1992* (Dublin: Irish Academic Press, 1995), were both based on this collection. In addition, a comprehensive reference book on Irish official publications from 1922 to 2002 will be published by the Irish Academic Press later in 2005.

Introduction

WHEN, IN 1972, the Commission on the Status of Women in Ireland issued its *Report to Minister for Finance*, it ushered in a new era of social policy in the Republic of Ireland. The report not only articulated an agenda for the equal treatment of women, but also triggered increasing political activism among women in Ireland. Not since the women's suffragist movement in the early twentieth century had a demand for women's rights emerged in such a self-conscious and coherent way. Over the period from the report's appearance up to the end of the century, pressure from the women's movement emerged from all points of the ideological spectrum and made an impact on all points of the policy spectrum. The policy directives of the European Community (which became the European Union in 1993) also facilitated the demand for equality after 1973, as did the modernisation of the economy after 1960 and the revolution in education after 1965.

These combined pressures confronted a culture, a church and a political system that held traditional views on the role of women. From the founding of the Irish Free State in 1922, legislation had included restrictions on the freedom of women in respect of reproductive rights, marriage, family law, employment and welfare. These policies were supported by the permeation of society by sexist attitudes and paternal religious authority, grounded in a particular image of women and a paternal view of society. The values embodied in the Constitution and laws of Ireland created a tension between the ideal of a liberal state, with an emphasis on individual rights and liberties, and the ideal of a Catholic state, with a cohesive community vision and church doctrine woven into the fabric of the Constitution. Politically, women were denied equal treatment in terms of rights, yet culturally they were venerated as the centre of the family and symbolised by the figure of Mary the Mother of God. They were excluded from any significant roles in business, religion or politics, and were to be sheltered from the hard edges of the world, yet idealised as the dominant figures in the home, and the primary repositories of the enduring religious and social values that were said to bind Irish society together. This paradoxical juxtaposition was based on the mixture in Irish society of the values of the Catholic Church and traditional agrarian culture. The church influenced legislation that reinforced the cultural role that women held in a traditional rural society.

When the question of women's rights emerged onto the political agenda, the issues of birth control, divorce and abortion flared into bitter political contests. However, the demand for equal treatment of women was not confined to such highly conflictual constitutional issues. Women's issues eventually engaged virtually every aspect of Irish public policy, from the behaviour of the police (the Gardai) in rape cases to the content of school textbooks, from workplace discrimination to hospital treatment, from the bedroom to the prison cell. The agenda of women's rights in fact mirrored the extensive agenda of individual rights being developed in what was becoming a modern, pluralistic society. Thus the quest for the equal treatment of women was, and remains, a critical pressure in modernising Ireland. Modernising is understood here as emphasising the equality of individuals and their attainment of the latitude to make choices about their lives, in particular by exercising the right to participate in decisions that affect them.

The report of the Commission on the Status of Women serves as a marker for women's rights in Ireland for, like Janus, it looked both backward and forward. The document looked backward in that it charted the laws and conditions that had affected women since the creation of the Free State. In each of the major policy areas, the report portrayed women as holders of a secondary status in which they were kept by law, by established practice, by custom and by regulation. The report was also forward-looking, in that it set a primary agenda for the equal treatment of women through its recommendations for ending the exclusion or marginalisation of women. The report set the agenda on equal pay, equality of treatment in employment, equality of treatment in social welfare policy and equality under the law. Other issues, such as those relating to education and political participation, were also covered but were not given the same weight. Thus the major agenda of the report focused on issues that fell within the realm of fairness or equality in a liberal state. While firm in its clarity on the secondary status of women, the report was hardly an expression of militant feminism.

The intention of this book is to identify the cases, laws, regulations and practices that pertained to women on a wide variety of public policy issues. The report of 1972 is the point of departure, as it provided a review of the situation of women from 1922 to 1972. We examine the recommendations of the original report and of subsequent government reports in particular domains, such as childcare or health. We also return to the overall agenda on the status of women when looking at the report of the Second Commission on the Status of Women, issued in 1993. In subsequent chapters we deal with the more elusive forms of discrimination that are a function of values, habits and practices. We map the status of women in the law before 1972 and the changes in their status as a result of the changes since 1972. We rely specifically on major government reports as barometers of the specific policy changes and evolving recommendations. These reports provide a sequential picture of the agenda of women's issues as represented by the collective effort of the commissions and agencies considering these issues.

The policy issues for women over the 75 years covered by this book are myriad. Unlike, say, economic development, which lends itself to a comparison of various government strategies to foster growth, changes in the status of women fall into a wide range of categories, from workplace practices to issues of constitutional law. We follow the agenda set down by the report of 1972 and begin in Chapter 1 with the issue of equal pay. Chapter 2 follows the report with a discussion of equal treatment in the workplace; Chapter 3 considers social welfare; and Chapter 4 deals with the legal status of married women with respect to property and money. Chapter 5 looks at the contentious constitutional issues of birth control, divorce and abortion. We turn in Chapter 6 to the issue of violence toward women, specifically rape and domestic violence. The remaining three chapters review education, health and political participation.

The pattern of the changes in public policy toward women breaks down into three broad stages. The first encompasses the period from 1922 until 1972, when women were excluded from the corridors of money and power, and restricted in the domains of employment, finance and marriage. The quest for, and achievement of, formal equal treatment for women under the law mark the second period, from 1972 until 1985. The policies at issue then were those concerning differential treatment on pay, jobs, pension, taxes and related topics. The third period, from 1985 until 1997, saw attempts to address the more difficult and more deeply imbedded restrictions on the equitable treatment of women, and the absence of opportunities in realms such as in education and health. The 1972 report is central to charting the period of exclusion, serving, so to speak, as a virtual indictment of practice in the early years of the state. The report, with its recommendations for change, was also a symbol of the period of the 'equality contract', as the state adopted its recommendations for change. However, the report gave way to other policy documents by the mid-1980s, as pressure from the women's movement and women's groups, from bureaucrats within the state, and from European Union directives changed and expanded the women's rights agenda. The publication of the report of the Second Commission on the Status of Women in 1993 reflected a much expanded agenda of women's concerns. Although the 1993 report does not ignore the issues of work and welfare, it ranges far and wide over such issues as the treatment of women prisoners, the provision of legal advice to rape victims and the manner in which the Gardai should treat children in domestic abuse cases.

Each chapter of this book is organised chronologically through the display of policy from 1922 to 1997, the first 75 years of the existence of the state. At the same time the book moves from the establishment of formal equality, covered in the earlier chapters, to the equity agenda of the past decade and a half. The closing chapters consider both the policies and practices that still restrict women's opportunities, and recommendations for changes in behaviour and attitudes to encourage women's achievements.

The period in which changes occurred in public policy pertaining to women was also a period in which Ireland was undergoing significant changes in other aspects of life. The Republic of Ireland entered the European Community in 1973 and European law began to bear increasingly on Irish policy, including regulations on the equal treatment of women. Since 1960 the economy had been expanding, leading to a significant rise in standards of living. Increased economic growth meant increased economic opportunities for women. In addition, the prevalence of television after 1960 brought about greater exposure to the wider world of secular values and culture. The transformation in the Irish education system after 1965 also brought about wider opportunities for women in their choice of career. These changes operated in a synergistic way and the women's movement was fuelled by changes in other facets of Irish life.[1] Simultaneously and reciprocally the whole of Irish social life was affected by political demands for changes in the treatment of women.[2] This book will make reference to such interactions, but its coverage is confined predominantly to the official documents that record progress on policies with respect to women over the first seventy-five years of the existence of the Irish state.

CHAPTER ONE

Women's pay and employment: practice and problems

HISTORICAL BACKGROUND

THE FIVE DECADES reviewed in the report of the first Commission on the Status of Women in Ireland (1972) constituted a period of great stress on the Irish state. Established under a treaty with the United Kingdom, signed in 1921, and a constitution written in 1922, the new Free State was born in violence. Those in the independence movement, Sinn Féin, who opposed the adoption of the Anglo-Irish Treaty, came into confrontation with their comrades who had accepted the treaty's provisions on the partition of the island, the payment of annuities to Britain, the use of Irish ports by the British Navy and the taking of an oath to the Crown by officeholders in the new state. The Civil War that followed was short but violent. The section of Sinn Féin that accepted the treaty, now called Cumann na nGaedheal, was attempting to establish order, restore the damage from the war with Britain and guide the economic, educational, health, transport and agricultural systems under conditions of both contested independence and continuing violence. The agenda was full and the governing party was not going to stray too far from the values that had guided the independence movement and the wider society up to that point. The political culture, that constellation of values undergirding the political system, drew from the traditional society and from the values of the Catholic Church. Neither was at all progressive when it came to the role of women. The Catholic Church of the early twentieth century in Ireland was largely the product of Paul, Cardinal Cullen, who, in the middle of the nineteenth century, had shaped the church in an ultramontane, hierarchical and Jansenist mould. The church was marked by ritual, dogmatic fidelity and a view that the state was to embody the values and doctrines of the church, as befitting a Catholic society. Within a decade the church's positions on divorce, contraception, censorship and education had been codified in law.

Cumann na nGaedheal was grappling with the problems of creating and managing a new state in which a segment of the public was still not committed to the legitimacy of that state. The issue of the partition of Ireland was resolved by the acceptance of the border specified in a further treaty in 1926. The section of Sinn Féin under Eamon de Valera, which had not accepted the treaty of 1921, split again: de Valera created a new party, Fianna Faíl, and entered the political process of the Free State that he had previously considered illegitimate. By 1932 Fianna Faíl was the majority party and held power.

In the decade after the founding of the state the dream of economic prosperity that had been promised with the end of British rule did not materialise. The state struggled with the tasks of balanced budgets and public spending while relying on agriculture as the engine of growth. The global depression after 1929 had not helped Ireland's underdeveloped and fragile economy. When de Valera took power he set out to come as close as he could to undoing the treaty of 1921. The first step was the cessation of the promised annuity payments to Britain. London retaliated by imposing a trade embargo on Ireland, which was reciprocated by Dublin. The resulting 'Economic War', which lasted until 1938, was no contest and drained Ireland's already poor economy. The protectionist policy adopted by de Valera in the 1930s was designed to foster the development of Irish industry and create the kind of rural, agricultural society that was idealised in his and other romantic versions of Irish nationalism.

De Valera eliminated the oath to the Crown, the Governor General, appeals to the Judicial Committee of the Privy Council and the payment of annuities from the Constitution of 1922, but he wished to go further, and sought to have a constitution that blended liberalism, Catholic social thought and Catholic doctrines. Adopted in 1937, the new Constitution specifically noted the special place of the Catholic Church, constitutionally forbade divorce and, in 'The Directive Principles of Social Policy', established the central place of women in the family, and of the family in the Irish state and society.

The outbreak of the Second World War in Europe in 1939 brought Britain into conflict with Germany, and Ireland was placed in the position of having to become an ally of its former colonial master if it joined the coalition against Germany. Not being ready to accept that degree of attachment to Britain while the partition of Ireland was still in place, de Valera chose neutrality. This fostered greater separation between the two parts of Ireland, as the North was a crucial staging area for the Battle of the Atlantic and Ulstermen served in Britain's armed forces. After the war Ireland was unwilling to join the North Atlantic Treaty Organisation and began to elevate neutrality to a principle of foreign policy. The grave nature of these decisions did little to bring the status of women onto the political agenda in southern Ireland, while in the United States and Britain women served in critical roles in factories and in government.

After the war, despite a brief surge in economic growth, Ireland's economy stagnated and a new wave of emigration began, lasting throughout the 1950s. The dream that had inspired the independence movement before 1922 appeared to be hollow, as Ireland was emptying of people, had a stagnant agricultural economy and had an encapsulated, inert culture. Some Irish leaders recognised that Ireland had to move beyond the policies that had prevailed since 1922.

Nineteen sixty was a pivotal year in the modern history of Ireland, as a series of incentive-based economic plans were adopted by the Irish government from that year until 1973, triggering a run of steady economic growth. The growth was a product of government spending on industrial development, the abandonment of protectionism and encouragement of foreign investment. At the same time increasing income provided more opportunities for the Irish people. Television was introduced to Ireland. The increase in communication was also accompanied by educational reforms, begun in 1965, which increased significantly the number of students completing secondary education and the number going on to tertiary (higher and further) education. The full impact of these reforms was felt over the next twenty years and contributed to both economic growth and the rebirth of a women's movement in Ireland. The preparations to enter the European Community in 1973 put new issues on the Irish political agenda, such as equal pay for women, which were dealt with by the 1972 report on the status of women.

The years from 1922 to 1972 revealed the degree to which the prevailing political culture and the church's values, the absence of political consensus in the Civil War period, the economic depression and protectionism of the 1930s, the neutrality of the war years and the emigration drain of the 1950s were hardly conducive to a change in the status of women. Women's organisations in this period, such as the Irish Countrywomen's Association and the Irish

Housewives Association, were operating at the margins of women's rights. It must be said that there were some women with powerful roles, mainly because of the central role of the church in running institutions in Irish life: nuns ran schools, hospitals and orphanages. Yet they were, in a sense, invisible, embedded as they were in the church's structures, and their self-consciousness as models for women was in the realm of vocation and obedience rather than leadership.

EQUAL PAY

The report of the first Commission on the Status of Women in Ireland (1972) outlines the status of women in the Irish economy. Although the emphasis is on pay, a considerable range of employment data is first presented to outline the gender structure of the Irish labour market the in mid-1960s. Irish women then made up about 25 per cent of the labour force. Their participation rate was low by international standards, more than half of women in employment were under 30 years of age, most were unmarried and most held jobs in relatively low-paying occupations. Women were 'very poorly represented' among administrative, executive and managerial workers.

Statistical sources did not furnish the Commission with comprehensive data on wage and salary rates for men and women. Nonetheless, in the early 1970s quarterly data for the industrial sector, as well as data from parts of the 'distributive trades', services and the public sector indicated that substantial pay differentials existed. In March 1972 women industrial workers had hourly earnings that averaged about 57 per cent of men's earnings. In September 1970 90 per cent of women industrial workers earned less than IR£16 a week, while 90 per cent of men earned more than that amount. The Commission noted that 'there has, in recent years, been an improvement in women's earnings as a percentage of men's' in industries employing 500 or more women. In the distributive trades and in the civil service women's earnings were about 75–85 per cent of men's wages.

The Commission then turned to the 'causes of unequal pay'. Some pay differences clearly reflected the fact that 'the employment of women tends to be confined to a comparatively narrow range of occupations with, on the whole, lower levels of skill and responsibility'. However, wages and earnings differed even in those instances where women 'are engaged on work which is the same or similar to that being performed by men'. Such differentials were not attributable to employment opportunities or promotion policies. In an interesting passage the Commission examines some half-dozen alternative explanations.

Commission on the Status of Women, *Report to Minister for Finance* (1972)

Causes of unequal pay

47. Women's earnings are, on average, considerably lower than the earnings of men. This situation is due in part to the fact that in Ireland, as in other countries, the employment of women tends to be confined to a comparatively narrow range of occupations with, on the whole, lower levels of skill and responsibility. Granted, however, that equality of opportunity for women in relation to training and promotion and access to certain employments is a very significant element in determining their earning power relative to men, it is nevertheless true that there are other factors which operate to depress women's wages and earnings even where they are engaged on work which is the same or similar to that being performed by men.

48. Among the more common explanations advanced for the payment of unequal pay to women who are performing the same or similar work as men are that:

(i)   women's rates of pay are the result of tradition and social attitudes;

(ii)   women workers are generally younger and consequently less experienced than men;

(iii) the employment of women involves a greater cost for the employer due to higher turnover and absentee rates;

(iv)   legal restrictions on women's employment render them less useful to the employer;

(v)   women are unable to carry out the heavier tasks due to their lesser physical strength; and

(vi)   the position of women in trade union organisation leaves them open to exploitation.

We deal with each of these points below.

TRADITION AND SOCIAL ATTITUDES

49. The circumstances existing at a particular period of time may give rise to the establishment of certain categories of employment in which

it is considered proper that women should be employed and to certain patterns of pay for them. The patterns thus established often outlive the influences which gave rise to them and in the normal course alter only gradually. At a time when it was not so common for women to enter industrial employment as it is now, social attitudes determined certain types of work which it was considered proper that women should undertake and sanctioned the view that even where their work overlapped that of men it was somehow worth less than men's work and that women ought accordingly to be paid less than men. After a time it became customary to pay women less than men and such a situation can continue indefinitely unless a great effort is made to end it and to enforce a right to equal pay.

It is undoubtedly true that a major factor affecting the comparison between men's and women's rates, both at present and in the past, is the attitude that men should be paid more than women because they generally have a family to support. It is often argued that a man's wage is regarded not as being the appropriate rate for the job but as being a 'family wage'. Children's allowances and allowances against income tax are not generally regarded as being adequate to meet the additional expenditure involved in supporting a family. The counter-arguments put forward by those who support equal pay are that many women are not free of financial responsibility for dependants, in particular, widows and deserted wives and single women with aged or infirm parents. In addition, it is argued that women are being asked to subsidise, in a completely unfair way, what should be direct State payments to persons with dependants and that this burden should be spread evenly and fairly over the whole community without regard to sex.

AGE-GROUPING OF WOMEN IN EMPLOYMENT

50. Many women spend their whole adult lives in employment but the majority do not. Even if a woman does continue in employment after marriage she will generally have to leave at some later stage to care for children. This results in a situation where the overall labour force at any time contains a high proportion of women in the younger age groups and with relatively short experience of their jobs as compared with men. Details of the age groups of women in the labour force, as returned in the 1966 Census of Population are given in Table 2 on page 22 [not shown]. Those figures show that in 1966 over 45% of women workers were under 25 years of age. The comparable figure for men was 21%. One would expect this

situation to be reflected in the relative average pay of men and women, even if only to the extent that women would not qualify for service pay to the same extent as men.

ALLEGED HIGHER 'COST' OF THE EMPLOYMENT OF WOMEN

51. Differences in rates of pay between men and women are sometimes defended on the grounds that the employment of women gives rise, for various reasons, to a higher 'cost' to the employer than the employment of men does. Among the factors alleged in this context are that women have higher absenteeism rates and a more rapid turnover.

ABSENTEEISM AND TURNOVER RATES

There is no published study on the question of absenteeism or turnover rates among women workers in Ireland. An investigation of absenteeism and labour turnover in Irish industry is at present being carried out by the Institute of Public Administration under the auspices of the Human Sciences Committee of the Irish National Productivity Committee but no report is available yet. An attempt was made in the survey referred to in paragraph 9 of this report to obtain information from the firms in the survey on absentee patterns among men and women but the information returned by the firms that replied to the questionnaire was incomplete and frequently not comparable. Some firms mentioned absenteeism among women as a disadvantage of equal pay but the number was very small – one out of ten in the Food industry, one out of twenty in Clothing, Hosiery and Shoes, two out of fifteen in Textiles and one out of four in Paper, Printing, etc. In reference to absentee rates among women, a recent report published on the status of women in Canada[1] states that while most studies indicate that women are absent from work more often than men the difference in absentee rates is so small as to be relatively insignificant – women being reported absent, on average, two days more than men in a year. An interview survey of women[2] between the ages of 16 and 64 in a sample of 10,000 carried out by the Government Social Survey on behalf of the British Ministry of Labour, in 1965, in which respondents were asked whether, apart from public and national holidays, annual holidays and any periods of illness, there were any times when they did not work, found that the great majority of gainfully occupied women worked continuously. Over 86% said they worked at all times and even among those responsible for children, where the percentage working continuously was lowest, it amounted to 78.6%.

52. In the survey referred to in paragraph 13 [not included] we attempted to get a general picture of absentee rates among women in the organisations seen but only about half of the firms interviewed were able to provide information on this matter. Some of the remaining firms indicated that they had just recently begun to examine the problem and that as yet they had not any conclusive data available. Where information was available the methods of calculating absentee rates varied considerably. Some companies had obtained frequencies and percentages to describe the situation for the total enterprise or to compare the behaviour of men and women, but the typical picture presented was a qualitative, descriptive account of the absentee pattern, using 'high', 'low', 'no problem' or 'no difference' categories. Critical factors identified as affecting absentee rates were sex of the worker, the nature of the work, age and marital status. About one quarter of the companies that supplied information on this subject said they had compared the absence behaviour of men and women and that they had experienced higher rates for women than for men. The remainder found no significant difference and in a few cases it was higher for men than for women. Managers of some companies isolated the repetitive nature of the work as the primary factor associated with absenteeism and since many women are engaged on unskilled highly repetitive work this may account for an overall higher level of absence. In some cases the age of the worker was seen to be closely correlated with absentee rates, the younger workers, male and female, tending to have higher rates than the middle age group. One company which experienced a drop in the absentee rate attributed this change to raising the entry age. With regard to married women, a mixed picture emerged. Two companies who stated that absenteeism is higher for married women, had only employed married women on a part-time basis. The Women's Advisory Committee of the Irish Congress of Trade Unions stated that they had no reason to believe that married women were any less stable than single women. On the whole, the information obtained in the survey did not support the belief that absenteeism is primarily a female problem. On the contrary, other factors, such as nature of work, age and marital status, were mentioned as critical variables. Accordingly, statements concerning absenteeism can only be meaningfully understood and acted upon if comparisons of men and women are derived from groups engaged in similar tasks, and account is taken of the other factors mentioned. It is only when

organisations view the problem as being affected by a number of variables that adequate solutions can be explored, and reliable conclusions drawn concerning male/female differences.

A question concerning turnover rates (number who left the employment in a year as a percentage of the number employed) included in the Commission's survey on the cost of equal pay in the private sector indicated that the turnover rate for women was, on the whole, considerably higher than for men. In one industry however – the Textile Industry – the turnover rate for single women was lower than that for single men. The replies also revealed that the turnover rate for single men was consistently higher than for married men. Age and the nature of the work appear to be factors affecting absentee and turnover rates among both sexes and a detailed study would probably show a tendency towards increased incidence for both men and women in the younger age groups and in less responsible jobs.

Information obtained in the survey referred to in paragraph 13 [not included] tends to support this view. As in the case of absenteeism, labour turnover data was supplied by about half of the companies interviewed with most informants providing non-specific and descriptive information and some supplying more precise information in the form of percentages. Approximately one-quarter of the firms that did give information on turnover rates said that labour wastage was higher for women than for men. The true causes of leaving are, however, often complicated and may be obscure even to the leaver, as well as to management. The factors most frequently mentioned were marriage and the nature of the work. The common pattern, especially in the case of clerical workers, is for women to leave work on marriage. For some this may be voluntary but many girls have no choice and are forced to leave the organisation on marriage. Consequently, firms who stated that turnover was very high for women compared with men are, of course, creating such a situation by imposing a marriage bar. There was substantial agreement among some informants that labour turnover for female workers is strongly associated with job monotony and lack of stimulation at work and that women tend to leave undemanding jobs and seek more interesting and varied work elsewhere. Some companies stated that the labour turnover for married women is higher than that of single women. The question of labour turnover of married women at work cannot, however, be isolated from the type of work and the nature of the work contract of the married female employee, e.g. whether part-time or full-time, temporary or permanent. The type of work made available to them is, in general, part-time, low-skilled and frequently held on an insecure basis. All these factors are precisely the ones which tend to lead in any case, whether the employee is single or married, male or female, to a higher than average turnover rate. The limited career prospects available to women were also mentioned as an important factor affecting turnover. Barriers to promotion for women are numerous, and consequently one would expect such blocks to work backwards and to generate dissatisfaction among women. Organisations tend to ignore this and hence women have only the choice to leave the employment, or to remain on as dissatisfied workers. Companies where the turnover of women was described as 'low' offered a variety of explanations for this including better than average working conditions and wages, introduction of age-related scales and shortage of female employment in the locality. In general, the work-life pattern of women – with many working for a few years after finishing school and then leaving the labour force for marriage and child-rearing – does increase the labour turnover rate for women. Obviously, changes in company rules with regard to employment after marriage and the provision of maternity leave would be a major factor in reducing labour turnover among women. Women leave jobs for reasons other than marriage, for example for other work which is better paid, for improved working conditions, for a more convenient locale and so on; but these considerations also influence turnover rates among men and we have not obtained any evidence to prove that their effect on turnover rates for men is any less than for women.

In any event, whether there is or is not a significant difference between men and women in relation to absentee and turnover rates, it does appear that a blanket differential in their rates of pay could hardly be regarded as an efficient or fair method to take account of it. Different patterns of absenteeism and turnover among male workers are not reflected in their pay rates. It seems to us that absenteeism and labour turnover, whether among men or women, is a personnel problem to which specific remedies may be applied. These remedies should, however, apply equally to men and women.

LEGAL RESTRICTIONS ON WOMEN'S EMPLOYMENT

53. These provisions are of some importance where work is organised on a continuous shift basis as it may limit the extent to which women may be employed interchangeably with men and

thus decrease the value of their services to an employer or entirely restrict their entry to certain occupations. In addition, as the rate of pay for shift work and night work is generally substantially higher than the ordinary basic rate, the restrictions operate to reduce women's average earnings as compared to those of men. Legal restrictions on women's employment are considered in greater detail in Chapter 4.

PHYSICAL STRENGTH

54. The lesser physical strength of women has, in the past, excluded them completely from many types of heavy industry and has, as a consequence, increased the supply of women's labour relative to the demand for it in other kinds of employment. In addition, it may happen that where men and women are employed on work of a similar nature, men receive a higher rate because they are required to perform any heavy tasks which may arise from time to time. Improvements in mechanical handling procedures have tended to diminish the importance of physical strength as a requisite for certain jobs and will most likely continue to do so.

TRADE UNION ORGANISATION

55. The relative weakness of trade union organisation among women as compared to men is also sometimes named as a contributory cause of women's lower earning power. In relation to trade union membership and trade union activity among women, the Irish Congress of Trade Unions has informed us in its written submission that a survey carried out by the research service of the Congress during the course of 1970 indicated that there were about 100,000 women trade unionists in the Twenty-six county area, representing over one-fourth of all trade unionists. The Congress stated also that while there was no information available about the extent of women's participation in trade union activity, there were strong reasons for believing that their participation was even less than among men. A recent survey had identified only seven women full-time officials who were engaged in negotiating wages and conditions of employment for members, out of a total of 230 such officials. Out of approximately 229,000 women employees at work in 1966, an estimated 90,000 – about two out of every five – were then members of trade unions. Even excluding private domestic service the proportion was still considerably less than one-half. The proportion of male employees in trade unions is about two-thirds. We have no doubt that the growth and maintenance of the present

earnings differential between the sexes is assisted by the relative weakness of trade union organisation among women and, more importantly, their much lesser involvement in trade union activity than men.

56. The Commission attempted, in the survey referred to in paragraph 13 [not included], to get a general picture of the extent of women's involvement in trade union matters and the implications that this has for the whole question of equality of opportunity for women in employment. In general, the companies taking part in the survey stated that their female employees were members of trade unions but variations did, however, emerge across different categories of workers. Industrial and factory female workers were strongly unionised as also were technical staff. Union membership among clerical workers did not appear to be so widespread in the private sector organisations and not infrequently the situation obtained that factory workers in a company were unionised while the office staff were not. In the semi-State organisations the majority of clerical staff are in membership of a trade union or staff association. There was strong agreement among management that active participation by women in trade union matters appeared to be extremely low. Even in the companies where women workers constituted a majority, trade union affairs still fell mainly to the male employees even though all the women workers, or a substantial number of them, were members of the union. The overall picture which emerged was that female shop stewards were comparatively few and that the involvement of women in any negotiations was minimal. In two organisations employing a large number of clerical workers where women constituted approximately 50% of the work force and would have had the same educational experience as their male colleagues, the female/male ratio in negotiation teams were one out of eight and one out of five respectively. The participation and representation in union activities of women in factory work appeared to be even less than that of women in the clerical field. There were, however, exceptions to the foregoing pattern; pockets of active women were located across some of the larger organisations. Frequently, however, this involvement expressed itself not in terms of female shop-stewards filtering grievances but rather acting as strong members of union or association committees and of works councils.

We were not able to isolate any predominant reason for the general low level of participation of women in union affairs. Management do not appear to have given much thought to the subject and the common response is that women are perceived as not being interested in trade union affairs or that women regard industrial bargaining as a male preserve and that a girl would have to be very dedicated to enter it. We discussed this matter with representatives of the Women's Advisory Committee (WAC) of the Irish Congress of Trade Unions who agreed that many women are reluctant to come forward to act as shop stewards or members of deputations. This situation was in turn reflected in the limited number of women who attended courses for trade union officials and their low attendance as delegates at annual conferences. They noted that a major barrier to the participation of women in trade unions is the attitude of many male trade unionists and they felt that if women are to build up confidence to seek opportunities in the work environment, the attitudes of men would have to undergo radical changes, in the direction of becoming more receptive and supportive of women's needs and demands. The WAC were of the opinion that the awareness and interest of women in trade union matters could be greatly increased if the schools civics courses included information about trade unions and thus prepared the ground for constructive membership later as workers. They felt that day release with pay, for educational purposes, should be made more readily available to women workers. While many employers were helpful about day release it was their experience that employers were reluctant to grant it in the areas where it was most needed. The Committee were considering trying to organise training in future for potential as well as existing women shop stewards to try to overcome some of the diffidence which exists among women concerning their abilities in this kind of work.

The Unions were perceived by the individual women workers interviewed in the survey as being male preserves and, apart from a few respondents, informants described themselves as non-active in Union affairs. A general feeling appeared to prevail that the Unions are not very concerned about women and, in particular, it was felt that Unions do not press for the same financial remuneration for women workers as they do for men. There was general agreement among those in membership of Unions that the Unions failed to communicate with them and that the Union did not focus very much on women. Informants mentioned that women were apathetic about getting involved in Union affairs because they lacked information to stimulate interest.

57. In general, it does seem that Unions do seek changes which benefit women workers, where the women themselves are actively

involved in Union matters and press their Unions to achieve the demands. It is clear, however, that trade unions must re-examine the role of women in their own organisations and face up to the challenge of adapting themselves to facilitate constructive participation by their women members. At present it appears that trade unions may be merely duplicating conditions of lack of opportunity for their female members which are similar to those experienced by women in their work situations.

Attitudes to equal pay
58. In considering the question of attitudes to equal pay we have had regard to the views expressed in the written and oral submissions made to us, to references to the subject in published reports and to Ministerial statements of policy in relation to the principle of equal pay. A report published in 1970 by the Economic and Social Research Institute (Paper No. 56 – Views on Pay Increases, Fringe Benefits and Low Pay) which contains certain information on attitudes to equal pay, obtained in a sample survey of over 1,000 adult male employees, is considered at paragraph 63 below. As that survey was confined to men we decided to obtain, on as wide a base as possible, the views of women concerning equal pay. Arrangements were, accordingly, made to include questions on the matter in a survey of the participation of women in the labour force being carried out by the Economic and Social Research Institute for the Department of Labour and the findings are considered in paragraph 64 below. This survey, which covered a sample of 5,054 women, was not, however, comparable to the survey of men referred to above as the women surveyed were not confined to employed women and the sampling procedures differed.

59. All the submissions received by us, both written and oral, referring to equal pay have been in favour of the application of the principle and we have not had any representations opposing it. The terms used to describe equal pay have, however, varied. The most commonly used have been 'equal pay for equal work', and 'equal pay for work of equal value'. Among the larger organisations from which we received submissions, the Irish Congress of Trade Unions recommended the adoption of the principle of equal pay for work of equal value and the Federated Union of Employers recommended that the EEC definition of equal pay be used. (This definition is set out at paragraph 33 [not included]). In relation to the civil service, the Civil Service General Council Staff Panel and the individual civil service organisations from which we received

submissions all supported the abolition of sex-differentiated and marriage-differentiated scales in the public service. It has been pointed out to us by certain of the women's organisations that, in their view, some unions had not in the past been in favour of equal pay but their attitude on the matter had changed as they had found that women were being placed in jobs formerly filled by men because they were a cheap source of labour. It has also been represented to us that an intensive programme of public education should be introduced to help change the attitudes that exist in relation to the remuneration of women.

60. In August, 1966, the three political parties represented in Dáil Éireann agreed that an informal committee should be set up to review the constitutional, legislative and institutional bases of Government. It was agreed between the political parties that participation in the Committee would involve no obligation to support any recommendations which might be made, even if made unanimously, and that members of the Committee, either as individuals or as party representatives, would not be regarded as committed in any way to support such recommendations. In its interim report [*Report of the Committee on the Constitution*], published in 1967, the committee recommended that Article 45 of the Constitution should, in setting out the directive principles of social policy, include a provision establishing the principle of equal pay for men and women for work of equal value.

61. The group appointed by the Minister for Finance in September, 1966, to examine and report on the organisation of the Departments of State at the higher levels referred in its report (the 'Devlin' Report) [*Report of the Public Services Organisation Review Group*, 1966-1969] to the practice of sex-differentiation and marriage-differentiation of pay in the civil service under which, in general, women and single men receive lower rates than married men in the general service and some departmental grades and women receive lower rates than men (married or single) in professional and technical and other departmental grades. They pointed out that, should we enter the EEC, sex-differentiation, at least, would be contrary to the provisions of the Treaty of Rome and they recommended that a full examination of the problems involved should be made in the hope that a solution, possibly on a phased basis, might be found. The Group considered that this could make a useful contribution to the problems of recruitment and retention of staff, particularly in the case of professional and other highly qualified officers.

62. Ministerial statements of Government policy concerning equal pay have been made in the Dáil in response to numerous questions asked over recent years relating to matters such as the Government's intentions in regard to Article 119 of the Treaty of Rome should Ireland accede to the EEC and whether it was intended to ratify the International Labour Organisation Convention No. 100 concerning equal remuneration for men and women workers for work of equal value. The response to such questions has been that the Government's policy in relation to pay and conditions for workers is that they should, as far as possible, be negotiated freely between employers and unions and it has been pointed out that trade unions desiring to obtain equal pay for women workers could do so when pay agreements were being negotiated with employers. In reply to a question put to the Minister for Finance in July, 1969, concerning equal pay for men and women in the State service the Minister said that a recent pay agreement had provided the same minimum increase for men and women in the public service and that, accordingly, a start had been made in applying the principle of equal pay. Ministerial replies to Dáil Questions concerning equal pay asked since the establishment of this Commission have generally stated that the matter would be examined by the Government when the report of the Commission became available. We have already referred, in paragraph 6 [not included], to the statement concerning equal pay made by the Minister for Finance in the 1972 Budget Statement.

63. In 1968 the Economic and Social Research Institute undertook, on behalf of the Minister for Labour, a survey of views on income differentials and income increases to provide material for an assessment of prevailing attitudes to questions of pay and their bearing on the development of an incomes policy. The first report of the enquiry [carried out by Dr Hilde Behrend, Ann Knowles and Jean Davies – members of the staff of the University of Edinburgh – in collaboration with the Economic and Social Research Institute], to which we refer in paragraph 58 above, was published in August, 1970, and contains the findings of the survey about views on pay increases, fringe benefits and lower paid workers of a national sample of 1,084 adult male employees. The report stresses that the views obtained were those of male employees only and that no women were included in the survey. While no direct question concerning the respondents' attitudes to equal pay for the same work or work of equal value was asked, respondents were asked four consecutive questions as to what

they thought would be a fair minimum (basic) wage for married men, single men, married women and single women. The report states that higher figures – taking the medians of the distributions – were given for a married man than for a single man and higher figures for men than for women. The great majority of respondents – 79% – felt that a single man should have a higher rate than a single woman and 86.7% felt that a married man should have a higher rate than a married woman. A substantial minority of 25% felt that single men and women should have the same minimum rate. Forty per cent felt married women should have the same as single women, 39% felt they should have more and 21% thought they should have less. Only 58 respondents (5.4%) considered that each of the four categories – married men, single men, married women and single women – should have the same minimum rate. The survey did not specifically raise the question of dependants (although assumptions by the respondents on this matter must have affected the replies given) and did not attempt to ascertain what the respondent's views on a fair basic wage for each of the categories would have been if the additional financial responsibilities imposed by dependants were offset by adjustments in taxation or social welfare.

64. As stated in paragraph 58 above, the Commission arranged for the inclusion of questions on attitudes to equal pay in a survey of the participation of women in the labour force being carried out by the Economic and Social Research Institute for the Minister for Labour. The survey covered a sample of 5,054 women mainly between 21 and 64 years of age in both urban and rural areas and was not confined to women in employment. Two questions relating to equal pay for the same work were put to each respondent. The first question asked respondents to decide, assuming the present taxation and allowance system, whether various pairs of employees (a single woman compared with a single man, for example) performing the same work should be paid the same rate of pay by their employer or whether one should be paid more than the other. The second question posed the problem of equal pay in a theoretical way and introduced the concept of adjustments in taxation and social welfare allowances to take account of different responsibilities in relation to dependants.

The replies to the first question, in which respondents were faced with specific cases and were asked to assume existing arrangements regarding taxation and social welfare allowances, showed a substantial majority in favour of the same rate of pay for (i) a single woman compared with a single man, (ii) a widow with dependent children compared with a married man and (iii) a single woman with dependants compared with a married man. Almost 52% of the respondents felt that a married woman should get the same rate of pay as a married man. A majority of respondents felt that a married man and a widow with dependent children should be paid more than a single woman.

The replies to the second question showed that the great majority (70%) of the respondents were in favour of equal pay for the same work, with persons with dependants paying less in taxes and getting extra allowances compared to persons without dependants. Twenty per cent of the respondents felt that even where the person with dependants is paying less in taxes and getting extra allowances, he or she should still get a higher rate of pay. A small minority of about 6% felt that both categories should get the same rate of pay and should pay the same amount in taxes and get the same allowances.

The replies given to the first question when classified by reference to the replies given to the second question show a large degree of consistency in that the persons who chose the 'same rate of pay' in the various parts of the first question were more likely to select the 'same rate of pay' options in the second question.

65.   It is, we feel, clear that there is already a very large body of opinion in favour of equal pay for men and women. It is also clear, however, that there is a general feeling that persons with dependants should have a higher total income than those without dependants. The findings reported in the Economic and Social Research Institute survey, referred to at paragraph 63 above, suggest that there is an assumption among men that the sex-differential is needed to ensure that family responsibilities are provided for and, accordingly, it would seem that the application of equal pay without account being taken of the additional income requirements of those with dependants to support would be likely to give rise to subsequent strong pressures to restore the former differentials. The results of the survey referred to in paragraph 64 also indicate that the successful introduction of equal pay and its acceptability will require changes in the existing taxation and/or social welfare codes to provide against a lowering of the relative standard of living of persons with dependants.

Having sketched the pay differential issue the Commission presented survey-based information indicating that 'it is, we feel, clear that there is already a very large body of opinion in favour of equal pay for men and women'. A persistent concern once again appeared, however. It was also clear that 'there is a general feeling that persons with dependants should have a higher total income than those without dependants'. However, the Commission argued that this should be accomplished not by paying a higher 'family wage' to men, but by providing adjustments through social welfare allowances.

While there was widespread support for the principle of equal pay, the Commission pointed out that its introduction would have costs – direct and indirect – as well as benefits. The Commission considered in some detail both the advantages and adverse effects of the proposal. In the Commission's view, the advantages 'for women themselves and the community as a whole' warranted the implementation of the equal pay principle. It was noted, however, that the advantages were likely to be realised mainly in the long run, whereas the adverse effects were likely to manifest themselves in the short term (a political consideration not expressly stated in the report). Needing to conform to the directives of international bodies, armed with evidence of wide pay differentials in Ireland and confident of widespread support, the Commission recommended legislative action on various aspects of the equal pay principle.

Commission on the Status of Women, *Report to Minister for Finance* (1972)

The implications of equal pay
138. The introduction of equal pay will have significant implications, both for women themselves and for the community as a whole. It is not possible, however, to predict accurately what these will be and we must therefore confine ourselves to a general consideration of some of the potential implications of equal pay without being able to draw precise conclusions.

The advantages of equal pay
139. The advent of equal pay may be expected to produce some or all of the following effects:
(a) an expansion of the employment opportunities for women in skilled, technical and professional employments;
(b) a restructuring of the female labour force with the general effect of promoting a more efficient use of women workers;

(c) increases in female labour productivity;
(d) contribute to relieving shortages of labour in the economy; and
(e) an increase in the real output of the economy and perhaps a
     moderation of the rate of inflation generally (in so far as (d) is
     achieved).

These effects are all potential long-term advantages to women
and to the community which might be expected to result from the
implementation of equal pay. The way in which each of them might
be brought about and how they could affect the female labour force
and the community is considered in paragraphs 140 to 151 [not
included]. There are also potentially adverse effects which might
result from the implementation of equal pay and these are
considered in paragraphs 152 to 170 [not all included].

Adverse effects of equal pay
152. The following adverse effects may result from the introduction of equal pay:
(a) a rise in the domestic price level;
(b) displacement of female labour from employment;
(c) indirect 'spillover' and 'facility' costs.
154. A rise in prices will generally result in:
(a) a redistribution of income in a regressive manner;
(b) additional inflationary pressure;
(c) a possible adverse effect on the balance of payments.

Conclusions
170. Some of the possible effects of equal pay have been discussed
in this section but it is not possible to predict with any certainty the
exact effects its introduction will have. The task of clearly
distinguishing these effects from the multitude of other influences
at work in the economy is so difficult as to be virtually impossible.
The experience of other countries is not well documented and, in
any case, variations in economic, social and institutional circumstances in different countries obviously affect the pattern of events
which equal pay may be expected to bring about. We are, however,
reasonably confident that there are considerable advantages to be
gained from equal pay both for women themselves and the
community as a whole. It is necessary to note, however, that the
advantages of equal pay are likely to accrue mainly in the long-term
while most of the adverse effects will occur within the phasing-in
period. In the short-term, therefore, the net impact of equal pay

may be expected to be adverse but, over time, the balance of effect should become progressively more favourable.

Summary of recommendations
580. The following is a summary of our recommendations.

EQUAL PAY
GENERAL
That a policy of equal pay be followed.

CIRCUMSTANCES IN WHICH EQUAL PAY SHOULD APPLY
Equality of treatment between men and women should apply in any of the following circumstances:
(a) where women are performing the same jobs as men or where men and women are completely interchangeable between jobs;
(b) where the jobs performed by men and women are of a similar nature but contain differences which occur only infrequently or are of small practical importance in relation to total job content;
(c) where it is established, by any of the means outlined in paragraph 94 [not included], or by an Equal Pay Commissioner of the Labour Court that the jobs performed by men and women are of equal value in that the demands (for instance in relation to skill, physical or mental effort, responsibility and working conditions) made on a woman are equal to the demands made on a man in respect of the work each performs.

LEGISLATION
Legislation should be enacted to ensure the effective implementation of equal pay.

SETTLEMENT OF DISPUTES
A dispute concerning equal pay should be referred to the Labour Court by any of the parties involved to investigate it and make an award. The Court should be enabled to appoint Equal Pay Commissioners to carry out the investigation. An award by the Court should be effective from the date of the award and should be recoverable from the employer as a civil debt.

If the dispute concerns the provisions of a collective agreement and the Court is satisfied that discrimination exists in the agreement it should refer the agreement back to the parties concerned to amend it. If the amendment is not made within a reasonable time the Labour Court should have power to amend the agreement to remove the discrimination. The agreement as so amended should be the effective document and should have full force and effect and any loss resulting to an employee from an employer's failure to comply with the amendment should be recoverable from the employer as a civil debt.

(5) SEX-DIFFERENTIATED AND MARRIAGE-DIFFERENTIATED SCALES IN THE PUBLIC SERVICE

(i)   where scales are differentiated on the basis of sex, as apart from the content of the work, steps should be taken to place women on the appropriate 'man' scale.

(ii) where scales are differentiated on the basis of marriage, steps should be taken to abolish the single ('A') scales and to place all affected officers on the appropriate married ('B') scales.

(iii) the differentiation that exists between the pay of married men and that of women and single men in the grade of Clerical Officer in the local authority service and health service and in the grade of School Attendance Officer should be discontinued.

(6) PHASING

(i)   Where men and women are performing the same or similar work or work of equal value:

(a)   the rate of pay of the women concerned should be increased annually by 5% of the appropriate male rate existing immediately prior to each such annual increase; in the case of occupations in which pay is differentiated on a marriage basis, the appropriate male rate is the married rate;

(b)   in addition, agreements for other increases in rates of pay should provide for the same absolute increase for men and women;

(c)   the full application of equal pay should be completed not later than 31 December, 1977, and the phasing arrangements recommended should be adjusted, as necessary, to ensure this.

(ii) The Employer-Labour Conference should, in reviewing the terms and operation of the National Agreement, make provision for the introduction of equal pay as proposed in this report. If such provision is made by the Conference, the legislation proposed in paragraph 98 should take account of any phasing arrangements agreed. If such provision is not made by the Conference the legislation should provide for the introduction of equal pay on a phased basis as outlined above.

(7) JOB EVALUATION

The Employer-Labour Conference should take steps to encourage the wider use of job evaluation. The Equal Pay Commissioners referred to in paragraph 99 should be familiar with job evaluation.

To monitor developments on these and other recommendations the Irish government established the Women's Representative Committee in 1974. Its reports of 1976 and 1978 provide a useful overview of changes effected in the early years of what Eileen Connolly has called the Irish government's 'equality contract'.[3] We refer to these policy developments in Chapter 2, following a presentation of the Commission's deliberations on 'Women in Employment'.

WOMEN IN EMPLOYMENT

The Commission recognised that a number of legal barriers had long prevented women from fully participating in the Irish labour market. These concerns were addressed in turn. First, however, the panel explored the 'more subtle forms of discrimination' that hampered women's access to jobs, promotion and training. Such discrimination was rooted in attitudes toward, and assumptions about, women in employment held by management, fellow workers and perhaps the public in general.

In its search for information on this issue the Commission decided on an 'interview survey' of management representatives from both the public and the private sectors. It was not a random sample of employers, but rather a survey of selected organisations engaged in a wide range of activities. Moreover, these firms had 'a substantial number or a substantial proportion of women employees'. All told, the firms surveyed employed 107,000 people, one third of them women. The Commission's focus was on equality of opportunity for women. The members stated quite clearly that equal pay initiatives would count for little if women were denied equality of access to jobs, training and promotion. The panel interviews with employers took place in March and April 1972. In addition, a small sample of forty women workers from various occupations presented their views on employment issues.

Commission on the Status of Women, *Report to Minister for Finance* (1972)

Managerial views

181. A variety of reasons were offered by management to justify male-only job categories. On the clerical side, job difficulties in terms of intellectual content were referred to frequently. Such jobs were variously described as jobs 'with responsibility', jobs requiring 'decision making', 'harder', or 'difficult' jobs, the underlying assumption being that men more than women excel in work with these intellectual demands. At the same time, female jobs are described as routine. These jobs are invariably the less important ones, lower in status and lower in financial reward than the vast majority of male jobs. In some cases a trend emerged towards recruiting few male clerical staff or reducing the proportion of male clerks employed and a primary reason given for this was that conditions would be created which would enhance the career structure for men. The same outcome resulted in other firms where a policy of female-only jobs in clerical areas had been adopted on the grounds that women prefer and are better than men in this type of work. An important consequence of this kind of change is a trend towards increasing the number of females at the lower level office jobs – typing, card-punching, etc. – and a trend towards filling 'jobs with promotional potential' with men. In such companies, men tend to be recruited at levels described as 'executive' or 'administrative' with a view to career development and promotion to managerial positions. Other criteria by management in assigning men and women to different jobs included economic considerations, tradition and expected length of stay. Another basic assumption underlying job allocation as between the sexes is that female staff are expected to have a short working life – mainly as a stop-gap between school and marriage. Consequently, it appears that the vast majority of females are recruited to positions where it is felt that the type of work will suffer least by discontinuous service. In other words, female staff are not encouraged to prolong their working life with any one company and some women may react by conforming to this expectation. In this connection it is interesting to note that one

firm which had in the past recruited men only for clerical jobs, recently had begun to recruit females into these grades in order to reduce the 'stability' of the system. It appears that firms desire a certain level of labour turnover, a flow-through of people in jobs to reduce the forces towards inertia. It may well be that, in certain instances, women employees are fulfilling this organisational need. Only one firm had given any serious thought to the question of 'optimum length of stay' in any one type of job in their organisation. In general, most companies fail to analyse the question of appropriate learning and working time for any one job.

182. On the industrial side, the nature of the work is most frequently mentioned in explaining job categorisation between men and women – men do heavy, dirty or dangerous work and deal with larger and heavier components than women. Traditional divisions are common and it appears that these are rarely questioned or attempts made to change them. Sometimes, in the past, work may have been dirty or involved handling heavy objects but now may have changed as a result of technological progress. Nevertheless, the attitudes relating to whether a man or a woman should be assigned to the job still remain. Unskilled and semi-skilled factory assembly jobs are generally assigned to female workers, the typical reason given being that women are better at these jobs than men – the jobs are monotonous but require dexterity. This implies either that the level of boredom tolerance for women is higher than for men or else that their concentration is better. Other factors which emerged affecting the assignment of jobs as between men and women were restrictions brought about by trade unions and the legislative restriction banning night shift work for women.

Recruitment
184. Many organisations appear to attract female clerical staff and office workers primarily on the basis of intangibles such as the overall image of the company as modern and progressive and the status of a few secretaries to top personnel. The general impression is that organisations have in the past tended to select highly qualified girls and then assign them to undemanding low-responsibility jobs. Employers are extremely slow in utilising the female resources they seek and are recruiting. They fall far short of extending women in the jobs to which they assign them. In one or two organisations a start has been made on redressing this situation but even in these instances the raising of the ceiling for the development of women has been barely perceptible.

Training

197. Some firms stated that in training there was no discrimination in favour of men – that women employees received a 'fair share' in proportion to their number at different organisational levels. In general, where firms stated that there was no difference in training for men and women, in practice they were referring primarily to those jobs in which men and women are interchangeable, and not in terms of opening up new areas and new jobs to women. It emerged that only two undertakings appeared to provide, within the recent past, equal training opportunities for men and women. Frequently, management stated that in their experience, women were not 'interested in training' and 'were not prepared to take on responsibility'. It appears that where management perceived women from this perspective that somehow it justified their own lack of initiative in focusing on the development of their women employees. One major barrier to the training of women is the expectation that their length of stay with the organisation will be short and this is the most frequent argument for the non-training of women employees. No company, however, spelled out what constitutes a desirable length of stay from the organisation's point of view, for either men or women.

198. Few firms emerged as having seriously analysed and examined the role of training in relation to the position of their female employees. In general, women are recruited for special qualifications and skills which they have acquired prior to entering the organisation and there is little interest shown in developing their potential any further. A few firms, however, are initiating constructive change in the traditional approach to the training of women. These firms appear to have integrated the training process as an intrinsic part of their overall organisational growth programme on the basic assumption that women as well as men have potential which is worth developing. In one such concern, an important change in the design of training courses is that of having women trained as Trainers, so that they are now in the role of teaching men and women, in special techniques, from all levels of the organisation, including managers. This development is one of the most significant and fundamental changes which has been initiated in this field. The learning conditions themselves reflect the values which it is hoped that the trainees will learn in these situations. If women are trained and appointed as trainers and given organisational status, then the trainees will also accept them in that role and will accord them the same status.

Promotion

199. The general pattern of promotion for females in typing jobs – where many of them are situated – is a movement up within this structure, for example, from Junior Typist to Senior Typist to Personal Secretary. In other words, typing remains a basic requirement for the promotional jobs in this area. In practically all firms, Personal Secretary to top management was described as a status job and one which staff in the female grades sought to achieve. In some large employments in the public sector, there is a promotion line from typist to a clerical grade but in view of the large number of women in the lower grade only a small fraction move upwards.

204. In general, management perceived women workers as having a low level of motivation and an important factor frequently mentioned was the lack of interest of female employees in promotion. The lack of career orientation of younger staff was also seen as an important element in lowering their interests in study leading to special qualifications. Typical comments in this area were that young female staff don't think in terms of a career or avail of opportunities to study to the same extent as male staff so that when promotion opportunities come along they are not qualified to take them up. Implicit in the practices of some firms was an attitude to women as having limited ability and potential. One company was explicit on this and indicated that they set a definite promotional ceiling for women because of women 'lacking ability'. Representatives of some semi-State organisations stated that older male staff tend to think in terms of women lacking ability but that this prejudice is slowly changing.

Management expectations regarding women workers also play an important role in matters affecting their career development. The most important of these is the expected length of stay of female staff. We have already noted the adverse effects that management's expectation of an average 'short-stay' by women can have on their training. This in turn reduces their promotional opportunities. This expectation is pervasive and not only affects the promotion and training of females with no special qualifications but can hinder the recruitment of female graduates.

206. We have noted also an undercurrent of uncertainty as to the type of consequences that could ensue if women had the same promotion opportunities as men. Generally, this centred on the possible unfavourable reaction of male employees if some of their promotional outlets were lost to women with a consequent deterioration in morale in the organisation. A further matter affecting women's opportunities is the question of their

acceptability in certain jobs. This concept, the criteria of which are difficult to identify, was mentioned frequently to account for the almost total absence of women in Sales, Marketing and Commercial divisions of organisations. One marketing organisation, when probed further on the issue, spoke of the 'attitudes of the customer' and 'attitudes of Irish Industry' as the reason why top management perceived women in the sales/marketing area as being unsuitable and unacceptable. It is worth noting at this point the experience of the large Banking organisations, which have recently reorganised the promotional avenues for women. The job of the 'Cashier' in the Irish scene was traditionally a male job. Within the past two years women, young and old, are taking on this job, which brings them into direct contact with customers. The customers' response appears to be very positive, so that this major change on the part of the organisation was easily accepted by the customer. It could be that Managements who anticipate negative reactions to women representatives in jobs involving direct contact with the customer, could very well be misjudging this response, and the main problem for management appears to be one of coping with internal change, regarding allocation of people and assignment of women to new areas, rather than one of reaction from outside the organisation.

208. In general, the great majority of firms appeared to be reluctant to initiate any change with regard to improving the career prospects of women. A general fear of unforeseen consequences appears mainly to account for this, allied to a gross lack of analysis of the issues involved and a failure to face up to the basic assumptions underlying the existing situation for women in these concerns. In those organisations where change has occurred it has not happened by chance; the impetus for change appears to have been that management at the highest level has, as part of a general re-think about staff organisation and development, realised that long-term career planning and development for women, aimed at the full utilisation of their potential, is in the best interests of the organisation and have set out actively, and with a certain urgency, to pursue this policy. Where positive programmes of career development for women have been initiated, the indications are that women are eager to take advantage of the new opportunities which become available to them.

Interviews with individual women workers
214. In general, the orientation and attitudes of women were seen as barriers to women progressing in employment. There was a

clear recognition that these barriers could not be isolated and understood apart from the overall cultural context in which they are embedded and that the social institutions moulding the attitudes of both men and women to women at work would require appropriate changes so that outmoded attitudes and values would be discarded and more positive and less rigid attitudes to women in employment adopted.

215. There was general agreement among those interviewed that management's role in creating work conditions and an attitudinal climate favourable or unfavourable for women employees is a crucial one. Management's approach towards women appeared to be spread over a wide spectrum of behaviour. On the one hand, a picture emerged of managers who exhibited a certain degree of openness with positive attitudes towards women employees. Such managers were usually located in firms where organisational changes were in progress necessitating an analysis of the whole organisational system. On the other hand (and the more frequent experience), management came across as a major inhibiting force with extremely close attitudes towards women, discouraging their progress in the organisation or their trial on new areas of work. One area singled out by a number of interviewees for special comment was the Personnel Department. There was a strong feeling that the Personnel Department should be more approachable and supportive of individual cases and problems. One solution suggested by some informants was that where the Personnel Manager was a man, his assistant, at least, should be a woman.

221. Factors relating to women themselves which were seen as limiting women's promotional opportunities included the lack of clear-cut job goals for women and the short-term perspective of women towards employment. In addition, women's fear of appearing too 'pushy' and hence not feminine was frequently referred to and a definite perception of the need for women to be more ambitious and competitive was evident.

Attitudes to married women at work
223. While a formal marriage bar affected a number of the interviewees, in general it was possible for both factory and office staff to retain their jobs after marriage. The pattern appeared to be one in which the female employee left on pregnancy and did not seek to return. None of the firms where the respondents worked had any special arrangements for maternity leave or for return to employment after maternity.

224. A wide range of sentiments were voiced by informants concerning the appropriate relation between work and marriage. There was, however, a strong feeling evident that the mothers of young children, up to say 5 years of age, should stay at home to care for them. Distinctions were made between the needs and responsibilities of the married woman with young children and those of the older woman who wished to come back to work after, say, ten years or so in the home and it was felt that organisations should adapt to provide employment for mature women. In some cases, however, an unfavourable reaction to the employment of married women, based on the fear that such employment would hinder the career prospects of single women, was evident.

225. Among the reasons given for working after marriage the most frequently mentioned was economic necessity arising from the high cost of living, especially housing. A reason mentioned by a number of married informants was the feeling that they gain in status and respect particularly since housework has low prestige and isolates them from social interaction. Some single respondents hoped for a complete switch from their pre-marriage employment, emphasising work that would be more interesting and more worthwhile.

Attitudes to change

227. Finally, an attempt was made to explore with those interviewed the kind of changes with regard to women at work they would like to see introduced in the near future. The informants focused on issues which directly concerned themselves and their own work role and there was considerable consistency in the areas which they mentioned as requiring immediate action.

228. There was overall agreement that the equal pay principle should apply to work of equal value. Informants recognised that the introduction of equal pay would not benefit everyone since many women are not employed on the same or similar jobs as men and, accordingly, it was suggested that many jobs in which women are engaged should be upgraded and objective criteria used for evaluating and comparing their jobs with those of men. Payment by age was strongly criticised by some informants who felt that it worked against the young female worker who would have devoted five or six of the 'best' years of her life to the job.

229. The role of education and past learning experience in orientating girls towards a narrow range of jobs was severely criticised and demands were made for opening up a wider range of job alternatives for women and for a break away from the present sex-

typing of jobs. The role of schools in providing appropriate career guidance for girls was stressed. Career guidance should be built on sound educational guidance at earlier stages, and be capable of opening up new horizons soundly based on the potential and ability and motivation of the girls. Professional informants who had teaching backgrounds were acutely aware of the inadequacies of teacher training in the field of Career Guidance, and suggested that teacher training courses, both in Training Colleges and in the Universities, should incorporate special courses on Vocational Development, which would open up more career and job possibilities, rather than channelling them into traditional areas. Many informants indicated that since the life-pattern of women was undergoing many unforeseen changes, they should be trained to think of work not merely as a stop-gap between school and marriage, but in terms of returning at later stages or in continuing part-time or full-time work even during the early stages of marriage. It was mentioned that women should have more specialist training to give them flexibility, so that they are not tied to a specific task in a specific organisation.

The survey findings were said to 'confirm that women are not participating on equal footing with men in employment and that in many areas they are being deliberately discriminated against'. While stating that 'a start must certainly be made in bringing about changes in attitudes to women's employment', the Commission sought immediately 'to take steps to end discriminatory practices against women in employment'.

The Commission recommended that the Labour Court be assigned the task of investigating complaints of discrimination against women in the private and public sectors. The Commission examined two major restrictions on women's employment. One was the 'marriage bar', which required women to retire from employment on marriage, or prohibited the employment of married women. Moreover, in many instances, upon marriage women were barred from participation in occupational pension schemes. These restrictions were sometimes embodied in collective agreements in the private sector. In the civil service the 'marriage bar' provisions were contained in the Local Government Act 1941, the Civil Service Regulation Act 1956 and the Civil Service Commissioners Act 1956. The Commission recommended the prohibition of such practices and the repeal of the earlier Acts.

The second questionable area involved restriction on

women's night-time work in industry, a provision of the Conditions of Employment Act 1936. The Commission held that for women, the provision 'affects both their opportunity for employment and their earning capacity'.

The Commission then turned to a consideration of additional factors that affect women's employment opportunities: the wording of advertisements, eligibility for occupational pension schemes, training and counselling for entry (or re-entry) into the labour market, and day care for children. Having identified the barriers to women in employment, the Commission offered its complete recommendations on women in the workplace.

Commission on the Status of Women, *Report to Minister for Finance* (1972)

249. There is, we believe, a clear need here for some agency to investigate complaints of discrimination against women, either in the private or the public sector, in relation to their access to employment or in training or promotion in employment and to take action to remedy the discrimination if a complaint is justified. We accept that there are many difficulties to be resolved in determining the exact terms of reference under which any such agency would operate and it may, we feel, be necessary to establish its sphere of operation gradually, proceeding by way of case experience at conciliation level, for a start, to the establishment of criteria by which it can be gauged whether discrimination on the basis of sex exists in any particular case and then to the determination of the enforcement remedies which should be available where it is not possible to reach a satisfactory settlement by way of conciliation.

252. One of the matters investigated in the survey referred to in paragraph 13 [not included] was the compulsory retirement of women on marriage. in general, females employed in clerical jobs in service industries. banks, local authorities and semi-State bodies are required to resign their employment on marriage. Of the semi-State organisations interviewed, only two have eliminated the marriage bar, so that their female clerical staff can, if they choose, continue on in full-time employment after marriage. In two firms, a marriage bar was imposed on females in clerical and 'skilled' areas, but not in unskilled jobs. In the hotel industry, in unskilled and semi-skilled jobs in manufacturing (particularly in food, electronics and textile industries) and in some clerical areas, the marriage bar did not apply. When the different practices relating to the operation of a marriage

bar in the companies were examined, it became evident that companies which stated that a marriage bar was in operation frequently had a situation similar to that of an organisation in which the 'no marriage bar' condition obtained. In other words, while the marriage bar rule applied in theory, in practice it was relaxed, and female employees were allowed to remain on in the employment for a certain period of time after marriage. The length of stay after marriage varied, but, in general, did not appear to exceed two years. In the majority of cases, the period of stay after marriage was in a purely temporary capacity and where pension schemes operated, the married woman was precluded from continuing in the scheme. The reasons put forward to explain the existence of a marriage bar were complex and sometimes inconsistent. For example, one company which spoke of the need for a marriage bar to enable married women to fulfil their home responsibilities, was willing to employ the same women part-time, during the lunch hour rush period, and made the point that the company has the added advantage of recruiting only efficient employees to return to work in this part-time, temporary capacity. For some companies, the rationale for maintaining a marriage bar was couched in economic terms and decisions in the matter were often related to the supply and demand position for single women workers. In some cases, the companies indicated that a conflict existed between their own preferences with regard to the employment of married women, and those of the trade union concerned. Differences presented themselves where the companies indicated that they would favour removing the marriage bar while the trade unions were in favour of retaining it. It is difficult to measure with any exactness the degree to which the attitudes of certain trade unions in this matter reflect the attitudes of their female members but it appears that not infrequently the situation does arise where trade unions hold opinions contrary to those of many of their female members, particularly in 'male dominated' organisations where the men are concerned with maintaining the status quo while the female employees and/or the company may favour change.

Maternity leave
In this country, all women who are compulsorily insured are insured for the purpose of maternity benefit. Women engaged in a non-manual capacity earning over IR£1,600 a year and women engaged in permanent employment in the civil service, the teaching profession or any local or public authority are not in compulsory insurance and are not accordingly insured for this purpose. Maternity benefit

consists of two separate types of payment. Firstly, there is a maternity grant which is a sum of IR£4 payable in respect of each confinement either on the husband's or on the woman's own insurance; if both are insured, two grants may be payable. In addition to the maternity grant, a maternity allowance may be payable but only on the woman's own insurance. This allowance at present is IR£5.55 a week and is payable for a total of 12 weeks – six weeks before and six weeks after confinement (if the confinement occurs later than expected, the allowance continues to be payable until the expiration of the 6th week after confinement). These arrangements do not confer any right to maternity leave from her employment on a woman. In the survey referred to in paragraph 13 [not included], the great majority of the organisations interviewed that stated they did not impose a marriage bar, as well as those that had relaxed the resignation on marriage condition, were in fact operating a 'maternity bar'. In other words, female employees could remain on after marriage until they required leave of absence for maternity, at which stage their employment was terminated. It was clear from management that this attitude was communicated either directly or indirectly to married women workers and, accordingly, there was little pressure from them for the grant of maternity leave, either paid or unpaid. We did not find any instance in the organisations surveyed where a woman would be granted paid maternity leave by her employer. In the private sector, the only areas where a rough pattern of granting maternity leave arises are in the hotel industry and in some unskilled or semi-skilled jobs in manufacturing industry. There is, however, no question of any right having been established by such employees to return to their jobs after a birth and the practice is very much affected by the supply position of women workers. The employer does not grant any pay for the period of leave but the employee is entitled to social welfare maternity allowance for a period of 12 weeks if she satisfies the appropriate contribution conditions. Very recently, two of the semi-State organisations interviewed, which employ a high proportion of female clerical staff, have drawn up regulations governing the retention of married women and the grant of maternity leave. In both cases the maternity leave is unpaid and extends for ten weeks in one organisation and 12 weeks in the other.

Restrictions on women's employment
271. There are certain restrictions imposed on the employment of women which do not apply in the case of men. These may be divided into two categories. Firstly, there are those restrictions

which prohibit or control the employment of women in certain dangerous or unhealthy occupations and secondly there is the general restriction placed on the employment of women on industrial work during certain hours at night.

272. The Factories Act 1955 is the principal legislative provision regulating the employment of women in the first category mentioned. The Act prohibits the employment of women and young persons on certain processes connected with lead manufacture and sets down the provisions under which women and young persons are to be employed on processes involving the use of lead compounds. Women and young persons are also prohibited from cleaning prime movers while in motion.

We have not received any representations that the legislative provisions governing the employment of women in dangerous or unhealthy occupations should be abolished or altered in any way. We have no information that any of these restrictions are unreasonable and we do not, accordingly, recommend that any change be made in them.

273. A legal restriction on the employment of women between the hours of 10.00 p.m. and 8.00 a.m. and a provision that there must be an interval of at least 11 hours between spells of work for them is contained in the Conditions of Employment Act 1936 (Part III Section 46). These restrictions do not apply in the case of adult male workers. The Act applies to workers engaged in industrial work generally but excluding mining and certain specified categories of employees. The Shops (Conditions of Employment) Act 1938, which applies to employment in wholesale and retail shops, warehouses, hotels, licensed premises and refreshment houses (restaurants, cafés, etc.) does not place any restriction on the night work of adult men or women. The Mines and Quarries Act 1965 provides for an absolute prohibition on the employment of women underground, and, in the case of women otherwise employed in mining for an interval of not less than 12 hours between periods of employment, including a continuous period of seven hours falling between 10.00 p.m. and 7.00 a.m.

274. The Conditions of Employment Act 1936 contains provisions enabling the appropriate Minister, following consultations with representatives of employers and workers, to make regulations declaring any specified form of industrial work to be excluded industrial work for the purpose of the part of the Act relating to conditions as to times of work. Exclusion regulations have been made to allow women in various specified industries to work earlier

than 8.00 a.m. and later than 10.00 p.m. in most cases not earlier than 7.00 a.m. or later than 11.00 p.m. but, in a small number of cases, as early as 6.00 a.m. and as late as 12 midnight, subject to a minimum break of 11 hours.

Newspaper advertisements
281. One of the most conspicuous areas of discrimination against women is in the matter of newspaper advertisements by employers and employment agencies seeking staff. Every day produces a number of advertisements which discriminate against women in one form or another. The discrimination may consist of a straightforward invitation to men only to apply for the job or an outline of the qualifications which the 'successful man' will be required to have. The discrimination may occasionally be more oblique than this and consist of the specification in the advertisement of a male scale only. We have noted this practice in certain recent advertisements for public service appointments particularly for professional posts such as for archaeologists. The reason underlying such format would appear to be that the rates of pay applicable to such posts have been differentiated on a sex basis with a higher scale for males and it is considered more attractive to show the higher rate only in the advertisement for the post. We believe that such advertisements may mislead qualified women into believing that the particular post is open only to men and discourage them from applying.

282. We received from one of the women's organisations a sample of employment advertisements taken from Irish newspapers showing that in many cases invitations to apply for jobs, particularly the more attractive ones, were being directed specifically to men, and advertisements asking women to apply were mainly for lower-level less remunerative jobs. In order to get a more extensive coverage of the subject we arranged with the School of Public Administration to examine the situations vacant advertisements in three daily newspapers covering the period from October 1970 to March 1971; we are very grateful to the students of the School and to the School authorities for their co-operation in this matter. The results of that survey prove that discrimination in such advertisements is extremely prevalent. Of approximately 2,800 advertisements examined, 1,234 (44%) were apparently or specifically confined to male applicants, that is the advertisements referred to the required person as 'he' or 'the man sought' or specifically requested men applicants. Of the remaining

advertisements, 37% were open to both men and women and 19% were confined to women – the majority of posts confined to women being in the clerical, secretarial and typing area. Excluding craftsmen posts, the highest proportion of advertisements confined to men applicants occurred in the managerial category (246 out of 370) and the next highest in the commercial category – mostly sales representatives (181 out of 291).

Pension schemes
285. The Economic and Social Research Institute Survey referred to in paragraph 284 [not included] showed that in the sample chosen, only 27% of female wage earners were in pension schemes as compared with 67% of male wage earners. This position was repeated, but to a lesser extent, among salary earners where 41% of women and 78% of men were covered by a pension scheme. The comparatively lower percentage of women covered by occupational pension schemes reflected the more stringent eligibility requirements for females for entry to the schemes. Among wage-earners, 44% of the schemes did not allow females to enter the scheme until they had reached 25 years of age as compared with 3% of schemes having the same provision for males. The corresponding figures for salary earners were very much the same – 51% and 2%. The reasons advanced for this situation are that many employers do not include females until they reach the age at which their expectation of marriage begins to decline and that, in addition, death-in-service benefits are not considered as important for females because the proportion who have persons wholly dependent on them is lower than the corresponding proportion among males.

Employment of married women and re-entry of women to employment
296. There has undoubtedly been a very marked change of attitudes in recent years towards the question of women working after marriage. Many women now expect to continue working after they get married and at least up to the birth of the first baby. There has also been a change in attitudes towards women re-entering employment when their family responsibilities start to diminish. In the ESRI survey referred to above, 74% of the women interviewed approved of married women working, although a very substantial proportion of them felt that certain conditions should exist before a woman re-entered employment. The condition specified by the

largest number of respondents was that the woman should have no young children to look after or that she should be in a position to get help with children. Of 529 husbands of non-farm married women (working and non-working) contacted in the sample, only 183 disapproved or would disapprove of their wives working. It seems likely that although the present labour force participation rate of married women is very low, this change in attitudes allied to the lower average age of marriage, the general reduction in the average size of family and the consequential lower average age of the mother when the last child is born will bring about a marked change in this position in the coming years. There will be a large increase in the number of mothers in the 30-35 age group whose children are not in need of their full care and attention and who will probably be anxious to resume employment. The position will also be affected by the general trend towards longer participation in formal education; as indicated in paragraph 522 [not included], there is a tendency for labour force participation rates of women to rise with increasing educational attainment.

299. Public opinion in Ireland traditionally resisted the employment and promotion of married women on two grounds. One was the belief that outside work was incompatible with the responsibilities of a mother and housewife. This objection has been greatly modified and diminished in recent years, and, in our judgement, rightly. The other objection has been that in conditions of less than full employment the employment of married women will reduce the employment prospects of men, single women and widows and notably the promotion opportunities of widows and single persons. The latter part of this objection seems to us to be without foundation. If married women were to have no prospect of being promoted, or admitted to skilled work, or even of being employed at all, girls and younger women will inevitably be treated as temporary, short-term workers who have no long term prospects in their occupation and are therefore not worth training or promoting. Younger and single women are thus likely themselves to be the worst sufferers if opportunity for older married women is denied.

Day care for children
Many married women who find that they must re-enter employment, or mothers who are ill or hospitalised for any length of time, are faced with the task of finding suitable care facilities for young children. The most satisfactory solution to this problem is where arrangements can

be made for parents or other relations to undertake responsibility for them while the mother is working or incapacitated. Frequently, it is not possible for the mother to make this kind of arrangement and she must either try to avail of professional child-minding facilities or else depend on older children to look after the younger ones outside school hours. This latter solution is clearly a very unsafe and unsatisfactory one but representations have been made to us that, in certain areas, it is not an infrequent occurrence where mothers are working and that the responsibility lies with the State and other authorities for not providing suitable crèche and day-nursery facilities where young children can receive skilled care if the mother is forced by economic necessity to resume work. By the term 'crèche' we mean a centre where children in good health up to between 2 and 3 years of age are cared for during all or the greater part of a normal working day by qualified, mainly professional, personnel. In referring to day-nurseries, we mean a similar type of centre catering for children of from about three to six years of age. The same overall standards of professional qualifications of staff are not necessarily required for the day nursery as for the crèche. Pre-school playgroups, which are mainly organised on a commercial basis and which take children usually from two to three hours a day, are, we feel, of very limited value in enabling the mother to take up employment although they are very important in freeing mothers from the strain of continuous child-minding and allowing them some freedom of movement outside the home during the day which they might not otherwise achieve.

580. The following is a summary of our recommendations.

(8) Promotion of women in the Civil Service and the Local Authority Service

Boards formed in the Civil Service and the Local Authority Service and by the Civil Service Commission and the Local Appointments Commission for the selection of staff for promotion, should, where possible, be composed of both men and women.

(9) Access by women to apprenticeships

The Department of Labour and An Chomhairle Oiliúna should initiate discussions with employer and trade union interests with a view to the formulation of proposals under which existing restrictions (imposed either by trade unions or employers and trade unions) on the entry of women to skilled occupations which are exclusively male at present, would be removed over a number of years.

(10) PERMANENT MACHINERY FOR ACTION AGAINST SEX DISCRIMINATION IN EMPLOYMENT

(i)   The Labour Court should be given responsibility for investigating complaints from individual women or from trade unions, associations or other groups of women, of discrimination against them on the basis of sex in relation to their access to employment or in their training or promotion in employment;

(ii)   the Court should itself be enabled to initiate investigations of such discrimination and to appoint officers to specialise in this area;

(iii)   the Court should be given power to enforce the production by an employer of any documentation or statistics it requires for the purpose of its investigations;

(iv)   if the Court is satisfied that discrimination on the basis of sex exists, it should try by way of conciliation to reach a settlement with the employer concerned to remove the discrimination. As soon as sufficient experience is gained by the Court in its investigation and conciliation functions in this matter, but in any case not later than three years after the commencement of these functions, the Court should report to the Minister for Labour on the criteria which, in the light of its experience, it has established for determining whether discrimination on the basis of sex exists. In that report, the Court should indicate the legal or other powers which it considers necessary to have in order to enforce its findings in cases where it is not possible by way of conciliation to influence an employer to desist from discrimination. The report should be published by the Minister for Labour.

(11) THE MARRIAGE BAR

(i)   A woman should be allowed to continue in her job irrespective of any change in her marital status.

(ii)   Provisions in collective agreements or service contracts requiring women to retire on marriage or restricting the number of married women that may be employed should be declared illegal. An employer should not be allowed to require an employee to resign on marriage.

(iii)   The exclusion of a woman from participating in a pension scheme on the grounds that she is married should be prohibited.

(iv)   Statutory provisions requiring the retirement of women from employment on marriage or prohibiting the employment of married women should be repealed. From the enactment of this legislation it should be illegal for any employer to compel an employee to retire on marriage or for any employer or trade union to place any restriction on the recruitment or retention of married women.

(v) The recommendations concerning the prohibition of restrictions on the employment of married women to apply also in the case of widows.

(vi) Married women, like single women or widows, should be entitled to equal pay with men in any of the circumstances outlined in paragraph 92 [not included].

(12) MATERNITY LEAVE

(i) A woman who is in insurable employment and who satisfies the appropriate contribution conditions should have an entitlement to a total of twelve weeks maternity leave, as a minimum, of which not less than six must be taken after confinement. Payments to such a woman during the period of maternity leave should be made from the social insurance fund as at present.

(ii) In addition to the maternity leave referred to in the previous recommendation, a mother should be entitled, at her option, to a further four weeks maternity leave from her employment but without pay and without entitlement to social welfare benefit; she should be allowed to take this optional leave either before or after the confinement.

(iii) The Department of Labour should, following consultation with employer and trade union interests, formulate regulations giving effect to the principle that an employer should be prohibited from dismissing a woman from employment on the grounds of her pregnancy and that a woman should have the right to return to the same employment, but not necessarily to the same job in that employment, without loss of seniority or promotional level, or pension rights, on the expiration of the periods of maternity leave recommended; these regulations should be applied by legislation.

(iv) Women who are not in insurable employment should be entitled to paid maternity leave for a period of twelve weeks, as a minimum, of which not less than six must be taken after the confinement; the amount of pay should be negotiated between employers and the appropriate workers' organisations having regard to matters such as length of service, etc.

(13) RESTRICTIONS ON WOMEN'S EMPLOYMENT

(i)   The desirability of Ireland's continued ratification of Convention No. 89 of the International Labour Organisation concerning the night work of women employed in industry should be kept under review by the Government. Should the Government decide at any time to denounce the Convention, the employment of women on industrial work at night should only be permitted where agreement on the matter has been reached between the employer and the Trade Union concerned.

(ii) Consideration should be given to the repeal, at the earliest opportunity, of section 16 of the Conditions of Employment Act 1936, which enables regulations to be made, after consultation with representatives of employers and workers, prohibiting the employment of female workers on any form of industrial work, or fixing the proportion of female workers that may be employed on such work.

(14) NEWSPAPER ADVERTISEMENTS

(i)   The Government should, in relation to employment under its control, ensure that job openings are not advertised in a manner which expressly or impliedly [sic] limits them to male or female applicants, except where sex is a bona fide occupational qualification or where women are not permitted by law to be employed;

(ii) The Government should consider whether it would be practical to introduce legislation to enforce such conditions in relation to private employment.

(15) OCCUPATIONAL PENSION SCHEMES

(i)   Where a woman is ineligible to enter an occupational pension scheme before a certain age or before she has a certain number of years' service in an employment, and where such a condition does not apply to a male employee, then if the woman remains in the employment to pension age her pensionable service should include the years during which she was precluded, solely by reason of her sex, from joining the pension scheme.

(ii) The compulsory retirement age for women from any insurable employment should be not lower than the age at which the social welfare retirement pension is payable.

(iii) The amount of the lump sum which a widow may receive

under a pension scheme without compulsion to purchase an annuity should be substantially increased.

(16) EMPLOYMENT OF MARRIED WOMEN AND RE-ENTRY OF WOMEN TO EMPLOYMENT

(i)   The targets of national employment policy should be enlarged to ensure that every category of willing and available worker can be employed, and the programmes of the Industrial Development Authority and other development agencies should be directed to this enlarged target.

The Department of Labour should have a small number of staff in the placement service specially assigned to advise women on all aspects of re-entry to the labour force and a close liaison should be established with women's voluntary organisations interested in this question. The service should be promoted as widely as possible in the press and on radio and television. In addition to advising enquirers on a postal basis or by personal interview the advisory service should also arrange special information talks in suitable centres (for instance, the Vocational Schools) throughout the country.

(iii) The Department of Labour and the employer and trade union organisations should initiate detailed studies to identify areas where it would be beneficial to introduce part-time or flexible working hours and where this can be done without exploitation or unduly endangering the employment of existing staffs or their earnings or condition of employment.

(17) DAY CARE FOR CHILDREN

(i)   Where new housing schemes are being erected, provision should be made for the building of crèches or day-nurseries and the provision of facilities of this nature should be a condition for the grant of planning permission for such schemes where many women may have an economic necessity to take up part-time work.

(ii) Consideration should be given by the Department of Education to the setting up of a working party of qualified and experienced persons to examine the adequacy of the existing facilities and teaching services provided for children in the four and five year age groups attending school and to recommend ways in which the provision of extended day care for children from four years of age on school premises could be developed where there is a need for such a service.

(iii) Planning authorities should take steps, by public advertisement, to ensure that the necessity to obtain planning
permission, where a private residence is used for the purpose
of operating a playgroup, is known as widely as possible. If it
is apparent that this requirement is being disregarded,
provision should be introduced by legislation or regulation
requiring all existing and new playgroups to register with the
local authority in whose area they are situated and it should be
an offence to operate a playgroup without first registering in
this manner.

(iv) A small grant should be made available by the Government to
the Irish Pre-School Playgroups Association towards the cost of
publishing annually a register of playgroups recognised as
conforming to its code of standards and for which planning
permission has been obtained, if the Association undertakes
the task of compiling and publishing such a register.

CONCLUSION

In carrying out its mandate, the first Commission on the Status
of Women reported on a number of practices that still blocked
equal treatment for women in the Irish labour market when the
report was issued in 1972. These practices were found in every
aspect of employment: job search, hiring, promotion,
compensation and dismissal. As the passages from the report in
this chapter have shown, the Commission also presented the
government with a detailed list of measures calculated to
improve the standing of women in the workplace. The
following chapter traces responses to these recommendation in
the 1970s and also explores further developments in work-
related issues affecting women during the quarter-century after
1972.

CHAPTER TWO

Women's pay and employment: public policies since 1972

THE 'EQUALITY CONTRACT' BETWEEN THE STATE AND IRISH WOMEN

OVER A RELATIVELY BRIEF PERIOD following the publication of the report of the Commission on the Status of Women in Ireland (1972) the Irish Parliament acted on several central issues of pay and employment. This legislation included the Anti-Discrimination (Pay) Act 1974, which implemented the equal pay principle contained in the report's Recommendations 1, 2, 3, 4, 6 and 7. In response to its Recommendation 5 the civil service removed its sex-differentiated pay scales in 1973–74 and its marriage-differentiated scales in 1974. The 1974 Act also established the Equality Office of the Labour Court to deal with disputes over claims to equal pay. The Employment Equality Act 1977 created the Employment Equality Agency, which replaced the Labour Court as supervisor of compliance with the 1974 and 1977 Acts. The latter Act, combined with two others, barred a number of discriminatory practices in training, hiring, promotion and retention. The 'marriage bar', removed in the civil service in 1973, was prohibited in all types of employment; and the Unfair Dismissals Act 1977 and the Maternity Protection of Employees Act 1981 offered job protection to pregnant women and new mothers who sought to return to work.

Although such legislation and institutional initiatives resolved a number of work-related issues in the 1970s, several important concerns remained. Women still encountered obstacles to night-time employment; men and women continued to face different eligibility requirements for occupational pension schemes; and the movement toward adequate day care for children had barely begun.

In addition to these specific matters, the general view persisted that a number of barriers still stood in the way of women seeking equal opportunity in employment. The latter concern was addressed in a new review of women's status by a government-appointed body: *Irish*

Women: Agenda for Practical Action, a report published in February 1985 by the Working Party on Women's Affairs and Family Law Reform. In fact this document went well beyond employment issues as its authors attempted to provide 'a charter for the pursuit of equal opportunity policies for the years ahead'.

The wide-ranging nature of this 'charter' is suggested by the report's table of contents: there are several chapter headings on issues that were not considered in the 1972 report. The first chapter provides a concise treatment of 'the changing role of women' in Ireland and the challenges it poses for policy-makers. The Working Party acknowledges the progress made in removing 'basic economic and social discrimination against women', but asserts that there is need now 'to promote actively and to facilitate greater participation by women in economic and social life'.

Working Party on Women's Affairs and Family Law Reform, *Irish Women: Agenda for Practical Action (1985)*

1.1 Important changes have and are taking place in the role of women and in the contribution they are making to the economic and social life of the community. Even more important is the contribution they are capable of making, if measures are taken to promote and facilitate changes in their role. These changes are associated with more and younger married women in our population, less children per marriage, more married women at work, increased mobility of women, greater job opportunities and more diversified education for women. These fundamental changes are briefly analysed in this chapter as an introduction to discussing what needs to be done to take the best advantage of these changes for the economic and social development of the individual woman and of society as a whole.

1.2 Much progress has already been made in removing basic economic and social discrimination against women. There is, however, a wider range of measures open to society to promote actively and to facilitate greater participation by women in economic and social life. These measures require the provision of positive opportunities and facilities to enable women to participate to a far greater extent in the economic and social life of the community and, by so doing, demonstrate their great potential to improve nearly all aspects of life within the country. The underlying demographic, educational and labour force trends demonstrate clearly how inappropriate are the existing socioeconomic structures and why it is necessary to create new opportunities, facilities and attitudes if our economic and social growth is not to be seriously retarded by restricting the potential contribution women can make. In a country at our stage of development, it is essential that both material and human resources be utilised to the maximum, if we are to avail of the opportunities for increased economic and social development on which our future depends.

Within this widening agenda employment issues still receive priority of place. The Working Party emphasises positive steps to promote greater employment opportunities for women at a difficult time: while women's labour force participation rate was increasing, there was substantial unemployment throughout the European community.

2.78 It is now ten years since the Social Action Programme of the then newly enlarged European Communities focused attention on discrimination between men and women in employment. As is apparent from Part 11 of this Chapter [not included], action at Community level in the 1970s has ensured that basic principles such as equal pay for equal work, and equal treatment in employment and social security matters are now firmly established. However, despite these measures defining a floor of rights for women at work, there are signs that progress towards equal opportunities for women is losing momentum in the Community as a whole. It was for this reason that, during the Irish Presidency of the European Communities in the latter half of 1984, the opportunity was taken to promote a Community initiative in the social affairs area which would supplement and extend existing measures. This initiative is discussed in paragraphs 2.81 to 2.84 following.

2.79 Equal employment opportunities might appropriately be defined as a chance for all people to work and to advance on the basis of merit, ability and potential. Policies to achieve optimum use of human resources require a flexible and inventive integration of theory and practice. In the Working Party's opinion, the key point is that the theoretical commitment to equal opportunities in the workplace, which exists at present, has to be translated into practical action which will be seen to serve to promote the best interests of the organisation as a whole. That is the fundamental principle which informs the contents of this part of Chapter 2.

2.80 Positive action is a concept which has sometimes been misunderstood. It should be seen as an attempt to realise substantive equality of opportunity – as opposed to formal equality of opportunity, which is achieved when no legal or quasi-legal obstacle faces a woman as compared to a man.

Irish Presidency initiative

2.81 With the exception of the permissive arrangements relating to vocational training for women, the concept of positive action had not, prior to the Irish Presidency initiative, been explicitly incorporated in Community legislation. However, there was a general recognition that, while the difference between the Member States in terms of their political, economic, legal and social structures are numerous, the problems encountered by women are remarkably similar Community-wide. Some Member States have attempted to make progress by pursuing a legal approach. Others have quite consciously chosen to embody governmental will in other forms of institutional intervention. Nonetheless, the evidence of a slowing-down of progress in relation to equality of opportunity appears to be uniform across the Community as a whole.

2.82 Secondly, the successful promotion of an initiative in the area of positive action depends, crucially, on how sensitive and adaptable it is to the tradition and nuances of the institutional structures of each country. It is, therefore, necessary to acknowledge the importance attached to the autonomous role of employers and trade unions at the level of the undertaking, together with the great diversity of structures and tradition in the country. Thirdly, adoption of a Community instrument would mean having an explicit policy of encouragement, and a variety of different agents, including both sides of industry, should serve to bring about conditions likely to spark off voluntary programmes at the level of the undertaking. The adoption of positive action programmes could help break down hide-bound resistance to equalising opportunities by reviewing the nature of employment systems – for example, recruitment and selection practices, collective agreements, conditions of employment – and by examining the statistical impact of these regimes on men and women.

2.83 Adoption by Member States of a draft Recommendation on Positive Action in favour of Women was, therefore, a priority aim of the Minister for Labour during the Irish Presidency. This aim was achieved at the Council of Social Affairs Ministers in December 1984. Under the terms of the instrument, Member States are recommended to adopt a positive action policy, within the framework of national policies and practices, designed to eliminate de facto inequalities affecting women in working life and to promote a better balance between the sexes in employment, in order to:

(a)   eliminate or counteract the prejudicial effects on women in employment or seeking employment which arise from existing social attitudes, behaviours and structures based on the idea of a traditional division of roles in society between men and women; and

(b) encourage the participation of women in various occupations in those sectors of working life where they are at present under-represented, particularly in the sectors of the future, and at higher levels of responsibility.

A variety of approaches is provided for, as regards appropriate general and specific measures to be contained within the positive action policy, thereby affording sufficient flexibility to suit the particular social and economic conditions of the Member States.

Comment on EEC positive action measure
The Working Party acknowledges that specific actions are required to take account of the residue of discrimination which persists Community-wide affecting the role of women in employment and impeding their progress towards equality of status and reward with male workers. The Recommendation on Positive Action in Favour of Women seeks to do this and its adoption is, therefore, welcomed by the Working Party. The Working Party believes that the main benefits of the instrument are likely to come from the discipline of focusing attention at Community level on positive action and from the shared experiences arising from the monitoring arrangements which will be established by the EEC Commission.

Irish Government initiative
2.85 The Working Party also wishes to refer to an initiative taken by the Government at national level at the end of 1984 which was in keeping with the efforts made at Community level during the Irish Presidency in treating the Recommendation on Positive Action as a dossier of principal concern in the social affairs area. The initiative highlighted especially the Government's acceptance of the idea in the Recommendation that the public sector should take specific measures and set an example to the private sector in the area of positive action.

2.86 The Government's initiative in this area arose from an examination of the hierarchical structure in public sector organisations in Ireland which indicated a clustering of women employees at lower levels. From information received during 1984 from Government Departments, it was clear that, in the State-sponsored bodies operating under the aegis of the Departments concerned, the female workforce was largely concentrated in the narrow range of clerical/secretarial occupations. That applied equally to the minority of those State-sponsored bodies (referred to at paragraph 2.92 below) which had initiated and implemented programmcs and strategies to encourage women to develop their potential and to aspire to executive/managerial positions indicative, perhaps, of the short length of time during which such programmes had been in operation and suggestive of the need for constant vigilance in their application.

2.87 The Working Party is of the opinion that a significant difficulty arises for women at the foot of the traditional hierarchical structure of organisations. By their nature, hierarchical structures can offer development to fewer and fewer people as they progress up through the system. As the organisation narrows in towards its apex, more people have to adjust to going no further upwards. If a class of people, for whatever reason, never make it beyond the bottom few rungs of the ladder, then members of that class tend to lower their expectations and motivation in a measure of self-protection against frustration. In Ireland, where the group clustered at the bottom of the hierarchy comprises mainly women, this can be taken to represent the underuse of a central organisational resource in that the technical and managerial ability of nearly a third of employees is being almost totally by-passed. When formulating the scope of positive measures, therefore, it is necessary to look at ways and means of altering the distribution pattern of women in the workplace.

2.88 Against the background of the hierarchical structure of Irish public sector organisations referred to in paragraph 2.86, the thinking behind the Government's initiative was that a commitment to the principle of equality of opportunity by the Board of the State-sponsored body, which has the full and active commitment of management and of those who exercise supervisory functions in the body, should be supplemented by a policy of specific encouragement to women in the workforce to participate in training and promotional opportunities and to articulate their needs and requirements through appropriately established channels. The Government approved proposals on these lines in November, 1984, which envisaged proceeding in three stages. First, the Government would endorse a policy statement outlining the mechanism which should be used to translate principles of employment equality between men and women into specific action within the organisation, including the designation of a specific officer for that purpose. Secondly, the Board of Directors of each State-sponsored body would be asked to adhere to the policy enunciated by the Government and to disseminate its intention to do so to all members of staff and applicants for employment in the organisation, and to all contracting agencies and bodies. Thirdly, each State-sponsored body would be required to include information regarding progress on measures taken in its annual report – or, in the case of bodies which did not produce an annual report, the submission of an annual statement of progress to the Minister of the parent Department and the Minister for Labour.

RECOMMENDATION

2.89 The Working Party welcomes the Government decision in this regard and recommends that it should be given practical effect throughout the State-sponsored body sector as a matter of priority. In the interests of activating a joint response at company level to the Government initiative, we endorse the recommendation of the Employment Equality Agency in its Code of Practice that organisations drawing up an equal opportunities programme should consult the recognised trade unions in the enterprise and provide for joint union/management review of the programme on a continual basis.

Additional initiative in the Civil Service

2.90 A further development in this general area which is worthy of highlighting here is the fact that, shortly after taking up office, the Minister for Labour initiated an exercise to compile a profile of grade placements and upward mobility within his own Department. The purpose of the exercise was to identify constraints to achievement of equal opportunity for women in the Department and, based on an analysis of the data yielded by this exercise, to design mechanisms to eliminate such constraints. In terms of overall Civil Service Organisation, data relating to equal opportunity aspects of Civil Service recruitment and promotion have been made available to staff interests. This arrangement has been made at General Council under the Civil Service Conciliation and Arbitration Scheme and any further discussions can be pursued under the Scheme.

RECOMMENDATION

2.91 The Working Party welcomes these developments and recommends that employers in both the public and private sectors take similar initiatives.

2.92 Prior to the initiatives treated at paragraphs 2.85 to 2.91 above, positive action programmes in Ireland had been located mainly within those Irish companies which are associated with multinational enterprises such as Digital and IBM. The existence of such programmes can be attributed mainly to the corporate policies of the parent companies. However, initiatives had also been taken in some State-sponsored bodies such as Aer Rianta, the ESB, RTÉ and the IDA. In the case of the ESB, a number of recommendations pertinent to positive action were made in a report commissioned by management and these are taken account of at paragraph 2.96 below. In the case of RTÉ and the IDA, a review of the position in regard to the provision of equal opportunities was undertaken by joint working groups representative of management and workers. Indeed, the equal opportunities model adopted by the IDA provides for an on-going union/management input in the scheme, as endorsed by the Working Party in their Recommendation at paragraph 2.89 above.

2.93 These programmes accord with the contention at paragraph 2.82 above that the successful promotion of an initiative in the area of positive action depends crucially on how sensitive and adaptable it is to the tradition and nuances of the institutional structures of each country. For that reason, the position in Ireland has a voluntary or collective bargaining foundation. That also holds good for Britain, where a Programme of Action for Equal Opportunities for Women in the Civil Service has recently been introduced. The mechanisms on which the programme is based are: firstly a Civil Service Equal Opportunity Policy Statement which has been agreed with Departments and the Council of Civil Service Unions; secondly, the designation in each Department of an officer or officers with responsibility for the full scope of equal opportunity matters; thirdly, existing joint management and trade union machinery will be used to review and stimulate progress in the achievement of equal opportunity. Under the programme of action, a considerable amount of flexibility is given to individual Departments with a view to making progress, in agreement with trade union interests, on the restructuring of work patterns, career development, child care and maternity/paternity provisions and a number of other areas such as pensions and occupational health. The expectation is that alongside practical initiatives and promulgation of the Equal Opportunity Policy Statement, the publication of the programme of action and the designation of Equal Opportunity Officers will create the publicity necessary to begin to influence attitudes.

2.94 In contrast to the voluntarist tradition in Ireland and Britain, a highly regulated statutory framework is to be found in the United

States and Sweden. For over a decade now in the United States, the law has required not just equal opportunities for women and minorities as of the present, but that affirmative or positive action be taken to undo the effects of past discrimination, i.e. the scope and format of the administrative and enforcement machinery in the equal opportunities field derives from the experience of the evolution of civil rights measures introduced in the 1960s. Under the Affirmative Action Regulations, employers are obliged to monitor the flow of all categories of employees throughout their organisations. When this statistical checking reveals blocks to free movement upwards that affect some groups – for example, women – and not others, the organisation is obliged in law to introduce mechanisms and programmes to remove those blocks. In the case of Sweden, the Equality Act of 1980 requires not only a ban on discrimination, but also requires all employers to work actively to promote equality at the workplace. Under the latter, the goal is to distribute men and women as evenly as possible among different categories of employees. The aim is that each sex shall be represented by at least 40% of the employees for the distribution to be considered even and an Equal Opportunities Ombudsman exists to ensure that the Act is complied with. Although it is too early to evaluate the success of the Swedish experience, the initial progress made under the Act has indicated that it has been a workable instrument for greater equality between the sexes.

Positive action strategies

2.95 Under section 22 (b) of the Employment Equality Act 1977, provision has been made whereby the Labour Court might, in determining the appropriate remedy in a case of discrimination, have regard to steps which an employer might take to avoid the re-occurrence or continuation of discriminatory practices. In this connection, the Working Party considers it appropriate to draw from certain research available in the area of positive action, as well as from international experience, to put forward an indicative list of the key elements involved in strategies for positive action. In so doing, we have had regard to the Government's Policy Statement on Equality of Opportunity between Men and Women in Employment, which is outlined in Appendix 2.2 [not included], to the Code of Practice of the Employment Equality Agency and to the following research: two studies prepared for the EEC Commission, to help in the deliberations in relation to formulation of the EEC Action Programme and a study which was carried out within the UK Civil Service.

INDICATIVE LIST OF KEY ELEMENTS IN POSITIVE ACTION STRATEGIES

2.96 Drawing from the research referred to above, the following is
an indicative list of key elements in positive action strategies:

(i)   The desirability of the provision of 'infrastructural' or support-
      ing structures – such as child care facilities, opportunities for
      part-time work, flexible working hours, reinstatement
      possibilities, and special leave provisions – which would
      provide workers with family ties with the possibility of
      participating more easily in employment.

(ii) RECRUITMENT

(a)   Recruitment literature and publicity material should be
      reviewed to see if there is any way in which more emphasis
      could be placed on the opportunities for women in technical/
      technological/management jobs;
(b)   selection boards should include women members to the
      maximum extent possible;
(c)   guidance for selection boards should be revised to give more
      detailed information on the avoidance of discrimination; inter-
      viewers should be made familiar with interviewing techniques
      designed to secure equal treatment of each applicant;
(d)   the recruitment manager should, as far as practicable, monitor the
      results of the recruitment process to ensure that equality prevails;
(e)   efforts to attract women applicants to non-traditional job areas
      should be strengthened, with regular reviews of progress.

(iii) PROMOTION

(a)   As with recruitment boards, promotion board interviewers should
      be made aware of biases which can occur; specific training should
      be given on equal opportunities aspects of selection;
(b)   members should be required to record the reasons for their
      decisions to ensure that the concept of equal opportunities is
      applied.

(iv) TRAINING

(a)   Departments/firms should encourage women to attend courses
      and make the maximum use of the training opportunities
      available;
(b)   women, because of their level of qualifications, experience of
      life/work patterns, may have personal training requirements
      which may not be successfully met by existing training
      programmes; specifically, because of traditional lack of

confidence etc. of women, an 'assertiveness' training element
is needed in most courses;
(c) there is a need for special training for male managers in their
role of supervising female staff members;
(d) there is a need for special training and career planning for
women in 'dead-end' jobs, to help them to re-launch their
career, or enter a different career stream within the
organisation.

(v) ALLOCATION OF DUTIES
It is necessary to ensure that women are not assigned to narrow or
restricted areas of work or to particular locations, which might
restrict their lateral, let alone vertical, mobility within an
organisation; there should be comprehensive guidelines devised for
personnel divisions to help avoid this.

(vi) MOBILITY
Policies on mobility should be implemented as flexibly as possible;
studies show that organisations sometimes expect a greater deal of
mobility from their executives than is really necessary.

(vii) STATISTICS
From the point of view of planning and monitoring an equal opportunity policy, data on the female staff in an organisation is needed, such
as: the distribution of women by type of job, grade, pay, qualifications,
the proportion of women attending training courses and comparison
of the percentages of men and women achieving promotion.

TYPICAL POSITIVE ACTION PROGRAMME
2.97 Taking account of the indicative list of key elements contained at
paragraph 2.96 above, the process of developing a positive action
programme in an organisation would typically involve the following
stages:
(i)   the Department/firm would, following consultations with trade
union/employee representatives, draw up a policy which
would commit it to creating an environment conducive to
equal opportunities; this policy would be well publicised
among staff and in advertising for the filling of posts;
(ii) an executive of the company would then be appointed to
assume responsibility for the programme; the executive would
be supported in the task by a working party composed of
representatives from management, staff and unions;

(iii) relevant data would be collected and analysed;
(iv) targets would be set to remedy discriminations and disadvantages and specific measures introduced to achieve greater equality, along the lines indicated in paragraph 2.96;
(v) a 'feedback' network would be established and regular monitoring and updating, where necessary, of the programme would take place; and
(vi) the programme would be submitted to the relevant Equality Agency for appraisal and review.

EMPLOYMENT

8.15 While many women running a home see their role as full-time 'homemakers', particularly when their children are growing, for an increasing number the possibility of employment outside the home at some time in the future is a consideration. In the study of women and work in Ireland already referred to, 37.6% of the women working full-time in the home indicated that they would like to work or go back to work outside the home at some point. Looking towards a longer-term perspective, 60% of this group stated that they wanted their daughters to combine the wife/mother role with a career. For the women themselves, the strongest correlation of intention to enter the labour force was found to be a woman's age, with younger women being significantly more likely to express such an intention. Other relevant factors influencing desire for future labour force participation were previous work experience, education, positive attitudes towards employment on the part of husbands and parents. In general, the presence of children was not seen as a deterrent to labour force participation. This bears out the reality, as indicated by the statistics, that the rate of increase in labour force participation by women has been particularly marked for women in the child-bearing age (15–44). This study concluded that there was a considerable potential labour force participation by women working full time in the home, which would require societal adjustments such as those discussed in the chapter on employment (i.e. more part-time work opportunities, parental leave, child care facilities, flexible working hours).

COSTS ASSOCIATED WITH RETURN TO EMPLOYMENT

8.16 For women who wish to re-enter employment, however, there are both opportunities and obstacles. The growth of service type employment in recent years has created opportunities for women workers. Obstacles include gaps in training or education, due to prolonged absence from employment and the high cost of returning to work, particularly if children have to be cared for. Costs associated with working have been identified as follows: income tax, social security, pension contribution, meals and snacks, transport, gifts and social gatherings associated with work, medical expenses arising from the job, care of children, union and professional association dues, professional publications, clothing and hairdressing expenses, educational expenses, other. The extent of these costs would of course vary with a woman's income, but on any estimate, they are likely to be considerable and many women therefore work for a low net return. On the other hand, some of the costs may be perceived as benefits, (such as help with domestic chores, extra clothes etc.) and can therefore be seen to justify the low return. Also, the additional income of a wife returning to work improves the general standard of living of a family and in some cases is essential to maintain a basic standard of living, particularly during recessionary times. Wider community costs include retraining and educational programmes. As has already been discussed, women can be severely handicapped in their careers through lack of vocational guidance early in school life when important choices are made. Also many women are prevented from taking advantage of career openings through lack of educational qualifications, or out-of-date qualifications. While opportunities for adult education exist on a wide front, in practice adjustments in course timetables etc. are needed if women with family responsibilities are to benefit. Educational television can be of considerable benefit for women working at home. Adult education and retraining programmes have already been discussed in the education and employment chapters and the recommendations made in this context are re-emphasised. In relation to community costs, however, the OECD study, referred to earlier in this paragraph indicates that re-entry programmes for older women can be a very satisfactory investment for the community, their economic success depending on the value of the work the woman performs, the length and cost of training, the rate of labour wastage and the costs of substituting the services the women would have been performing in the home if she were not in paid employment.

On the basis of data on participation rates of women in the labour force, declining fertility rates and changing attitudes – becoming more positive towards married women in employment – the option of return to employment at a future date is likely to be considered by more and more women working in the home. The main constraint facing these women, however, is the unemployment situation. In the national survey of women and work carried out as background to the recent study prepared at Maynooth College, the results showed that, at present, when women working at home think of the possibility of taking up employment, the first obstacle that crops up is not the difficulty of managing the housework or minding the children but the difficulty of finding employment. Nonetheless the fact that attitudinal and other major changes have taken place which facilitate the re-entry of women presently working full time in the home into employment – even if employment opportunities are scarce at present – has implications for future employment policy and for the role of women generally in society.

RECOMMENDATION

8.18 For women who have been out of the labour force for some time, and who have therefore missed out on on-the-job training and promotion, the Working Party considers that there is a particular need for help at the point of re-entry in the form of training and counselling on career choices. One of the most important implications of the research completed in the area of women wishing to re-enter employment is that there are many women in search of employment opportunities who do not regard themselves as unemployed or who are not registered as such, making it difficult to determine exactly how big the female labour force is or what its characteristics are. For instance, the Maynooth study referred to explored the issue of the size and components of the female labour force by taking a broad and inclusive measure of income-related activities among women and by comparing the results of that measure with other measures of the female labour force, especially that contained in the five per cent sample estimates of the 1981 Census of Population. The differences in the results produced by the different measures were considerable: the activity rate among married women estimated in the Maynooth study was significantly higher than that in the 1981 estimates, the 'extra' female labour force being in three major groups: part-time employees, unpaid family workers on family farms and unemployed women who would normally report themselves as engaged in home duties. As regards official statistics, information from the 1979 Labour Force Survey shows that if all women working in the home, who in addition said either that they had occasional work outside the home or that they were seeking work outside the home, were included in an 'extended' labour force this would be 12% above the figure normally used.

Early in the 1990s the Irish government established a Second Commission on the Status of Women. Its task was to survey the outcomes of the 1972 Commission's recommendations, as well as to make recommendations of its own. The Second Commissions' *Report to Government* (1993) is a wide-ranging document, with eleven chapters yielding some fifty pages of recommendations. We consider here, once again, developments related to women and work. Other concerns in the 1993 report, such as health, education and legal status, will be addressed in subsequent chapters.

In reviewing the 1972 report's recommendations on pay and employment, the Second Commission pointed to a number of positive outcomes. The 'Equality Contract' Acts of the 1970s, mentioned above, were central factors in dealing with discrimination. The Employment Equality (Employment of Women) Order 1987 permitted night-time and Sunday employment for women in industry. The Commission also cited the Unfair Dismissals Act 1977 and the Maternity (Protection of Employees) Act 1981 as enhancing women's job security. The Commission also concluded that progress had occurred on women's access to training, employment counselling and the like.

The Second Commission considered the conditions of women in the workplace after twenty years and offered a dozen of its own work-related recommendations. These had to do with women's access to employment, equality of opportunity and the perceived need for an overall 'employment strategy for women'. The Commission saw 'flexibility' as a key to success in these areas, emphasising flexible hours of work, job-sharing and career breaks.

The Second Commission also called for a strengthening of the Maternity Act 1981 to conform to the EC Directive of 1992, and for an extension of such maternity benefits to adopting mothers. The Maternity Protection Act 1994 and the Adoptive Leave Act 1995 implemented these recommendations. Finally, the Second Commission urged the establishment of a statutory minimum wage as an anti-poverty measure, noting that Ireland and the United Kingdom were by then the only EC member states without any national minimum wage provision. The *Second Progress Report of the Monitoring Committee on the*

Implementation of the Recommendations of the Second Commission on the Status of Women (1996) notes that 'it is not proposed that a statutory minimum wage should be introduced'. The Commission's recommendation was said to be at variance with Ireland's 'voluntarist tradition of industrial relations', and in any case, not only had the system of Joint Labour Committees established minimum rates of pay in areas not covered by collective bargaining agreements, but recent economic development programmes and changes in the tax regime had targeted low-paid workers.

Second Commission on the Status of Women, *Report to Government (1993)*

In this Chapter the Commission addresses the issues facing women already in work or looking for employment. We are concerned that the Government should devise an approach to women's employment which would reflect the actual lifestyles and lifestyle trends of women and so take into account such factors as: the growing participation in employment by women with young children; structural and attitudinal barriers; problems caused by a segregated labour market and the low pay rates of many women.

We make the case for affirmative measures such as strengthened employment equality legislation; a national minimum wage; equal opportunities programmes; and specific encouragement for the entrepreneurial talents of women. We also consider in detail the issue of reconciling work and family obligations.

3.1.1 PROFILE OF WOMEN AT WORK

Among EC countries Ireland has one of the lowest rates of participation by women aged between 15 to 64 in work outside the home. The European Community average is 42% compared to 32.9% in Ireland. While, theoretically, all members of the population aged between 15 and 64 could be available for work, for a variety of reasons not all of them are. The 'labour force' is the measurement of people within that age group who are actually at work, or who are registered as unemployed, or who are seeking to enter or re-enter the world of work. Women make up 49.3% of the population aged between 15 and 64, but they account for only 32.3% of the labour force. While only 32.9% of women of working age are in the labour force 70.9% of men participate.

3.1.2 TRENDS IN LABOUR FORCE PARTICIPATION

The proportion of the labour force consisting of women has grown only slightly – from 29.1% to 32.3% – over the past ten years. However, there have been substantial changes in the nature of women's participation. More young, single women are staying longer in full-time education and therefore outside the labour force. This has been offset by increased participation of married women. (There has been a rapid increase in the proportion of the female labour force who are married, up from 30.2% in 1981 to 48.5% in 1991.) In this respect, Irish experience has reflected a widespread international trend.

The labour force participation of married women is an indicator of the evolving roles of women in society. Women have more diverse roles. It is no longer a clear divide between the role of mother in the home versus single working woman, but rather roles can comprise a number of de facto permutations and combinations of married/single, economically active/engaged in home duties, and with/without children. It is important to be aware of this increasing trend of diversity. While the largest labour force increase in recent years has been amongst married women, the number of single mothers is rising considerably. The incidence of marriage breakdown is also contributing to increased presence of lone mothers in the workforce.

In Ireland, as elsewhere, the net effect of these trends has been a marked rise in the labour force participation of women of childbearing age.

The emerging data for younger women suggests that there is now a greater tendency for women to remain in the labour force during the peak child rearing years. This may be due to a variety of factors which include the difficulty of re-entry to the labour force after voluntary interruption, economic reasons and the desire not to be isolated in the home.

A lower marriage rate suggests that there will be a continued strong presence of single women in the work force. While parenthood is a choice, other family responsibilities, notably ageing and infirm parents, affect single and married alike. By and large, elder care is an obligation that devolves firmly upon women. Given the fact that our population has started to age, this is likely to become a more urgent problem.

The increased presence of women, especially married women, over the past twenty-five years in the labour force has been a marked feature of employment growth in OECD countries. It has been closely linked to the growth of service employment over that period. In Ireland in 1987, 77% of all women's employment was in the services sector.

3.1.4 STRUCTURAL OBSTACLES TO WOMEN'S PARTICIPATION IN THE LABOUR FORCE

There are number of structural obstacles which are inhibiting the participation of women in the labour force.

Twenty-three per cent of registered unemployed in Ireland are women. This is in all likelihood a depressed figure since many women who would be interested in paid employment are not on the Live Register due to lack of entitlement to social welfare benefits. The high rate of unemployment generally inhibits many women who would like to become part of the labour force from taking the decision to seek work.

In cases where the partner is unemployed, the proportion of women in the labour force is lower than average. This is likely to be due to the fact that if a woman enters employment, the social welfare adult dependant rate paid to her husband for her maintenance ceases as soon as she earns more than IR£55 per week

International comparisons suggest women-headed households experience higher rates of poverty than any other group in society and yet, the whole thrust of income support payments for lone parents in Ireland has been to discourage them from participation in the labour force.

Employment equality legislation, in principle, enables women to exercise choice in their careers and at different stages in their careers. Ending paid differentials for the same job, the recognition of the rights of women at work, to be married without experiencing legal and administrative penalties, and the right to a maternity benefit are very important towards this end.

3.1.5 ATTITUDINAL OBSTACLES TO WOMEN'S PARTICIPATION IN THE LABOUR FORCE

In addition to the restrictive practices which prevailed before the enactment of employment equality legislation, and the structural obstacles outlined above, attitudes can also be a powerful deterrent to the realisation of equal opportunity. In Ireland, attitudinal change has been much slower than legislative change – research shows Irish opinion as being at the more sexist end of the EC scale, see Table 3.1 [designated Table 2.1 in this book].

Table 2.1
Proportions of survey respondents in EC member states having equal
confidence in both sexes for various occupations, 1987 (%)

	Bus or train driver	Surgeon	Barrister	Public representative	Average of the four
Denmark	86	85	82	86	84
Netherlands	75	83	75	79	78
France	77	70	70	68	70
United Kingdom	61	70	66	75	68
Belgium	67	66	64	67	66
Spain	56	65	69	67	64
Portugal	52	67	65	63	61
Germany (West)	57	55	59	64	58
Luxembourg	47	58	60	62	56
Greece	52	56	61	58	56
Italy	54	56	55	59	56
Ireland	43	51	50	61	51
EC 12	63	64	63	67	64

Source: Men and Women of Europe, 1987 Women of Europe, Supplement
No. 2 (Brussels: Commission of the European Communities, 1988)

It will only be possible for women to realise their opportunities if
attitudinal change occurs within two significant groups. These are:

(i)   for the work place to recognise that both women and men
      employees have domestic responsibilities and to make
      attempts to structure work to take account of this reality;
(ii) for men to assume co-responsibility for domestic and family
      commitments.

For too long work and family have been regarded as mutually
exclusive spheres of interest. Domestic commitments and work
complement each other in the life of any individual, even if the time
demands of each function do, of necessity, compete with each
other. In our view it is necessary to end this compartmentalisation
and to respond to the actual domestic pressures on women and
men in Irish society in the context of:

• training for work,
• the organisation of work,
• the practice of work, and
• child care, elder care and other family responsibilities.

The *Second Progress Report* (1996) on the implementation of
the Second Commission's recommendations noted some recent

developments. As part of a movement in the early 1990s to reform the equality legislation of an earlier period, the Second Commission had recommended a number of amendments and institutional changes. These were reflected in the Employment Equality Bill of 1996, which was aimed at expanding the grounds for a claim of discrimination in employment. Before it could be enacted, however, the Supreme Court declared the Bill unconstitutional. A revised Bill became the Employment Equality Act 1998, superseding the Pay and Employment Acts of 1974 and 1977.

The 1998 Act outlaws discrimination on grounds of gender, marital status, family status, sexual orientation, religious belief, age, disability, race or membership of the Traveller community. It also widens the scope of anti-discriminatory scrutiny to include 'all areas relevant to employment'.

The Act extends protection to the defence forces, as well as outlawing sexual harassment 'in the workplace and in the course of employment'. Employers are allowed to develop 'positive action measures to promote equal opportunities' for women. As monitoring body, the Equality Authority replaces the Employment Equality Agency that had performed that function since 1977.

PENSIONS

The first Commission on the Status of Women had considered another work-related issue: women's access to occupational pension schemes. The Commission had found that, while such plans were formerly found mainly in relation to state employment, by 1972 they had 'become an integral part of most companies' financing operations'. A study by the Economic and Social Research Institute showed that only 27 per cent of female wage earners were in pension plans, in contrast to 67 per cent of male wage earners. The Commission had ascribed the disparity to the more 'stringent eligibility requirements' for women. Accordingly, the Commission had recommended changes in the practices governing participation in occupational pension plans.

The Working Party of 1985 alluded to an anticipated European directive on equal treatment of men and women in pension plans, but it did not explore the question. Rather, the National Pensions Board was established in 1986 'to advise the Minister for

Social Welfare on the future regulation of occupational pension schemes'. The Board's *Report on Equal Treatment of Men and Women in Occupational Pension Schemes* (1989) held that the Anti-Discrimination (Pay) Act 1974 did not adequately protect women's pension rights. The Board cited both the European directive (86/378/EEC) and Article 119 of the Treaty of Rome as the legal basis for recommending legislation to govern pension schemes in Ireland.

The Pensions Act 1990 was developed on the basis of the Board's report. Part VII provided for equal treatment of men and women in occupational benefit schemes. In the *National Pensions Board Final Report* (1993, p. 89) the Board noted that the European Court of Justice had ruled that benefits related to occupational schemes constitute 'pay'. Thus, the equal pay article, Article 119, imposed a legal requirement for the equal treatment of men and women in such schemes.

CHILD CARE

An issue that remained largely unresolved into the 1990s was that of child care, a concern that affected women's participation in the labour force. The first Commission on the Status of Women had recommended the establishment of child care facilities in new housing schemes, as well as tighter regulation of child care groups. In the following two decades these themes were often repeated: the overall case for child care and the important questions of staff competence, as well as the safety, health and developmental concerns of the children served.

Commission on the Status of Women, *Report to Minister for Finance* (1972)

Many married women who find that they must re-enter employment, or mothers who are ill or hospitalised for any length of time, are faced with the task of finding suitable care facilities for young children. The most satisfactory solution to this problem is where arrangements can be made for parents or other relations to undertake responsibility for them while the mother is working or incapacitated. Frequently, it is not possible for the mother to make this kind of arrangement and she must either try to avail of professional child-minding facilities or else depend on older children to look after the younger ones outside school hours.

This latter solution is clearly a very unsafe and unsatisfactory one but representations have been made to us that, in certain areas, it is not an infrequent occurrence where mothers are working and that the responsibility lies with the State and other authorities for not providing suitable crèche and day-nursery facilities where young children can receive skilled care if the mother is forced by economic necessity to resume work. By the term 'crèche' we mean a centre where children in good health up to between two and three years of age are cared for during all or the greater part of a normal working day by qualified, mainly professional, personnel. In referring to day-nurseries, we mean a similar type of centre catering for children of from about three to six years of age. The same overall standards of professional qualifications of staff are not necessarily required for the day nursery as for the crèche. Pre-school playgroups, which are mainly organised on a commercial basis and which take children usually from two to three hours a day, are, we feel, of very limited value in enabling the mother to take up employment although they are very important in freeing mothers from the strain of continuous child-minding and allowing them some freedom of movement outside the home during the day which they might not otherwise achieve.

In 1983 a publication of the Department of Labour, *Child Care Facilities for Working Parents*, took up the issue, but little was done to attack the problem. Most of the proposals of the Working Party on Child Care Facilities dealt with controlling and regulating day care facilities. However, the report did recommend cooperation between employers and employees in establishing day care facilities at or near the workplace. In addition, the Working Party recommended that the state consider providing tax relief and grants to stimulate these initiatives.

The Second Commission on the Status of Women cited the limited implementation of the Child Care Act 1991. The Commission also suggested that Ireland had not kept pace with other developed countries in establishing community- and employment-based child care. In addition, the Commission provided a strong statement on the child care issue. It criticised the government for a lack of action and urged a deeper commitment to support of child care as a public policy function. It also cited the European Community's child care recommendations of March 1992 as a stimulus to policy development. The Commission's own recommendations were calculated to aid the Irish government in this area.

Second Commission on the Status of Women, *Report to Government* (1993)

4.1.1 INTRODUCTION

Child care can be described as the work and responsibility involved in caring for children and meeting their full range of needs, and how that work and responsibility is organised and divided. While child care is an issue that can affect both parents, realistically in our society at present the responsibility for child care devolves on women, whether married or lone parents. Therefore, it is women who are most adversely affected by the absence of accessible, affordable, quality child care supports. The Commission's perspective on child care is twofold. Firstly, we are concerned that the lack of supports for child care seriously limits women's potential to play an equal part in society and, if they wish, to pursue paid employment. Secondly, society has a responsibility to ensure the highest possible quality of care for dependent children; it is not enough to devolve responsibility for providing this on to mothers alone.

At present in Ireland, child care as a community or economic service is characterised by a virtually total absence of standards and protective legislation and by minimal financial support. The Commission seeks to make recommendations which will change this situation for the better by responding to the actual needs emerging in our society.

4.1.2 THE HISTORICAL CONTEXT

In Ireland until recent times child care was, in the main, carried out within the family by the mother, often supported by the extended family. The mother's fulltime career as homemaker complemented the role of the father as fulltime breadwinner. This model of child care was never universal. It excluded the children of widows who had no option but to find paid work. It also excluded families depending for their income on sectors of employment where traditionally it was easier for women than men to find work, for example in the clothing industry.

In modern societies organised child care is intended to replace the previous extended family, to provide support to families without many resources of their own, and to ensure provision of the stimulation and developmental activities necessary for children.

4.1.3 SOCIAL CHANGES

In Europe generally, very significant social changes have occurred since the Second World War. These include a generally improved economic climate, rising levels of educational qualifications for both women and men, fertility control for women, an attendant falling birth rate, a rise in the number of one-parent families, and the emergence of equality and equal opportunity for women as a civil and legal rights issue. These factors have interacted to result in increased labour force participation rates on the part of women and, in particular, in increased levels of employment of mothers outside the home.

In Ireland, these changes have also taken place, but on an even more dramatic scale, because they have been telescoped into the past twenty years. The labour force participation rate of married women has increased from 16.7% in 1971 to 26.9% in 1991 and the non-marital birthrate increased sixfold to 16.6% in 1991. Comparison of 1985 and 1988 European Labour Force Survey data shows Ireland as among those countries registering the greatest increase in participation of mothers with young children in the labour force. By 1990, 35% of mothers in Ireland with children under 7 years of age were in the labour force. This compares with an EC average of 53.3%.

4.1.4 THE CONSEQUENCES OF SOCIAL CHANGE

In developed countries a major impetus for the development of child care policy and of organised child care facilities has been the trend for more women of childbearing age to remain in the workforce or to seek to return to work. In Ireland these trends are also manifesting themselves. between 1971 and 1989 the participation rate of married women increased from 7.5% to 23.7%. In 1991, the rate increased to 26.9%.

4.1.6 CHILD CARE AS A SOCIAL POLICY ISSUE

Child care is an equality issue because the unequal distribution of responsibility presents barriers to participation by women with children in employment, education, and training. Child care is also an economic efficiency issue in that inadequacies in support and provision mean that some of the best educated and highly skilled human resources are not available in the marketplace, their absence due, not to choice, but to the absence of choice. This constitutes an inefficient use of investment in education and training. Finally, child care is a human rights issue for both women and children and for those men who wish to develop the nurturing aspect of their relationship with their children.

For the reasons set out above it is clear that child care – focusing on the needs of children, their quality of life, wellbeing and development – must be a major area of social policy, complementary to both equal opportunity policy, and to education.

4.1.7 THE CASE FOR CHILD CARE

In our view the question of child care must be tackled for the following reasons:

(i)   Social equity
(ii) Economic efficiency
(iii) Labour market trends
(iv) Supports for homemakers
(v)   Development of children

4.2 Government policy/EC policy

4.2.1 EXISTING INFLUENCES ON CHILD CARE

There are two significant influences impacting on the emergence of Government policy on child care. One of these influences is concerned with the health and welfare of children. The expression of government policy in this area can be found in the Child Care Act 1991. It is important to note that only Part VII of the Act, supervision of pre-school services, deals with child care in the general sense we have outlined. The other nine Parts of the Act are concerned with the welfare of children in need of adequate care and protection. In other words, there is only very limited recognition, as yet, by the Government that it has policy functions and obligations regarding child care for children who do not fall into the category of social need.

The other main influence on the piecemeal development of the child care debate in Ireland has been EC-led, with the elaboration under the Treaty of Rome of equal opportunities policies which have focused very significantly on the importance of child care facilities for women in employment.

To sum up: interest in child care as an issue has been led by two main considerations, the development and welfare of the child, and the need for supports for the caring parent, generally the mother. Such supports are important for all mothers but the need for them is more acute if the mother works, or wishes to seek work, outside the home. In the view of the Commission, these considerations complement each other and in our recommendation we aim to take account of both objectives.

4.2.2 WORKING PARTY ON CHILD CARE FACILITIES FOR THE CHILDREN OF WORKING PARENTS

In 1983 the Working Party on Child Care Facilities in its report to the Minister for Labour came up with a set of proposals for the provision and regulation of child care facilities. The core recommendation of this report was that: the overall aim of official policy should be the provision, as soon as possible, of a comprehensive day care service in each Health Board region to cater for the needs of working parents and others who have difficulties in having their children looked after.

Nobody pretends that it is easy to devise recommendations on child care which have the wholehearted support of all social partners, including Government. That does not excuse or explain the minimal policy initiatives on child care and the failure of successive Governments since 1983 to develop some of the Working Party proposals.

4.2.3 EC RECOMMENDATION ON CHILD CARE

An important stimulus has been given to the development of a child care policy in Ireland by the agreement of an EC recommendation on child care. In March 1992, Ireland, along with the other EC Member States, adopted a recommendation on child care to the effect that Member States should take, and/or progressively encourage, initiatives to enable women and men to reconcile their occupational, family, and upbringing responsibilities arising from the care of children. The recommendation sets out in broad terms the kinds of initiatives Member States might take towards that end. The recommendation also specifies that Member States should report to the EC Commission within three years of its adoption on the measures taken to give it effect. At paragraph 4.3.2 [not included] of this Report we make a number of recommendations on the kinds of initiatives the Government might take, so that it would be in a position to report progress to the EC Commission in three years time.

The Commission recommends that child care policy should be devised and implemented through a small policy unit in the Department of Health, advised by a Committee of senior officials drawn from the Departments of Education, the Environment, Labour, the proposed Department of Women's Affairs and the social partners. The Child Care Policy Unit should be established immediately and should be charged with the development and phased implementation of an integrated child care plan, and the administration of the child care development budget in order to realise those objectives.

Following the general recommendations that the government and the social partners should strive to reconcile work and domestic commitments, the Commission offered a number of specific recommendations. These included the development of workplace child care facilities; the establishment of a child care policy in the Department of Health; favourable tax treatment for the capital costs of setting up the facilities; and the development of local child care partnerships involving employers, unions and governmental authorities. There was also a call for a training and certification regimen for child care workers, and a recommendation that there be year-round child care provided by schools.

These recommendations covered familiar terrain, encouraging innovative initiatives by employers and calling for the government to be more 'proactive' in increasing the number of places in existing facilities. There was a perceived need for counselling for parents who were seeking child care services, and for child care to be made available for those attending state institutions of training and education.

Finally, *The Second Progress Report of the Monitoring Committee on the Implementation of the Recommendations of the Second Commission on the Status of Women* (1996) notes that by implementing all sections of the Child Care Act 1991 the government had substantially met the Second Commission's recommendations, notably by:

- establishing standards for pre-school services;
- providing child care services for disadvantaged children and children at risk;
- creating a Child Care Unit in the Department of Health, with IR£30 million in funding for the period 1993–96;
- establishing regional child care development offices as well as rural community centres; and
- making capital cost allowances for the development of child care facilities.

CONCLUSION

Three quarters of a century after the founding of the Free State, Irish law contained a battery of measures intended to promote equal and equitable treatment of women in the work place. These measures covered all facets of employment: advertising in relation to job search; pay, promotion and dismissal policies; maternity leave and child care; re-entry to the labour force; sexual harassment; and pensions. Despite this range of remedies for discrimination, opinions differed on the extent of the gains that women had experienced in the areas of pay and employment.

CHAPTER THREE

Social welfare and disadvantage

ELIMINATING DISCRIMINATION

Following its extensive treatment of employment and pay issues affecting women, the first Commission on the Status of Women turned to an examination of discriminatory practices in social welfare. This was a huge task: as Aileen Donnelly has noted, 'no other field of law affects so directly and so significantly such an overwhelming proportion of the population'.[1] The Social Welfare Commission had noted in the late 1980s that the social welfare system 'had developed in a piecemeal manner over several decades', and that, in many instances, 'gender was the basis for social welfare payments',[2] creating a likelihood of unequal treatment. Moreover, as in the case of pay and employment, European directives were becoming increasingly relevant to the Irish situation. Thus, the social welfare system was an obvious object of scrutiny for the Commission. In an introductory paragraph the Commission's report alludes to the complexity of the issue.

Commission on the Status of Women, *Report to Minister for Finance* (1972)

Women and social welfare

326. The various matters which have come to our notice regarding discrimination against women in the social welfare code are dealt with below. At the outset, we feel it is desirable that we should state our acceptance of the fact that schemes of social insurance and assistance cannot achieve complete equity as between individuals or between different groups of persons, nor is it possible, under any statutory scheme, to provide for all eventualities nor, having regard to national resources, to provide

complete protection for everyone in all adverse circumstances which may arise. We have endeavoured accordingly, in our recommendations on matters arising in this area, to take account of these constraints in so far as is compatible with our terms of reference which require us to make recommendations on the steps necessary to place women on an equal footing with men. Although women's position in society has altered noticeably over recent decades, it is nevertheless true that the average woman's life-pattern is and will remain, different from that of the average man. Accordingly, a narrow interpretation of our terms of reference to the effect that a woman must be eligible to receive every benefit available to a man would not, we feel, achieve, overall, the desired end. In this connection, it must be borne in mind – and does not appear to be generally appreciated by many of the bodies from whom we received submissions – that there is no predetermined actuarial basis for the social insurance scheme and that the benefits available are financed not only by the contributions of insured persons but by those of employers and by State grant from general taxation. In general therefore, our approach has been to indicate ways in which differences in treatment between men and women may be eliminated except where such differences are based on reasons which we consider are substantial and valid. We have, throughout, been conscious of the necessity to avoid the danger which exists that by eliminating one form of discrimination other types of discrimination may be brought into existence. At the same time, we have tried to ensure that women, or particular categories of women, (such as widows, deserted wives) are provided for in relation to the risks to which their position in society makes them particularly vulnerable.

Summary of recommendations
580. The following is a summary of our recommendations.

Women and social welfare
(18) RATE OF UNEMPLOYMENT AND DISABILITY BENEFIT PAYABLE TO WIDOWS IN RECEIPT OF WIDOW'S CONTRIBUTORY PENSION
(i) A widow should receive flat-rate unemployment and disability benefit at a rate which is not less than that payable to a married woman.
(ii) As an interim measure, while the implementation of the previous recommendation is being considered, the social welfare contribution for a widow should be appropriately

reduced while she is entitled to unemployment and disability benefit at half the ordinary rate. The employer's contribution should be maintained at the ordinary rate for a woman.

(19) MARRIED WOMEN IN THE SOCIAL INSURANCE SCHEME
(i)　A woman should retain any accumulated title to social insurance benefit after marriage but the present marriage grant should at the same time be abolished. The change should take effect concurrently with the legislation prohibiting the compulsory retirement of women on marriage recommended in paragraph 257 [not included].

A number of Acts in the 1970s addressed some of these issues. The Social Welfare Act 1973 relieved the employee social insurance contribution for widows receiving widow's pensions. (The Social Welfare Act 1990 provided for a phased reintroduction of this contribution.) The 1973 Act also allowed a woman to retain entitlement to social insurance contributions made before marriage. Under the Social Welfare Regulations 1973 women working in domestic service and agriculture became eligible for unemployment benefits on the same conditions as other workers. Finally, the 1973 Act provided a Social Assistance Allowance for unmarried mothers who keep their children. This provision became part of the Lone Parent's Allowance.

Three more statutes introduced important changes. The Social Welfare Act 1974 granted title to children's allowance to mothers rather than fathers. The Social Welfare (No. 2) Act 1974 introduced a Social Assistance Allowance for wives of prisoners serving terms of six months or more. The Social Welfare Act 1978 eased the unemployment insurance eligibility requirements for single women and widows.

In *Irish Women: The Agenda for Practical Action* (1985), the Working Party on Women's Affairs and Family Law Reform acknowledged that gains had been made but identified areas where, in its view, more had to be done.

Working Party on Women's Affairs and Family Law Reform, *Irish Women: Agenda for Practical Action* (1985)

Social welfare

6.1 The Irish social security system, in common with the experience in other countries, has evolved from the poor laws of an earlier age into the comprehensive system of the present time, encompassing social insurance, social assistance and health care. Inasmuch as many of the refinements of the system have taken place over the past thirty years, it must be acknowledged that successive Governments have, overall, demonstrated a commendable ability to react to the process of rapid social change over the period. Paradoxically, but perhaps not surprisingly, the system was slow to adjust specifically to the new role of women brought about by the economic and social development of our country from the late 1950s onwards. This fact was highlighted most clearly in the Report of the Commission on the Status of Women and, although much has been achieved to eliminate discriminations in the system since that Report was published, there are still a number of important areas which need to be tackled.

Commission on Social Welfare
6.2 In considering the issues to be discussed in this Chapter, the Working Party has noted the decision of the Minister for Social Welfare in August, 1983, to establish a Commission on Social Welfare. The Commission is to review and report on the social welfare system and related social services and to make recommendations for their development having regard to the needs of modern Irish society. In particular, the Commission is being asked to review the system of pay-related social insurance and health contributions and their effects on the provision of social security and employment.

6.3 While acknowledging the comprehensive review of the social welfare system which is being carried out by the Commission, the Working Party do not consider it inconsistent on their part to outline their own views on certain schemes under the system in the following paragraphs which they recommend for consideration by the Commission.

Issues for consideration
6.4 For the purposes of this Chapter, the Working Party considered the social security system insofar as it affects women under the following broad headings:
(i)   the remaining areas of discrimination in the Social Welfare Code;
(ii) family policy;
(iii) social insurance benefits for women who break their employment and for the self-employed; and
(iv) the Prescribed Relative Allowance and Single Women's Allowance.
It should be noted that other issues in the social welfare area

which are of crucial importance to women – such as assistance for one-parent families, and the question of whether there should be a single one-parent family allowance – have been dealt with in the chapters dealing with Single Parents and Women Working in the Home.

Remaining areas of discrimination in the social welfare code

6.5 As indicated in paragraph 6.1 above, much of the discrimination against women in the Social Welfare Code has been eliminated over the past decade or so. For example, single women may now claim unemployment assistance on the same basis as applies to married and single men, and steps have hitherto been taken towards eliminating the discrimination against married women by, for example, increasing the duration for which they can receive unemployment benefit. The elimination of any remaining discriminations in this area is required under the terms of the EEC Directive on the 'progressive implementation of the principle of equal treatment for men and women in matters of social security'.

EEC Directive on Equal Treatment for Men and Women in Matters of Social Security

6.6 This Directive provides that there should be no discrimination whatsoever on grounds of sex either directly or indirectly by reference to marital or family status. In particular, the Directive prohibits discrimination with regard to the scope of and conditions of access to the social welfare schemes, the obligation to contribute, the calculation of contributions and the calculation of benefits – including increases due in respect of a spouse and for dependants – and the conditions governing the duration and retention of entitlement to benefits. The schemes with which the Directive is concerned are sickness, invalidity, old age, accidents at work and occupational diseases and unemployment assistance. The Directive also refers to social assistance schemes insofar as they are intended to supplement or replace the other schemes covered by the Directive. In discussing the question of the application of the Directive in the Irish context, it must be borne in mind that Ireland is now obliged to comply with its provisions. While the arrangements which have been decided upon may not meet with the favour of all social welfare recipients, the fact that they entail substantial net additional cost to the Exchequer must be regarded as an earnest of the Government's commitment to the principle of equal treatment.

6.7 The areas where the principle of equal treatment are not observed in the Irish social welfare code at present, and which will require amendment to conform with the terms of the EEC Directive, have been identified as applying almost exclusively to married women. At present married women –

(i) receive lower rates of benefit than men in the schemes of disability benefit, unemployment benefit, invalidity pension and occupational injuries benefits;

(ii) can only receive unemployment benefit for a maximum of 312 days as against 390 days generally;

(iii) are effectively debarred from the unemployment assistance scheme (for a married woman to qualify for unemployment assistance either her husband must be dependent on her or she must not be a dependant of his); and

(iv) have conditions applied to them in the matter of adult and child dependants which are considerably less favourable than those applying to married men.

Government decision in relation to the EEC Directive

6.8 To eliminate these discriminatory features, the Government have now decided as follows:

(i) married women must be paid the same rates of benefit and for the same duration as men and single women; this proposal will result in about 40,000 married women receiving increases in their weekly entitlements; the vast majority would be on disability or unemployment benefit and these would – quite apart from the effects of the other proposals mentioned below enabling them to qualify for increases for dependants – result in increases of the order of IR£4-£5 per week for them;

(ii) unemployment benefit will now be paid to them for 390 days as against 312 days previously;

(iii) married women must be given entitlement to apply for unemployment assistance in the same way as other unemployed people who are capable of, available for and genuinely seeking employment. The unemployment assistance scheme is means-tested and, in common with all the other assistance schemes, the means of the applicant's spouse is considered in determining entitlement. The proposal removes the discrimination that exists and gives married women workers exactly the same entitlement as other unemployed workers.

Changes in traditional family patterns and in women's participation in the labour force brought about a need to revise family income support schemes. As the Working Party on Women's Affairs and Family Law Reform observed (p. 213 of its *Agenda*), there was a persistent problem facing many women: breaks in their employment hampered their 'building up entitlements to social welfare benefits'.

At the same time the Social Welfare Commission was exploring other issues as it undertook a long overdue review of the social welfare system.

Social Welfare Commission, *Report of the Social Welfare Commission* (1988)

1.2 Need for review
The present social welfare system represents the end result of an evolutionary process which began with the enactment of the first Old Age Pension Act in 1908. New schemes have been added and modifications and improvements made to the system in response to perceived needs and subject to available resources at various times (see Chapter 2). The extension of the system which now incorporates more than twenty individual schemes, has meant a corresponding increase in the numbers of people whose standard of living is dependent on social welfare and also in the level of funding necessary to finance the system. In 1966, there were 566,442 beneficiaries, i.e., recipients and their defendants, representing 20% of the total population, in receipt of weekly social welfare payments (excluding children's allowance). By 1985, the number of beneficiaries had increased to 1,318,155 or 37.4% of the population. Expenditure on social welfare in the period between 1973/74 and 1985 increased from IR£206 million representing 7% of GNP to IR£2,273 million representing approximately 14% of GNP. Despite the dramatic growth in the social welfare system in terms of the numbers affected and the amount of resources involved, the development of the system has progressed without any fundamental review. The reorganisation of the existing system which took place in 1947, when the Department of Social Welfare was established, represented no more than a rationalisation of the various existing agencies administering different elements of the system under one Department and the unification of the separate codes of unemployment insurance and national health insurance in a single comprehensive insurance system. The need for an overall review of the social welfare system was, therefore, clearly overdue. The fact that no such examination had previously taken place

during the life span of the system was indeed one of the principal difficulties which we had to face in undertaking our task.

The deliberations on remaining discrimination in the social welfare code reflected the influence of the important Third Equality Directive, issued by the European Community in 1979 (79/7/EEC). This required the Community's member states to treat men and women equally in social security plans providing protection against such risks as illness, unemployment or old age. The deadline for implementation of the directive was 23 December 1984. At that time Ireland had not acted to bring its social welfare code into compliance with the equality principle.[3]

The significance of the deadline became clear in the following year, when the European Court of Justice ruled that the Third Equality Directive had the force of law in Ireland. This decision resulted from a request by the Irish High Court for a ruling on a claim regarding unemployment payments in the Cotter and McDermott case. In effect, the ruling of the European Court meant that as from 23 December 1984 social welfare rules applied equally to men and women in Ireland. The Social Welfare (No.2) Act 1985 provided for gradual implementation of the Directive over a period from May to November 1986. The Act 'standardised levels and duration of unemployment/disability/injury/disablement benefits for men and women'.[4] Nonetheless, several issues remained unresolved. There was a continuing attempt to collect arrears of benefit payments for the period December 1984 to March or November 1986, and the new regulations themselves contained provisions that discriminated against women seeking increases in adult/child dependant allowances.

The Second Commission on the Status of Women (1993) did not devote a separate chapter of its report to social welfare matters. Rather, it dealt with these issues as they arose in a specific context, such as in relation to women in the home and women in situations of disadvantage.

The Second Commission's recommendations regarding women in the home indicate that social welfare legislation had removed a number of earlier discriminatory practices. The Second Commission aimed at such outcomes as a reduction in benefit recipients' disincentives to return to work and the provision of information on eligibility rules for the Family Income Support Scheme.

The Second Progress Report of the Monitoring Committee on the Implementation of the Recommendations of the Second Commission on the Status of Women noted the actions taken. Section 15 of the Social Welfare Act 1995 established regulatory powers to permit a higher level of earnings before an Adult Dependant Allowance was withdrawn from the spouse. This change was seen as alleviating the 'poverty trap', which tended to keep people in low-paying jobs or out of employment altogether.

Between December 1992 and December 1995 the number of families receiving Family Income Support increased by 48 per cent to 11,486, a result attributed to the impact of multifaceted advertising campaigns. The Household Budget Scheme 1993, operated by the Postal Service, permitted budgeted direct deductions from social welfare benefits to pay a variety of household bills, while the government's budgets of 1994 and 1995 provided increased funding to support projects and programmes of locally-based women's groups.

The Second Commission referred in its report to specific groups of women who are at a 'double disadvantage' – first by gender and then by specific circumstance. Chapter 5 of the report identified eight such circumstances, ranging from poverty to status as Travellers to prostitution. While several of these categories represented longstanding concerns, others reflected recent changes in Irish society, taking notice, for example, of the difficulties faced by young single mothers, disabled women and lesbian women. The problems facing women in rural Ireland were examined separately, in Chapter 6 of the report. Because the topic of rural women had been raised in an earlier document, *Irish Women: An Agenda for Practical Action* (1985), we begin there.

RURAL WOMEN

The Working Party on Women's Affairs and Family Law Reform devoted a chapter of its *Irish Women: Agenda for Practical Action* (1985) to 'the position of Women in Rural Ireland'. After noting recent demographic and occupational changes, as well as the paucity of systematic research data, the Working Party identified a number of 'key' issues affecting rural women. It also cited farmers' traditional attitudes to the role of women as an obstacle to change.

The Working Party's recommendations emphasised the development of employment opportunities as well as the need for education and training, an expansion of relief services in rural areas, and social security coverage for the self-employed, the majority of whom were farmers.

Working Party on Women's Affairs and Family Law Reform, *Irish Women: Agenda for Practical Action* (1985)

The position of women in rural Ireland
GENERAL REMARKS
7.1 Chapter One [not included] has already referred to the recent stabilisation in the rural population and to the relative improvement in economic and social conditions in recent times in rural Ireland. In terms of sex distribution, the latest Census shows women exceeding men in the towns, whereas in country districts the number of males exceeded females very considerably. The location of service and factory employment in the towns would largely explain the female predominance in the town population, whereas in the country districts, the predominance of men engaged in farming and farming related activities would be the main factor. The number of women in the labour force who classified themselves as having an agricultural occupation in 1981 was 12,700 or 3.6% of the female labour force, compared to 42,100 (or 14.7% of the female labour force) twenty years earlier. Rural women today, in terms of occupational status are most typically working either as farmers' wives or in service-type employment in the towns.

KEY ISSUES AFFECTING RURAL WOMEN
7.2 The disadvantages faced by rural women have recently been articulated through 'get-togethers' organised by the Council for the Status of Women but in general there has been little systematic research carried out in this area. Discussion of issues relating to the position of women in rural Ireland usually tends to focus on their role in farming and family businesses generally, education and training, relief services, legal and security provisions affecting farming women particularly, opportunities for employment, access to services and community involvement (including membership of relevant farming/rural organisations).

WOMEN IN FARMING

7.3 Regarding firstly the role of women in farming, there are at present 8,100 women farmers (5.8% of the total number of farmers), most of whom are likely to be the widows or daughters of male farmers. The majority of farming women are therefore farm wives, classified under the Census of Population and labour force data as being engaged in 'home duties'. The contribution of farm wives to the farm business is unrecorded in GNP statistics. The 1975 EEC Farm Structures Survey reported that spouses (on the whole, wives) contributed 47,000 agricultural work units or 14.5% of the total units, on Irish farms. In Farm Management Survey reports, labour inputs are aggregated to 'labour units' which do not distinguish between male and female labour. The contribution of a woman is counted as .67 of that of a male even where a woman is working on her own. In the 1978 Farm Management Survey, women are reported as working full-time at farm work in 2.5% of cases. The proportion of farms on which there was some labour input by women was much higher, ranging across the farm size categories as indicated in the following table [designated Table 3.1 in this book].

Table 3.1
Proportion of farms with labour input by women, 1978

Size (acres)	30	30–50	50–100	100–200	200+
Per cent	30.3	34.2	44.5	34.3	25.0

In the 1978 Farm Management Survey where the farmer was married (66% of the total) there was a female contribution on 44% of the farms. Even on farms where the occupant was single, 16% had a labour input by women, generally by the farmer's mother. Dairy farms showed the highest level of female participation, with women involved in 46% of cases. A recent research study confirms the contribution of farming women to the farm unit in the directly productive sector of the farm. The study indicated that nearly one-third of wives were seen to play a very important role in primarily male-type farm tasks and that their contribution to the farm production process appears to be highly significant in over half of all farms. Finally, in a study on part-time farming, the importance of the contribution of the part-time farmer's wife to labour on the family farm was highlighted, with an estimated 56% of part-time farmers' wives working on the family farm. On those farms they contributed 83% of the family labour provided by family members other then the farm operator. This percentage was somewhat lower on dairy farms (75%) than on drystock farms (84%).

On farms where the wife contributed labour, she did so for 41 weeks on average, with over 61% contributing some labour every week of the year. The farm activity in which they were most commonly engaged in was the general care of livestock.

CHANGING ROLE OF FARM WOMEN

7.4 For a number of reasons, considerable changes in the role of farm women have taken place in recent years. The growing commercialisation of farm production has considerably reduced the traditional farmyard tasks of the farm wife. Growing prosperity generally has brought improved material wellbeing in farm homes. Increasing numbers of farmers' wives are coming from backgrounds other than farming, as more male farmers inherit farms at a younger age and as farming has become a more appealing occupation. The research evidence shows that many of these women are more educated in the formal sense than their husbands. The reduction in the labour force engaged in agriculture has left farmers mainly dependent on their wives for help with farm tasks. In the more professional, business approach to farming, the wife is now mainly responsible for keeping the records and accounts which are so important for the efficient functioning of the farm. Research also shows that the decision making in relation to the farm and family reflect a high degree of involvement by the wife. It is significant particularly in relation to decisions regarding 'credit-use' for farm and home development, family living expenses and insurance for family members, home and farm. Involvement in farm business tasks is considerable.

FARMERS' ATTITUDES TO THE ROLE OF WOMEN

7.5 On the other hand, there is evidence that attitudes to the role of women can remain traditional even if, as is clear, that role is changing rapidly. In recent research carried out in West Limerick, one of the factors examined was 'lifestyles, values and attitudes to change and development'. Included under this heading were attitudes to the role of women, where respondents were asked to agree with statements such as 'it's a woman's job to do the work around the house' and 'I'd have more confidence in a male doctor or solicitor than in a female one'. The results showed not only a positive relationship between the age of the respondent and traditional attitudes to women, with older people having more traditional views, but indicated different attitudes based on socio-economic status. For example, only 29% and 43% of people in professional/administrative, and managerial/executive jobs respectively believe that 'It's a woman's job to do the work around the house', compared with 71% of farmers.

The Second Commission on the Status of Women also devoted a chapter of its report (1993) to the issues confronting rural women, arguing that their disadvantages stem from three unique factors: physical isolation and reduced access to services; the difficulties associated with the occupation of farming; and the changing circumstances stemming from rural development initiatives.

Second Commission on the Status of Women, *Report to Government* (1993)

6.1.1 ISSUES AFFECTING RURAL WOMEN

In this Chapter the Commission considers the issues affecting rural women, i.e. all women living outside urban areas. No more than urban women, rural women do not constitute a homogenous group. As well as farmers and farmers' wives, rural women are comprised of such categories as industrial workers, employees in public and private services, outworkers, fishermen's wives, self-employed, the wives of self-employed, relatives assisting on farms or in other businesses, etc. The Commission believes it is important to give consideration to rural women as a specific category of women for three reasons. Firstly, by virtue of their residence in rural areas women experience particular problems of physical isolation and access to services. Secondly, many of them are living on farms and face specific difficulties associated with the occupation of farming. Thirdly, the current emphasis on rural development as a means of revitalising rural economies gives rise to particular issues for women. We seek to address all of these issues in this Chapter.

6.1.2 RURAL WOMEN – SOME BASIC STATISTICS

According to the 1986 Census there were 1,271,898 women aged fifteen years or over living in Ireland and, of these more than half a million (518,476) were living in rural areas, i.e. 41% of all women. Men under the age of 65 outnumber women in all age groups in rural areas. Over the age of 65, women outnumber men. The main demographic indicators for rural and urban areas are shown in Table 6.1 [not included].

When compared to urban areas, there are proportionately more married, widowed and older women in rural Ireland. The lower proportion of separated women may reflect a tendency for separated women to relocate in urban areas.

6.2 Problems of access

6.2.1 Transport

One of the most consistent issues in submissions to the Commission concerning rural women was the problem of access to services and facilities. Many rural women live in areas far from centres of population. They experience a sense of isolation, often accompanied by feelings of loneliness and depression. Given the fact that most rural women do not work outside the home or farm, that many live in low income households and care for elderly relatives, the burdens on them can be very considerable.

In the last two decades there has been a dramatic reduction in public transport services in rural areas as population decline and increased private car ownership made many routes commercially non-viable. While there is a relatively high incidence of car ownership in rural households (72% according to the 1987 Household Budget Survey), women's access to the family car is often restricted, either because they are unable to drive, or the car is unavailable during the day. Women in carless households and elderly women may find that they have to restrict travel to a minimum and that they are effectively excluded from a range of services and social and educational facilities. It is not possible for elderly people to avail of their free travel entitlement if they live in areas where there is little or no accessible public transport. For necessary journeys to the doctor, dentist or other services, women are often reliant on the goodwill of neighbours or have to bear the cost of hiring a taxi for a relatively long journey.

The Commission recommends that the Department of Tourism, Transport and Communications, and the Department of the Environment, in consultation with other relevant Departments, should review options for improving access to transport for rural women with a view to developing a long-term integrated strategy. Specifically, the Departments involved should consider introducing, on a pilot basis, some of the models already successfully established in other countries. The possibility of introducing driving instruction into the school curriculum, or on short courses provided by training agencies such as FÁS, VECs, or Teagasc, should also be investigated.

6.2.2 Telecommunications and access to information

Telecommunications is another area where access is a problem. Problems of transport and distance to services are mitigated by the telephone and the service in rural areas has improved immeasurably over the past decade. However, the cost of long-distance calls means that many rural women are effectively disadvantaged in terms of telephone access to information and advice. There are particularly difficult psychological problems arising from the isolation of rural life. These need sympathetic and imaginative responses. One such response is the Irish Country-women's Association telephone helpline service which is grant-aided by the Department of Social Welfare. Two days a week calls from all parts of Ireland, charged as local calls, are responded to by a psychologist. Callers use a special number publicised through the organisation's own network but often used by non-members. The service, provided by a women's organisation with Government assistance, offers a model of a useful support scheme.

The Commission recommends:

(a)   the adoption of an information policy by the Government so that targeted information on Social Welfare and other State services is available at a low cost to the general public; the ultimate aim of this policy should be that information on State services is available for the price of a local telephone call;

(b)   adequate funding for, and supply of, information to the National Social Services Board so that it can fulfil the functions assigned to it.

6.2.3 HEALTH

A great number of submissions to the Commission concerned access to services. Health, both physical and psychological, figured prominently. The centralisation of hospital services has meant that rural women must often travel long distances for ante- and post-natal care, cancer screening, family planning, and other medical needs. There are two complementary ways of dealing with this problem. Firstly, by improving transport facilities as proposed in paragraph 6.2.1. Secondly, by mobilising services such as cancer screening, family planning, menopause clinics, and bringing them to local communities. The Commission suggests in Chapter 11 that services be brought to the people wherever possible. In particular, preventive health programmes and routine maternity care should be available locally.

A further feature of the health service which affects rural women particularly has been the system of block booking appointments which pertains in some hospitals. Where women have long distances to travel, and possibly taxi costs to pay or inflexible public transport times to meet, any unnecessary delay spent in attendance in a hospital waiting line can severely complicate women's lives.

The Commission recommends that the Health Boards establish mobile health centres which can respond to women's health needs and provide routine treatment, available to rural women on a regular basis in each Health Board area. Such mobile centres could locate at local health or community centres or at the multipurpose centres recommended in Section 4 of this Chapter [not included].

6.2.4 EDUCATION AND TRAINING

There has been some improvement in rural women's access to, and participation in, training and continuing education courses in recent years. Teagasc, the Agricultural and Food Development Authority, provided short courses on various aspects of agriculture and rural development for 5,956 adults in 1991. 852 or 17% of the participants were women. Women from rural areas have participated in FÁS courses and Vocational Education Committee (VEC) adult education classes and some women's groups have themselves organised courses with VEC assistance. Training courses run at An Grianan, the ICA residential college, usually are fully subscribed and the Government might consider establishing, or supporting the establishment, of a second such residential college. The County Enterprise Partnership Boards, which are in the process of being set up, should also support women's training for development.

In general, however, rural women's access to adult education and training courses is limited by remoteness from training centres and the lack of child care facilities. Just as much as any sector of the community, rural women should have access to training so that they can enhance their skills and increase their earning potential. FÁS, Teagasc, CERT, the VECs and other training agencies must plan for the specific needs of rural women and ensure that training is accessible to them..

Current EC Community initiatives such as LEADER, EUROFORM and NOW provide a new framework in which rural women's training needs can be addressed. Information technology can offer an effective means of overcoming obstacles of distance and access.

The Commission recommends that:

(a) the training needs of rural women, particularly adult rural women, should be examined so that Teagasc, FÁS and the Vocational Education Committees can respond effectively to expressed needs;

(b) the training needs of, and development opportunities for, women should also be addressed in the context of rural development initiatives which offer possibilities for developing the economic independence of rural women e.g. EC programmes such as LEADER, EUROFORM and NOW;

(c) the Government should support the establishment of a college along the lines of An Grianan, the ICA College, suitable for short-stay residential training courses. This could serve as a logical extension of the Department of Social Welfare scheme of grants for locally-based women's groups and might usefully serve as a bridge into more directly commercially-based initiatives;

(d) the County Enterprise Partnership Boards should ensure women's participation in training for development and in decision-making projects and initiatives; provision should also be made for the equitable representation of women and men on such Boards.

6.2.5 CHILD CARE

The need for child care services is set out elsewhere in the Commission's Report, but it important to point out that there is also a need to develop appropriate child care services in rural areas. Such services might best be provided in the context of multi-functional centres catering for the needs of women and children. These could be developed as part of a long term community care strategy.

6.3 Farm women

6.3.1 INTRODUCTION

Although farm women do not constitute a majority of rural women, specific disadvantages impact upon them which the Commission believe must be addressed. Before turning to consideration of farm women in detail, it is worth drawing attention to the fact that there are wide differences within the farming sector in Ireland in terms of the size of the farming operation and farm income. Only 20% of all farms in Ireland had farm incomes above IR£10,000 in 1990; on 60% of Irish farms, the farm income was under IR£5,000. Many farm families rely on off-farm income or social welfare payments to supplement their farm income.

6.3.2 NUMBER OF FARM WOMEN

It is possible to make some crude estimates from data from the National Farm Survey, 1990. According to this survey there are an estimated 173,500 male farm operators in Ireland and 64% of all farm operators are married. From this we can deduce that there are around 111,000 farm wives in the country. The great majority of women on Irish farms are therefore the wives of male farmers.

A survey of family farming recently carried out by Teagasc in counties in the West and East regions provides some interesting data on farm wives. Just over half of the wives in each region had young children, nearly a third are on farms where the husband has an off-farm job, and a considerable proportion are themselves engaged in off-farm work. Some key results from this survey are shown in Table 6.2 [designated Table 3.2 in this book].

Table 3.2
Some characteristics of farm wives in west and east regions (%)

	West	East
Children less than 16 years old	58	54
Leaving Certificate or higher	39	52
Agricultural training	0	2
Husband has off-farm job	31	30
Wife has off-farm job	23	17

Source: Based on a survey by Teagasc of 185 farm wives in the West Region and 204 farm wives in the East Region

6.3.3 ROLES OF WOMEN ON FARMS

Because farm wives' work is not directly remunerated, they are unlikely to be covered for social welfare in their own right and do not contribute to a social insurance scheme.

The picture emerging form the Gasson survey (1990) is reinforced by research from other countries where studies show that most farm wives are involved in the farm business and that their work input is very significant. Their involvement in manual labour usually depends on the size of farm and system of farming and is often considerable, especially on dairy farms. Many wives are responsible for farm accounts and the administrative aspects of the farm operation. Women frequently take on the administrative side of farm management; in many cases because they have a higher level of education than their husbands.

The Commission recommends that the work of farm wives on family farms should be given adequate recognition. To achieve this it is recommended that the work of women on farms be documented and appropriate categories devised so that this work can be included by the Central Statistics Office in the collection and publication of national statistics. Such categories could also be used as a basis for assessing farm women's contributions/entitlements to social insurance associated with their occupational position.

6.3.5 OWNERSHIP OF FAMILY FARMS

There is no specific legislation governing women farmers. Since most married women typically 'marry in' to a farm which their husband has acquired as a gift or inheritance, partnerships and co-ownerships which are common in other countries are comparatively rare in Ireland. Most women, therefore, do not have title to the farm on which they are working unless a couple takes a specific decision to transfer the farm into joint ownership. The Finance Act 1990 abolished the stamp duty requirement on gifts between spouses so that there is no longer any cost disincentive to joint ownership.

Yet joint ownership is still relatively unusual. This means, in effect, that very many farm women may work on the family farm all their lives and yet have no right to legal ownership of a share in the farm or the farm income. The only protection farm women, in common with other women, enjoy at present is the Family Home Protection Act 1976 which gives them a right of veto on the sale of the family home, and the Succession Act 1965 which provides for a minimum entitlement to part of the estate on widowhood. Ironically, in the event of legal separation, as opposed to marriage breakdown per se, farm women may not fare too badly as the Judicial Separation and Family Law Reform Act 1989 provides for a system of division of property.

In its First Statement to Government (April 1991), the Commission recommended the introduction of automatic joint ownership of the family home.

This recommendation was accepted by the Government and legislation to give it effect is currently being drafted. Furthermore, in this report to Government, the Commission is recommending introduction of a community property regime on marriage which would entail joint entitlement to all income and a right to a minimum half-share of the estate on death.

The Commission recommends the introduction of a community property regime; see Chapter 1 [not included] for a fuller discussion of the issues involved.

6.3.6 SOCIAL INSURANCE

Women on farms, whether farming on their own account, or as farm wives, fare badly in terms of social insurance compared to their counterparts in waged employment. Farmers are insured under the scheme for social insurance for self-employed workers. The contributions provide the insured (i.e. the farmer) with cover for Retirement and a Widows and Orphans Pension. In the case of woman farmers who are insured in their own right, there is no cover for maternity, sickness, optical or dental benefit, unlike their counterparts in employment. Farmer's wives are regarded as 'prescribed relatives' and are not eligible for social insurance cover unless they are legal partners in the farm business. Their only entitlement under the scheme, therefore, is a derived one, i.e. entitlement to a widow's pension.

Ireland lags very much behind other EC Member States in terms of social insurance cover for women on farms. In most Member States the range of cover for the self-employed is wider than in Ireland and, where insurance is not compulsory, farm women who are actively working on the farm can make voluntary contributions.

The Commission recommends that:

(a) women married to men excluded on the grounds of age from participation in the scheme of social insurance for the self-employed should themselves be able to make voluntary contributions if they are below the age of exclusion;

(b) the Department of Social Welfare should examine the scheme of social insurance for the self-employed with a view to moving towards a system of individual entitlements.

6.3.7 RELIEF SERVICES

It has been argued that the provision of relief services is a more appropriate response than social insurance cover for farm women in the case of absences through sickness or maternity or where women wish to avail of vocational training. Farm relief services are already well established in many of the EC Member States.

Although the Farm Relief Service is relatively well established in Ireland the service is, in effect, restricted to those who can afford to use it.

The Commission recommends that ways of improving women's access to relief services in cases of childbirth, sickness, and vocational training should be investigated, including the possibility of attracting EC Community funding for such services for women. Priority should be given to facilitating the further development of the existing farm relief services network. This is an issue which Teagasc, in conjunction with FÁS, should pursue in the context of LEADER or other EC rural development programmes.

6.3.8 AGRICULTURAL EDUCATION AND TRAINING

Most women enter farming as an occupation by marrying a farmer. The great majority will have been in a non-farm occupation prior to marriage. Farm women, therefore, need access to vocational training, particularly as the business side of farming becomes increasingly complex. Moreover, vocational training can also enhance the professional status of farm women and increase their self-confidence and self-worth.

Nearly 6,000 adults participated in short Teagasc training courses on various aspects of farming in 1990. Only 17% of the participants were women. This no doubt reflects the nature of the courses offered (certain course topics being perceived as in the male domain) but also difficulties for women in attending courses through not having access to child care or relief services.

The Commission recommends that Teagasc should draw up and adopt an equal opportunities programme which should include the following elements:

(a) a review of courses currently available to farm women with the aim of responding to the expressed needs of women;

(b) encouraging and facilitating more women students to take the Certificate in Farming and the Certificate in Agriculture. This should be based on a clear strategy with timescales and targets;

(c) providing increased access for adult farm women to vocational training courses in agriculture including skills courses for women 'marrying into' farms.

6.3.9 PARTICIPATION IN AGRICULTURAL ORGANISATIONS

Despite the fact that there is no formal discrimination against women participating in farm organisations and agricultural co-operatives, there are still few women in evidence in such organisations. In this regard, the farming organisations reflect the same traits as the other social partners, political parties, and major sporting organisations. As in these other areas, men dominate the public face of farming and agribusiness and this reinforces gender based stereotypes. Farming organisations tend to be structured on the basis of family membership. In principle this means that there are a considerable number of women members. However, the active membership, certainly in policy-making areas, has a much lower representation of women. While women involved in farming would have an obvious interest in committees dealing with family-centred issues, such as the IFA's Farm Family Committee, women also have a direct mainstream interest in committees dealing with commodities, agribusiness, rural development and other issues. The Commission believes it is important they should be represented on those kinds of committees in recognition of the extent and depth of the contribution they make to farm enterprise. Farming organisations, along with other important lobbies in our patriarchal society, should make extra efforts to encourage the active participation of women at grassroots and senior level within their organisations. The ultimate aim should be the securing of gender balance at the most senior levels within the 40%–60% range set out in the Commission's First Statement.

The Commission recommends that agricultural organisations should introduce a positive action programme to encourage women to become actively involved at all levels of their organisations, in particular, to assume more officer posts and to be included at national level as representatives for discussion of major economic issues.

6.5 Rural women and rural development

6.5.1 RURAL DEVELOPMENT MEASURES

Changes in the European Community such as the move to a Single European Market and the restructuring of the Common Agricultural Policy have led to a new emphasis on rural development as a way of strengthening rural economies. In this context, alternative enterprises, tourism and heritage development, community enterprises, and small business development, are being encouraged at EC and national level, particularly in the Operational Programmes associated with the reform of the Structural Funds.

The Commission recommends that all Operational Programmes for the Structural Funds and Community Initiatives which promote rural development should include an explicit recognition of the need to address the problems and concerns of rural women as well as measures designed to include women in projects to be funded.

6.5.2 WOMEN'S GROUPS

For over 80 years the Irish Countrywomen's Association has made a notable contribution to the lives of rural women by the formation of groups or 'Guilds'. These have progressed and changed over the years as rural life has changed. Assertiveness courses are now promoted alongside the teaching of arts and craft, and the ICA uses the strength of its large membership to become involved in social and economic policy issues. One outcome of this is that today's better educated and more confident women are forming groups related to the needs in their own communities. A survey in the west region in 1991 identified over 40 such groups with an average of 20 members. These groups have mainly been involved in adult education and personal development through programmes based on needs identified by the women themselves.

The activities and success of these groups have highlighted a clear need for multi-functional centres for rural women. Such centres could provide an integrated response to many of the problems already identified in this report – child care facilities, information and advice services, access to health services, training, information technology, small business infrastructure.

At a time when rural population decline is a major concern in many parts of Europe and 'bottom up' strategies are being advocated, such an approach to the problems of rural women in Ireland seems appropriate and cost effective.

The Commission recommends the establishment and support of multifunctional centres in the context of the development of community care and rural development. Ideally, such centres require funding for a core staff, overheads and administration. The users should also play a lead role in running such centres.

The *Second Progress Report of the Monitoring Committee on the Implementation of the Recommendations of the Second Commission on the Status of Women* (1996) did not identify specific legislation enacted to deal with the problems facing rural women. However, there were a number of initiatives taken up in response to the recommendations. These included improvements in rural bus service, as well as programmes dealing with vehicle ownership, operation and maintenance. Local offices of the social welfare services provided easier access to information in this area, and a programme introduced in 1995 was aimed at improving and expanding health centres throughout the country.

The *Second Progress Report* noted several developments pertaining to the training needs of rural women. In the mid-1990s a Rural Advisory Committee was examining these needs. FÁS provided training for rural women, while New Opportunities for Women (NOW) promoted equal oppor-tunities for women in employment and vocational training. Gender equality, both for beneficiaries and for participants, was also an objective of the Operational Programme for Local Urban and Rural Development.

WOMEN IN SITUATIONS OF DOUBLE DISADVANTAGE

The First Commission on the Status of Women did not include any discussion of issues affecting lesbian women, prostitutes or prisoners in its report (1972). Official consideration of these groups did not emerge until the report of the Second Commission on the Status of Women was published in 1993. Reflecting the change in the focus of public policy, from issues of formal equality to issues of equitable treatment, the Second Commission provided concise assessments of the difficulties other disadvantaged women encounter, putting them at risk even in the best of economic times. In each instance the Commission offered recommendations for change

The Commission noted, in particular, that there were no laws against lesbianism in Ireland, yet it also noted that 'open acknowledgement of same-sex orientation could be damaging in career and personal terms'. Evidence suggested that lesbians were not only socially stigmatised but were also threatened or attacked by those hostile to gays.[5] In relation to women prisoners, the issues identified by the Second Commission were in the areas of counselling, lock-up hours and the possibility of an open prison for women. With respect to prostitution, the Second Commission recognised that it was a complex problem, involving dysfunctional families, violence and drugs, and recommended a comprehensive programme of social rehabilitation.

Second Commission on the Status of Women, *Report to Government* (1993)

5.1 Women in situations of particular disadvantage
5.1.1 Double disadvantage
In this Chapter we consider eight categories of women with particular problems:

- women in poverty;
- older women;
- young single mothers;
- women with disabilities;
- lesbian women;
- Traveller women;
- women prisoners; and
- women involved in prostitution.

We make specific recommendations in each case as to how the problems of each of these categories should be addressed.

At first sight it might seem patronising to group together very disparate categories of women under the heading 'women in situations of particular disadvantage'. However, as the Commission considered the submissions received, it became clear that there were categories of women who, due to poverty, disability, age, etc., experienced more than the 'ordinary' inequalities all women have faced. The categories of women considered in this Chapter are, because of the way in which society is structured and organised, effectively prevented from taking part in economic and social life in the many ordinary ways other women are able to take for granted. These categories might well be defined as doubly disadvantaged and it is on that basis that the Commission felt they needed specific, focused attention with a view to drawing up recommendations.

Marginalised women demonstrate considerable strength and resilience in overcoming poverty, discrimination, racism and negative stereotyping. Apart from the individual strength needed to survive day to day, increasingly, women who experience exclusion are working together to gain equal rights with other women and towards equal rights with men.

5.1.2 CHARACTERISTICS OF WOMEN IN SITUATIONS OF PARTICULAR DISADVANTAGE

Taken together, the groups of marginalised women considered in this report constitute a sizeable population. It is not possible to hazard a guess as to just how many women fall into these categories. There is little statistical data available on some categories. Moreover, not all such groups are distinct so that there would be an element of double counting. While it has been necessary to target specific groups for consideration in this Report, this should not mask the reality that women may experience exclusion from society and opportunity in a variety of different ways.

The age, socio-economic status, geographical location, physical status, sexual orientation, and ethnic origin of many women determine their exclusion from making a full range of choices and from enjoying the rights and privileges of citizens. The concept of inclusion is key because it acknowledges the right to be different and to celebrate that difference. Social class, religion, sexual orientation, disability or other factors must not constitute a basis for the denial of rights and entitlements. There is also a need to ensure that the rights, choices and opportunities that all women enjoy in principle are effective in practice. An elderly woman, for example, has the right to free travel. However, if she lives in an isolated area she may not have access to any means of exercising that right.

5.1.3 NEGATIVE STEREOTYPING
The most invidious form of exclusion is the negative stereotyping which results from prejudice, ignorance, and fear and which focuses on finding scapegoats rather than addressing problems. Both women and men engage in negative stereotyping and its power cannot be overestimated. The elimination of gender-related stereotyping should benefit society as a whole. In order to achieve this, specific measures will be necessary to improve the status of all women. Categories of women who are doubly disadvantaged need additional measures directed towards ending their marginalisation and bringing them closer to social equality.

Marginalised women in their social situations are often isolated, lacking in self-esteem, and made to feel dependent and valueless. Authority figures often fail to realise the extent to which these women suffer from internalised oppression. Disadvantaged women can experience attitudes towards them, even from the most well-disposed people, as extremely patriarchal and patronising. In preparing this Chapter, and indeed the whole Report, the Commission wished to include rather than exclude, and to value the positive aspects of difference.

5.1.4 CONCLUSIONS
The Commission, in an attempt to evoke a positive response, has highlighted issues affecting marginalised women throughout the Report, and not solely in this Chapter. Further research is necessary into a number of categories of marginalised women so that informed policy decisions can be formulated. It is very important that the motivation and experience of marginalised women is used to bring about positive change. This means, inter alia, a strategy to train marginalised women in a variety of social, educational and health care jobs so they can assist in devising and implementing positive measures. Groups and organisations which represent the interests of marginalised women will also require additional support and funding. In the remainder of this Chapter the Commission considers the specific categories of women in poverty, older women, young single mothers, women with disabilities, lesbian women, Traveller women, women in prison, and women involved in prostitution. On

the basis of submissions received, research, and consideration of the issues arising, the Commission decided that these were the main categories requiring special consideration. People may feel that there are other such categories deserving detailed treatment. In such cases many of the existing recommendations in this Chapter may be applied to additional categories of disadvantaged women.

5.2 Women in poverty
5.2.1 Introduction

In 1987 an estimated 274,000 women lived in households with incomes of less than IR£48 per week per individual adult, as against 224,000 men. Women living in rural areas and those aged between 35-65 are most likely to live in poverty. Women particularly affected by financial poverty include:

- those rearing children on their own;
- women in low paid work;
- Traveller women;
- women who are homeless;
- elderly women, especially those living alone;
- women caring in a full-time capacity for elderly or ill relatives;
- social welfare dependants;
- wives of low paid workers or social welfare dependants.

5.2.2 INCOME AND STATUS

Stereotypes of low income families wasting money on drink, being promiscuous, rearing children who are in trouble either at school or in the street weigh heavily on women living in poverty. There is little credit given by society in general for the skill needed to live with dignity in areas which lack basic services and amenities and where poverty and disadvantage are concentrated.

Access to and control over an adequate income are fundamental to improving the situation of women in poverty. Three factors prevent this at present.

- only one-third of Irish women are in the labour force and earn an independent income through paid work;
- many women in work are in low-paid jobs which do not provide the opportunity or the resources for promotion and development;
- the manner of payment of social welfare payments, many of which reinforce dependent roles for women, since generally the woman is not the direct recipient of the payment.

The most important route out of poverty is economic independence. Given the high levels of unemployment and the heavy
concentration of registered unemployed in disadvantaged areas,
the prospect of a paid job remains a distant hope for many women
at present trapped in the poverty underclass. It is important to plan
for change and progress and to that end it is essential that we
establish the real rate of unemployment among women so that
labour market/ employment initiatives are directed at the right
target group. At present, one major reason why women do not sign
on at labour exchanges is because as 'non-workers' they are not
entitled to benefit. A recent study suggests that in Ireland 85% of
unemployed men are registered as opposed to 48% of unemployed
women. It has obviously been in the interest of successive
Governments to keep registered unemployment low, not least in
order to contain social welfare costs. This, however, has had the
effect of limiting women's eligibility for Government labour market
initiatives targeted at the registered unemployed. It is essential that
the real position of women's unemployment is both revealed and
discussed. The recent PESP – initiated Area Based Response to Long
Term Unemployment has an important role to play here.

5.2.3 CYCLE OF POVERTY

Young women from low income backgrounds who drop out of
school with no qualifications are ten times more likely to become
single mothers than those who come out of the system with a
Leaving Certificate. Single mothers, along with other groups of
people in disadvantaged situations such as Travellers or second-
generation unemployed families, become trapped in a cycle of
poverty from which it is increasingly difficult for both themselves
and their children to escape. Because of rules which limit, for
example, the eligibility of lone parents for State employment
schemes the effect of public policy towards lone mothers has
been to discourage their participation in the labour market rather
than to provide them with training and other supports which
might help them to hold a job (see Chapter 10 [not included]). It
is likely that a mix of cultural values and expediency produces
this treatment of lone mothers, i.e. a genuine concern for the
well-being of the child coupled with a readiness to keep these
women off the Live Register. Whatever the motivation, classifying
lone mothers as long term social welfare claimants rather than
facilitating them to earn a living helps perpetuate the cycle of
poverty.

5.2.4 HEALTH CONSIDERATIONS

Poverty and ill-health are linked. Women on low incomes are more likely to experience the following: shorter lifespan; depression; health hazards in the home and at work; violence; illness; greater likelihood of smoking and exposure to attendant illnesses; high infant mortality. They are less likely than other women to have:

- information about preventive health measures;
- access to and choice of contraception;
- choice of health service.

5.2.5 RECOMMENDATIONS ON POVERTY

The Commission recommends that:

(a) the Department of Social Welfare should introduce a system of individual payments to all adults in receipt of social welfare,

(b) any barriers to women working or participating in employment programmes, created by the current social welfare regulations should be reviewed and eliminated where necessary,

(c) participation in a FÁS programme by lone parents should not result in their losing out financially. There is a case for additional support for childminding costs while training,

(d) the PESP Area Based Responses to Long-term Unemployment should research the level of unemployment among women in catchment areas and take positive action to ensure that women have equal access to advice, training and work opportunities;

(e) child care services which may be introduced should have as a priority the support of low income families and women parenting alone,

(f) support for locally-based developmental opportunities should be increased and made available on a multiannual basis,

(g) the Department of Education should fund compensatory pro-grammes for pupils of schools in disadvantaged areas in order to help break the cycle of poverty, early parenthood and dependency,

(h) the health of women living on low incomes should be a priority for health service provision. Maternity services, post-natal clinics and screening services should be as locally based as possible,

(i) preventive health care programmes targeted at women on low incomes should be introduced,

(j) information on all methods of contraception including sterilisation should be freely available for women and choice of contraceptive method should be available to medical card holders,

(k) appropriate and timely legal protection should be available for women victims of domestic violence regardless of marital status,

(l) planning and housing should take account of women's needs with regard to access, transport, shopping, safety, play areas for younger children and teenagers, etc.

5.3 Older women

5.3.1 OLDER WOMEN IN IRELAND TODAY

At the 1986 census there were 384,355 people aged 65 and over in the country of whom two thirds (256,236) were women. The number is steadily rising, with more people living to 70, 80 and 90. In 1986, 37% of the elderly were over 75 years of age. This is expected to increase to 44% by the year 2006. Women's average lifespan in Ireland is 76 years at present, men's 71 years.

5.3.2 OLDER WOMEN AS A VALUABLE RESOURCE

The Commission would like to see greater recognition of the contribution older women make to the economic and social fabric: society should value older people as a resource, rather than seeing them as a problem.

Although there are many excellent organisations for the elderly in Ireland, none deal specifically with women's issues. Midlife and older women as a distinct entity with specific needs are largely invisible in terms of statistics, published and unpublished documents and research, inclusion in policies, plans and programmes. Elderly women have very low representation in the political process. In a society where the principal social value of a woman has been frequently/disproportionately defined in terms of reproductive potential and youthful beauty, social attitudes to elderly women can be dismissive at best. Many women need help and encouragement to come to terms with their new identity. Stereotypes surrounding older women can work heavily against them. Not many older women hold positions of authority. The elderly are usually portrayed as recipients of services, reinforcing their image as a burden rather than as a resource. Women take on many positive roles within Irish society, yet there is often little acknowledgement of their achievement in later years. Instead their life-long sense of duty and obligation is more often exploited than acknowledged. For example, inadequate child care facilities often means that a grandmother is called upon to act as unpaid childminder.

5.3.3 OLDER WOMEN'S RELATIONSHIPS

Many of the social taboos surrounding sexuality which confined women in the past have now gone. One of the last to remain however, is the taboo which relates to older women and sexuality. Older women can and do lead fulfilled sexual lives. Yet, the myths that older people are neither interested in, nor capable of, sexual activity still persist despite major studies which have shown that neither is true.

The biggest factors which determine whether or not you are sexually active as you get older are your health, whether you have a partner and happy sexual experiences in the past. A new openness with regard to sexuality and the older woman needs to be fostered.

5.3.4 LEARNING AND INTELLIGENCE

The stereotype of elderly women is widespread – their brains deteriorate, they become cranky and personalities change to become rigid and uniform. There is no evidence to suggest that women take on a particularly 'elderly' personality when they cross the threshold of 65 years. Age itself is not an important factor either in the development of personality traits or the ability to change or adapt. Disease rather than age has been identified as the important variable.

One of the reasons that it is important to debunk these stereotypes is their implication for the ability to learn. Increasing numbers of older women are seeking opportunities for adult education. Where daytime classes have been provided in one Dublin college, there has been a heavy demand from over 65s. The kinds of courses which might usefully be provided by VECs or other organisations include: basic financial management; basic computer technology; how to create a positive image of oneself as an older woman; how to make a useful contribution to the community locally and nationally; how to come to terms with one's own emotional and sexual needs and to build bridges with younger generations so that positive experiences are shared; how to enjoy one's later years; and the building of a new lifestyle with a retired spouse. Since many older women do not like going out at night, it is important that these classes should be provided in the daytime.

5.3.6 RECOMMENDATIONS ON OLDER WOMEN

The Commission recommends that:

(a) long-term social planning should take account of older women's need for appropriate housing, health, educational and other services, taking into account social and demographic changes and set within the context of the development of community care;

(b) the Social Welfare Code should be amended to allow homemakers to make voluntary contributions in respect of years spent caring for pre-school children, the elderly or disabled, to facilitate them to obtain contributory pensions and other benefits in their own right;

(c) Government policies affecting rural areas should have a social as well as economic element which would take into account the implications for elderly women of the rationalisation of services such as post and public transport;

(d) overall, policy for the aged should be set within the context of the United Nations Principles for Older Persons;

(e) a preventive health programme for the elderly and elderly women, in particular, should be introduced which emphasises the importance of maintaining physical and mental fitness while ageing;

(f) funding should be allocated to an organisation such as Age and Opportunity to support older women specifically to explore more positive attitudes to ageing through developmental programmes similar to those funded for locally based women's groups;

(g) in line with our recommendation at (a) above the situation of the elderly in our society needs to be tackled by a clear strategy. This would include such elements as residential homes in towns which should supply sheltered housing care and increased eligibility for carer's allowance;

(h) more daytime educational and development courses, including courses on personal financial management, should be available to older women, with hours coinciding when possible with those of available public transport.

5.4 Young single mothers
5.4.1 CHARACTERISTICS OF SINGLE MOTHERS

In 1991, non-marital births accounted for one in six of all births. In this regard, Ireland now approaches the EC average for extramarital births. Up to 1977, the vast majority of mothers of non-marital children were first time mothers. Thereafter an increasing proportion were women who had had children previously. In 1987, 75% of mothers who gave birth to a non-marital child were first-time mothers.

Internationally, studies of lone parents report a pattern of poor socio-economic status, marginal attachment to the labour force, and generally low standards of living. Irish evidence reinforces this pattern. Single mothers, particularly younger single mothers, tend to be from disadvantaged backgrounds to a disproportionate degree. They are more likely to be unemployed or never to have been employed and to reside in households with a high degree of unemployment. An unmarried mother is also likely to be younger than her married peer.

Typically, unmarried mothers are in receipt of social welfare payments, at least for a period of time, are medical card holders, and are local authority tenants. Between 1975 and 1987, it is estimated that 75% of potential claimants, i.e. women with first non-marital children who had not given their children up for adoption, were awarded the Unmarried Mother's Allowance (25,000 women).

5.4.4 RECOMMENDATIONS ON YOUNG SINGLE MOTHERS
There are very complex issues arising from this section but on the basis of careful consideration, a number of recommendations would seem to be imperative.

The Commission recommends:

(a) that a sex education programme should be developed by the Department of Education which will give young people, male and female, a sense of personal autonomy and responsibility in relationships. This should be complemented by targeted Health Promotion Unit advertisements in the media, pointing out to girls the disadvantages of early, unplanned pregnancies and pointing out to boys the responsibility for contraception; (see Chapter 9 [not included]);

(b) younger women in receipt of the Lone Parent's Allowance should be given education and training assistance, including the provision of child care at training centres, in order that they can earn a living rather than being regarded as social welfare 'pensioners' (see Chapter 10 [not included]);

(c) younger lone mothers need support mechanisms to help them cope, e.g. mutual support groups, short-term child care etc.;

(d) the Department of Social Welfare regulations should be reviewed to see if they unwittingly contribute towards fragmenting stable relationships.

5.5 Women with disabilities
5.5.1 REALITY OF LIFE FOR WOMEN WITH DISABILITIES
'Women with disabilities' is taken to mean women who have any disability whether physical, mental, developmental, psychiatric or

sensory. There are an estimated 150,000 women with disabilities in Ireland.

'Women with disabilities are rendered invisible in a host of different ways. First, they appear less and are literally less often seen in public. Second, even when they are not physically out of sight, they are psychologically out of sight. Third, as a minority group, they are often ignored and devalued by the majority.

Disabled women tend to be characterised as either helpless and dependent, or heroic and saintly, rather than as competent, sexual, and capable, 'full' women. Their invisibility, caused by their separation from mainstream life, gives rise to and reinforces such ignorant stereotypes.

Lack of access to most facilities, amenities and services in the community deny these women the basic rights and needs that enable women to have some level of control over their own lives. For example, women with disabilities are denied physical access or have access only with difficulty due to steps, narrow doors, high curbs, inaccessible public transport, etc. Some establishments, such as cinemas, deny access on the grounds that wheelchairs constitute a fire hazard, since, in the absence of designated areas for wheelchairs, they must often be left in the aisles. The non-provision of information in Braille or a lack of sign language interpreters can just as effectively exclude women with other disabilities from availing of services and amenities.

5.5.2 GENDER ISSUES IN DISABILITY

As with so many marginalised groups where men as well as women are affected, research into disability has tended not to take account of additional gender issues. However, the pattern of discrimination against women in general is replicated between women and men with disabilities. Research shows that women with disability are:

- less likely to be in employment than their male counterparts;
- less likely to be involved in a close sexual relationship;
- less likely to be receiving emotional or physical support;
- less likely to be in receipt of training for employment;
- likely to be poorer than men with a disability if relying on welfare benefits;
- likely to be earning half as much as men with a disability if in paid employment;
- under-represented in the decision-making structures of voluntary organisations, even those which provide support for people with conditions which affect more women than men.

Disability has consequences not just for the individual but also for the whole family. Where support systems do not exist or are inadequate, the disability impacts on the freedoms of other family members. Ongoing policy for people with disabilities should be based on respect for their rights as individuals and the right to make choices in their lives.

5.5.3 RECOMMENDATIONS

The Commission recommends that:

(a) the needs of the disabled should be mainstreamed i.e. taken into consideration in all strategic planning decisions related to the social and physical environment;

(b) the vocational development of women with disability should be enhanced by access to appropriate careers/counselling and to education and training which is not gender based and which does not reinforce stereotyped notions of women's work;

(c) national employment policies and targets should specifically take people with disabilities, particularly women, into account;

(d) the home help service should be available to all women with disability who require it. There should be an element of means-testing, so that a fee would be charged according to means to non-medical card holders (see Chapter 11 [not included]);

(e) research into the particular needs and situations of women with disabilities should be financed by the State.

5.6 Lesbian women

5.6.1 Introduction

It is widely accepted by social researchers that about 10% of the population has a homosexual orientation, with this figure occurring across different cultures, contexts, national samples, small scale studies, and different time periods. This is a substantial minority. In Ireland as in many other countries, it is also largely an underground minority. Even though the past decade has seen the development of an articulate gay rights movement it is still rare to find an openly gay man in Irish society; rarer still to find an openly lesbian woman. The issue, of course, raises complex issues of personal privacy but there is no doubt that there is a powerful taboo in operation; a fear that the open acknowledgement of a same-sex orientation could be damaging in career and personal terms.

There are no laws against lesbianism in Ireland. This does not mean that we live in a lesbian utopia. The taboo status of lesbianism functions as an unwritten law, suppressing not only the practice of lesbian sexuality but the awareness of its very existence. On the evidence of the 1990 European Values Study, lesbians and gay men in Ireland are right to be cautious. With regard to sexual orientation, Irish attitudes are consistently less tolerant than the EC average. However, it should be noted that, when compared to previous European Values Studies, the trend in Ireland is towards a more liberal attitude on homosexuality, with women being slightly more liberal than men.

5.6.2 LIMITING ATTITUDES

Submissions received by the Commission make the point that there is not a single open or 'out' lesbian woman in any position of power or public office in Ireland, and that only rarely have individual lesbians spoken out in the media so the vast majority of the population hears little or nothing factual and positive about lesbians.

It has been submitted to the Commission that lesbians are dismissed from jobs, lose custody of children, are evicted from housing, are rejected by their families, are beaten up and harassed, are ejected from political, religious or other social groups, and are barred from public places in Ireland – all for revealing their sexual orientation, or having been identified as lesbian. Our impression, however, is that it is the fear of some or all of these things happening, rather than their incidence, which is the central oppression in the lives of lesbian women. This is not in any way to denigrate the seriousness of the oppression.

This form of oppression results in situations of enforced and continuous secrecy, restrictions on social activities, and often isolation, fear, shame, guilt and ignorance about individual sexuality. Lesbian teenagers may have no positive Irish role models. Sexual orientation is not included as a category for protection in the Employment Equality Act or Unfair Dismissals Act. Lesbian partners are in the same situation as heterosexual cohabitees in that their relationship does not have legal sanction.

No lesbian organisations established for the support and development of lesbian women receive Government funding.

5.6.3 DIVERSITY AND VARIETY

The Commission believes that diversity and variety in Irish cultural and social life is to be welcomed. 'Different' does not equate with 'threatening'. The idea that groups of law-abiding Irish women are coerced into silence and secrecy about a core attribute of their personality is repugnant. We welcome the trend towards greater tolerance and openness indicated in the European Values Study

5.6.5 RECOMMENDATIONS ON LESBIAN WOMEN
The Commission recommends:
(a) that legislation should be enacted to decriminalise homosexual acts between consenting adults, in line with the European court of Human Rights judgement in the Norris case and the subsequent commitment in the agreed Programme for Government 1991–1993. (While the Irish legislation relates only to men, and not to women, its continuing existence helps contribute towards a climate in which all homosexual relationships are regarded as aberrant);
(b) the inclusion of sexual orientation as a category for unlawful discrimination in the amended employment equality legislation and Unfair Dismissals Act;
(c) the inclusion of a module on homophobia (prejudice and hatred of lesbians and gay men) in the proposed sex and relationship education course in second level schools (see Chapter 9 [not included]);
(d) that lesbian groups should be eligible for consideration for funding from the Department of Social Welfare's scheme of grants for local women's groups involved in development, support and self-help activities. The same criteria should be used in assessing applications from lesbian groups as are used in assessing applications from any other women's groups.

5.7 Traveller women
5.7.1 CHARACTERISTICS OF TRAVELLERS
The Health Research Board's study on the Vital Statistics of Travelling People, 1987, drew a picture of Travellers as a group who marry at a very young age and have many children. In 1987, for example, the birth rate for the Irish population as a whole was 16.6 per 1,000 people. For Travellers, the birth rate was over double this at 34.9 per 1,000. The average family size for the whole population was 2.3 compared with 5.3 for Travellers. From before birth to old age, Travellers have high mortality rates, notably from accidents, and congenital problems. The stillbirth rate for Ireland was 6.9 per 1,000 births in 1982; for Travellers it was almost three times this at 19.5 per 1,000. Moreover, the infant mortality rate (i.e. deaths in the first year of life) was 7.4 per 1,000 for the Irish population generally compared with 18.1 per 1,000 for Travellers. The life expectancy of women

Travellers is 65 years compared to 77 years for females generally, i.e. the life expectancy of Travellers now is what it was for Irish people generally in the 1940s. Those members of the travelling community who do not live in houses (approximately 50%) have even higher mortality rates especially among females, and in particular, from accidents, than housed Travellers.

Travellers face particular disadvantage characterised by high rates of illiteracy, poor health, low life expectancy, heavy domestic responsibilities and very poor living conditions. Traveller women, in particular, shoulder the burden of managing their households. Many women face the daily grind of rearing children by the roadside, without basic amenities such as water, sanitation, drying facilities, hard-stands for trailers, etc.

While younger women might prefer a house to roadside living, they can face isolation among the settled community and have difficulty in remaining in regular contact with their own community. Discrimination means that they can be excluded from many services and amenities such as cafes, pubs, shops, launderettes and hairdressers.

5.7.2 TRAVELLER NEEDS
Earlier policies directed towards assimilation of Travellers into settled society were well intentioned, but have not worked, not least because those members of the settled population alongside whom Travellers were settled, were very often in circumstances of considerable deprivation themselves. The days are now over when assimilation to the settled population seemed to be the answer both to the hardships borne by Travellers and to the challenges they presented to local authorities and planners. Their history, music, and oral traditions; their strong sense of community; their strong family values and mutual support in times of difficulty – are often unknown to, or unappreciated by, the settled community.

Because Travellers are at the margins of Irish society, because of the migrant nature of many of them, and because of the somewhat uneasy relationship between Travellers and the settled population – the response of State services and provision to the sometimes complex needs of Travellers has been mixed. Some local authorities have made good provision for Travellers in terms of halting sites and facilities. Others have sought to ignore the problem altogether.

5.7.3 DEPRIVATION
The reality is that Travellers live day-to-day in situations of extreme deprivation. This presses hardest on women Travellers

because they take – or are left to assume – major responsibility for the care of their families. Government policy for over twenty years has been for the provision of proper accommodation for Travellers in houses or serviced caravan sites, according to the wishes of Travellers themselves. As noted in paragraph 5.7.2 above, implementation of this policy by local authorities on the ground has been sporadic. In particular, it remains the case that provision of accommodation has for some years been at a slower rate than the increase in the number of Traveller family units and there are sizeable numbers of Traveller families (1,166 in 1990) still living in unacceptable conditions in unserviced sites on the roadsides of Ireland. The physical hardships of Traveller life are compounded by the discrimination on the part of the settled community which Travellers come up against on a daily basis. Finally, received Traveller culture itself has sexist and patriarchal elements, which Traveller women have to contend with and challenge.

5.7.4 RECOMMENDATIONS ON TRAVELLER WOMEN
The Commission recommends:

HEALTH

(a) training for health care workers on the special needs of women Travellers, along with outreach and localised services geared to meet health needs related to Traveller's lifestyles; the Commission welcomes the Eastern Health Board's planned provision of a mobile clinic for Travellers as an example of this type of initiative and recommends extension of this facility to other Health Board areas;

(b) that education on family planning services geared to Travellers' special needs should be provided to GPs;

(c) that in view of the Traveller tradition of marrying close blood relatives a genetic counselling programme should be developed which is targeted at Travellers;

(d) that Traveller women should be supported in relation to the health care of their children through targeted programmes.

ADULT EDUCATION

(e) that adult education and training programmes should be developed and provided for Traveller women, building on the experiences gained already from such developmental programmes as are operated, e.g. by FÁS. These should include access to crèche facilities. Designed in consultation with

Traveller women, such courses should reflect their particular identity. Every effort should be made to train and employ Traveller women to assist in the running of such courses.

TRAINING FOR SERVICE PROVIDERS TO TRAVELLERS

(f) training for service providers to Travellers and the design and implementation of a code of conduct for service providers in a wide range of areas, in order to ensure equal treatment.

ACCOMMODATION FOR TRAVELLERS

(g) the urgent development of a national plan for Traveller accommodation which will take account both of the needs of Travellers who wish to settle, through the provision of group housing schemes, and those who wish to continue a nomadic lifestyle, through providing adequate sites and facilities;

(h) that an integral part of this national plan should be mandatory consultation with Travellers and especially Traveller women by local authorities before decisions regarding the design and location of sites and housing schemes are made;

(i) that safety issues should be given a high priority in the planning and design of housing sites. The Preventive Code of Practice developed by Dublin County Council to reduce risks to families from fires on serviced sites should be implemented and monitored by all local authorities.

5.8 Women prisoners
5.8.1 The penal system and women
It is above all important to stress that women prisoners represent only a very small part of the total prison population. In the course of preparing this Section, Commission members had the opportunity to visit the women's prison in Mountjoy Gaol. At that time (July 1992) there were 35 women in custody, most of them for drug-related reasons. Also at the time of our visit, a building which will house the women's prison within Mountjoy was being refurbished so that women prisoners were housed in temporary, although not makeshift, accommodation.

The starting point for a consideration of the particular problems of women offenders must be the Report of the Committee of Inquiry into the Penal System, July 1985, which addressed itself to the Penal System as a whole but made a number of recommendations specifically about women prisoners. Unfortunately, a number of the problems that the Committee identified still need to be addressed. The Committee of Inquiry stated that women in custody were mainly young, and the victims of an array of personal problems. That situation has not changed since 1985. Characteristically, women offenders have a background of poverty, low educational attainment, and specific social problems, notably drugs. This means that they have specific needs but it also means that many women offenders spend repeated short spells in prison which makes participation in rehabilitative education and training programmes very problematical.

5.8.5 SHORTCOMINGS IN THE PRISON SYSTEM
The main shortcoming in the women's prison system was identified in the 1985 Committee of Inquiry Report, i.e. the lack of an open prison for women which could accommodate the majority of women prisoners. Seven years on, there is still no open prison for women. This is completely unacceptable, however sympathetically the temporary release provisions of the Criminal Justice Act 1960 are applied. While it is also desirable, in principle, to separate women on remand from women under sentence, and to separate juveniles from adult prisoners, the Commission recognises that because the overall size of the women prison population is so small this policy might impose conditions of isolation on remand prisoners which, in effect, could be considered as an additional unwarranted punishment. Again, an open prison might provide some flexibility to tackle this problem. Other areas which give rise to concern are that there is no provision for a halfway house pending release and there is a lack of follow-up services after release.

5.8.6 RECOMMENDATIONS ON WOMEN PRISONERS
The Commission recommends that:
(a) relevant and properly resourced educational, training, recreational and work opportunities, including a garden or greenhouse, should be available to women prisoners;
(b) a programme of research and evaluation in the field of criminal justice as it affects women both at court and in prison should be undertaken immediately, so that its conclusions can inform policy-making;
(c) the lock-up hours for women prisoners should be examined with a view to enabling them to associate and watch television later in the evenings than they currently can;
(d) the Department of Justice should make an immediate commitment to the development of open prison facilities for women

prisoners, a half-way house and follow up services after release;

(e) the possibility of providing a family room where prisoners could spend a longer time with their children should be examined.

5.8.7 VICTIM SUPPORT

In addition to the recommendations in section 5.8.6, the Commission recommends that measures should be taken to provide adequate systematic support to victims of petty and personal crime, most of whom are women. Such measures should include:

(a) improving funding for victim support schemes;
(b) guaranteeing counselling support to all victims who request it;
(c) emphasising reparation to victims in sentencing, where appropriate.

5.9 Women involved in prostitution

5.9.1 INCIDENCE OF PROSTITUTION

Because prostitution in Ireland is largely undocumented, it is very difficult to form a reliable estimate of the numbers of women involved. However, it is clear from the testimonies which do exist and from research carried out elsewhere, that the lives of prostitutes are characterised by a sense of powerlessness, few opportunities, no voice in society, no choices in life and very little hope.

The Commission received one submission on the situation of women involved in prostitution in the Dublin area from an order of religious sisters who provide support in a low-key, practical way over a long time horizon to women involved in prostitution. This submission urged the adoption of strategies which recognise the dignity of all women irrespective of their condition, based on women's right to choice, self-determination, non-stigmatisation and non-victimisation.

Case studies of over 200 women involved in prostitution in Dublin suggest that women often suffer sexual and physical abuse, resulting not only in physical injury but also in emotional pain and low self-esteem. In some cases, this impression is reinforced by Court evidence. Financial pressures, unemployment, a lack of education and poor housing were also shared common experiences. A quotation from *Lyn: A Story of Prostitution*, which deals with the lives of Dublin prostitutes, conveys the isolation and risk of casual violence graphically:

My jaws would clench and I would take a deep breath as I took up my position on the path. Then I'd look to my left, then my right, across the road: 'Is that someone hiding in the garden over there? Who's that in the parked car? Are there two or three men in it?' Then I'd turn and peer into the bushes along the banks of the Canal. 'Looks OK. No, did that bush move? What's that noise? Coulda swore I saw someone lurking behind that tree, or was it an optical illusion?'

Getting into a car was even more scary. Your heart raced as you assessed the client. And as you got in the car, you check that it had a door handle on the inside and a window catch, in case you had to get out in a hurry. The silent ones were the worst. 'Why doesn't he speak?' So you small-talked, and I mean small talk. And if your client was the silent type your palms were sweating with fear and you heard yourself asking inane things in an effort to get him to say something so you could hear the tone of his voice. Was there any kindness in it? If he made any sudden moves you jumped out of your skin even though he was only reaching for his wallet.

5.9.2 A STRATEGY TO TACKLE PROBLEMS

We make the point in Chapter 1 [not included] that any prosecution which might be taken for prostitution should be even-handed, as between the prostitute and the man. In this section, we are concerned with health and social supports for the women involved. This strategy must be based on recognition of the dignity of the women concerned. That the term 'common prostitute' has fallen into disuse is a welcome development. Fundamentally, a strategy devised to assist women involved in prostitution must be based on practical assistance measures, support, and initiatives geared to reintegration into society, e.g. through training for work. This is not easy to do. While it is possible to train women in skills with which they might earn a living it cannot be easy for them to find work when most of their past must, in effect, remain a closed book. The most useful approach might be development of a cooperative or cooperatives and training for legitimate forms of self-employment. It would make sense in developing an intervention strategy to build on the goodwill, experience and resources of voluntary bodies already active in providing assistance, and on the experiences of the women themselves and on their sense of solidarity.

We do not underestimate the scope of the problem. Prostitutes can have very complex problems deriving from a mix of socioeconomic disadvantages exacerbated by violence and drug-taking. The question we have to ask ourselves as a society is whether we are content to see women remain as part of this underclass without opportunities either to leave it or to improve their existence.

5.9.3 RECOMMENDATIONS ON PROSTITUTES

The Commission recommends that:

(a) an integrated approach involving the Departments of Health, Education, Social Welfare, and Justice and interested voluntary organisations should be adopted in order to provide health and welfare services and information to women involved in prostitution. Every effort should be made to encourage women involved in prostitution to participate in decision-making regarding the type and level of service they require and in designing 'social rehabilitation' programmes;

(b) as a first step in this strategy the setting up of a drop-in centre or centres should be funded. The services provided would include short-term accommodation as well as opportunities for self-help and building self-esteem, along with relief from isolation, informal education and advice, medical and social assistance; these services could usefully be provided in association with voluntary bodies already engaged in helping women in prostitution;

(c) a rehabilitation centre should be established for women who want to get out of prostitution. The development and operation of this centre should draw on the experiences derived from the implementation of recommendations (a) and (b) above and the Centre should provide counselling and training for future employment.

The *Second Progress Report of the Monitoring Committee on the Implementation of the Recommendations of the Second Commission on the Status of Women* (1996) listed a number of recent initiatives taken to aid disadvantaged women. For those in poverty, there were training courses and temporary work experience programmes with expanded child care support. Plans were evolving that would improve access to health care and family planning services. In order 'to help break the cycle of poverty' various school programmes had been put in place to alleviate or prevent 'educational disadvantage'.

Housing and health services were found to be central concerns for elderly women in particular. In response, the government established the Department of Environment's Task Force on Special Housing Aid for the Elderly in 1982; and the Housing Act 1988 identified the elderly as a separate class to be considered in local authorities' housing programmes. Overall, there has been a significant increase in the funding for housing for the elderly.

According to the *Second Progress Report*, health policy for the elderly was 'consistent with the United Nations Principles for Older Persons', which meant, in effect, supporting home care for the elderly where feasible, and providing 'specialist and extended care facilities to meet their (later) needs'.[6] In addition, the *Second Progress Report* noted proposals for promoting healthy ageing and for increasing the number of general hospital departments specialising in medicine for the elderly. We include coverage of other aspects of the health care of the elderly in Chapter 9.

The Second Commission on the Status of Women cited the wide-ranging needs of Traveller women, among them needs for health services and family planning, education, training and housing. Its report emphasised the need for specially trained service providers for the Travelling community. It also urged that local authorities consult with, and encourage participation by, Traveller women in designing projects.

The *Second Progress Report* also provided a lengthy review of responses to the Second Commission's recommendations on Traveller women, drawing heavily on the *Report of the Task Force on the Travelling Community*, published in July 1995.

Task Force on the Travelling Community, *Report of the Task Force on the Travelling Community* (1995)

1.1 Traveller women have played particular and significant leadership roles within their own community and representing their own community. A Traveller woman stood for election to the Dáil in response to anti-Traveller campaigns in Dublin in the early 80s and secured a considerable vote. In 1994 a Traveller woman was elected town commissioner in a west of Ireland town. A number of Traveller women have been accorded various national awards and commendations. Traveller women have produced widely acclaimed poetry, art and crafts. However, the central contribution which women make to the well-being of the Traveller community is largely unrecognised.

1.5 The establishment of the First and Second Commissions on the Status of Women represent an acknowledgement by the Government of the need to pay particular attention to the role, status and contribution of women to our society. They are also an acknowledgement that women are not automatically included in, but in fact are more likely to be excluded from, general policies and programmes. The Task Force acknowledges a similar requirement and position with regard to Traveller women.

4.4 'Settled' people's responses to Traveller women's difficulties are often to blame them for their own situation. A Traveller woman writing in 1989 (Ref. 8 [not included]) said: 'Settled women look down on Traveller women and give out about them for the oppression they suffers. But what a lot of Settled women don't see is that Travelling and Settled women are in the same boat when it comes to the way they are looked down on and treated in society by men.'

4.5 This process of blaming can often be a feature of Traveller women's experience in dealing with the various social services – medical, social work, accommodation, social welfare or schools. Some of those they deal with promote and support their fight to their Traveller identity. Others, often unconsciously, undermine it. Traveller women can be left with the message that their problems can best be solved if they cease to be Travellers. This leaves Traveller women in an impossible and unenviable situation, effectively being blamed for being Travellers.

Traveller women, on the other hand, like so many other women from minority groups experiencing oppression, may be left with little opportunity to address their own situation as women. Challenging this oppression is often seen as attacking the culture, which is already under threat from the outside, and therefore must be supported internally by all members. This ignores the fact that cultures are not stagnant, but are dynamic relationships which change with time as the lives and experiences of their members change.

4.7 It is widely recognised that young women from minority groups can experience particular discrimination, especially at times of major changes in their culture. The UN placed a particular focus within this Year of Tolerance on promoting their rights. The current tension between traditional approaches and modern developments evident in Traveller culture (and in Irish society as a whole over the past 20 years) has particular implications for young Traveller women. It is essential that young Traveller women have their particular education and developmental needs met in ways that do not blame them for being Traveller women, but which acknowledge the changing dynamic of Traveller culture and the crucial importance of equality for Traveller women in the future.

8.1 Recommendations

HR.1 In implementing each of the recommendations addressed in this Report the gender dimension should be examined in order to ascertain how policies and practices in each area contribute to or block progress for Traveller women. Proposals for future initiatives in each area must be monitored in terms of their impact on equality for Traveller women. Each must outline its objectives, targets and likely outcomes for Traveller women.

HR.2 The Government should make resources available for the collection and collation of data on Traveller women through specific research projects. In these projects Traveller women and Traveller women's groups should be subjects, rather than objects, of the research. The research should build on local profiles and accounts already produced and on other research underway so that any study complements rather than repeats, and addresses gaps not heretofore the subject of detailed scrutiny.

HR.3 In line with the recommendations of the Second Commission on the Status of Women, Government policies on this matter and EU Directives, progress for Traveller women is recognised as a priority in the move towards equality for all women. It is also recognised as essential if progress is to be made for all Travellers. This necessitates a particular focus on Traveller women by any body set up as a consequence of the Task Force Report and in all Government Departments concerned with its implementation. It also requires a particular focus on Traveller women in procedures and legislation adopted towards the implementation of the Report of the Second Commission on the Status of Women.

HR.4 The special needs of different groups of Traveller women should be looked at separately acknowledging that not all Traveller women are the same, for example, the specific situation of young, Traveller women referred to at paragraph 4.7 above.

HR.5 (i) Particular issues which affect the human rights of Traveller women must be urgently addressed. Institutionalised violence towards Traveller women requires detailed examination and responses. Culturally appropriate ways to support Traveller women who experience violence within their community, and to respond to the issue of male violence, need to be worked on with Traveller women. Such work should take into account the responses already being made by voluntary groups, refuges and Women's Aid. The Department of Health should provide resources for pilot projects in this area.

(ii) There should be no discrimination or exclusion of Traveller women wishing to access these services.

(iii) Resources should be made available by the Department of Health to expand and improve existing facilities in these areas. This should ensure provision for family units of different sizes.

(iv) Those working in this area should have access to training in order to ensure their understanding of Travellers and their way of life.

(v) The child care needs of Traveller women should be researched and addressed.

HR.6 Traveller women's economic roles in their community should be acknowledged and resourced so that any economic progress for Travellers is supportive of, rather than at the expense of, Traveller women.

HR.7 (i) Targeted responses to Traveller women's needs in a variety of areas such as health, education, training and personal development are required as a prerequisite towards progress and equality. These should be designed and delivered in partnership with Traveller women's organisations. They should be flexible and capable of integrating local work already underway and building on the knowledge of existing groups.

(ii) Ongoing targeted initiatives for Traveller women, as outlined above, should be built into mainstream programmes of FÁS and other State agencies. Staff on such programmes should be selected and managed by Traveller women's organisations.

Sexual orientation was excluded as grounds for dismissal in the Unfair Dismissals (Amendment) Act 1993. Units on sexual orientation have been included in upper-level secondary school materials on relationships and sexuality education. The Second Commission's recommendation that funding be provided for lesbian groups by the Department of Social Welfare turned out to be irrelevant, since lesbian groups had not been excluded and in fact had been funded.

With respect to the Second Commission's recommendations on women prisoners, the government undertook to set aside sections of Castlerea for women and to build a new women's prison, although the implementation of these undertakings was delayed. It also undertook to revise the Prison Rules for women. The recommendations on aid to victims were implemented with increased funding for the Association for Victim Support and the provision of compensation for victims in the Criminal Justice Act 1993.

With respect to the Second Commission's recommendations on prostitutes, in 1991 the Eastern Health Board started the Women's Health Project, which targets women in prostitution, providing advice, medical testing and a drop-in clinic. The Congregation of the Good Shepherd created an organisation, Ruhama, to provide counselling and comfort to prostitutes, and the Eastern Health Board provided IR£20,000 to support its work in 1994 and 1995.

CONCLUSION

The widening agenda of women's issues is very evident in this chapter on social welfare. Reports by government-appointed bodies have increasingly focused on the concerns of specific groups of women, concerns that exacerbate the general problems of gender discrimination. While job-creation programmes retain a central strategic place in the recommendations, it is also clear that a number of varied tactical approaches are needed to aid diverse constituencies.

Despite such efforts, a report published by the Combat Poverty Agency in 1999 indicated that the risk of poverty for women had not declined.[7] The National Women's Council of Ireland attributed this condition to the gender-biased construction of the social welfare system, which remained in place despite reforms. The Council recommended that the model of social welfare based on 'male breadwinners' and women's dependency be changed to one promoting 'individualisation', that is, a system in which 'all qualifying social welfare claimants and their partners receive their payments individually, i.e. assessment on a joint basis, payment on an individual basis'.[8]

CHAPTER FOUR

Married women

In this chapter we address a topic introduced in Chapter 3: the legal status of women in marriage and in the home. In this instance, while the issues do not raise constitutional questions, they nonetheless pertain to such important matters as property rights, financial concerns and guardianship of children. Using Nuala Jackson's approach, they are issues that involve economic security for married women and questions of parenthood.[1]

The report of the first Commission on the Status of Women (1972) identified a number of specific issues within its general framework. These included such considerations as the legal status of married women, the partners in marriage, community of property, guardianship of infants and succession.

At the outset of its examination of these matters the Commission noted the relevance to Ireland of the United Nations Declaration on the Elimination of Discrimination against Women.

Commission on the Status of Women, *Report to Minister for Finance* (1972)

Women and the law
437. The United Nations Declaration on the Elimination of Discrimination against Women, adopted on 7 November, 1967, and voted for by Ireland, states that, without prejudice to the safeguarding of the unity and the harmony of the family, which remains the basic unit of any society, all appropriate measures, particularly legislative measures, shall be taken to ensure to women, married or unmarried, equal rights with men in the field of civil law, and in particular: (i) the right to

acquire, administer, enjoy, dispose of and inherit property, including property acquired during marriage; (ii) the right to equality in legal capacity and the exercise thereof; and (iii) the same rights as men with regard to the law on the movement of persons. The Declaration also provides that women should have equal rights with men during marriage and at its dissolution and that parents should have equal rights and duties in relation to their children, in all cases the interests of the children to be paramount. In relation to criminal law the Declaration states that all provisions of penal codes which constitute discrimination against women shall be repealed.

The Commission also cited Irish legislation of the 1950s and 1960s that, in its view, had 'removed the vast bulk of such discrimination' that had existed in law. Nonetheless, the Commission indicated that considerable confusion remained regarding 'the present general status of women in civil law'.

441. There have been many references in the submissions made to us concerning the legal status of women. Apart, however, from the matters referred to in paragraph 440 [not included], we have received little evidence of any overt discrimination against women in civil law and none in relation to the criminal law. There are cases, however, where the law, though equal between the sexes, may bear more heavily on a woman than on a man. Up to comparatively recent times a considerable amount of discrimination in law existed against women. The enactment of such legislation as the Married Women's Status Act 1957, the Guardianship of Infants Act 1964 and the Succession Act 1965 removed the vast bulk of such discrimination. Certain instances of discrimination, such as in regard to the eligibility of women for jury service, still exist and are dealt with below. It is apparent to us from the submissions received that not a little confusion exists concerning the present general status of women in civil law and we have accordingly, in addition to dealing with specific instances of discrimination, decided to deal briefly with the background and the present position of the more important matters of a legal nature that have been raised with us.

The Commission then outlined this general status by detailing the nature and significance of the Acts alluded to above. The Commission provided its own recommendations for further action to counter discrimination against women. Its first concern was the legal status of married women.

LEGAL STATUS OF MARRIED WOMEN

442. Originally, at common law, a married woman's existence was treated as being merged in that of her husband, the theory of the law being that in consideration of the husband's undertaking to support and maintain his wife he became entitled to her property. Accordingly, any property held by her at the time of her marriage or acquired thereafter became either absolutely or temporarily the property of her husband as did any cash or chattels. A married woman could not make a valid contract and her husband could be held liable on foot of contracts entered into by the wife before marriage. Torts committed or debts incurred by the wife before or during the marriage could also be held to be the liability of the husband.

443. This underlying principle, with certain reliefs granted in the Courts of Chancery and by various Married Women's Property Acts, obtained up to the enactment of the Married Women's Status Act 1957, which made wide changes in this field of law. This Act provided that a married woman would be capable of contracting and made her liable personally for her torts, contracts and debts, except for contracts entered into or debts incurred as agent of the husband. It provided also that a married woman would be capable of acquiring, holding and disposing (by will or otherwise) of any property and would be subject to the law relating to bankruptcy and to the enforcement of judgements and orders as if she were unmarried. The property of a married woman now belongs to her as if she were unmarried and can be disposed of accordingly. A husband and wife are now treated as two separate persons for all purposes of acquisition of any property.

Married women, therefore, now enjoy the same legal position as single women and men in regard to their property and in relation to their ordinary rights in contract and tort.

THE PARTNERS IN MARRIAGE

444. There is a presumption in law that where a husband and wife are living together, the wife has authority to contract on his behalf in all matters concerning the supply of necessaries for the husband, herself and the household. The goods and services so contracted for must be suitable in kind, sufficient in quantity and necessary in fact according to the conditions in which the husband chooses his wife and family shall live. In deciding what are necessaries of life, the criterion is not primarily the husband's means but the standard at which he decides his family shall live. Where the husband supplies the wife with necessaries or with the money to buy them

he has the power to cancel the authority of his wife to contract on his behalf or to pledge his credit.

445. It has been represented to us that the position outlined in paragraph 444 can, and sometimes does, give rise to considerable hardship on the wife and that she is far from being placed on an equal footing with her husband. While her husband is alive the work she does in the home does not give her any real economic status within the home whereas the work performed by the husband outside the home puts him in the position of forcing his wife, if he so chooses, to live at the very lowest economic level. The day's work of a housewife looking after children at home is fully committed to the purposes of the family and the Constitution recognises this. The day's work of the husband in earning an income is on the other hand, in the eyes of the law, committed to the purposes of the family only to the limited extent outlined above. He has the right to profit fully from his wife's work at home. She, in the eyes of the law, can claim from the profits of his work only necessaries plus such further addition to the family's standard of living as he – not she – may decide.

446. How husbands and wives manage their family affairs is normally a matter for themselves alone. But the law has to make assumptions about what is to happen when things go wrong and a case comes into Court. We consider that the Common Law position as outlined in paragraph 444 can discriminate against wives. With a view to improving this position, we recommend that in future the legal obligation to support the family should rest on both husband and wife according to their means and capacity. In the event of any dispute coming before the Courts it should be for the Courts to decide whether reasonable arrangements have been made between the husband and wife as to the disposal of the family income in respect of (a) their current standard of living and (b) provision for the domestic home, family emergencies and old age.

447. In relation to the family residence, it is the case in most marriages that the home, which is normally the principal item of family property, is owned by the husband and any mortgage repayments on it are generally made from his income. There is some indication that this position is changing gradually and that a greater number of young married couples are placing the home in joint ownership. We welcome this development as it affords a measure of protection for the wife in relation to the disposal of the home and we feel that the trend should be encouraged.

448. Where the matrimonial home is in the sole ownership of the

husband it may happen, in exceptional cases, that severe hardship and distress is caused to the wife where the husband, for one reason or another, decides to dispose of it. At present he may do this without his wife's knowledge or consent and his wife may find, without any notice whatsoever, that she and any children involved have no longer any place to live.

449. We do not wish to interfere in any way with the present freedom of action of the normal married couple to dispose by mutual agreement of their home as and when they wish. We do consider, however, that the wife should be afforded some protection where she complains of hardship likely to be caused by the sale of the home without her consent.

450. There are, we consider, two acceptable alternative courses by which the protection referred to in paragraph 449 may be achieved. The first is to provide that neither spouse of the marriage may dispose of the matrimonial home without prior consultation with the other spouse and that where it is not possible to reach agreement a period of time should be allowed to expire before any further action is taken. The Courts should have power during this period of time, on application made by either spouse, to decide, if it is considered that undue hardship would be caused to the other spouse or to any dependent children of the marriage, by the disposal of the home, that such disposal may not be proceeded with. By undue hardship we envisage, for instance, circumstances in which the affected spouse would be left without any accommodation or would be asked to accept accommodation which the Courts did not consider was a suitable alternative. This type of interference by the Courts with the legal rights to the matrimonial home is not unique. In New Zealand for instance, the Matrimonial Property Act 1963 gives the courts wide discretion to interfere with legal or equitable rights to the matrimonial property on the grounds of fairness or justice. Under that Act, the courts may make such order as appears just in settling property disputes between a husband and wife at any stage of marriage, 'notwithstanding that the legal or equitable interests of the husband and wife in the property are defined or notwithstanding that the spouse in whose favour the order is made had no legal or equitable interest in the property'. Where the dispute concerns the matrimonial home, the courts must have regard to the respective contributions of the husband and wife to the property concerned, but such contributions need not be of a monetary nature – they can be by way of the provision of services, prudent management or any

other means. In Denmark, the spouse who has the title to the matrimonial home may not sell or mortgage it without the consent of the other spouse and in France neither spouse may dispose of the matrimonial home or its contents without the consent of the other spouse.

451. The second way in which the protection sought could be achieved would be to introduce a system of co-ownership of the matrimonial home under which the home would legally be regarded as being jointly owned by the husband and wife, by virtue of the marriage bond, except where an agreement to the contrary had been entered into by the spouses.

The advantages of co-ownership are that it would recognise the partnership element in marriage by giving the spouses equal interests in the principal family asset. We can see many difficulties and anomalies arising, however, from the automatic sharing of one asset – for instance where the home formed an integral part of a farm or other business venture. In general, we consider that while co-ownership appears to be a desirable protection for the married woman we do not feel that we are qualified to determine whether such a system is a practical one or is desirable in the context of the overall legal system in Ireland nor to detail the basis on which it should apply.

452. On balance, we feel that the system outlined in paragraph 450 would be the easier to introduce and to operate and would be less likely to lead to anomalies or injustices in individual cases. We recommend, accordingly, that neither spouse should have power to dispose of the matrimonial home without prior consultation with the other spouse and where agreement is not reached a period of time should be allowed to expire before the disposal is proceeded with. The courts should have power during this period of time, on application made by either spouse, to decide whether undue hardship would be caused to the other spouse or to any dependent children of the marriage by the disposal of the home and whether the disposal may or may not be proceeded with. In the case of a mortgaged home, where either spouse fails to keep up the mortgage payments the other spouse should be entitled to keep up the payments and thereby acquire a share in the equity of redemption. We recommend, in addition, that the system of co-ownership of the matrimonial home outlined in paragraph 451 should be further investigated and if it should prove to be a workable one, consideration should be given to its introduction as an alternative to the foregoing recommendation.

453. In the event of a separation being effected, and an arrangement for alimony provided for, we recommend that in such case the wife should, in addition thereto, have a claim to the value of a moiety of the matrimonial home.

SAVINGS FROM HOUSEKEEPING ALLOWANCE

454. In Ireland, a wife is not entitled to ownership of any savings which she may effect in money given to her by her husband for housekeeping purposes. Such savings, or any goods bought with them, belong in law to her husband. In Britain this Common Law position was altered by the enactment of the Married Women's Property Act 1964. That Act provided that if any question arises as to the right of a husband or wife to money derived from any allowance made by the husband for the expenses of the matrimonial home or for similar purposes, or to any property acquired out of such money, the money or property shall, in the absence of any agreement to the contrary, be treated as belonging to the husband and the wife, in equal shares. We recommend that a similar provision be introduced here.

As the first Commission noted, the 1957 Act established the equality of married women with respect to the ability to contract, to acquire, hold and dispose of any property. The Commission noted that the disposition of property should also be considered. Thus the topic of partners in marriage was centred on the issues of earnings and the home. The Family Home Protection Act 1976, which was passed largely in response to the Commission's recommendation, prevented the sale of a house occupied by a married couple without the consent of both husband and wife. In addition, the Family Law (Maintenance of Spouse and Child) Act 1976 provided for an application to the court for support of spouse and children when it has not been provided. This Act also established the joint ownership of money saved from housekeeping

It was against this background that, in 1985, the Working Party on Women's Affairs and Family Law Reform noted the Law Reform Commission's recommendations on property ownership and the special circumstances of debt on the home, which can force the sale of the home in an arrangement that is unjust to one spouse.

**Working Party on Women's Affairs and Family Law
Reform, Irish Women:** *Agenda for Practical Action* **(1985)**

Reform in progress

10.8 The Working Party is pleased to record that substantial reform
is in progress departmentally in the sense that amending legislation
is either in course of preparation or proposals from the Law Reform
Commission are under active consideration in many of the family
law areas where, in the view of the Working Party, action is
required; we are, however, very much aware that reform has in
some instances taken considerably longer than was anticipated.

10.9 The Working Party has been assured by the Departments
substantively concerned that the submissions received by the
Working Party will be fully taken into account in preparing
amending legislation. The situation on individual items is as set out
hereafter:

(A) MATRIMONIAL PROPERTY (FAMILY HOME)

10.10 The law relating to the property relationship between spouses
was included within the ambit of the Law Reform Commission's
First Programme of Law Reform and was the subject of specific
recommendations in the Commission's First Report on Family Law
[LRC I – 1981].

10.11 The Commission recommended that where a spouse,
whether directly or indirectly, makes a contribution in money or
money's worth to the acquisition, improvement or maintenance of
the family home, then, subject to agreement, arrangement or
understanding between the parties, he or she will acquire a
beneficial interest (or an enlarged share in the beneficial interest) of
such an extent as appears just and equitable to the Court. In this
regard a 'contribution in money or money's worth' should in the
Commission's view include, inter alia, the contribution made by each
spouse to the welfare of the family including any contribution made
by looking after the home or caring for the family. Under the present
law this contribution would not generally be regarded as conferring
any beneficial interest on the spouse making the contribution.

10.12 The Commission also recommended that section 12 of the
Married Women's Status Act 1957 (which enables disputes between
spouses as to ownership and possession of property to be decided
in summary proceedings in the High Court or Circuit Court) should
be repealed and re-enacted in a more extended form, designed to
ensure that the Court can do justice in cases that might be regarded

as falling outside the present scope of section 12, as where the defendant spouse had disposed of the property before application was made to the Court and has not made just and equitable payment to the plaintiffs in respect of the property.

(B) MATRIMONIAL PROPERTY (GENERAL)

10.86 References are contained earlier in this chapter [not included] to the Government's proposed legislation which will generally give each spouse equal rights of ownership in the family home and contents. There are, however, other aspects of matrimonial property to which the Working Party wishes briefly to refer. These are the questions of a community of property between husband and wife and the special situation of the family home in respect of what we might term the judgement mortgage procedure – this latter aspect also was referred to in the submissions received by the Working Party.

10.87 The Report of the Commission on the Status of Women referred to the concept of a community of property involving joint ownership of family property to be realised at the end of a marriage and recommended that this matter should be further investigated. The Law Reform Commission indicated in its First Report on Family Law, that after deliberating at some length on the question of whether their proposals for change should be extended so as to cover all property (including property other than the family home), and having regard to the broad range of policy and legal issues that such a step would involve, the Commission did not propose that such an extension should be made at present. The Commission did, however, feel that the matter could best be dealt with in the context of 'community of property' between husband and wife, and stated that they intend to publish a Working Paper in due course on this issue. The Working Party welcomes the proposal of the Law Reform Commission in this regard.

10.88 The Working Party would like to refer secondly to the position of the family home in relation to the Family Home Protection legislation on the one hand and the Judgement Mortgage (Ireland) Act 1850 as amended by the Judgement Mortgage (Ireland) Act 1858 on the other hand.

10.89 Under section 3(1) of the Family Home Protection Act 1976 the purported conveyance by a spouse, without the prior consent in writing of the other spouse, of any interest in the family home to any person except the other spouse is, subject to certain statutory exceptions, void. Further protection is provided by section 5 of the Act in that, where it appears to the court, on the application of a spouse, that the other spouse is engaging in such conduct as may lead to the loss of any interest in the family home or may render it unsuitable for habitation as a family home with the intention of depriving the applicant spouse or a dependent child of the family of his residence in the family home, the court may make such order as it considers proper, directed to the other spouse or to any other person, for the protection of the family home in the interest of the applicant spouse or of the child.

10.90 Section 5 also provides that, where the applicant spouse or a dependent child of the family has been deprived of his residence in the family home by conduct that resulted in the loss of any interest therein or rendered it unsuitable for habitation as a family home, the Court may order the other spouse or any other person to pay to the applicant spouse such amount as the Court considers proper to compensate the applicant spouse and any such child for their loss or make such other order directed to the other spouse or to any other person as may appear to the Court to be just and equitable. These provisions are obviously very desirable and give very great protection to a spouse in respect of action by the other spouse which might result in the loss of the family home.

10.91 It has, however, been argued that the effect of the Judgement Mortgage Acts is seriously to weaken the protection that is given by the 1976 Act. The effect of the former Acts is to enable a creditor who obtains a judgement for debt in court against a land owner, e.g. a house owner, to convert the judgement into a type of mortgage against the property – hence the expression 'judgement mortgage'. The creditor first files in the Court in which judgement was entered an affidavit containing details of the judgement. A mortgage affecting the debtor's interest in the property can then be created by registering in the Registry of Deeds (or in the Land Registry, in the case of registered land) an attested copy of that affidavit. Nevertheless, the judgement mortgagee must apply to the Court to have the property sold (an ordinary legal mortgagee does not so have to apply to the Court) and he takes the property subject to all rights and burdens – and one such burden could arise where a spouse with a beneficial interest in the property is in occupation.

10.92 These restraints apart, the burden of the argument that is made is that the Judgement Mortgage Acts enable a family home to be sold over the head of an innocent spouse, who may have had no knowledge of the debt that led to such an event, let alone have consented to the debt. This is perceived as an injustice and gives rise to a demand for a change in the law, perhaps by way of an amendment of the Family Home Protection Act 1976 to provide that a judgement mortgage should not be capable of being registered against a family home unless, at some prior stage, the other spouse consented to the debt. The idea here is that lending institutions generally would be aware that they could not ultimately hope to rely on the security of a family home unless, at some stage prior to registration, they received the written consent of the other spouse.

10.93 The Working Party, having carefully considered this argument, finds itself unable to support it. In the first place, an amendment of the kind suggested would go well beyond the purpose and spirit of the Act, which was and is to protect a spouse, and the children, against dispossession from the family home by the deliberate act of the other spouse. It is clear from the debates in the Oireachtas that preceded enactment into law of the measure that the Provisions of the Act were framed strictly to that end, and the longstanding borrowing, security and bankruptcy arrangements were consciously being left untouched.

10.94 Accordingly, any legislative changes of the kind under discussion would represent, not just an amendment of the 1976 Act, but a fundamental policy change, carrying wide implications. For example, a judgement mortgage does not arise only on foot of a formally negotiated loan (to which, in principle, the consent of the other spouse might perhaps be made a requirement). It can arise in relation to any form of money debt, whether originating as a trading debt, money due for services rendered, damages awarded in an action for a tort or in any other fashion. In few, if any, such cases could the question of the other spouse's consent arise: the logic of a thorough-going family home protection law would then require something on the lines of what is sometimes called 'homestead legislation' which (where it has been tried) does not appear to have conferred benefits commensurate with its restrictive and sometimes crippling effects on many business transactions.

10.95 Apart from what is said above, however, recent developments have in any event overtaken the argument for change of this kind. For one thing, recent case law suggests that a spouse who is in actual occupation of a family home and who can prove beneficial ownership in part of that home has rights of occupation as co-owner of the home which would appear to be binding on a judgement mortgagee seeking a sale. In addition, a judgement mortgagee when seeking a sale in such a case proceeds under the

Partition Acts: however, recent decisions of the High Court have indicated that a sale of a family home under those Acts will not be made unless the Court is satisfied that it should dispense with the consent of the other spouse under the Family Home Protection Act. But, most important of all, the effect of the Proposed Matrimonial Home legislation will be greatly to strengthen the position of the non-owning spouse, once the Act is passed, and to put the question of sales by judgement mortgagees into an entirely different context.

PROPOSALS ON COMMUNITY OF PROPERTY

Sections of the Commission's report (1972) called for a form of co-ownership of the family home at the end of marriage. The Working Party's *Agenda* (1985) endorsed the Law Reform Commission's recommendation that the spouse acquire a 'beneficial interest' in the home and that the spouse not be deprived of that benefit by a mortgage foreclosure. In response to a recommendation of the Commission, the Judicial Separation and Family Reform Act 1989 protected the interests of the respective spouses in the family property following a judicial separation.

Commission on the Status of Women, *Report to Minister for Finance* (1972)

COMMUNITY OF PROPERTY

455. We have referred in paragraph 443 to the fact that husband and wife are treated as separate persons for all purposes of acquisition and ownership of any property. It is frequently argued, however, that this situation does not provide any real equality as most married women are still engaged for the greater part of their working lives on home duties and that the law as it stands does not take this contribution into account in so far as property rights built up by the husband from his paid employment during marriage are concerned. It is reasonable to argue that such property rights of the husband would be less if his wife's services in the home were not available to him. This general argument must, of course, be qualified to the extent that the wife is automatically entitled where the husband dies intestate to inherit either the whole or two-thirds of the estate, depending on whether there are issue or not; where the husband dies testate, she is

entitled to one-half of the estate where there is no issue and to one-third where there is issue. These succession provisions for the widow are more generous than in Britain and, as far as we are aware, are also in advance of many other countries where the position frequently is that the widow has no automatic legal right to share in the assets accumulated by the husband.

Legal provisions under which husband and wife share certain of their assets on the termination of marriage have been enacted in a number of other countries and are sometimes referred to as 'Community of Property'.[2] Countries having such systems include France, Germany, the Netherlands and the Scandinavian Countries. The systems vary considerably in detail as between the different countries but a factor common to all of them is that either during the marriage or on its termination certain of the spouses' property forms a community in which each has an equal interest. A further common factor is that the spouses are free at the beginning of the marriage (and sometimes later) to agree between themselves that the community system should not apply to them.

456. In all the legal systems referred to in paragraph 455 the sharing of property either brought into or acquired during the marriage takes place only at the end of the marriage and to this extent the reference to such systems as 'community of property' may mislead. During the marriage each spouse can acquire, deal with and dispose of his or her own property. No system has introduced joint management in respect of all property during marriage.

457. In Ireland, a husband and wife are free to enter into any voluntary agreement they wish concerning the ownership and management of their property and income. We do not consider that a 'community of property' entailing joint ownership and joint management of property or other assets either brought into or acquired during marriage, however desirable, is feasible or practical in all or even a majority of cases. A system of community of property entailing joint ownership of family property to be realised at the end of marriage does, however, appear to be feasible and of value. We have noted in paragraph 455 that the provisions for widows under the Succession Act 1965 are relatively favourable; in view, however, of the not insignificant number of legal separations referred to in paragraph 563 [not included], the advantages that a community system would confer on widows in relation to estate duty and the possibility and value of building into such a system safeguards against one spouse or the other

misusing the right to administer his or her property during marriage, we think that more may be required and we recommend that such a system of community of property to be realised at the end of marriage should be further investigated.

> In its report (1993), the Second Commission on the Status of Women expressed concern about the unfair disposition of family property and called for a community property form of co-ownership.

Second Commission on the Status of Women, *Report to Government* (1993)

1.5.1 PROPERTY RIGHTS ON MARRIAGE

In our First Statement, the Commission recommended that legislation should be introduced to provide for joint ownership of the family home by a married couple. The Government accepted the recommendation and legislation is expected very shortly. The Commission considers that this is only a first step in providing a suitable regime of marital property in order to eliminate inequality in the traditional marriage.

> The source of the inequality is the division of labour between homemaker and wage earner which usually results in the economic subordination of the wife. If the state is to rectify this situation there would seem to be no realistic alternative to the adoption of sharing principles within marriage. A scheme providing for the compulsory sharing of wealth, inspired by the idea of equality, would not, in this writer's view, be opposed to the values which underpin the prevailing conception of marriage. It would, depending on the particular scheme adopted, bring about radical change in the present system of separate property but such change would be in no way inimical to marriage founded on the true equality of the spouses. As it is, there is already compulsory sharing at death. But death ought not to be the only terminating event that triggers sharing. (*Key Issues in Irish Family Law* by Paul A. O'Connor, 1988)

Since the Succession Act 1965, a spouse is entitled to a legal share of one-third in the assets of a deceased spouse who died testate, if there is issue, regardless of whatever the will provides, and to one half if there is no issue. In the case of intestacy a spouse is entitled to two-thirds if there is issue, or the entire estate if there is no issue.

1.5.2 DIVISION OF PROPERTY IN THE EVENT OF JUDICIAL SEPARATION

Many people may not realise that a form of deferred community property has already been part of Irish legislation since the passing of the Judicial Separation and Family Law Reform Act 1989. This entails division of the property by the court in the case of judicial separation with no predetermined share. The court is given power to order a division of property as well as periodic payments when granting a judicial separation. In doing this the court takes into consideration such matters as the contribution of a spouse to the welfare of the family, the age of dependent children, the conduct or misconduct of the spouses, length of the marriage, and the effect on the earning capacity of each spouse by the marital responsibilities assumed.

The Commission does not propose that there should be a change in this law where there is a judicial separation. The complex issues which arise on the breakdown of marriage would probably not be met by a simple division of the family assets. But the Commission does believe that a system of community property should be introduced for existing marriages.

1.5.3 COMMUNITY PROPERTY

Many of the submissions to the Commission spoke of the low self-esteem felt by the wife and mother at home and the lack of appreciation for all she does. In spite of the words in the Constitution extolling her role in society, the status of the woman in the home will not be improved until she is given access to money and power. In all justice the wife working in the home is entitled to a share in the family income as of right, instead of just being 'maintained'.

This recommendation builds on the recommendation already accepted by the Government that the family home should be owned jointly by both spouses regardless of how the family home was provided. The protection afforded by the Family Home Protection Act 1976 would continue to be available.

The Commission recommends a regime of community property giving joint entitlement to all income from any source during marriage and a legal right to a half share in the deceased's estate where a spouse dies testate. Under the present law, this represents an increase of one-sixth where there is issue but there is no change where there is no issue. There should be no changes where the spouse dies intestate.

Any regime of community property should apply automatically unless the spouses opt out of the arrangement, either wholly or partially. This is in line with the existing law under the Succession Act 1965 where spouses are entitled to opt out of their legal right share, and also with the recommendation in the First Statement relating to joint ownership of the family home. If there is an opting out, it should be valid only if there has been independent legal advice.

1.5.4 OTHER IMPORTANT ASPECTS OF COMMUNITY PROPERTY

There are other aspects for which provision would have to be made.

(i)   In order to protect family assets it should not be possible to alienate or charge any lands, premises, assets, business enterprise, savings or investments without the consent of the other spouse, though some discretionary limit would have to be fixed by law below which no consent would be necessary. Consent should not be unreasonably withheld and there should be provision for the Court to dispense with consent in appropriate cases, as in the Family Home Protection Act 1976;

(ii) there should be a legal right to information about income and assets so that a spouse can ascertain the real position from employers, financial institutions, etc;

(iii) control and management of community property should be based on title, i.e. exercised by the person in whose name the property is vested. If owned jointly, it should be jointly managed;

(iv) there should be no liability for the pre-marital debts of one spouse by the other spouse.

The list does not pretend to be exhaustive and the drafting of any law on community property would require careful study to deal with any anomalies that may be thrown up.

1.5.5 BENEFITS OF DISCUSSION AND AGREEMENT ABOUT FINANCIAL MATTERS

Persons who have decided to live together without marriage can and often do regulate their ownership of property and other financial aspects of their lives together by private contract. If there were an automatic regime of community property for married couples, they too would have to discuss financial matters prior to marriage and make an informed choice if they decided they would not avail of the provisions of such a law. Secretiveness about money produces distrust and suspicion. This type of openness should, therefore, contribute to a healthy marriage.

1.5.6 RECOMMENDATIONS

The Commission recommends the immediate introduction of a regime of community property in marriage providing for:

(a) joint ownership of the family home (see First Statement);

(b) joint entitlement to all income;

(c) a legal right share of one half of the estate where the other spouse dies testate (i.e. having made a will);

(d) no change where the other spouse dies intestate (i.e. not having made a will);

(e) a legal prohibition against alienation or charging, any lands, premises, assets, business enterprise, savings or investments without the consent of the other spouse, above a given discretionary limit; there should be provision for the court to dispense with this consent;

(f) a legal right to information about income and assets;

(g) control and management of property to be based on title;

(h) no responsibility for pre-marital debts of the other spouse;

(i) a right to opt out, on getting independent legal advice;

(j) no change to the existing law on division of property on marital breakdown.

In 1993 the Oireachtas (Irish Parliament) debated a Matrimonial Home Bill that provided for 'the automatic joint ownership by spouses of the family home'. However, the Supreme Court ruled the bill unconstitutional in January 1994. The Department of Equality and Law Reform, as well as the Review Group on the Constitution, took up the question after the Court's decision.

The Monitoring Committee on the Implementation of the Recommendations of the Second Commission took note of this decision in its *Second Progress Report.*

Second Progress Report of the Monitoring Committee on the Implementation of the Recommendations of the Second Commission on the Status of Women (1996)

Following the Supreme Court decision that the Matrimonial Home Bill 1993, which provided for the automatic joint ownership by spouses of the family home, was unconstitutional, the Department of Equality and Law Reform has been considering the legislative options in relation to encouraging such joint ownership. It is unlikely that the Department will be in a position to bring forward proposals in this area quickly given the constitutional complexities which attach to the matter. At the moment, the proposal which is being considered most actively relates to legislative measures which would facilitate the transfer of family homes into the names of both spouses. This matter has also referred to the Review Group on the Constitution for consideration.

The Supreme Court decision on the Matrimonial Home Bill also has implications for the introduction of the wide-ranging regime of community property which is envisaged in the Commission's Report. Any such introduction would represent a radical change in existing property law and the time required for critical examination of this issue will inevitably be lengthy.

GUARDIANSHIP OF INFANTS

A much-contested issue was the guardianship of infants. The first Commission on the Status of Women surveyed the problem in its report.

Commission on the Status of Women, *Report to Minister for Finance* (1972)

GUARDIANSHIP OF INFANTS

458. The Guardianship of Infants Act 1964 altered the statutory and common law position which the wife held vis-à-vis that of the husband with respect to guardianship and custody of their infant children. Prior to that Act the wife was not the legal guardian during their joint lives and had no entitlement to the custody of the children. She had not the same rights as the father to appoint a testamentary guardian, that is, to appoint a guardian by will. A guardian appointed by her could not act jointly with the father after her death but could act only after the death of both parents. The 1964 Act gave the mother equal rights with the father in all matters affecting the guardianship and custody of their children. While this was new to the statute law, it was the logical outcome of the statement in the Supreme Court judgement in the Tilson Case (1951) I.R.1 that, pursuant to Article 42 of the Constitution, parents have a 'joint power and duty' in respect of their children's upbringing. The Act provides that both parents are joint guardians during their lives and that either of them may appoint a testamentary guardian to act with the survivor on his or her death.

The mother of an illegitimate child is now the guardian of that child, whereas prior to the Act the child had, strictly speaking, no guardian, although the mother prima facie had the custody.

A mother seeking to have the names of her infant children (up to 16 years of age) entered on her passport can only do so with the consent of the father. The same provision applies equally to the father. Representations have been made to us on this point by a number of bodies but we do not see that it constitutes discrimination.

The Guardianship of Infants Act 1964 brought a significant change in women's legal position as parents.[3] The Act gave the mother equal rights with the father in all matters affecting the guardianship and custody of their children. This change in statutory law reflected the decision in the Tilson case of 1951, which held that parents have a 'joint power and duty' regarding their children's upbringing. The 1964 Act also provides that 'the mother of an illegitimate infant is now the guardian of that infant'. However, the 'joint power and duty' applies only to married couples. The natural father of an illegitimate child has no such right during the mother's lifetime.

In its *Report on Illegitimacy* (1982), the Law Reform Commission recommended that equal rights of guardianship be accorded to the natural mother and the natural father, regardless of marital status. In 1986 the European Court of Human Rights found Ireland's gender discrimination based upon marital status to be incompatible with the European Convention on Human Rights. In response, section 6A of the Status of Children Act 1987 permitted the natural father of an illegitimate child to apply for guardianship of the child.

Nevertheless, the K. v W. case of 1990 demonstrates, as Nuala Jackson points out, that 'the rights of the father of a non-marital child would appear to be constantly variable and in no sense certain' (p. 140). Nuala Jackson also argues that the father's inferior position does not necessarily benefit mothers, because the primary parenting role limits 'her opportunities to develop in other ways' (p. 142).

As noted above, for married parents the decision in the Tilson case and the Guardianship of Infants Act 1964 provided for the joint guardianship of their children. However several court decisions indicate that a 'maternal prejudice' tends to operate in custody cases involving the children of separated parents. Here, too, the view that the mother is the primary care giver creates a dilemma: if she accepts the full responsibility for child care her career prospects diminish; if she does not conform to the 'maternal prejudice' model she risks losing custody of the children.

SUCCESSION TO A HUSBAND'S ESTATE

The Succession Act 1965 was the third piece of legislation against gender discrimination cited by the first Commission on the Status of Women in its review of developments affecting the status of women. The Act, which came into effect in January 1967, established that a widow was entitled to a share of her deceased husband's estate. Until then a husband could disinherit or not adequately provide for his wife and children. The Commission recommended that the Act be amended so that the courts could take particular notice of the provision made for an elderly or disabled spouse. The proposed amendment was considered in the late 1970s but the Second Commission noted in 1993 that no amendments to the Succession Act 1965 had been introduced. The Second Commission called for the surviving spouse to receive one half of the estate, rather than the one third specified in the 1965 Act.

Commission on the Status of Women, *Report to Minister for Finance* (1972)

Succession
459. It was possible, before 1967, for a husband to make a valid will which disinherited or did not adequately provide for his wife and children. The right to dispose of his property freely by will overrode the claim of the widow and children. The Succession Act 1965 (which came into operation on 1 January, 1967), reformed the law relating to succession to property of deceased persons and in particular the devolution, administration, testamentary disposition and distribution on intestacy of such property. The Act provides that where there is no issue of the marriage and where one spouse dies intestate the remaining spouse takes the whole estate. Where an intestate dies leaving a spouse and issue, the spouse takes two-thirds of the estate and the remaining one-third is distributed among the issue if they are in equal degree of relationship. If a husband dies testate leaving a spouse and no children then the spouse has

a right (known as a legal right) to one-half of the estate. If the testator leaves a spouse and children, the spouse has a legal right to one-third of the estate. The legal right of a spouse in this regard has priority over devises, bequests and shares on intestacy and is, in effect, a debt payable out of the estate. Any child of a testator is entitled under section 117 of the Act to apply to the court to have just provision for him out of the estate. The court is not permitted to make a provision for a child that will interfere with the legal right share of a surviving spouse, and it may interfere with a devise or bequest to the spouse only in the case of a child who is the step-child of that spouse. Subject to this, the surviving spouse is entitled to take the whole estate where it is bequeathed to her or him by the testator.

Section 121 of the 1965 Act is designed to prevent a person from disinheriting his spouse or children by disposing of his property before his death. The section provides that, if a deceased person has made any disposition of his property under which the beneficial ownership vests in possession within three years before his death or later (other than a testamentary disposition or a disposition to a purchaser) for the purpose of defeating or substantially diminishing the share of his spouse, whether as a legal right or on intestacy, or the intestate share of any of his children, or of leaving any of his children insufficiently provided for, the court, on application by or on behalf of the spouse or child, may order that the disposition shall, in whole or in part, be deemed to be a devise or bequest made by the deceased in his will and to have had no other effect. So far as a spouse is concerned, this means that the disposition will be reckoned as part of the estate out of which the spouse will be entitled to a legal right share. In the case of a child, the disposition will be included in the estate in respect of which the child will be entitled to bring an application under section 117. The court has power to make such further order in relation to the disposition as may appear to be just and equitable having regard to all the circumstances. The court may not interfere with a disposition made to the spouse of the disponer except on an application made by a child of the disponer who is not a child of the spouse. In the case of a disposition made to a child of the disponer, the court may not make an order under the section if the spouse was alive when the disposition was made and consented in writing to it. Provisions somewhat similar to those contained in section 121 are to be found in the French, German and Swiss Civil Codes.

Where the estate of a deceased person includes a dwelling in which, at the time of the deceased's death, the surviving spouse was ordinarily resident, the surviving spouse may, subject to certain conditions, require the personal representatives in writing to appropriate the dwelling and any household chattels in or towards satisfaction of any share of the surviving spouse and of the shares of any infant children for whom the surviving spouse is a trustee under the Act or otherwise. If the share or shares are insufficient to enable such an appropriation to be made, appropriation may be required partly in satisfaction of the share or shares in the deceased's estate and partly in return for payment of money. The court may, if in the special circumstances of any particular case it considers that hardship would otherwise be caused to the surviving spouse or to the surviving spouse and any such infant child, order that appropriation to the spouse shall be made without the payment of money or subject to the payment of such amount as the court considers reasonable. [*Infant here means children under legal age.]

Some people are under the impression that a will that does not make adequate provision, or makes no provision, for a surviving spouse or child is, for that reason alone, invalid. This is not so. The will is still valid, but it operates and takes effect subject to the legal right of the spouse and the claim of the child, in the same way as the payment of legacies under a will is subject -to the satisfaction of debts due out of the estate. Moreover, where the legal right of a surviving spouse has not been renounced in an ante-nuptial contract or in writing after the marriage, the spouse may elect to take either any devise or bequest made in the will together with any share on intestacy (if the testator dies partly testate) or the share as a legal right. Section 115 of the 1965 Act, in addition to providing for the right of election, also imposes on the personal representative the duty to notify the spouse in writing of this right.

The administration of the assets of the estate (whether solvent or insolvent) of a deceased person is dealt with comprehensively in section 46 of, and the First and Second Schedules to, the Act. Subsection (6) of the section provides that a claim to a share as a legal right or on intestacy in the estate is a claim against the assets of the estate to a sum of money equal to the value of that share.

We consider that special cases may arise affecting elderly or disabled spouses where the Courts should have power to look generally at the disposal of the estate and to adjudge, having regard to the circumstances of the case, whether the disposal was a provident one and if it considers that it was not so, to alter it. We recommend, accordingly, that the Succession Act 1965 be amended to give the Courts power to decide whether adequate provision has been made from the estate for an elderly or disabled spouse in the same way that they have power under Section 117 of the Act to decide whether just provision has been made for a child of the testator.

MAINTENANCE FOR DESERTED WIVES

The first Commission on the Status of Women also pointed to other family law concerns affecting the economic security of women. These pertained to deserted wives, wives of prisoners, unmarried mothers and women whose husbands had obtained a foreign divorce. In each of these instances the Commission recommended changes in eligibility requirements and levels of allowances payable under the social welfare code. Moreover, the Commission sought provision for reciprocal enforcement of court maintenance orders between Ireland and the United Kingdom.

A concern that legislation had not adequately addressed up to 1972 was maintenance provisions for deserted wives. It is true that the Married Women (Maintenance in Case of Desertion) Act 1886, the Enforcement of Court Orders Act 1940 and the Courts Act 1971 permitted a deserted wife to obtain a maintenance order against her spouse. However, in many instances the order was not enforceable. The first Commission noted that Ireland 'had no reciprocal arrangements for enforcement abroad of maintenance orders made by our Courts'. Accordingly, the Commission recommended a review and a tightening of maintenance procedures.

Commission on the Status of Women, *Report to Minister for Finance* (1972)

Deserted wives
460. A wife who is deserted by her husband may obtain a maintenance order against him in the District Court. Prior to 15 December, 1971, the relevant legislation governing such orders was the Married Women (Maintenance in Case of Desertion) Act 1886, as amended by the Enforcement of Court Orders Act 1940. Under this legislation the maximum amount which the District Court could award was originally fixed at IR£2 p.w. This was

increased to IR£4 by the 1940 Act. The Courts Act 1971, however, gave the District Court power to make an award of up to IR£15 a week in support of the wife depending on the husband's means and on any means the wife may have. In addition, the Act gave power to the District Court to make an award of up to IR£5 a week in support of any child of the husband and wife up to age 16 years. The Act also gave concurrent jurisdiction to the High Court but without any financial limitations. The costs of proceedings in the High Court are at the discretion of the Court but as the wife will under rules of Court due to be made by the Superior Court Rules Committee, be able to proceed by way of summary application the costs should in any case be quite small and the procedure fairly expeditious.

461. At present, Ireland has no reciprocal arrangements for the enforcement abroad of maintenance orders made by our Courts. Accordingly, if a deserting husband has taken up residence in Britain or elsewhere abroad there is little to be gained by the wife seeking a Court Order against him for maintenance. However, as members of the European Communities we will become parties to the EEC Convention on Jurisdiction and the Enforcement of Civil and Commercial Judgements (including maintenance and affiliation orders). The Convention is now being negotiated in final form with Ireland, Britain and Denmark. The Convention, which has already been ratified by the six original Member States, provides for direct jurisdiction in each State and for the free circulation of court judgements. There are also two modem Conventions prepared by The Hague Conference on International Private Law. The first of these Conventions covering the Recognition and Enforcement of Decisions relating to Maintenance Obligations was finalised at the Twelfth Session in October, 1972. The second Convention on the Applicable Law in the case of Maintenance Obligations will be finalised at the Session due to take place in March, 1973. The EEC Judgements Convention is, of course, designed to operate between Common Market States whereas the Hague Conventions (if ratified) will operate between States that are not Members of the European Communities and between a State that is a Member of the Communities and a non-Member State.

462. The Social Welfare Act 1970 made provision for the payment out of public founds of an allowance to a wife who has been deserted by her husband and who satisfies certain other prescribed conditions. The Act also empowers the Minister for Social Welfare

to specify by regulations the conditions which a woman must satisfy to be regarded as a deserted wife for the purposes of the regulations. One of these conditions is that the wife must have made reasonable efforts within the means available to her to trace her husband and to secure support and maintenance from him. Court action is one means of securing support and maintenance but the taking of such action in all cases where possible is not insisted on as a prerequisite condition for the receipt of the allowance. Each case is judged on its merits and if a woman is in a position to take court action, without incurring undue strain, financial or otherwise, and if there is a reasonable hope of her obtaining maintenance by this action, she would be expected to take it.

463. We recommend that every effort should be made to establish at the earliest possible time reciprocal enforcement of court maintenance orders between Ireland and Britain.

464. Prior to 1971 an Irish husband who deserted to Britain could not obtain a divorce there unless he could prove a matrimonial offence by his wife. Since 1 January, 1971, however, an Irish husband who can prove a change of domicile to Britain (that is, if he resides in Britain with the intention of continuing to reside there for an indefinite time and has no genuine intention of returning permanently to live in the Republic) may obtain a divorce on the grounds that he and his wife have 'lived apart' continuously for at least five years. Such divorces come within the jurisdiction of the British Courts as both husband and wife are regarded as being domiciled in Britain by virtue of the fact that a wife automatically acquires her husband's domicile. A petition for divorce on foot of separation can be opposed on the ground that a decree would result in grave financial or other hardship or that it would in all the circumstances be wrong to dissolve the marriage and, additionally, there is a right to seek financial support. The British Legal Aid system may be tended to such proceedings even though the wife is not resident in Britain. In the case of Mayo-Perrott v. Mayo-Perrott (1958) I.R.336, the Irish Supreme Court, affirming a decision of the High Court, refused to enforce an order for costs arising from a British Divorce, holding that as the decree for costs could not be severed from the divorce decree and as Article 43.3.2 of the Constitution precluded such actions in this country, the claim could not succeed. Recently, however, the Irish High Court in a Succession Act case recognised a divorce granted in England. (See per Kenny J. in Haden Crawford Caffin Deceased, 22 December, 1971 (unreported).)

465. If the husband does obtain a divorce in the manner outlined in paragraph 464, the Department of Social Welfare in Ireland regard the wife, for social welfare payment purposes, as being no longer married and therefore no longer entitled to a Deserted Wife's Allowance nor to a contributory widow's pension if her husband should die. In view of the difficulty in reconciling the decisions of the Irish Courts in the matter of the recognition of foreign divorces, we consider that this position is anomalous in the extreme having regard to the obligations of private international law, and we recommend that steps should be taken and any necessary legislation enacted at the earliest opportunity to remedy it and that divorced wives should be treated for social welfare purposes not less favourably than if they had remained deserted wives.

The estimated cost of this recommendation, without taking account of any increase in the incidence of claims, is approximately IR£17,000 a year.

There were several immediate responses to the recommendations. The Social Welfare (Deserted Wives Allowance) (Amendment) Regulations 1974 reduced the qualifying period from six to three months. Wives of prisoners serving sentences of six months or more gained a Social Assistance Allowance in the Social Welfare (No. 2) Act (1974). The Social Welfare Act 1973 provided an allowance to an unmarried mother who keeps her child. The Maintenance Orders Act (1974) brought about the reciprocal enforcement of those orders between Ireland and the United Kingdom. A later Act, the Jurisdiction of Courts and Enforcement of Judgements (European Communities) Act (1988), extended the mutual recognition and enforcement of maintenance orders to other member states of the European Community. Later still, the Social Welfare Act (1990) stipulated that all lone parents who are bringing up children be subject to the same means test and payment, regardless of their marital status.

The Second Commission on the Status of Women recommended improvements in maintenance enforcement procedures. The Maintenance Act 1994, ratified in 1995, extended reciprocal enforcement of maintenance orders to countries subject to European Union and United Nations conventions.

Second Commission on the Status of Women, *Report to Government* (1993)

1.5.7 THE ENFORCEMENT OF MAINTENANCE AWARDS

The remedies available in practice to enforce the payment of court orders for maintenance consist of imprisonment on foot of an order for committal, or attachment of earnings. Neither is ideal. Imprisonment may be the answer where there are sufficient assets to pay but there is, nevertheless, deliberate default. Generally speaking, it will only make a bad situation worse. Attachment of earnings involves the employer in the marital affairs of his employee. If the employee leaves that employment, further orders will have to be sought.

A form of automatic enforcement is in existence in the province of Manitoba, Canada:

> The programme has a computerised system for monitoring maintenance payments. All accounts enrolled in the programme are automatically monitored by a central computer. In the event that maintenance is not paid enforcement proceedings are immediately commenced – it is not necessary for the maintenance creditor to initiate proceedings. The usual action taken is garnishment of the debtor's earnings. The debtor can also be compelled to complete a financial statement and provide particulars in respect of his employment, income, and financial circumstances. As a last resort the debtor can be summoned before the Master of the Family Division of the Court of Queens Bench where he is required to show cause why he should not pay. As to the effectiveness of the system, approximately 85% of orders registered in the computer system in 1984 were collected. The system also operates expeditiously. Defaults in the payment of maintenance are detected within 10 working days after the payment is due and enforcement proceedings are commenced within one month of the first default. The reason for the success of the Manitoba system depends in part on the fact that the maintenance creditor does not have to institute proceedings. (Paul A. O'Connor, *Key Issues in Irish Family Law*, 1988)

The Commission believes that the State should play an active part in ensuring that money due on maintenance orders is paid promptly. The State, in the long term, would benefit because if women receive payments promptly it will reduce the cost to the State of providing Social Welfare. It is not only deserted wives who are eligible for maintenance payments. An unmarried mother is also entitled to apply for maintenance for her child under the Family Law (Maintenance of Spouses and Children) Act 1976, as amended by the Status of Children Act 1987.

If the State ensures that fathers pay maintenance, it may well have the effect that fathers will take an interest in the welfare, upbringing and education of their children, which they would otherwise neglect. This would, however, have to be carefully monitored to ensure that fathers did not manipulate involvement with the child as a means of control over the mother.

Maintenance Orders made by the Irish Courts can be enforced effectively in other EC countries through the Brussels Convention. Ireland has signed the Lugano Convention which would provide for enforcement in the EFTA countries as well as the EC countries, but Ireland has not ratified this convention and brought it into our law.

The Commission recommends:

(a)   that the State institute an automatic enforcement programme prosecuted by the State to ensure payment of maintenance orders:

(b)   that the Government ratify the Lugano Convention and enact appropriate legislation to extend the reciprocal enforcement of Maintenance Orders to EFTA countries.

TAXATION OF MARRIED WOMEN

Finally, the first Commission on the Status of Women reviewed two more issues affecting married women's status and economic well-being: taxation of married women, and women's access to loans and mortgages.

The first of these issues, taxation of married women, involved such complex questions as the income and estate tax status of married couples, rates of personal allowances, and earned income relief. The Commission assessed these matters and made a three-part recommendation.

Commission on the Status of Women, *Report to Minister for Finance* (1972)

Taxation of married women
405. In the area of taxation, the question of the taxation of married couples is one which has been raised most often in the submissions

received by us and is clearly an area in which there is a widespread sense of discrimination and grievance. It has been represented to us by many of the parties making submissions on this matter that the present system of taxation of married women is a strong disincentive to women to remain in or re-enter the labour force after their marriage. In this context, it is interesting to note that the survey carried out by the Economic and Social Research Institute and referred to at paragraph 11 of this report [not included], showed that 34% of the working married women in the non-farm sample felt that the most helpful policy to assist married women who are interested in working would be a change in the existing tax laws.

412. The present allowance system gives the wife who enters employment a higher tax allowance than the wife who works at home. This difference in tax treatment between wives in paid employment and wives working at home was considered by the Income Tax Commission in its seventh interim report (1962) and that Commission recommended that the wife's earned income allowance, as such, should be discontinued. This change would have obviated the existing anomaly in treatment between the working wife and the non-working wife but it would not, of course, have improved the married couple's position relative to two single persons. In the second White Paper on Direct Taxation, published in 1963, the Government indicated that the termination of the allowance would be considered either as a separate matter or in conjunction with any future review of the allowance. No further action was, however, taken on the matter.

413. The preceding paragraphs have referred to current anomalies between the income tax position of a married couple and that of two single persons. It is true of course that the existing system, while it does have these results, maintains an equity in treatment between one married couple and another. If the allowances available to a single person were available in full to each married partner then the operation of a separate ceiling (£500) on earned income relief for each spouse could, depending on the proportion in which the income is divided between the spouses, result in a greater tax burden on one married couple than on another having the same aggregate earnings.

414. The present difference in income tax treatment between the various conjugal categories is, we consider, discriminatory against the married woman, who, we feel, has the right to expect that the same level of personal allowance will be extended to her as to a single person. We recommend, accordingly, that a standard rate personal allowance be introduced which would apply equally to all persons

whatever their marital status except as provided for in paragraph 415. We recommend, in addition, that the allowance should be available to a spouse for use against his or her own income or to be used in whole or in part against the other spouse's income.

415. Widowed persons at present receive a higher personal allowance than that available to a single person. Due to the special circumstances affecting widowed persons, male or female, we recommend that such persons should receive a personal allowance which is higher than the standard rate personal allowance recommended in paragraph 414.

416. In relation to earned income relief, we recommend that a married woman should in future be allowed earned income relief at the rate of one-quarter of earned income subject to a maximum of IR£500 or such ceiling as may be in force at any particular time. Earned income relief for a husband should in future be allowed only against income earned by him and earned income relief for a wife should be allowed only against income earned by her.

417. We recommend that the changes proposed in paragraphs 414 and 416 should be phased in over a period of not more than 5 years.

> The Second Commission on the Status of Women (1993) noted that the Finance Acts 1974 and 1980 had amended tax rules in accordance with the recommendations of the first Commission. However, other gender-related taxation issues remained. The Second Commission addressed them in its report under the heading of 'Taxation and Women in the Home'.

Second Commission on the Status of Women, *Report to Government* (1993)

2.4 Taxation and women in the home
2.4.1 EQUITY IN TAXATION ISSUES
There are a number of taxation issues arising in relation to women which have implications both for household income and for the choice or lack of choice faced by a homemaker about returning to paid employment.

Since 1980, arising from the Murphy case, it has been the practice that married couples have been jointly assessed for tax on their joint income, using double the allowances and double the rate bands applicable to single persons, unless they opt for individual treatment or assessment, or are separated. In many cases, when both husband and wife are in paid employment, both sets of tax free allowances and tax bands apply to the husband's income while the wife's income is taxable in its entirety, apart from her PAYE allowance, where applicable. In effect the structure leads to a lower effective tax rate on the first earner in a couple, and a much higher rate on the second earner.

One significant consequence of joint assessment is that if a homemaker married to an employed man wishes to return to work she may face paying tax at the higher rate, 48%, on most or all of her income plus PRSI contributions, and this can act as a disincentive to return to work, especially if the job is low paid. If a woman has not been used to dealing with the Revenue Commissioners she may not even be aware of the right to separate treatment and separate taxation. In the case where a husband may have preferred his wife to stay at home rather than go out to work, it may be a condition of the wife's 'permission' to go out to work that she does not claim her own allowances and thereby lower his take-home pay.

In 1986 Child Tax Allowances were abolished, although reintroduced in 1989 for low-paid households. Ireland seems to be anomalous among OECD countries in not having child tax allowances. We do, of course, have Child Benefit but most OECD countries have both a universal benefit and a tax allowance provision.

When the present system of taxing married couples was introduced in 1980 by the Finance Act 1980, one of the state justifications for extending double bands and allowances to non-working as well as working spouses was so as not to differentiate between families where the wife works outside the home and families where the wife is a full-time homemaker. However, when the Finance Act 1980 provisions are combined with the Finance Act 1986 provisions abolishing Child Tax Allowances the upshot is that a married couple with no children receives the same tax allowances as a married couple with children. The Income Tax Code as presently applied cannot thus be held to be supportive of families with dependent children or of the principle of horizontal equity. Where the operation of the Code can be considered effective is in providing a disincentive for women to return to paid employment.

These are very complex issues that we have touched on here. They have been considered to some extent in the December 1991 NESC study on Women's Participation in the Irish Labour Market and we believe they require a full examination at policymaking level. Policy measures such as this could most appropriately be considered by the

Department of Women's Affairs, the establishment of which is recommended in Chapter 7 [not included].

2.4.2 CHILD TAX ALLOWANCE FOR LOW-INCOME FAMILIES

An important change was made in the 1989 Budget when a IR£200 child exemption limit was introduced for low-income families in addition to their other allowances. This was raised to IR£300 in 1990. In the 1991 Budget the exemption was set at IR£300 for each of the first 2 children and at IR£500 for subsequent children. PRSI is however, payable. At present the general low income exemption limit for a married couple is IR£6,800 which is twice the low income allowance for a single person; to give examples, no income tax is payable by a married couple with two children if their income is IR£7,400 or less, i.e. IR£6,800 plus IR£300 plus IR£300, or by a married couple with four children if their income is IR£8,400 or less, i.e. IR£6,800 plus IR£300 plus IR£300 plus IR£500 plus IR£500. The budgetary changes in the last few years represent a form of selective reintroduction of child tax allowances.

This initiative helps to tackle the unemployment trap, whereby a person with a number of dependent children, is as well off unemployed as working in a low-paid job because of entitlement to Social Welfare child dependant allowances. The initiative is, therefore, fully endorsed by the Commission. In the Commission's view a more graduated cut off rate for this tax allowance should be introduced in order to lessen any disincentive to the full-time homemaker to seek employment.

The Commission recommends continuation of the child tax allowance for low-income families, but with the introduction of a more graduated cut-off point to lessen the disincentive effect on women seeking employment.

2.4.3 TAX TRANSFERS BETWEEN MARRIED COUPLES

It seemed to the Commission that the idea of translating the tax-free allowance and tax bands of the homemaker spouse (we will call her the wife for the purposes of simplicity) into a tax credit payable direct to her had a lot of merit. The thinking behind this would be to effect a cash transfer within the household – from the husband to wife – in a way that would mean no additional gain or loss to the Exchequer. However, when the Commission investigated the issue we were advised by the Department of Finance and the Revenue Commissioners that implementation of the proposal was fraught with difficulties, among them the following:

- the first area of difficulty relates to the marginal tax rate, i.e. the highest rate of income tax paid by the husband on his income. In principle it might be possible to implement a system of tax credits in a revenue-neutral way if a single universal rate of tax applied but, in our actual system, payment of a tax credit to the wife would mean that in many cases the husband's marginal rate of tax would be altered;
- if the tax credit were applied at the standard rate of tax, the Department of Finance estimate (1991 figures) that there would be an additional tax take by the Revenue Commissioners of IR£19 million. If it were applied at the marginal rate, there would be a tax loss by the Revenue Commissioners of IR£33 million;
- there are 116,134 taxpayers in the married couple one-earner category whose income is below the exemption limit for tax. This represents almost one-third of such couples. Thus the poorest third of all homemaker wives would not be eligible for this transfer of income within their own household;
- the question arises as to whether participation in the tax credit scheme should be compulsory or voluntary, particularly if participation or non-participation in the scheme could mean a slight tax advantage or disadvantage;
- it would be extremely difficult to forecast if taxpayers were to have a tax liability in the coming tax year, and attempting to recover credits paid where, in fact, no liability had arisen would be even more difficult.

Women in the home
2.4.4 TAXATION: DIFFERENT CATEGORIES OF HOMEMAKERS
The arguments put forward in paragraph 2.4.3 are weighty ones and taking account of them, the Commission feels that it cannot make a straightforward recommendation that the homemaker spouse's tax free allowance and tax bands should be converted into a tax credit payable direct to her. However, this begs the question that the Income Tax Code as currently operated does not take account of the situation of different categories of women in the home.

In this Chapter, one of the Commissions' major concerns has been to make recommendations that would lessen the economic dependency of women in the home. All women in the home will benefit from the community of property recommendation set out in detail in Chapter 1. In the context of social welfare payments, we make recommendations on the payment of Social Welfare

Dependant's Allowance direct to the non-working spouse and on the payment of the Family Income Supplement direct to the primary caregiver. Implementation of these recommendations will mean a degree of economic independence for full-time homemakers in low-income households.

Women who are in paid employment, by definition, have some economic independence. Lone mothers, widows etc. are already in receipt of social welfare payments in there own right. This compares with the remaining category of women in the home, full-time homemakers in average to higher income households, who have no direct payment into their hand.

This would seem to reinforce the case for recognising different categories of women and their roles in the application of the Income Tax Code, while maintaining the principle of equity in taxation. A number of the arguments made against the transferred tax credit principle in paragraph 2.4.3 lapse if the tax credits apply solely to full-time homemakers in average to higher income households.

The introduction of this method of tax credit transfer could be accompanied by the establishment of the right of women in the home to obtain cover in their own right for retirement and old age pensions based on the husband's income.

The Commission believes it is important to generate an informed debate on this issue and indeed on other issues related to the taxation treatment of married women raised in the Callan and Farrell NESC report on Women's Participation in the Irish Labour Market already referred to at paragraph 2.4.1. The general proposal the Commission has outlined would, at the very least, establish the principle of some remuneration for the full-time homemaker's contribution to the household.

The Commission recommends that the Income Tax Code should be reviewed with the objectives
(a) of lessening the disincentive to married women to look for employment; and
(b) using the Income Tax Code as a means of transferring income from a breadwinner spouse to a full-time homemaker spouse.

2.4.5 TREATMENT OF MARRIED WOMEN BY THE REVENUE COMMISSIONERS

At present, when a couple marry, the Revenue Commissioners presume they opt for aggregation of income for tax purposes, unless either of them indicate to the contrary. There are advantages to aggregation in that the couple can take optimal advantage of both sets of tax-free allowances and lower tax bands. However, under the aggregation system as currently administered, all documentation is in the husband's name and all correspondence is issued to the husband. A disadvantage of aggregation, as currently applied, is that the wife cannot assume responsibility even if both partners agree that she should do so. Many submissions to the Commission have expressed serious resentment at this procedure. Many submissions also expressed annoyance at the difficulty of a woman retaining her maiden name in dealing with the Revenue Commissioners.

The Commission recommends that:

(a)   on marriage the Revenue Commissioners adopt the principle of separate treatment as the norm, rather than joint assessment;

(b)   in cases where couples opt for joint assessment all correspondence should be jointly addressed to husband and wife;

(c)   whatever the taxation option decided on by the couple, correspondence to the wife should use her own family name if that is her preference;

(d)   all income tax forms should require the same information from women and men.

ACCESS TO LOANS AND MORTGAGES

Women's access to sources of short-term and long-term credit clearly relates to the process of acquiring property. In response to 'a number of representations made to us that women are discriminated against', the first Commission on the Status of Women took up this question in order to discover if gender was a determining factor in the granting of loans. While no evidence of overt discrimination came to light, the Commission did note that women's loan applications were likely to be 'vetted with a greater degree of caution' than those of men. The Commission also recognised that 'generalisations about the earning capacity of women' might discriminate against a female applicant in a specific case. The Commission called for the introduction of a process by which a complaint of discrimination could be examined.

Commission on the Status of Women, *Report to Minister for Finance* (1972)

Loans and mortgages

473. We have had a number of representations made to us that women are discriminated against as compared with men when they apply for

credit facilities or for mortgage finances, particularly the latter.

474. In order to find out what is happening, we wrote to 16 major Banking, Insurance, Building Society and Hire Purchase organisations, enquiring whether any distinction is made by them in considering Applications for loans, mortgage finance or hire purchase facilities from female applicants as compared with male applicants.

475. In the case of applications for loan facilities, the Banks have indicated that, in general, such loans are made available irrespective of the sex of the applicant and that the main criteria are that the applicant is a person of integrity, has ability to repay over the normal period of credit and is able to make collateral security available if this is considered necessary. In relation to capacity to repay, a Bank would, in assessing a young unmarried female applicant's request for medium-term facilities, have regard to the possibility of the applicant's marriage and the possible resultant cessation of earning capacity. This would not arise where short-term facilities are requested. Apart from this, none of the Banks has indicated any difference in treatment between a man and a woman.

476. In the Building Societies, the guidelines adopted in considering applications for mortgage finance include stipulations that the income of the applicant must be suited to the amount of the loan applied for and that for long-term loan commitments the applicant must have reasonable security of employment. These and other criteria apply equally to men and women. One Building Society has indicated, however, (and it is assumed that this applies equally to the others) that in the case of an application from a married woman, where no personal income exists, the husband must enter the mortgage as a guarantor for the repayments. A married woman can, however obtain a loan to purchase a property where she has sufficient income in her own right, without the provision of a guarantor.

477. The conditions governing the provision of mortgage finance by the Insurance Companies to a woman vary somewhat but, in general, the Companies contacted indicated that they do not differentiate between applicants on a sex basis. One Company whose general policy was not to accommodate single applicants, whether male or female, stated that an additional degree of caution was exercised in respect of young single women as in the event of such a woman marrying she might be obliged to resign the employment on which the loan was based and approved. Another Company indicated that in the case of a female applicant they usually liked a male relative to join in the mortgage as security.

478. The Hire-Purchase Companies contacted said that in assessing an application the main criterion is the capacity of the applicant to meet the repayments and that the sex of an applicant only affects the application insofar as this consideration is affected. In the case of unmarried or widowed applicants, with their own income, applications would be considered on the individual merits of the applicant. In the case of married women, however, it is probable that the husband's signature as guarantor would be sought, whether or not the wife has her own income, to protect against a discontinuance of the wife's income due to home and family commitments.

479. The Housing Act 1966 provides for the making of loans and supplementary grants by local authorities to persons for the provision of houses. While the precise conditions included in local authority house-purchase loan and supplementary grants schemes are a matter for each local authority, the Department of Local Government has informed us that the general policy is to determine the eligibility of applicants on the basis of their need for housing and their income, rather than on their sex. No additional requirements are imposed on female applicants as compared with male applicants.

480. In general, it appears that approvals or rejections of applications for bank loans and mortgage and hire-purchase finance from women are based on business criteria which apply equally to men but that applications from women are vetted with a greater degree of caution. It is not, we feel, unreasonable that, for instance, a married woman without any independent income should be asked to provide a guarantor, whether this be her husband or some other person. There may be cases, however, where decisions as to whether the normal criteria are met by a woman are based on generalisations about the income-generating capacity of women which are irrelevant to the particular case under consideration and which amount to discrimination on the basis of sex. In such cases we feel that some channel should exist to have the complaint of discrimination on grounds of sex investigated and we recommend that this function be placed with the Restrictive Practices Commission. We are conscious of the fact that criteria other than the ability, or probable continuing ability, of the applicant to repay the advance are used in reaching a final decision on the application – for instance the belief of the organisation about the integrity of the individual concerned – and we do not see that a loan-institution can be forced to advance monies if this is in

conflict with their judgement of these other criteria. Nevertheless, in those cases where the Restrictive Practices Commission finds that the refusal (or the imposition of conditions which amount to a refusal) is in its opinion, and having regard to the general record of the concern in granting credit facilities to women, based solely or mainly on grounds of sex, we would hope that the institution concerned would review the application favourably in the light of this finding.

> In 1978 a review of the first Commission's recommendation noted that the Examiner of Restrictive Practices investigates complaints 'subject to his right to do so not being challenged'. In fact, no investigation had been carried out to that date. In the same document, the Women's Representative Committee commented that discrimination still existed and that legislation was required to deal effectively with the problem. This would be best accomplished, in its view, by 'rationalising the Restrictive Practices Commission, the National Prices Commission and the Office of the Director of Consumer Affairs into one Agency'.
>
> In 1985 the Working Party on Women's Affairs and Family Law Reform also addressed the question of alleged discrimination in credit applications. However, the Working Party expanded the scope of possible discriminatory practices to cover 'Goods and Facilities and Services'. In light of its consideration of this wider spectrum of issues, the Working Party recommended the formation of a new consumer protection agency to combat discrimination. This more general approach to consumer protection was also taken up by the Second Commission on the Status of Women in 1993 (see Chapter 5 of this book for its recommendations on equal status legislation).

CONCLUSION

Of the women's policy issues surveyed in this book the legal status of women is perhaps the most complex. In general terms this involved 'economic security for married women and questions of parenthood'. The first Commission on the Status of Women in 1972 alluded to this complexity by noting an anomaly. While legislation in the 1950s and 1960s had removed the vast bulk of discrimination in these areas, considerable confusion remained about the general status of women in the civil law. The Commission undertook the dual task of clarifying women's rights under the law in Ireland and also making recommendations to counter discrimination against women. The Family Home Protection Act (1976) and the Family Law (Maintenance of Spouse and Child) Act (1976) responded to these concerns. The enforcement procedures ofthe latter Act were strengthened by further legislation in the 1980s and 1990s.

Nonetheless the Working Party on Women's Affairs and Family Law Reform of 1985 noted that the legislation on family law was in preparation but certainly was slow in coming. The Working Party's recommendations dealt with matrimonial property. That issue continued into the 1990s with the recommendations ofthe Second Commission on the Status of Women for a regime of community property in marriage and joint ownership of the family home. However, the Matrimonial Home Bill before the Irish Parliament was declared unconstitutional by the Supreme Court in 1994.

Married women's economic security was further enhanced after 1972 by measures that provided more equitable tax levies and greater access to loans and mortgages. The guardianship and custody of children was a major area of concern. The Guardianship of Infants Act of 1964 gave equal rights to the mother and father in these matters. That Act applied to married couples while the Status of Children Act of 1987 provided equal rights to the natural mother and natural father regardless of marital status.

CHAPTER FIVE

Constitutional issues

DIVORCE

During the period of the union with Great Britain within the United Kingdom (1801–1922), divorce was handled by way of private bills in the British Parliament. After 1922 the responsibility fell to the new Irish legislature. However, when three private bills for divorce were introduced the first Prime Minister of the Free State, W.T. Cosgrave, after consulting the Catholic bishops, refused to allow them to go forward. Then, in 1925, he arranged for the passage of a motion that prevented the Joint Committee on Standing Orders from considering any such bills in the future. Divorce was effectively banned without any legislation to that effect.

In 1937, when de Valera created the new Constitution, he was determined that the document should reflect Catholicism as a pillar of Irish nationalism. Thus Article 41 contained a flat prohibition of divorce: 'No law shall be enacted providing for the grant of a dissolution of marriage.' From this point on a constitutional amendment, rather than an ordinary legal reform, would be required if divorce was to be permitted. There the matter stayed for just about fifty years.

Critics of Article 41 saw it as an embodiment in the Constitution of the Catholic doctrine that marriage is an inviolate and permanent union. Yet the Constitution also included a formal assertion of jurisdiction over the whole island of Ireland: not only the South, where a minority were not Catholic in any case, but also the North, where two thirds of the population were not Catholic.

Article 41 also created legal problems over the nature of marriage, as the Catholic Church allowed annulment of a marriage (a declaration that the marriage had never been valid), leaving some people married in the eyes of the state but not in those of the Church. The state also recognised foreign divorces, which were not recognised by the Church, leaving some people divorced in the eyes of the state but not in those of the Church. When new relationships were formed the issues of property, inheritance and child custody became unclear, and many people were left in a legal limbo. The effects of separation or desertion were serious: there were higher rates of poverty among lone parents and the problems that accompanied the absence of stability and opportunity, such as crime, drugs and homelessness, all fell far more heavily on the shoulders of women.

Marriage in Ireland in previous generations had been a union of older people who had not had an opportunity to get to know each other very well. Fulfilment for women was expected to come from their children, not necessarily from love and companionship. The social changes in Ireland in the period after 1960 were raising questions as to the appropriateness of the constitutional provision on divorce as education, employment opportunities and the expectations of young people about marriage shifted rapidly. Reflecting the social change, and the lingering issue of non-Catholic minorities, the Committee on the Constitution, in its report issued in 1967, called for the dropping of Article 41.

Committee on the Constitution, *Report* (1967)

Articles 41.3 and 44.2 – Provisions relating to marriage
123. Article 41.3.2 provides that 'no law shall be enacted providing for the grant of a dissolution of marriage'. This universal prohibition has been criticised mainly on the ground that it takes no heed of the wishes of a certain minority of the population who would wish to have divorce facilities and who are not prevented from securing divorce by the tenets of the religious denominations to which they belong. It is also argued that the Constitution was intended for the whole of Ireland and that the percentage of the population of the entire island made up of persons who are Roman Catholics, though large, is not overwhelming. The prohibition is a source of embarrassment to those seeking to bring about better relations between North and South since the majority of the Northern population have divorce rights under the law applicable to that area. It has also been

pointed out that there are other predominantly Catholic countries which do not in their Constitutions absolutely prohibit the enactment of laws relating to the dissolution of marriage. Finally, attention is sometimes drawn in discussing this subject to the more liberal attitude now prevailing in Catholic circles in regard to the rites and practices of other religious denominations, particularly since the Second Vatican Council.

124. It would appear to us that the object underlying this prohibition could be better achieved by using alternative wording which would not give offence to any of the religions professed by the inhabitants of this country. An example of such an alternative would be a provision somewhat on the following lines: 'In the case of a person who was married in accordance with the rites of a religion, no law shall be enacted providing for the grant of a dissolution of that marriage on grounds other than those acceptable to that religion.'

It would probably be necessary to add a clause to the effect that this was not to be regarded as contravening any other provision of the Constitution prohibiting religious discrimination. This wording would, we feel, meet the wishes of Catholics and non-Catholics alike. It would permit the enactment of marriage laws acceptable to all religions. It would not provide any scope for changing from one religion to another with a view to availing of a more liberal divorce regime. While it would not deal specifically with marriages not carried out in accordance with the rites of a religion, it would not preclude the making of rules relating to such cases.

125. In coming to this conclusion we have examined a great deal of published material on the subject, and in particular the decisions reached at the recent Vatican Council. It is important to note in this connection that the existing prohibition of dissolution of marriage deprives Catholics also of certain rights to which they would be entitled under their religious tenets. There are several circumstances in which the Catholic Church will grant dissolutions of valid marriages or will issue declarations of nullity. We understand that many thousands of cases are dealt with under these provisions every year either at Rome or by diocesan and metropolitan courts throughout the world. The absolute prohibition in our Constitution has, therefore, the effect of imposing on Catholics regulations more rigid than those required by the law of the Church. This conflict is referred to in a number of publications by Catholic authors.

126. It can be argued, therefore, that the existing Constitutional provision is coercive in relation to all persons, Catholic and non-

Catholic, whose religious rules do not absolutely prohibit divorce in all circumstances. It is unnecessarily harsh and rigid and could, in our view, be regarded as being at variance with the accepted principles of religious liberty as declared at the Vatican Council and elsewhere. It would seem, therefore, that there could be no objection from any quarter to an amendment of the Constitution on the lines which we have indicated in Paragraph 124 above, and we unanimously recommend that such an amendment be made.

127. If this basic change were made in subsection 2 of Article 41.3, it would be necessary to look again at the provisions of subsection 3. That subsection reads as follows:

> No person whose marriage has been dissolved under the civil law of any other State but is a subsisting valid marriage under the law for the time being in force within the jurisdiction of the Government and Parliament established by this Constitution shall be capable of contracting a valid marriage within that jurisdiction during the lifetime of the other party to the marriage so dissolved.

The wording of this provision created some difficulties during the passing of the Constitution in 1937 and it has been the cause of some confusion since that time. The position of divorced persons who re-marry in this State and of their partners and offspring is, of course, of vital importance in relation to the Succession Act and other matters, and it is desirable that any cause of doubt be removed. In the case of M.-P. v. M.-P. (1958. I.R.336) two Supreme Court judges discussed its effect in regard to the recognition in this country of an English decree as valid to dissolve a marriage and, unfortunately, their views differed very considerably from each other. We have considered these views carefully and have also noted with interest the subsequent decision of the English courts in B. v. B. (1961. 3 All E.R.225). In addition, we have examined the findings of a working party representative of the Attorney General's Office and the Department of External Affairs which reported in 1940 on this provision. We are led to the conclusion that the best course is to delete subsection 3 entirely; in that event, the recognition of foreign divorce decrees will be a matter for determination in accordance with private international law, the principles of which have been fairly well established. It is worth noting in this connection that in Article 29.3 of the Constitution this country specifically accepts the principles of international law.

'The State shall not impose any disabilities or make any

discrimination on the ground of religious profession, belief or status.'
Under the Marriage Acts different conditions are prescribed for
marriages performed in accordance with the rites of (i) the Church of
Ireland, (ii) the Presbyterian Church, (iii) other Protestant Churches,
(iv) the Jewish religion. These conditions relate to prior residence,
district where the marriage is to be celebrated and place and time of
the marriage. No similar conditions are laid down in connection with
Roman Catholic marriages. It appears that the Marriage Acts are now
being revised but that it may be necessary to continue with the
differentiation between the different kinds of marriage ceremonies.
The abolition of the conditions relating to the marriage of non-
Catholics is not regarded as an advisable step as some of the smaller
denominations are not sufficiently organised to ensure that parties
who present themselves for marriage are, in fact, free to marry.

129. The opinion has been expressed that these provisions
constitute discrimination on the grounds of religious profession or
belief within the meaning of Article 44.2.3 and that at least the penal
provisions of the existing code would be declared not to have been
carried over under the Constitution. We recommend that this
difficulty be removed by adding a suitable provision to this part of
the Constitution to the effect that the prohibition on religious
discrimination shall not prevent the enactment of different
procedural rules relating to different kinds of marriage ceremonies
with a view to ensuring that all legal rules are complied with by the
parties concerned.

By the late 1970s it was becoming more apparent that
relationships among couples were changing. The inclusion in
the Census of 1981 of a category for 'separated people' revealed
that the idealised uniformity of marriage in Ireland was not as
widely practised as had long been assumed. By the 1980s public
opinion polls were showing a shift toward accepting a divorce
law, with as many as 61 per cent of respondents favouring
change in a survey conducted in May 1986.

Bills had been brought forward in the Oireachtas
(Parliament) in the 1980s to eliminate the constitutional
prohibition of divorce. Although none was successful, they
prompted the Fine Gael government of Garret Fitzgerald to
offer a referendum in 1986 on the question of allowing divorce
legislation. The government had to address the policy
anomalies in family law that arose from not having a divorce
law, while not risking antagonising those who still held dear the

support for the family enshrined in Irish cultural and constitutional values.

In 1985 a joint committee of the two houses of the Oireachtas (the Dáil and the Seanad) had examined the issue, and outlined the status of the law with respect to separation in Ireland and the proposed new law that would be put into place if the referendum result favoured it.

Joint Committee on Marriage Breakdown, Report (1985)

7.8.1 In this Chapter the Committee will deal solely with the question of divorce. Elsewhere in this report other solutions and remedies for the problems caused by marital breakdown are discussed in full. Here the Committee will examine what are considered to be the substantive arguments for and against divorce, condensed from the 700 written submissions and oral evidence heard from 24 different groups. The object of the Committee in this regard is to put before the Oireachtas as clearly and succinctly as possible the options which are open and to express the views of the Committee on those options.

7.8.2 In using the expression 'divorce' we take it to be synonymous with the expression 'dissolution of marriage' as used in Article 41 of the Constitution. We feel that the former expression is more widely used by the majority of people and for this reason we feel that its use in this Chapter will bring about greater clarity.

7.8.3 In discussing divorce as a remedy for marital breakdown it is perhaps as well at the beginning to identify the difference between divorce and other remedies available in connection with the breakdown of a marriage. At the moment there is in existence legislation which deals with disputes as to the custody and upbringing of children, the maintenance of dependent spouses and children, and the protection of spouses and children at risk of violence and neglect. Further, there is provision for deciding ownership of assets of the parties to a marriage and for the grant of a decree of judicial separation or nullity in certain circumstances. The Committee has in other Chapters of this report suggested changes which will improve the effectiveness of these remedies as a response to the problems of marital breakdown. Should divorce be introduced following the carrying of a referendum the present response to marital breakdown would be altered in one very important way. It would give the courts the power to dissolve a valid marriage and thus the parties to that marriage would thereafter be free to remarry. The granting of the right to remarry would appear to the Committee to be the essence of a divorce jurisdiction as it is the main difference between divorce as a method of solving the problems caused by the breakdown of a marriage and other less far-reaching legal remedies.

Statement of current legal position

7.8.4 At present divorce, with the right to remarry, is not possible under the Civil Law of the State due to the provision contained in Article 41.3.2 of the Constitution which states: 'No law shall be enacted providing for the grant of a dissolution of marriage.' Under the terms of this provision the Oireachtas cannot enact legislation which permits divorce and, as a result, persons who contract valid marriages under the Civil Law remain married until the death of one or the other party.

7.8.5 When a valid marriage irretrievably breaks down the spouses cannot obtain any final legal recognition that their marriage is at an end and they cannot remarry. As has been pointed out above they can avail of limited legal remedies such as judicial separation, the conclusion of a deed of separation, or one or other spouse may obtain a Barring Order. Sometimes a spouse may simply desert the other spouse but, in any event, no matter which of these courses they pursue neither spouse would be free to enter into a new and valid marriage until the death of the other spouse.

7.8.6 Freedom to remarry can arise if the parties obtain a foreign decree of divorce provided this decree is recognised in this State. The law regarding recognition of foreign divorces is complex and it is not appropriate to enter into a lengthy discussion on this area of law. Suffice it to say that the State will only recognise a divorce obtained in a foreign jurisdiction if both parties to the marriage were domiciled in that foreign jurisdiction at the time of the divorce. Married couples living permanently in Ireland whose marriages have irretrievably broken down cannot obtain any divorce decree outside Ireland that will validly terminate their marriage under Irish law.

7.8.7 The prohibition on the enactment of legislation to permit divorce contained in the Constitution must remain part of the law until such time as a referendum is held and the majority of those voting at that time decide in favour of removing the ban on divorce contained in the Constitution. In the event of such a decision being made by the electorate the result of such a referendum would not, by itself, provide for divorce. It would then become necessary for the

Oireachtas to enact divorce legislation if divorce were to be made available. In this context it can be noted that the 1922 Constitution did not prohibit the Oireachtas from enacting divorce legislation and that no such legislation was enacted in the period from 1922 to the coming into force of the present Constitution in 1937.

ARGUMENTS IN FAVOUR OF DIVORCE

7.8.11From the numerous written and oral submissions, including personal submissions, made to this Committee, the following is a synopsis of the main arguments in favour of the introduction of divorce in this country:

(a) that the prohibition on divorce is an injustice to those persons whose marriages have irretrievably broken down and who have become involved in other relationships or wish to become involved in other relationships. They feel it to be such an injustice because

(1) they cannot achieve any recognition of their new relationship or any adequate legal definition of their status;
(2) there is no legislation in force to provide protection for parties to and the children of such a relationship, for instance, in the areas of maintenance, succession and in respect of violence and neglect;
(3) the children of such a relationship are illegitimate; and
(4) the parties suffer substantial disadvantages in such areas as taxation and the right to social welfare benefits.

It is argued that this injustice not only has adverse effects on the immediate parties to the relationship and any children that they may have but that the existence of unregulated second relationships after the breakdown of a marriage also has adverse effects on the community at large.

'We find people changing their names by deed polls to their boyfriends' names. They are coming in wanting to know why their children are regarded as illegitimate in the law. They are losing respect for the law. These are people who are basically law-abiding citizens and who have very strong religious views, but who find they have got themselves into second relationships. They feet that they want to marry. They want the commitment of marriage and they do not have that right at the moment. It is from the viewpoint of practitioners of family law that we have seen the problems that these second relationships caused – the fact that there is no legal protection for them and particularly for the children who are left and the women are left in a most vulnerable position. We feel that if divorce was to be brought in they would have the option of remarriage which would in fact help the parties to have a greater commitment to each other and it would mean that the law would apply to and protect these relationships as well.'

'Marriages should be supported through all their stages as active social relationships, but only as long as they are capable of being so. Failure to accept that the parties to a marriage which has broken down irretrievably have the right to divorce and remarry can cause hardship. Inter alia, this failure confers an uncertain status on new relationships arising after marriage breakdown; it also leaves unprotected the interests of couples and their children with regard to maintenance, security and continued parenting.'

'This Article (41.3.2) enshrines Roman Catholic teaching (in common with Article 41.3 regarding the definition of what constitutes a family) and taken together we believe that they constitute a threat arising from the pressures exerted by the growing number of stable relationships not recognised as family units under the present Constitution.'

(b) All the minority churches and religions (with the exception of the Church of the Latter-day Saints) do not favour the retention of the blanket prohibition on divorce in the Constitution and consider the availability of divorce legislation as a basic right notwithstanding that certain of those churches as a matter of internal discipline disapprove of divorce. It is argued that Civil Law in this area should not reflect only the views expressed by the church of which the majority of the population are members, and that by so doing at present it discriminates against members of other churches and religions and those who profess no religious faith.

'We recognise that too easy recourse to divorce may lead to widespread abuse and that the utmost care is required in legislation on these matters. Nevertheless, we hold that blanket prohibition of divorce is also the cause of serious abuse, much personal suffering, and grave social injustice. Attempts to suppress recognition of this situation do nothing to promote well-ordered marriage and family life.'

'The nature of marriage is to be lifelong and ideally this should always be so, but we recognise that human nature is frail and that some marriages fail to develop and break down irretrievably.

'We do recognise that circumstances can occur where relationships deteriorate to such an extent that it may be right to end a marriage, and for this reason we would welcome a change in the constitutional position on divorce. The demand for divorce to be legal may come only from a minority of the Christian people of this country. However, we see no reason why the Constitution or legislation should deny the minority their wish in this matter, bearing in mind that provision is made for divorce by other nations within the Council of Europe. We believe that legal provision should be made for divorce as a civil right for those whose marriages have broken down irretrievably and who wish to avail of it. The period of marriage before which a divorce is not allowed should be five years. Knowledge of this fact may prevent many rash and unsatisfactory marriages taking place. There should be an interval of 6 months after application for a divorce before proceedings can start, during which time counselling should be available. We do feel strongly however that divorce must always be seen as the last resort.'

The existing machinery suffers from the defect that it deals only with matters which, important and even vital though they may be, are only ancillary to the root problem, that of status. Persons whose marriages have broken down and who have struggled through the complex legal machinery find themselves substantially poorer but without the one remedy which they really want, namely the freedom to marry.

(c) That the constitutional ban on divorce and the absence of divorce legislation in this country since the foundation of the State has not prevented marital breakdown from occurring and that in the past decade the level of marital breakdown has increased.

'I do not believe that the absence of divorce law in any way stops marriages breaking down. Marriages go on breaking down by persons pursuing their own personal causes quite independently of what the law says or does not say.'

(d) That the breakdown of a marriage is due to the collapse of the relationship between the parties and that divorce does not cause that collapse, but merely affords a facility to give legal recognition to the fact that a marriage has ended, while leaving the parties thereto free to remarry. It is suggested that confirmation of this assertion can be obtained from an examination of the statistics in regard to marital breakdown in the Republic of Ireland and Northern Ireland. Despite the fact that divorce has been available in the North of Ireland since 1937, it has been suggested that the level of marital breakdown in the Republic of Ireland appears to be similar to the proportional level of marital breakdown in Northern Ireland.

> 'Our views on that (divorce) are that there clearly are cases where divorce is the only solution to the problem of irretrievable breakdown. We feel that conciliation should be part of that divorce procedure. Our family system differs from other European countries in that families here are larger and only 10 per cent of the married women work outside the home, so there would be financial considerations involved.'
>
> 'Gingerbread, through our members, recognises that marital breakdown occurs and that marriages do end. Irretrievable breakdown should be accepted as a basis for separation. If this is done, people in this situation have a right to finally choose to completely end their legal contract of marriage. We believe that this is a basic human right.'

(e) To deny the right to remarry to a battered wife or husband has no social advantage to the State and is in fact detrimental to society in general and lacking in compassion.

(f) That the absolute prohibition on the introduction of divorce legislation in the Constitution has the effect of imposing on Catholics regulations more rigid than those required by the law of the Church. The relevant Canons in the Code of Canon Law state as follows:

Article 1: The Dissolution of the Bond
Can. 1141 A marriage which is ratified and consummated cannot be dissolved by any human power or by any cause other than death.
Can. 1142 A non-consummated marriage between baptised persons or between a baptised party and an unbaptised party can be dissolved by the Roman Pontiff for a just reason, at the request of both parties or of either party, even if the other is unwilling.
Can. 1143 S1 In virtue of the Pauline privilege, a marriage entered into by two unbaptised persons is dissolved in favour of the faith of the party who received baptism, by the very fact that a new marriage is contracted by that same party, provided the unbaptised party departs.
S2 The unbaptised party is considered to depart if he or she is unwilling to live with the baptised party, or to live peacefully

without offence to the Creator, unless the baptised party has, after the reception of baptism, given the other just cause to depart.

Can. 1149 An unbaptised person who, having received baptism in the Catholic Church, cannot re-establish cohabitation with his or her unbaptised spouse by reason of captivity or persecution, can contract another marriage, even if the other party has in the meantime received baptism, without prejudice to the provisions of Can. 1141.

The facility of dissolution of the bond of marriage in the above circumstances, which is allowed under Canon Law, is ineffective at Civil Law.

(g) That it is the factual breakdown of a marriage and not the availability of divorce that has an adverse effect on children. It is suggested that in certain circumstances the integration of a child into a new loving family unit can reduce the trauma resulting from the breakdown of his or her parents' marriage.

'What is clear is that it is the effects of separation in marital conflict rather than divorce which constitutes a crisis for the child. Therefore, whether or not divorce is introduced, we urgently need to consider how we might respond to the many Irish families for whom separation may become a reality.'

(h) That divorce is not the source of financial hardship to parties whose marriage has broken down. Such financial hardship results from the need to finance two separate homes, which in turn results from the need to live separate and apart. The forming of a relationship with a third party can either ease or exacerbate such financial difficulties.

ARGUMENTS AGAINST DIVORCE

7.8.12 The following, in our view, is a synopsis of the main arguments presented to us against the introduction of divorce and against the holding of a referendum to facilitate such introduction. It is argued:

(a) That the introduction of a divorce jurisdiction would as it were open the flood gates and that the rate of divorce and the incidence of marital breakdown would be greatly increased. In other words, the introduction of divorce, rather than contributing towards a solution of the problem of marital breakdown, would merely cause multiplication of it.

In support of this argument it was suggested that it was the experience of practically every modem state in the western world which has introduced divorce on the grounds of irretrievable breakdown that the rate of divorce has multiplied, in some cases several times over.

> 'I think our view would be – we know very often from certain experience – that there are many incidents of marital breakdown but what concerns us basically is, in the light of evidence we have of experience in other countries , would the price we would pay in society be too high if we institute divorce legislation? In trying to solve the problem of a vulnerable society would we be opening the door to a further deterioration in the State, in the family and in our society? That is the point that concerns us.'

(b) That the introduction of divorce would fundamentally change the nature and perception of marriage by making it into a temporary as opposed to a permanent union between a husband and wife. The effect of this is to undermine the institution of marriage and the family and since the family is the fundamental unit of society, it is said that society itself is undermined and destabilised.

> 'Marriage in Canon Law is seen as a covenant by which a man and a woman establish a partnership of their whole life which by its own nature is ordered towards the wellbeing of the spouses and towards the procreation and upbringing of children. Its essential properties are unity and indissolubility (cf. Cans. 1055 and 1056).'

(c) That the introduction of divorce would reduce the protection at present given to the institution of marriage and the family under Article 41 of the Constitution.

(d) That the introduction of divorce would cause persons who were having difficulty in their marriage to work less hard at achieving a solution to those difficulties. In this respect it is pointed out that only a minority of marriages collapse and that to extend the facility of divorce and remarriage might undermine the stability of successful marriages.

> 'Divorce, once introduced. cannot be withdrawn. And it is to be feared that, once it was available as a solution (as a safety valve, so to speak), there would be little real urgency and little real energy

devoted to the effective support of marriages through proper education, material support measures and adequate remedial help.'

(e) That the introduction of divorce would have a detrimental effect on child development and would increase the number of children whose upbringing is damaged by the fact that they come from a broken home. In this respect it is pointed out that the process of the disintegration of a marriage is a traumatic experience for children of all ages and that they suffer because of it. However, if one of the parents remarries it is argued that the situation is exacerbated in that the children have to cope with the problem of forming new relationships with step-parents and step-brothers and step-sisters. Sometimes this can result in conflicts of loyalty and emotional tension between children and new and former parents.

'Apart from objections of principle and religious belief, it is our view that the hard evidence internationally indicates that divorce is not an acceptable solution to the question of marriage breakdown or disharmonies. The problems caused by the initial divorce and the subsequent legal interpretations and implications for wives and children make it clear that divorce far from being a remedy nearly always exacerbates the difficulties.'

(f) That women and children suffer financial hardship as a result of the introduction of divorce. This argument is based on the proposition that in general it costs more to look after two homes and two families than it costs to look after the original home and family. An inevitable reduction in the standards of living of the parties involved must take place. As the wife often obtains custody of the children she is financially in a particularly vulnerable position, being unable to take up full-time employment. It is suggested that the reality of divorce would be that the wife and children of the broken marriage would lose out financially and have to suffer the consequences of a reduced lifestyle.

'To introduce divorce into the Republic, where divorce has been unknown since the establishment of the Free State in 1922, would be an interference with the existing constitutional rights of spouses. A withdrawal of these valuable rights, which were guaranteed to the partners and children of existing marriages, would be unjust and intolerable.'

(g) That the introduction of divorce would be contrary to the religious views of the vast majority of the people residing in the Republic of Ireland and contrary to the teachings of the church of which the overwhelming majority of the population of the Republic of Ireland are members.

'Divorce would have a disastrously destabilising effect on Irish society. We suspect that this would happen here faster than in neighbouring countries.'

The Committee is of the view that the best way to discuss the strengths and weaknesses of these various arguments is in the context of an analysis of the possible effects of firstly the retention of the current constitutional position and secondly the removal of the present constitutional ban on divorce.

EFFECTS OF RETAINING THE CURRENT CONSTITUTIONAL POSITION

7.8.13 If the changes which the Committee believes to be necessary in other Chapters of this report are implemented it can be anticipated that persons entering into marriage in the future and some of those who are now married may be afforded a greater hope of stable and harmonious marriages. Changes such as the provision of improved education for relationships, an increase in the age for marriage, community-based support for marriage and the provision of more extensive marriage counselling can be expected to, at the very minimum, slow down the rate of increase of marriage breakdown and, hopefully, will substantially reduce that rate.

7.8.14 It is, however, recognised by the Committee that the implementation of its proposals in this area will have little, if any, impact in effecting a reconciliation between couples whose marriages have already irretrievably broken down. One of the difficulties in dealing with this whole area is that there is no accurate computation of the numbers of marriages which have actually broken down.

The highest estimate which has been put to this Committee is that 36,000 marriages have broken down in Ireland to date. This estimate would represent approximately 6% of the total number of marriages if it is correct. Figures available from the Central Statistics Office suggest that the figure could be considerably lower than this.

Figures obtained from the 1981 Census of Population conducted by the Central Statistics Office show a return of 14,117 persons who categorised themselves as neither married nor single. This category would include persons who obtained divorces in other countries but also included a number of persons whose legal status appeared to be married, but were separated.

The 1983 Labour Force Survey, also conducted by the Central Statistics Office, provided an estimated figure for separated persons as 8,300 males and 12,800 females. A further 5,500 males and 10,900 females were estimated to be married but not usually resident with the other spouse. In 1984 approximately 8,100 women were receiving deserted wives' benefit or allowance.

Even if a marriage failure of 6% were accepted it should be noted that this would still leave Ireland with the lowest figure for marriage breakdown in Europe. While some comfort can be taken from this fact, nonetheless it must be recognised that there are a significant number of people who find themselves in a situation of marriage breakdown. Further, even with the improvements which we hope will take place it is inevitable that some marriages will continue to breakdown.

7.8.15 It would also appear to be inevitable that some of the persons whose marriages have irretrievably broken down will form relationships with third parties. At the moment the parties to such a relationship, and any children of the relationship, are afforded little or no legal protection. In order to remedy the problems they encounter, and to put their relationships on a footing which gives to the parties involved and the children the type of legal protection which the law provides by way of statute in the case of married couples, the parties are in effect thrown back on drawing up contracts between themselves which set out their mutual rights and obligations. Such contracts can be of some assistance in the area of maintenance but the parties still find themselves in a considerably inferior position to that of a married couple who have all the enforcement procedures contained in the Family Law (Maintenance of Spouses and Children) Act 1976. There must be some question whether such contracts would be contrary to the constitutional protection afforded to the family and for this reason contrary to public policy. This view would call into question the enforceability of such agreements. In relation to protection from violence or abuse the parties must rely on the law in regard to injunctions, rather than the more effective and comprehensive legislation in regard to Barring Orders.

7.8.16 The making of mutual wills can give parties to such a second relationship some succession rights but such rights are subject to the rights of their spouse or children under the Succession Act, 1965. In normal circumstances the maximum benefit that can be obtained by a surviving member of a second relationship upon the death of the other party to that relationship is one-half of the estate of the deceased, where the deceased had no children by his marriage, or two-thirds where there were children of the marriage. Even this two-thirds, however, will be shadowed by any claim made by the children of the marriage for part of their parents' estate pursuant to the provisions of Section 117 of the Succession Act, 1965.

7.8.17 The Committee recognises that if the current law remains unchanged there will be a significant number of persons, whose marriages have broken down, who are obliged to resort to alternative forms and mechanisms in second relationships, in order to extend the appearance of a 'marriage' to their relationship. In the context of the present legal situation these efforts are doomed to be at best partially successful. However, it has been suggested that most of the problems experienced by persons in such second relationships can be relieved by the enactment of appropriate legislation. For example, it was pointed out that the abolition of the concept of illegitimacy would be a substantial step forward. It was also suggested that legislation could be enacted to provide appropriate rights to maintenance and protection by way of a Barring Order in respect of the members and the children of such relationships.

7.8.18 The problem with such an approach, in the view of the Committee, is that it would appear that there would be great difficulty in defining what type of relationship, and which persons involved in a relationship, should be covered and protected by the suggested legislation. For example, should the protection of such legislation be extended to a person who has formed a relationship for a short period of time, perhaps a number of weeks, with a party whose marriage has broken down? A question must arise whether it would be necessary to give evidence of a stable relationship, extending over a certain period of time, before such legislation could be invoked and if such a condition is to be necessary how such a stable relationship is to be defined. Also such legislation would have to deal with the difficult question of the relative priority which is to apply, between the spouses and children of the marriage of a party, and the partner and children of any subsequent relationship of that party. The nature of such a priority could make the protection in regard to matters of finance and succession more illusory than real. In any event, such legislation could only extend legislative protection, as opposed to constitutional protection, which covers the members of a family based on marriage. For these reasons it is the view of the Committee that simple legislative reforms cannot adequately solve the problems at present experienced by parties to a relationship, one or both of whom is still legally married to another person.

7.8.19 The Committee feels that it is inevitable in the context of the retention of the current constitutional position in relation to divorce that many adults, whose marriages have irretrievably broken down, will form stable permanent relationships with other men and women, and that the parties to such relationships, and the children of such relationships, will continue to lack any adequate legal status and protection. The parties to such relationships will be unable to remarry even though they may wish to do so and this fact, at least in their eyes, will, in all probability, appear to be harsh, unecessary and unjust. It is also recognised by the Committee that representatives of most of the minority religions in this country, who made submissions to the Committee, sincerely believe that the current constitutional position discriminates against members of their churches and religions, and presumably they will continue to hold this belief as long as the present position continues.

THE EFFECT OF REMOVING THE CURRENT CONSTITUTIONAL BAN ON DIVORCE LEGISLATION

7.8.20 The Committee is satisfied that it is impossible to say with any degree of certainty exactly how many people would apply for decrees of divorce if divorce legislation were enacted. One of the difficulties in this regard is the lack of any definite statistics as to the exact extent of marital breakdown in this country. There are a number of factors from which it is argued that there would not be a flood of divorce applications. Since the vast majority of people in the country are members of religions that actively disapprove of divorce, it can be expected that a certain proportion of persons who have experienced marital breakdown would not be anxious to avail of the remedy of divorce on account of their religious beliefs. Also, even on the highest figures presented to the Committee it would appear that the rate of marital breakdown in this country is lower than that of any other country in western Europe. Experience in other countries, where the majority of citizens are Catholics, and in which divorce has been introduced, for example, Portugal, has been that, following an initial large number of applications for divorce, the numbers of applications have not continued at the same high level. This would seem to indicate that the large number of applications immediately following the introduction of divorce reflects applicants whose marriages had broken down, perhaps for many years, and who were, up to then, unable to avail of the remedy of divorce. It should be borne in mind, however, that it is very dangerous to predict what might occur in this country from the experience of other countries.

7.8.21 Further, it is argued that regard must be had to the fact that legislation can have a profound effect upon human behaviour and that changes in legislation in this area could produce a significant change in patterns of behaviour that have been applicable up to this time. It is the view of both the Committee, and of a great majority of those who made submissions to it, that divorce rates of the kind that prevail in other countries would not be desirable in this country. Marital breakdown figures in this country have not as yet reached the level of those in other countries in the western world, and it is to be hoped that, given the type of positive support and active help for marriages which this Committee suggests in other Chapters, such levels would not be reached.

7.8.22 It has been suggested to the Committee that one of the consequences of the deletion of the prohibition on divorce from the Constitution would be that the protections and safeguards for the institutions of marriage and the family would be weakened. In the Committee's view, such protections and safeguards can take a number of distinct and yet interlinked forms. The first means by which the State can safeguard marriage is by upholding the protection of marriage and the family which is enshrined in our constitution. Secondly, such protection can be given in a practical way, by the introduction of measures to provide better reparation for marriage, and by the provision of proper back-up services with suitable facilities, to help married couples who are experiencing difficulties. The Committee has already expressed the hope that such increased practical help will be made available. Finally, the State can safeguard marriage by the introduction of suitable legislation aimed at preventing the causes of marital breakdown. A clear example of such legislation would, in the Committee's view, be the introduction of an Act to raise the minimum age for marriage.

7.8.23 At present clear constitutional protection for the institution of marriage and the family based on marriage is provided in Article 41 of the Constitution. It is worthwhile at this stage to quote in its entirety the text of Article 41:

Article 4 1.1.1 The State recognises the Family as the natural primary and fundamental unit group of Society, and as a moral institution possessing inalienable and imprescriptible rights, antecedent and superior to all positive law.

Article 41.1.2 The State, therefore, guarantees to protect the Family in its constitution and authority, as the necessary basis of social order and as indispensable to the welfare of the Nation and the State.

Article 41.2.1 In particular, the State recognises that by her life within the home, woman gives to the State a support without which the common good cannot be achieved.

Article 41.2.2 The State shall, therefore, endeavour to ensure that mothers shall not be obliged by economic necessity to engage in labour to the neglect of their duties in the home.

Article 41.3.1 The State pledges itself to guard with special care the institution of Marriage, on which the Family is founded, and to protect it against attack.

Article 41.3.2 No law shall be enacted providing for the grant of a dissolution of marriage.

Article 41.3.3 No person whose marriage has been dissolved under the civil law of any other State but is a subsisting valid marriage under the law for the time being in force within the jurisdiction of the Government and Parliament established by this Constitution shall be capable of contracting a valid marriage within that jurisdiction during the lifetime of the other party to the marriage so dissolved.

7.8.24 This Article is the fundamental basis of the various legal protections enjoyed by the family. It has been the bulwark which has from time to time been relied upon to prevent discrimination against the family as an institution. It has been urged on this Committee that any amendment of the Constitution which might be proposed to allow the introduction of divorce legislation should ensure that the rights of the family as set out in Article 41 are not diminished. The Committee accepts this view and is of the opinion that any such amendment should be drafted in such a way as to ensure that the basic emphasis of Article 41 is not altered; it should continue to place a duty on the State to protect the family and the institution of marriage, to recognise the family as the natural primary fundamental unit of society.

7.8.25 If divorce were to be introduced, the Committee believes that it would not be sufficient merely to remove the negative prohibition on divorce contained in Article 41.3.2 of the Constitution because it would be still possible for the remainder of Article 41 to be relied upon to have any such divorce legislation struck down as being unconstitutional. If a referendum were to take place the Committee believes that the proposed amendment to the Constitution should not simply ask whether the constitutional prohibition on divorce contained in Article 41.3.2 of the Constitution should be removed or should be retained. To ensure that no constitutional ambiguity results from any such referendum, the Committee is of the view that any amendment to be voted upon should be in a positive format, replacing the present Article 41.3.2 with a provision specifically authorising the Oireachtas to legislate for the dissolution of marriage.

OPINIONS OF THE COMMITTEE

7.8.26 The current constitutional position cannot be changed without a referendum being held. For such a referendum to be held enabling legislation would need to be enacted by the Oireachtas. Having regard to the many submissions and arguments heard by the Committee the question arises as to whether a referendum should be held.

7.8.27 The Committee feels that it is important to state clearly that support for the holding of a referendum does not necessarily imply support for divorce. It is perfectly logical and reasonable for a person to hold a view that a referendum on the question of whether or not the Oireachtas should have the power to introduce legislation for divorce should take place, whilst at the same time holding the view that any such legislation would be unnecessary or undesirable at this time. For example, a person may for personal or religious reasons dislike the concept of divorce yet feel that it is the democratic right of the people to decide on the issue. Equally the Committee feels that it is open to a person to believe that divorce legislation is necessary or desirable in this country but that a referendum would not be appropriate at this time, perhaps on the ground that such a referendum would have divisive effects in the community or from a belief that such a referendum would be doomed to defeat at this time.

7.8.28 Most of the submissions made to us when dealing with the question of divorce have concentrated on the arguments for and against divorce legislation but in many cases do not deal separately with the arguments for and against the holding of a referendum. A number of facts can be identified in relation to the holding of such a referendum. It is almost 48 years since the present Constitution came into force. Since then the Irish people have never been afforded a democratic opportunity to express their views as to whether they wish the current constitutional prohibition on divorce to be retained. Many people in this country are affected by the problem of marital breakdown. Strong arguments can be made both for and against the introduction of a divorce jurisdiction and a national debate is currently in progress about this question. It is likely that this debate will continue regardless of whether or not it is in the context of an actual referendum to reform the Constitution. Since Article 41.3.2 constitutes an absolute bar on the enactment of any divorce legislation, any move towards the introduction of divorce requires constitutional change, which in turn requires the holding of a referendum. It is necessary, however, to balance against these considerations the fact that the holding of a referendum on the question of divorce is likely to be socially divisive, in that deep divisions of opinion exist in the community in respect of this issue. Such divisions are already apparent to some extent with certain groups taking up a pro and anti divorce stance.

7.8.29 Having considered submissions and bearing in mind the factors set out above, the Committee is of the view that a referendum should be held; this was a decision of the majority of the Committee. A minority of the Committee believes that this matter should be decided by the Oireachtas as a whole without a recommendation from the Committee. So as to ensure that no constitutional ambiguity results from any such referendum, the Committee feels that any amendment to be voted upon should be in a positive format.

7.8.30 The Committee is also of the view that any amendment should be drafted in such a way as to ensure that the basic emphasis of Article 41 is not altered, in that the Article should continue to place a duty on the State to protect the family and the institution of marriage and to recognise the family as the natural primary and fundamental unit group of society.

7.8.31 The outcome of a referendum is a matter for the people. By that outcome they will decide whether the Oireachtas should be free to introduce divorce legislation in this country.

7.8.32 The Committee has decided that it will not express any views on the wider question of whether divorce legislation is either necessary or desirable in the State at present. Some members of the Committee are of the belief that a view should be expressed as to whether divorce legislation is either necessary or desirable. From the internal discussions of the Committee it is clear that it would not be possible to reach a consensus on this question. The Committee believes, however, that by setting out the arguments for and against divorce and by analysing those arguments in the context of the effects of introduction or non-introduction of divorce we have made a useful contribution to this debate, so as to assist members of the Oireachtas and the general public in reaching an informed view in regard to this important question. The Committee feels that it can also further this process by analysing the nature of any possible divorce legislation.

THE NATURE OF POSSIBLE DIVORCE LEGISLATION

7.8.33 The Committee believes that it would not be appropriate or feasible for it to recommend the details of any divorce legislation which might be provided in the event of a change in the Constitution. However, having heard and received detailed submissions from a wide variety of groups, organisations and individuals, the Committee feels that it should indicate its view as to what should be the main feature of any such legislation. The Committee is of the opinion that the situation of divorce on demand would not be appropriate in this country and would not be acceptable to the people. Adequate safeguards must be built into any legislation to take account of the State interest in fostering and protecting marriage and the family. Also the Committee feels that there is an obvious need to ensure in any such legislation that proper provision is made for the protection of dependent spouses and the welfare of the dependent children who might be affected by the grant of a decree of divorce. The Committee sees these factors as essential in considering any divorce legislation.

7.8.34 The constant theme in the opinions and observations of this Committee has been the need as far as possible to reduce the adversarial element in marriage breakdown. The Committee consequently feels that any divorce law should be based on the concept of marital breakdown. The Committee believes that this approach would reduce the acrimony and bitterness and would assist separated parents in the continuing relationship between themselves and their children.

7.8.35 The Committee has already discussed the concept of irretrievable breakdown in the context of judicial separation. If judicial separation and the dissolution of marriage are both to be granted on the basis of irretrievable breakdown, then it would appear logical that there should be some link between the two reliefs. The Committee believes that the grant of a decree of judicial separation should be a first step, whereby a person could apply after a fixed period of time, from the granting of a judicial separation, for a decree of divorce.

This approach would have a number of advantages. To see the remedy of judicial separation as a first step, which spouses would be required to negotiate as a prerequisite to petitioning for a decree of divorce, would have the effect of giving time to the parties to consider their respective positions and the implications for any children of the marriage. Further, there would be a period of time after the judicial separation had been obtained, for all would be decided at the date of the judicial separation. This would ensure that the interests of the dependent members of the family and particularly the children would be protected from an early stage.

The conditions that the Committee went on to propose were very restrictive: the court would be able to dissolve a marriage only if it had failed with no possibility of reconciliation. Provisions would also have been made for the issues concerning the property and custody of the dependent spouse and children to be determined by a family tribunal.

The ensuing campaign over the proposal to amend Article 41 was very intense, as it drew together the conservative opposition around the idea that divorce was a challenge to the fundamental values of Irish society. As the campaign went on, the government, reluctant to challenge either Catholic doctrine or what was still thought to be majority popular sentiment, did not make its case for change on the issue of principle, but sought the amendment as a form of technical 'fix' for the problems of separated couples. The Catholic Church issued a statement declaring that, while voters should vote according to their consciences, the proposed amendment would weaken the family. Survey results indicate that public opinion underwent a startling reversal in little more than two months, moving 27 percentage points from a majority in favour of change to a majority against.

The referendum on the proposed amendment was held on 26 June 1986. The amendment provided for the possibility of dissolving any marriage that had failed for at least five years with no reasonable possibility of reconciliation, provided that adequate and proper provision was made for any dependent spouse or child. The result was that 63 per cent of those voting opposed the amendment. The only constituencies that had majorities in favour were in Dublin, while the rural vote was overwhelmingly negative. The public, it appears, had made a distinction between the removal of the prohibition of divorce from the Constitution, and the rules and laws that would apply in the specific circumstances of divorce. In opinion polls the latter element of the proposal was supported by fewer people (51 per cent) than the former element (71 per cent), and the result reflected this divergence.[1]

Public attitudes at around the time of the referendum debate were examined by the Second Joint Committee on Women's Rights of the Oireachtas. It found that negative attitudes to divorce, and hence the majority against the amendment, were heavily influenced by religiosity, rural location, older age and belief in the lifelong nature of marriage. The Joint Committee concluded:[2]

> What this analysis shows is that while many issues were debated extensively in the media concerning the effects of divorce on the economic situation of the wife and on the psychological state of the children, etc., the key issue which, in the final analysis, determined voting behaviour was people's underlying attitude about marriage itself, i.e., whether or not they see it as a lifelong commitment and whether or not they feel people have a right to a second chance at happiness if their first marriage has failed. However, the results showed that attitudes concerning marriage as a lifelong commitment were closely tied into issues concerning the economic and social consequences of divorce for the wife.

The major piece of legislation that came in the wake of the referendum was the Judicial Separation and Family Law Reform Act 1989. The debate in 1986 had served to call attention to the deficiencies in the realm of family law and a private bill tabled in 1987 became the basis for the new Act. It broadened the grounds for judicial separation, introducing a 'no fault' provision, and allowed the courts greater discretion in the allocation of property, the making of orders for maintenance and the arrangement of lump sum payments, taking into account the contribution of the spouse. The Act also provided for greater informality in separation hearings and for mediation for couples. Some felt that if this Act had been in place before the referendum the amendment might well have been passed.

After nearly a decade, eliminating the prohibition on divorce returned to the national agenda and was again put to the people in 1995. Fianna Fáil, still the largest party in Irish politics, had moved away from its longstanding opposition to amendment, and in 1991 another commission had examined the question of divorce with an eye to avoiding the problems that had emerged in connection with the first referendum. Its report, and the government's White Paper based upon it, reviewed the difficulties created by the lack of a divorce law, as well as the measures taken to deal with the circumstances of separation and marital breakdown since 1986.

Government of Ireland White Paper, *Marital Breakdown, a Review and Proposed Changes* (1992)

Chapter Three: Overview

JUDICIAL SEPARATION

3.19 *The Judicial Separation and Family Law Reform Act 1989* abolished the action for divorce *a mensa et thoro* and replaced it with a new action for *judicial separation* which can be obtained on wider grounds and with better provision for financial relief for spouses and dependent children.

3.20 The old remedy of a divorce *a mensa et thoro* could be applied for by a spouse on the (fault-based) grounds only of adultery, cruelty, or unnatural practices on the part of the other spouse. A spouse may apply for a judicial separation on (one or more of) the grounds of adultery; unreasonable behaviour; desertion for one year; separation for one year where the other spouse consents to a decree being granted; separation for 3 years; absence of a normal marital relationship for a period of at least one year immediately preceding the application.

3.21 The Act contains extensive provisions in relation to financial/property orders in favour of spouses and dependent children. These include powers to order maintenance; secured maintenance; lump sums; transfer of property, including the family home, between spouses (and dependent children), and that a spouse may occupy the family home for life. On the granting of a decree of judicial separation, or at any time afterwards, on application to it, the court is empowered in certain circumstances to extinguish the succession rights of a spouse.

3.22 While the legal effect of a decree of judicial separation is that it is no longer obligatory for the spouses to cohabit, a judicial separation does not legally end the marriage and, accordingly, does not permit remarriage.

DOMICILE AND FOREIGN DIVORCES

3.23 *The Domicile and Recognition of Foreign Divorces Act 1986* changed the law in relation to the recognition here of divorces obtained abroad (domicile is a legal concept used to determine which country's law it is appropriate to apply to establish a person's status in law e. g. whether a person is married or not, and is dealt with further in Chapter 8 [not included]). Before the 1986 Act came into force a woman was regarded as acquiring, on marriage, the domicile of her husband; now a married woman's domicile is established in the same way as anyone else's. Also, before the 1986 Act came into force, a foreign divorce would be recognised here generally only if both spouses were domiciled in the foreign jurisdiction when the divorce proceedings were commenced there; now for a divorce to be recognised here only one of the spouses need have been domiciled in the foreign jurisdiction which granted the divorce. A person who obtains a foreign decree of divorce which is recognised in Ireland is, of course, free to remarry here.

Chapter Ten: Divorce: issues which arise
INTRODUCTION

10.1 Article 41.3.2 of the Constitution of Ireland states that no law shall be enacted providing for the grant of a dissolution of marriage. If divorce were to be introduced here, therefore, an amendment to the Constitution would be required. This Chapter discusses issues which arise in considering whether the avenues of legal redress open to those whose marriages have broken down should be extended to include divorce. Chapter 11 considers approaches which might be taken to amending the Constitution to allow for the introduction of divorce and Chapter 13 [not included] contains a commentary on the Scheme of the Family Law (No. 2) Bill which the Government considers it would be appropriate to introduce should an amendment to the Constitution be put to the people and be accepted by them.

MARRIAGE AND THE BREAKDOWN OF MARRIAGES

10.2 The European Convention on Human Rights provides that men and women of marriageable age have the right to marry and to found a family according to the national laws governing the exercise of this right. Though the right is subject to national laws, the European Court of Human Rights has held that the right must not be reduced or restricted in such a way or to such an extent that the right is impaired.

10.3 The vast majority of persons in Ireland who get married go on to live together in a lifelong union. There is, however, a minority whose hopes and expectations of a permanent union are dashed.

Marriages break down; couples separate. Some arrange a legal separation by means of a separation agreement. Others get a judicial separation. A number get divorced abroad. Some of those divorces are recognised here; very many are not. A very small number get civil annulments – a remedy which is of necessity limited, based as it is on the state of affairs prevailing at the time the marriage itself is entered into rather than on any subsequent events. The breakdown of a marriage is normally a process which brings with it a painful, emotional, psychological and financial crisis. Both spouses face having to make substantial changes in their style and standard of living and arrangements must be made for the care and upbringing of any children. There are extensive social and legal provisions, including Church and voluntary programmes, for the support of persons whose marriage has, for any number of reasons, got into difficulties or, ultimately, broken down. Social policies are formulated to promote and strengthen the family and where breakdown occurs social welfare and other arrangements are in place to provide support for those in need. Our separation laws encourage spouses to avail themselves of counselling and mediation and there is now more informality in family law proceedings in the courts. The courts have very wide powers to redistribute property between the spouses and children, to order financial relief for dependants (and, in certain circumstances, to extinguish succession rights).

10.4 The Government is concerned with the preservation of stable marriages and the avoidance of marriage breakdown. It must also be concerned to ensure that where marriages do break down, there is in our law and social policies a proper response to the matter. It would ultimately be a matter for the people to decide in a Referendum whether the law should go further than at present by allowing persons, whose marriage has broken down irretrievably, to have, in certain circumstances, their marriages legally ended, thus leaving them free to remarry.

LEGAL POSITION IN THE ABSENCE OF DIVORCE
JUDICIAL SEPARATION

10.5 Under existing law a spouse whose marriage has broken down may obtain a judicial separation from the courts. The effect of the decree is that the spouses are no longer obliged to cohabit (section 8 of the Judicial Separation and Family Law Reform Act 1989). The decree does not end the marriage and the decree may be rescinded by the courts at any time in the future on a reconciliation between the spouses and the resumption of cohabitation. The granting of a judicial separation decree does not permit remarriage.

CIVIL DECREE OF NULLITY

10.6 A party to a marriage who obtains a civil decree of nullity is entitled to remarry. In this connection a distinction must be drawn between a marriage which is *void* and a marriage which is *voidable*. In the case of a marriage which is *void* (e.g. for absence of consent or lack of capacity) there is no need to obtain a decree of nullity from the courts since there never was a marriage in the first place (although it may be advisable to seek a declaration from the courts that a marriage was void in order to remove any doubt in the matter). In the case of a marriage which is *voidable* the marriage continues to subsist until the court grants a decree of nullity. The effect of the decree is that the marriage is rendered void *ab initio* i.e. as never having taken place. The essential difference between a decree of nullity of a voidable marriage and a decree of divorce is that in the case of the former the ground on which a decree is applied for (e.g. physical impotence) has to exist at the date of the marriage: events or acts subsequent to the marriage are never a ground for a declaration of nullity. In the case of divorce it is events or acts subsequent to the marriage which would usually form the grounds for the decree.

FOREIGN DIVORCES

10.7 A person who obtains a foreign decree of divorce or nullity which is recognised in Ireland is, of course, entitled to remarry in the State. On the other hand, an Irish citizen who obtains a foreign decree of divorce or nullity which is not recognised in Ireland and who enters into a second marriage, whether in Ireland or elsewhere, may be guilty of bigamy under Irish law. Because the recognition here of foreign divorces requires at least one of the parties to be domiciled abroad – see section 8.21 [not included] – very few foreign divorces will, in practice, receive recognition and it is probable that many of the divorces that have been obtained by Irish persons abroad are not, in fact, recognised by our law.

CHURCH ANNULMENTS

10.8 Where in the case of a voidable marriage there has been a church annulment but there has not been a civil annulment the marriage remains a subsisting valid marriage under the civil law of the State. A party to a subsisting valid marriage who enters into a second marriage, knowing the other party to the first marriage to be alive, commits (under section 57 of the Offences against the Person Act 1861) the offence of bigamy.

10.9 In practice, the number of decrees of nullity granted each year by the Catholic Church averages around 200 (covering the 32 counties). In about 75% of cases a prohibition on 'remarriage' in the Church is imposed on one or both parties on the basis, it is understood, that the defect which caused the nullity is judged to be serious enough to put at risk the validity of a future marriage. The veto may be lifted by the local Bishop only if he is satisfied, after investigation, of the person's fitness for marriage in all essential respects. Further details in relation to the number of Catholic Church decrees of nullity are contained in Appendix 3.8 [not included].

10.10 A suggestion sometimes made to the effect that the state law of nullity should give legal recognition to Church decrees of nullity raises fundamental questions of principle including constitutional issues. Even if the grounds for nullity available under civil law and canon law were identical it would be inevitable that there would be differences in decisions in individual cases.

EFFECT OF DIVORCE

10.11 The granting of a decree of divorce has two functions: first, it enables couples whose marriages have broken down irretrievably to end legally what is often referred to as the 'empty shells' of their marriages; and, secondly, it allows people to remarry. It cannot, of course, affect in any way the religious status of a marriage. In practice not all of those who obtain a divorce in other jurisdictions marry again. For example, in 1986 in England and Wales there were over 2 million divorced people who had not remarried (Stone: *Road to Divorce*).

A 'RIGHT' TO DIVORCE?

10.12 Some people advance the proposition that divorce is a basic human right. It is nevertheless the case that no such right has been recognised under either the European Convention on Human Rights or the United Nations International Covenant on Civil and Political Rights. In particular, in the case of *Johnston and Others v. Ireland* (1986) the European Court of Human Rights held that the European Convention did not include any guarantee of a right to divorce. In a separate case – *F. v. Switzerland* (1987) – the Court held, however, that a limitation on the right to remarry, following a divorce, would be in breach of the Convention. The Court held to be in violation of the Convention a law enabling a court, when granting a divorce where fault was proved, to fix a period of up to 3 years during which the person at fault would not be entitled to remarry.

THE LEGAL POSITION OF 'SECOND' UNIONS

10.13 Some parties to marriages which have broken down go on, in the absence of a means to bring their marriages legally to an end, to set up 'second unions' outside of marriage.

10.14 The children of unions of this kind have been given full legal protection by the Status of Children Act 1987 (which was discussed in Chapter 7 [not included]) under which all children are entitled to the same maintenance, succession etc. rights whether or not their parents are married to each other.

10.15 Neither party to a 'second' union enjoys the same legal protection available to the parties to a marriage. They have no right to be maintained by the other, the father is not the guardian of any children of the second union (unless he succeeds in an application to court under the Status of Children Act, 1987 – see section 7.12 [not included]) and they have no automatic rights of succession to each other's estate when one of them dies. The remedy of a barring or protection order is not available to either party against the other. In this situation a person seeking the protection of the law must rely on the common law remedy of an injunction to bar the other party from the home. (However, unlike the barring and protection order, breach of either of which gives the Gardai power to arrest without warrant the spouse in breach and bring that spouse before the court, breach of an injunction does not, by itself, render a person liable to arrest or criminal prosecution: committal proceedings must be initiated by the person in whose favour the injunction was originally granted.) Likewise, the presumptions which operate in the area of matrimonial property do not apply to parties to a second union (an example would be the presumption – unless and until the contrary is proved – that spouses have agreed that the indirect contribution of one spouse to the acquisition of the family home by the other spouse confers on the first-named spouse a beneficial interest in the home to the extent of the contribution made). Instead, the general rules relating to the contributions of one person to the acquisition by another of property apply.

10.16 As a general proposition it follows that, since the remedies available in family law were introduced on the basis that the ordinary rules of law did not give sufficient protection to spouses, parties to a second union outside marriage – who must rely on the ordinary rules – do not have as high a level of safeguards and entitlements as spouses have. The special protection afforded by the law to spouses may be seen as reflecting the provision in Article 41.3.1 of the Constitution to the effect that the State pledges itself to guard with special care the institution of marriage, on which the Family is founded, and to protect it against attack. On the introduction of divorce the full benefits of family law would apply to the parties of 'second unions' where the parties marry. On the other hand, following a divorce neither party to the marriage which has been dissolved retains the legal rights (or owes the legal duties) of a spouse arising out of that marriage – although there may remain legal obligations such as maintenance. Consequently, a principal issue to be addressed, if divorce were to be introduced, would be the safeguarding as far as possible of the position of divorced dependent spouses (as well as the position of dependent children).

PROTECTION OF SPOUSES AND CHILDREN

10.17 Where marriages break down and couples separate this inevitably has financial consequences for families. There are already comprehensive provisions in the Judicial Separation and Family Law Reform Act 1989 which aim at the protection as far as possible of spouses and dependent children and these are adaptable for any divorce legislation. One of the issues raised during the 1986 Divorce Referendum was the possible adverse effects, particularly on family farms and family businesses, of any proposals for the division and redistribution of family property following divorce. In this regard the Government would propose that property transfer provisions on the lines of those already in force in the case of judicial separation would apply in the case of divorce if a referendum to allow divorce were to be held and was successful.

10.18 In many cases there will be only one income and little property and it is likely that, no matter what the legislation provides, it will prove difficult for a spouse who divorces and remarries to support a first and second family, with consequent disadvantages particularly for the first family. While many of these difficulties exist already in cases of judicial separation, divorce – as distinct from separation – may in some cases tend to add to the difficulties since it enables a spouse, through remarriage, to create new legal responsibilities towards a second spouse. Problems are likely in practice to be greatest in the case of wives who have given up careers on marriage and who may find it difficult to re-establish themselves in employment after a long period of marriage – young wives who have remained in employment during marriage are likely to have less difficulty in coping financially after divorce. The court will be empowered under the legislation that is proposed, in the event of divorce being approved by the people, to make whatever orders are necessary in the circumstances in order to ensure that the interests of the first spouse are protected as far as possible.

10.19 It is clearly important that the court in divorce proceedings should give as much thought as possible to arrangements for children. The Judicial Separation Act attempts to safeguard children by providing that before granting a decree of judicial separation the court must be satisfied that the arrangements made for the welfare of each child are proper in all the circumstances. The court is empowered to deal with the arrangements whether or not the parents desire it to do so. It is proposed that similar provisions would be included in any divorce legislation.

While the breakdown of a marriage and the circumstances giving rise to it can be expected inevitably to be difficult for children their legal rights are not affected by divorce because after divorce parents remain guardians of their children, though the court may have to decide which parent is to have custody as it does in separation cases; and children remain entitled to inherit from their parents where there is no will and, where there is a will, remain entitled to apply to have proper provision made out of the deceased parent's estate where such proper provision has not been made by will or otherwise.

DIVORCE IN OTHER JURISDICTIONS
10.20 Appendix 3.9 [not included] sets out information on the grounds for divorce in a number of European countries and statistics in relation to the number of divorces granted. As will be seen from the information contained in the Appendix, there are considerable variations on the circumstances in which divorce is permitted in other European countries. The following table, which sets out, for the years shown, the divorce rate in a number of European countries per 1,000 married couples also shows wide variations among those countries in the prevalence of divorce.

Table 5.1
Divorce rate per 1,000 married couples in various european countries for selected years

	1961	*1971*	*1981*	*1985*
England/Wales/Scotland	2.1	5.8	11.5	13.2
Belgium	2.0	2.8	6.1	7.3
Denmark	5.7	10.8	12.1	12.6
France	2.9	3.5	6.8	8.1*
Germany (Fed. Rep.)	3.6	5.2	7.2	8.6
Greece	1.5	1.7	2.5	
Italy	2.5	0.9	1.1	
Luxembourg	2.0*	2.6*	5.9	7.2
Netherlands	2.2	3.7	8.3	9.9
Portugal	0.4	0.3	2.8	3.7
Spain		1.1		

(Note: figures marked * are for the closest year for which figures are available.)

Chapter 11: Divorce: possible approaches to a constitutional amendment

INTRODUCTION

11.1 This Chapter sets out possible approaches which might be taken to amending the Constitution so as to remove the prohibition on divorce. A proposal to amend the Constitution must be introduced in the Dáil as a Bill and if such a Bill is passed by both Houses of the Oireachtas it must be submitted to the people for approval in a referendum.

It was the view of a majority of the Oireachtas Joint Committee on Marriage Breakdown (1985) that a referendum should be held on divorce. In 1986 a Government Bill containing proposals to repeal the Constitutional ban on divorce and for its replacement with a new provision (enabling divorce in certain circumstances) was passed, unopposed, by both Houses of the Oireachtas. Details of that constitutional amendment proposal are contained in Appendix 3.10 [not included]. In the subsequent referendum 63% of those who voted were against the proposal to amend the Constitution.

11.3 In the context of the continuing debate about divorce the Government is concerned to ensure that the people, who would have to decide in any further referendum whether they wish to amend the Constitution to enable divorce legislation to be introduced, should be fully informed about the legal and other

implications of the matter. In addition to the information already set
out, the Government has decided to publish in this White Paper
details of

(a)   forms which a constitutional amendment in relation to divorce
      might take;
(b)   the Scheme of a Bill (the Family Law (No. 2) Bill) which the
      Government believes it would be appropriate to enact if a
      constitutional amendment – in any of the forms outlined –
      were to be passed by the people.

The forms which a constitutional amendment might take are
discussed in the rest of this Chapter. Chapter 13 contains a general
commentary on the Scheme of the Family Law (No. 2) Bill which is
contained, together with explanatory notes, in Appendix 2 [not
included].

11.4 The Government proposes to proceed with a divorce
referendum after a full debate on the complex issues involved and
following the enactment of other legislative proposals in the area of
family law which are outlined in the White Paper. The Government
will consider the responses to the options contained in this White
Paper in advance of finalising its proposals on this matter.

OPTIONS FOR CONSTITUTIONAL CHANGE

11.5 A key question which arises in determining an appropriate
approach to a constitutional amendment is whether it should be
drafted so that the actual form of divorce legislation should be left
entirely at the discretion of the Oireachtas or whether the
amendment should entrench in the Constitution provisions which
would establish the circumstances in which divorces could be
granted and thus take that decision out of the hands of the
legislature. The entrenchment approach has clear drawbacks. What
may prove to be desirable changes in the circumstances in which
divorces could be granted and which would normally be dealt
with by way of amending legislation might not in practice be
proceeded with if a referendum were necessary on each occasion
and such an approach could be seen to represent a needlessly
restrictive restraint on the legislature in responding to changing
circumstances. There is also the argument that a Constitution is
more properly concerned with statements of fundamental principles
and that the enshrinement in it of the level of detail generally
contained in legislation itself could be regarded as inappropriate. On
the other hand it has been argued that, in the absence of an
entrenchment provision in the Constitution, there would be nothing

to prevent the Oireachtas from providing for a very liberal divorce regime without direct reference to the people.

11.6 The following sections of this Chapter set out 5 possible approaches to amending the Constitution. The first example would leave it entirely up to the Oireachtas to decide on the provisions of any divorce legislation; examples 2, 3 and 4 attempt to meet the criteria that an amendment should establish in broad outline the circumstances in which divorce could be granted but at the same time should be sufficiently specific so as to avoid criticisms that it does not in reality impose effective restrictions; example 5 would insert in the Constitution the actual precise grounds for divorce (this would mean, of course, that any widening of these precise grounds to permit easier or wider divorce in future years could come about only after a further referendum). The amendment in each case would be in substitution for the present Article 41.3.2 of the Constitution. The periods of time used in the examples of amendments could, of course, be varied if this were to be considered desirable.

EXAMPLE 1: GROUNDS FOR DIVORCE A MATTER FOR OIREACHTAS
11.7 'Provision may, however, be made by law providing for the grant of a dissolution of marriage subject to any conditions prescribed by law.'

Commentary: This example leaves it entirely up to the Oireachtas to decide on the provisions of any divorce legislation. This approach was discussed in section 11.6. If such an amendment were to be made to the Constitution the Government would be in a position to introduce legislation allowing for divorce based on one or more of the grounds included in the following example amendments viz.

- absence of normal marital relationship for 5 years
- separation for 5 years
- judicial separation or entitlement thereto plus a period of 2 years
- irretrievable breakdown on proof of specified 'fault' and 'no fault' grounds.

EXAMPLE 2: ABSENCE OF NORMAL MARITAL RELATIONSHIP FOR 5 YEARS
11.8 'Where, and only where, such court established under this Constitution as may be prescribed by law is satisfied that a normal marital relationship has not existed between the parties to a

marriage for a period of at least 5 years, there is no reasonable possibility of such a relationship being resumed, and any other condition prescribed by law has been complied with, the court may in accordance with law grant a dissolution of the marriage, provided that the court is satisfied that adequate and proper provision, having regard to the circumstances, will be made for any dependent spouse and for any child of or any child who is dependent on either spouse.'

Commentary: This formulation is somewhat similar to the formulation rejected in the 1986 Referendum. The main difference is that 'absence of a normal marital relationship for a period of 5 years' replaces the 'failure of the marriage' concept (the latter concept is unfamiliar to our law whereas the former is well known). Breakdown of marriage to the extent that the court is satisfied in all the circumstances that a normal marital relationship has not existed between the spouses for a period of at least one year immediately preceding the date of the application is a ground for the grant of a decree of judicial separation.

A constitutional amendment along these lines would mean that the absence of a normal marital relationship for a period of five years would be the sole ground for a divorce although, if considered necessary, the legislation could include examples of situations – e.g. actual separation of the spouses for 5 years – where 'absence of a normal marital relationship for 5 years' would be presumed to exist. It would not require actual separation in order to be invoked.

The concept of a normal marital relationship is widely used in the High Court in nullity cases and the lack of capacity to form or maintain such a relationship is fully investigated in these cases. It can refer not only to physical incapacity but also the capacity to sustain an emotional and psychological relationship. Its proposed use in the case of judicial separation was criticised by some on grounds of vagueness. Almost 50% of all judicial separations granted in the period since the Judicial Separation Act came into force on 19 October 1989 to December 1990 were granted on that basis. This does not necessarily mean, however, that that was the only ground pleaded. Indeed, this ground is in many cases being pleaded along with one of the other grounds of adultery, unreasonable behaviour, desertion or separation which in practice form the basis of the finding of 'absence of a normal marital relationship' in those cases.

If the concept were to be used in a constitutional amendment on divorce it would eventually fall to be interpreted by the High and/or Supreme Courts in the constitutional context. Some might argue that a liberal interpretation would, in effect, amount to what might be regarded as divorce on the demand of one spouse, to the extent that a claim by one of the spouses that there has been an absence of a normal marital relationship might tend to be regarded by the court as *prima facie* evidence of the fact and not be investigated in detail, particularly if the application for divorce is undefended (although there is the restriction that such a breakdown would have to be claimed to have existed for at least 5 years). On the other hand a strict interpretation might require investigation in every case – whether defended or not – as, indeed, happens at present in the case of petitions for nullity. (At present about 20% of judicial separation applications are undefended.)

It would be difficult to define in legislation the many circumstances covering the absence of a normal marital relationship although it might be possible to use the phraseology used by the courts at present in nullity cases e.g. the absence of a physical, emotional or psychological relationship. In any event this might be otiose since these are the criteria already used by the courts, albeit in nullity cases.

EXAMPLE 3: SEPARATION FOR 5 YEARS
11.9 'Where, and only where, such court established under this Constitution as may be prescribed by law is satisfied that the parties to a marriage are living apart from one another and have lived apart from one another for a period or periods to be prescribed by law but which shall amount in total to not less than 5 years, there is no reasonable possibility of cohabitation being resumed, and any other condition prescribed by law has been complied with, the court may in accordance with law grant a dissolution of the marriage, provided that the court is satisfied that adequate and proper provision, having regard to the circumstances, will be made for any dependent spouse and for any child of or any child who is dependent on either spouse.'

Commentary: Separation as the sole ground would be simple, objective and judgementally neutral. On the other hand it might in some cases encourage people to separate in order to obtain a divorce thereby reducing the chance of a reconciliation. In addition, it might present problems for the less well off who might have difficulty in separating (though separation would, of course, have to be defined as including separation in two households but under the one roof but this, naturally, would be more difficult to prove). The legislation would be straightforward: providing for 5 years separation as the only ground; defining separation (as in section 2(3) (a) of the Judicial Separation Act); allowing for short breaks in the separation (see section 2(2) of the Judicial Separation Act); and making any other provision deemed necessary. In this type of approach divorce would not be possible until there had been 5 years separation, even in a case where adultery, unreasonable behaviour or desertion represent the real grounds giving rise to seeking a divorce (in the previous example even in such cases a divorce would not be possible until there was an absence of a normal marital relationship for 5 years).

EXAMPLE 4: JUDICIAL SEPARATION OR ENTITLEMENT THERETO PLUS A PERIOD OF 2 YEARS

11.10 'Where, and only where, such court established under this Constitution as may be prescribed by law is satisfied that a marriage has irretrievably broken down, and any other condition prescribed by law has been complied with, the court may in accordance with law grant a dissolution of marriage, provided that the court is satisfied that adequate and proper provision, having regard to the circumstances, will be made for any dependent spouse and for any child of or any child who is dependent on either spouse. A marriage shall be regarded as having irretrievably broken down if, but only if, a decree of judicial separation in respect of that marriage has been granted in accordance with the law for the time being in force at least two years before the date of any application to the court for a decree of divorce, or one or more of the grounds warranting the granting of such decree have existed for a period of at least two years before the date of any application to the court for a decree of divorce, and there is no reasonable possibility of reconciliation between the spouses.'

Commentary: In this case a divorce would not be granted unless the court was satisfied that the marriage was irretrievably broken down. This would be proved only (a) if a decree of judicial separation has been granted at least two years before the application for a divorce or (b) one or more of the grounds warranting the granting of a decree of judicial separation has existed for more than two years before the application for divorce, and there was no prospect of a reconciliation.

A two-stage approach to divorce is a common feature of arrangements in some other jurisdictions (where there is, for example, a time lapse between the granting of a *decree nisi* and a *decree absolute*). It also appears common in some European Countries for divorce to be preceded by judicial separation.

In practice, a two-year waiting period between the granting of a judicial separation and an application for divorce could represent a period of reflection which in some cases might lead to reconciliation. Where a judicial separation had been granted, custody, maintenance and property matters would have been settled but, before granting a divorce, the court could look at these matters again in the context of divorce with the advantage of being able to assess how the judicial separation arrangements had worked out in practice, making whatever adjustments it considered were warranted.

In the Statement of the Government's Intentions at the time of the 1986 Referendum it was indicated that, except for transitional arrangements which were to apply in particular cases, a separation agreement would have had to be approved by a court or a judicial separation secured at least two years before an application for divorce could be made. However, the actual wording of the amendment at the time would not have imposed this requirement. The present amendment example would involve enshrining in the Constitution a requirement that a judicial separation had been granted at least two years previously, or that one or more grounds warranting the granting of a judicial separation had existed for a period of at least two years. The formulation has the further advantage that it avoids the need to spell out specific grounds for the granting of a decree and allows the Oireachtas a certain degree of flexibility to respond to changing circumstances. While it might be argued that it would allow the Oireachtas to vary the grounds for divorce by liberalising further the grounds for judicial separation it has to be borne in mind that these grounds are, in fact, quite liberal as they are. In any event – as with the periods of time specified in other examples – the waiting period could be increased if this were considered desirable. In addition, the situation in which a divorce would be available could be confined to judicial separations granted or capable of being granted in certain (defined) circumstances only.

An alternate approach to this type of formulation might be to confine it to cases where a judicial separation had actually been granted (or a separation agreement had been made a Rule of Court under section 8 of the Family Law (Maintenance of Spouses and

Children) Act 1976). However, this approach would require someone seeking a divorce who had not already obtained a judicial separation to go through two sets of court proceedings: one for a judicial separation (or to have a separation agreement made a Rule of Court) and another, two years later, for a divorce.

EXAMPLE 5: IRRETRIEVABLE BREAKDOWN ON PROOF OF SPECIFIED 'FAULT' AND 'NO FAULT' GROUNDS

11.11 'Where, and only where, such court established under this Constitution as may be prescribed by law is satisfied that a marriage has irretrievably broken down and any other condition prescribed by law has been complied with, the court may in accordance with law grant a dissolution of the marriage, provided that the court is satisfied that adequate and proper provision, having regard to the circumstances, will be made for any dependent spouse and for any child of or any child who is dependent on either spouse. A marriage shall be regarded as having irretrievably broken down if, but only if,

(i)   a spouse has committed adultery
(ii) a spouse has behaved in such a way that the other spouse cannot reasonably be expected to live with that spouse
(iii) a spouse has deserted the other spouse for a continuous period of at least three years immediately preceding any application to the court
(iv) the spouses have lived apart from one another for a continuous period of at least three years immediately preceding any application to the court and both parties consent to a dissolution being granted
(v)   the spouses have lived apart from one another for a continuous period of at least five years immediately preceding any application to the court or
(vi) the court is satisfied in all the circumstances that a normal marital relationship has not existed between the spouses for a period of at least three years immediately preceding the date of any application to the court, and there is no reasonable possibility of reconciliation between the spouses.'

Commentary: This example provides for irretrievable breakdown as the sole ground for the grant of a divorce; irretrievable breakdown would be proved by any of the matters from (i) to (vi) and, in addition the court would have to be satisfied that there is no reasonable possibility of reconciliation between the spouses. As in the case of judicial separation, adultery and unreasonable behaviour would be sufficient for the grant of a divorce with, however, the additional need to convince the court that there is no possibility of a reconciliation. The inclusion of these grounds would enable a spouse, having established fault on the part of the other spouse, to obtain a divorce without having to wait a specified time period as in grounds (iii) to (vi) of the amendment example. On the other hand, the absence of a time period might encourage spouses to divorce too quickly or to use fault rather than no fault grounds in order to obtain an earlier divorce. So as to provide protection against newly marrieds rushing into premature divorces Head 4 of the Scheme of the Family Law (No.2) Bill based on this amendment example contains a provision to the effect that no application for divorce shall be made before the expiration of the period of 3 years from the date of the marriage. (There would be a similar provision in the case of an amendment based on judicial separation – amendment example 4.) It would be possible to enshrine this in the amendment but its inclusion either in the amendment or (as proposed) the legislation might be open to the argument that it is unfair to 'wronged' spouses. As against that, the absence of any time limit could tend to lead, in practice, to a situation where divorce is readily available to an unacceptable extent. In the case of the four other grounds in the Judicial Separation Act (desertion, separation where there is consent to a decree being granted, separation where there is not consent and absence of normal marital relationship) two years would be added to the periods stipulated in these grounds for the purposes of divorce i.e. from one year to three in the case of desertion, separation with consent and absence of normal marital relationship and from three to five years where there is separation but no consent to a decree. It would not of course be necessary to include all the grounds for the grant of a judicial separation for the purposes of divorce and the strictness of a divorce 'regime' could be determined by the precise grounds to be included (or omitted).

The enshrinement of this level of detail in the Constitution is particularly open to the criticisms which were mentioned earlier in this Chapter: what may prove to be desirable changes in the circumstances in which divorce could be granted and which would normally be dealt with by way of amending legislation might not, in practice, be proceeded with if a referendum were necessary on each occasion and such an approach could be seen to be a needlessly restrictive restraint on the legislature in responding to changing circumstances. There is also the argument that a Constitution is more properly concerned with statements of fundamental principles and that the enshrinement in it of the level of detail generally contained in legislation itself could be regarded as inappropriate.

In 1995 a new proposal was placed before the people to eliminate the prohibition of divorce from the Constitution and replace it with one of the examples offered in the White Paper, *Marital Breakdown.* The key provisions were that the couple had to have lived apart for four of the past five years; that there was no reasonable likelihood of reconciliation; and that the court was satisfied that appropriate provision had been made for a dependent spouse or children.

The campaign leading up to the second referendum was no less hard-fought than the campaign in 1986 had been. The opponents of the amendment focused on claims that damage to society would follow from the indulgence of individuals' wishes at the expense of the common good. The supporters of the amendment emphasised the realities of broken marriage and remarriage, couples living together, the legal tangle in the absence of a divorce law and the denial of individual rights by the state (as distinct from the Catholic Church). The government published a document entitled *The Right to Remarry* and spent IR£60,000 on its own campaign, which was seen by the opponents of divorce as unfair since it was an expenditure of public money to promote one side in the debate. The Catholic Church and the Anti-Divorce Campaign were intense in their focus on the alleged deterioration of Ireland into a secular society and the risk that the family unit would be destroyed.

As the day of the referendum, 24 November 1995, approached, support for the amendment began to be eroded. Public opinion polls indicated a fall in support from the amendment from 69 per cent of respondents to 45 per cent. The result of the referendum itself represented a paper-thin margin of victory for the amendment, which won 50.3 per cent of the votes cast. The positive shift from the result in 1986, however, was more than nearly 14 percentage points, reflecting better legislative preparation by the government, and the increasing influence of the women's movement (although women in general displayed more conservative views on both occasions).

Not all matters concerning divorce had been clarified by the amendment (now generally referred to as the Fifteenth Amendment). A Constitutional Review Group raised one further issue in its report (1996, pp. 334–37): that of the recognition of foreign divorces. The amendment had eliminated subsection 3.2 from Article 41 of the Constitution but had not eliminated subsection 3.3, which recognises foreign divorces granted to people who are domiciled in another state. The Review Group's report recommended that the subsection be retained, since, in its view, it was necessary for the Oireachtas to have the express capacity to lay down guidelines for recognising foreign divorces even where the criteria would not meet other requirements of the amended Article.

In 1996 the Oireachtas passed another statute sponsored by the government of the day, the Family Law (Divorce) Act. The number of applications for divorce in 1997 was 1,200 – somewhat less than might be expected given the fact that in 1996 more than 50,000 women had indicated that they were separated from their husbands. The first legal divorce in Ireland was granted in 1997.

CONTRACEPTION

The state had hewed to the Catholic Church's doctrine on divorce since 1922. Contraception was another area of convergence between church and state in which Catholic doctrine was embodied in public policy and had a direct effect on women.

The first legislative initiative affecting the issue of contraception in the new state was the Censorship of Publications Act 1929, which was primarily directed at stemming the tide of cheap tabloid newspapers from Britain, but included a provision in section 7 banning all literature that advocated the 'unnatural prevention of conception or the procurement of abortion or miscarriage' and 'the use of any method, treatment or appliance for the purpose of such prevention or procurement'. Next, the Criminal Law (Amendment) Act 1935, which sought to regulate prostitution, also included provisions that forbade the importation, distribution or advertisement of contraceptives. The Censorship of Publications Act 1946 reiterated the prohibition on advertising or otherwise providing information on birth control.

The report of the first Commission on the Status of Women (1972) dealt with the issue of contraception as a matter of family planning. It recommended that information and advice be provided to married couples, and that their 'medical requirements' in relation to family planning should also be met – a veiled reference to contraception.

Commission on the Status of Women, *Report to Minister for Finance* (1972)

570. Our attention has been drawn to various international instruments which include references to family planning. Particular attention has been drawn to the Proclamation of the United Nations International Conference on Human Rights in Teheran in 1968 and the United Nations Declaration on Social Progress and Development, 1969. The Proclamation of Teheran proclaimed that 'parents have a basic human right to determine freely and responsibly the number and the spacing of their children', and a Resolution of that Conference considered that couples have a right to 'adequate education and information' in this respect. The Resolution referred to was adopted with 49 votes for, no vote against and with 7 abstentions (by no means all the United Nations Countries attended the Conference). Ireland voted for the Resolution.

The United Nations Declaration on Social Progress and Development stated that on the basis of the principles set forth in the Declaration, the achievement of the objectives of social progress and development requires the mobilisation of the necessary resources by national and international action, with particular attention to such means and methods as, inter alia,

the formulation and establishment, as needed, of programmes in the field of population, within the framework of national demographic policies and as part of the welfare medical services, including education, training of personnel and the provision to families of the knowledge and means necessary to enable them to exercise their right to determine freely and responsibly the number and spacing of their children. (Part 111, Article 22 (b))

In an intervention before the vote, Ireland made the point that the inclusion of 'and means' created difficulties of a moral character for a number of delegations. Ireland requested a separate vote on these words, and the words were retained with 60 votes for and 16 votes against (including Ireland) and 17 abstentions. A further separate vote on that part of Article 22(b) after 'demographic policies' resulted in its retention with 64 votes for and 20 votes against (including Ireland) and 13 abstentions. The text of Article 22 (b) as a whole was adopted with 67 votes for, 6 votes against and 26 abstentions. Ireland was one of the countries which abstained. Ireland abstained also in the vote on Part III as a whole of the Declaration. The Declaration as a whole was adopted with 119 votes for (including Ireland), no vote against and 2 abstentions. Acceptance of the Declaration as a whole is subject to any reservations on specific provisions indicated by vote or by intervention in the debate. Neither the Proclamation nor the Declaration referred to is legally binding.

571. Reference has also been made to the relevance of the European Convention on Human Rights and Fundamental Freedoms (1950) in this matter. In Article 12 of that Convention it was declared that men and women of marriageable age have the right to marry and found a family, according to the national laws governing the exercise of this right. While the Convention does not mention expressly any right of family planning, this does not exclude an inherent right, outside the Convention, of parents to plan their family.

572. We consider that parents have the right to regulate the number and spacing of their family and that such right can only be exercised with the full agreement of both husband and wife and is not the exclusive right of one or the other.

573. As to the methods which may be adopted by parents in the exercise of this right, it must remain a matter for their mutual selection and be influenced by their moral conscience. In their approach to finding a solution to such a complex problem involving diverse human emotions in an intimate relationship, it is desirable that husband and wife should have available to them adequate enlightenment as to their rights and responsibilities. We wish to make clear that this consideration and the recommendations contained in the following paragraph should not be understood or implied as envisaging the withdrawal of legal restrictions reasonably necessary for the protection of public morality. We recognise that amending legislation would be involved in the implementation of our recommendations.

574. We recommend, accordingly, that:
(i)   Information and expert advice on family planning should be available through medical and other appropriate channels to

families throughout the country. Such advice should respect the moral and personal attitudes of each married couple;
(ii) medical requirements arising out of the married couples' decisions on family planning should be available under control and through channels to be determined by the Department of Health.

The McGee case changed the prevailing interpretation of the Constitution and increased the pressure for a change in the law concerning the availability of contraceptives. In McGee v. Attorney General, 1973, the court considered the case of Mary McGee, a 27-year-old woman, married to a fisherman, who had four children. Her doctor advised her that another pregnancy would endanger her life or result in paralysis and issued a prescription for spermicidal jelly. Deciding not to have any more children, Mrs McGee ordered the spermicidal jelly from the United Kingdom. It was seized by customs officials as a shipment in violation of the Criminal Law (Amendment) Act 1935. The Irish Family Planning Association aided the McGees in bringing their case to the High Court, on the grounds that a married couple with justifiable medical requirements should be able to purchase such a product. The High Court dismissed the claim, but the Supreme Court overturned the High Court's verdict on appeal. It based its decision on Article 40.3.1 of the Constitution:

> The state guarantees in its laws to respect, and, as far as practicable, by its laws to defend and vindicate the personal rights of the citizen.

The Supreme Court's view was that this provision implied a right to privacy, such that the seizure of Mrs McGee's shipment was an invasion of her right to marital privacy. The discovery of a right to privacy by the Supreme Court was consistent with a process of evolving interpretation that has also discovered other implied rights of citizens, such as the right to work and the right to free movement.

The decision in the McGee case struck down the prohibition in the 1935 Act and allowed the importation of contraceptive products for married couples. However, it left open the question of the need for new legislation to bring the law into line with the decision. The Catholic Church still opposed any change in the law on contraception, viewing it as a sin: John Charles McQuaid, Archbishop of Dublin, called it 'a curse upon the country'. The Fianna Fáil government of the day resisted legislating on the subject, despite pleas from Senators, including the future President of Ireland Mary Robinson (then a Labour Party politician).

Since 1963 the contraceptive pill had been available in Ireland, where doctors prescribed it ostensibly to regulate women's menstrual cycles. The Irish Medical Association estimated in 1978 that 48,000 women in Ireland were on the pill. The number of people seeking family planning also rose after the first family planning clinic was opened in Dublin in 1969. Public opinion was also shifting. Surveys suggested that only one third of Irish people favoured the sale of contraceptives in the early 1970s, but by the late 1970s that proportion had increased to two thirds. Demonstrations were organised by the Women's Liberation Movement and a group of women went to Belfast in May 1971 to purchase contraceptives, daring the government to arrest them on their return with the banned products. The government did nothing and the 'Condom Train' became a public embarrassment.

There had been an attempt to liberalise the law under the Fine Gael/Labour government led by Liam Cosgrave, which had been in power at the time of the McGee case. Its Control of Importation, Sale and Manufacture of Contraceptives Bill was introduced in 1974. However, the governing coalition was so divided that members of the government, including Cosgrave himself, voted against the bill and it was defeated. In 1976 the Contraceptive Action Programme was founded to keep the issue at the top of the agenda through signature drives and meetings.

The next Fianna Fáil government brought in a new bill in 1978 after consulting with a wide variety of groups, including the Catholic bishops. The Health (Family Planning) Bill called for the dispensing of contraceptives on the basis of a doctor's prescription when the doctor was convinced that it was necessary for family planning or medical reasons. Advertising and importation were limited to chemists (pharmacists). Restrictive as it was, the bill provoked considerable controversy before its passage: it was too much for the Catholic Church and other conservative elements in society, and too little for liberals and radicals, while some constitutional scholars argued that it was simply unnecessary.[3] The bill was passed in 1979 and came into effect in 1980.

The government then felt compelled to turn a blind eye to the extensive violation of the new Act, as condoms became widely available from family planning clinics and on university campuses. The fact that they were not available in all the rural parts of the country, and that some doctors were uncomfortable in the role of moral arbiters, caused the government to introduce a new Health and Family Planning Bill in 1985. Once enacted, this allowed the distribution of condoms by regional health boards and clinics, and allowed anyone over 18 to get them without a prescription. Nevertheless, vending machines were still illegal and family planning was not available in rural areas.

The matter was still not settled, however, as the AIDS crisis hit Ireland, as it did other countries, in the early 1990s. Members of the Irish Family Planning Association courted arrest by selling condoms in a music store in order to dramatise the issue of availability. Eventually, the Health (Family Planning) (Amendment) Act 1993 redefined the issue, shifting the sale and use of condoms from the area of birth control to the area of public health. The Act legalised the sale of condoms from vending machines, removed the age limit for purchase, and removed all other remaining controls over the sale and supply of condoms.

ABORTION

Abortion was against the law in Ireland under Section 8 and 9 of the Offences against the Persons Act 1861. Most people in Ireland were decidedly not pro-choice, a position that made little headway in 'natalist' Ireland. In the 1970s the Irish women's movement focused on the question of contraception, not abortion.

Nevertheless, the attempt to put an anti-abortion provision into the Constitution was in part provoked by the rise of the women's movement, which had generated a strong reaction among conservative and religious groups. Conservative groups interpreted the appearance of the more radical groups, such as Irishwomen United, as an indication that Ireland was awash in secularism and consequent moral decay. The Dublin Well Women's Centre and the Women's Right to Choose movement were seen as part of a pro-abortion lobby by such groups. In addition, conservatives thought that, given the attitudes to abortion in other countries, abortion might be allowed in Ireland in the near future, under a directive from the European Community concerning individual rights. There was also the real, if unlikely, possibility that an Irish court might find a right to abortion in the Constitution, just as courts had discovered other implied rights in that document.

In 1981 the Pro Life Amendment Campaign (PLAC) was founded by such groups as the Society for the Protection of the Unborn Child (SPUC), Opus Dei and the Responsible Society. The PLAC sought to gain the support of the mainstream political parties for an amendment to the Constitution that would expressly forbid abortion. The matter seemed straightforward, since the campaign was supported by both the main parties, Fianna Faíl and Fine Gael (while the third party, Labour, was divided on the question and in any case tended to follow Fine Gael, its coalition partner). The wording of the proposed amendment was drawn up under the Fianna Faíl government of Charles Haughey, which held power up to 1983:

> The state acknowledges the right to life of the unborn and, with due regard to the equal right to life of the mother, guarantees in its laws to respect, and, as far as is practicable, by its laws to defend and vindicate that right.

However, a report on the amendment by the Attorney General, Peter Sutherland, raised some questions for the Fine Gael/labour coalition that took office under Garret FitzGerald in 1983. Sutherland and others had pointed out that the wording was capable of being interpreted by the courts as not allowing any operation on a pregnant woman that might pose any risk at all to the foetus, even in cases such as ectopic pregnancy; the possibility had also been raised that the amendment might actually allow abortion, since the word 'unborn' was not defined. Although FitzGerald raised these issues the PLAC, Fianna Faíl and the Catholic Church all preferred the original wording, and the amendment went forward from the Oireachtas in that form.

The Catholic Church took the position, as it usually did on constitutional amendments, that, although Irish voters should vote in accordance with their own consciences, it was the obligation of the Church to inform the consciences of good Catholics on matters of faith and morals. Meanwhile, although the amendment had originally been intended and perceived as a cross-party initiative, Fine Gael and the Labour Party both came to oppose it, although not as actively as the Anti-Amendment Campaign, a loose collection of groups centred around Senator Mary Robinson. The opposition contained a diverse set of interests, which ran from those opposing any government having a voice in decisions about women's bodies, to those who were opposed to abortion but sought remedies in birth control and education, rather than constitutional law. The campaign was very divisive: Tom Hesketh, in his book *The Second Partitioning of Ireland*, likened it to the Irish Civil War.[4]

The result of the referendum, held on 7 September 1983 with a voter turnout of 55 per cent, was 66.9 per cent in favour of the amendment. The only constituencies that returned a 'No ' vote were in Dublin and, as in the divorce referendum in 1986, rural Ireland was overwhelmingly in support of maintaining the doctrinal position of the Catholic Church in the law.

After the referendum SPUC brought suit against clinics that offered nondirective abortion information and counselling. In both cases, Attorney General v. Open Door Counselling *et al.*, 1988, and SPUC v. Grogan *et al.*, 1989, the Supreme Court took the new anti-abortion clause (Article 40.3.3) as meaning that the Constitution protected not only the life of a specific unborn child but also the unborn in general. Accordingly, no information or advertising could be presented in Ireland about abortion, nor could information be provided about travel elsewhere for the termination of a pregnancy. The distribution of the names and addresses of abortion providers in Britain, and the means of reaching them, were thus impermissible, as any such information would assist in the destruction of the life of an unborn child.

Appeals against these decisions went to the European Court of Justice, which found in a review of SPUC v. Grogan in 1991 that a provider of abortion in a country where abortion is legal has a right to advertise in any other member state of the European Community (as the European Union was known until 1993). Moreover, in 1992 the European Court of Human Rights (which has no connection with the European Court of Justice) decided, in Open Door Counselling, Dublin Well Women's Centre and Others v. Ireland, that the European Convention on

Human Rights allowed the dissemination of information on abortion, and access to that information, in Ireland as elsewhere in Europe, since restraint on such information was an infringement of the right to freedom of expression.

These cases, and the X case discussed below, triggered the submission of three more proposals for constitutional amendments to the people of Ireland on one day, 25 November 1992. The first proposal was that the subsection on abortion (Article 40.3.3) added to the Constitution in 1983 should itself be amended by adding the words:

> This subsection shall not limit freedom to obtain or make available, in the State, subject to such conditions as may be laid down by law, information relating to services lawfully available in another state.

This amendment (now generally known as the Fourteenth Amendment) was passed with a 60 per cent majority. Conditions were laid down by law three years later, in the Regulation of Information (Services Outside the State for Termination of Pregnancies) Act 1995. This requires that all courses of action open to a pregnant woman be made available when information is provided, and prohibits direct advocacy of abortion in the course of providing information or counselling.

The other two amendments submitted to the Irish people that November developed from one of the most distressing cases brought before an Irish court in the twentieth century. A girl of 14 had been raped by an older family acquaintance. After charges were filed the girl's family sought an abortion in London, but notified the Garda that they were doing so in case medical evidence was needed for the rape charges to proceed. The Garda notified the Attorney General, who issued an injunction to prevent the girl from leaving Ireland on the basis of Article 40.3.3. By then the girl was already in Britain, but her parents complied with the order and returned to Ireland. As the girl was threatening to take her own life, her parents brought the case, X v. Attorney General, 1992, in the High Court. The Attorney General's intervention was upheld by the High Court, which based its decision on the grounds that, while it was uncertain that the girl would indeed kill herself, it *was* certain (at least in the minds of the judges) that an abortion would have terminated the life of an unborn child.

The parents of girl X sought clarification through an appeal to the Supreme Court. It decided to overturn the High Court's decision by a majority of four to one, based upon the 'real and substantial risk' to the life of the distraught girl. The decision resolved the X case but left ambiguities in the interpretation of Article 40.3.3 with respect to the question of issuing an injunction to prevent travel outside the territory of the Republic of Ireland for the termination of a pregnancy where it was unclear that there was a real and substantial threat to the woman's life. Thus one of the proposals submitted in November 1992 was that yet another clause be added to Article 40.3.33: 'This subsection shall not limit freedom to travel between the State and another state.' This clause, now known as the Thirteenth Amendment, was passed with a majority of 62 per cent.

The third proposal submitted in November 1992 dealt with the question of a threat to the life, rather than to the health, of a pregnant woman. If this amendment had been passed abortion would have been permitted, but only if

> such termination is necessary to save the life, as distinct from the health, of the mother where there is an illness or disorder of the mother giving rise to a real and substantial risk to her life, not being a risk of self-destruction.

The final phrase was understood by all concerned to be a reference to the X case. This attempt to reverse the decision of the Supreme Court failed, with 65 per cent of those voting being opposed, although it was unclear to what extent the X case affected voters' decisions, and many would have voted against any possibility of abortion on principle.

Accordingly, the criteria laid down by the Supreme Court in the X case remain operative alongside the two new clauses inserted in the Constitution in November 1992. A woman may now receive information about abortion services outside the Republic (typically, this means services in the United Kingdom), and may not be prevented from travelling abroad to have a pregnancy terminated on the grounds of a real and substantial threat to her own life, but abortion within the Republic itself is still a criminal offence.

In its report (1993) the Second Commission on the Status of Women considered the question of equality of treatment and called for legislation to guarantee equal legal status for women and men. The Commission noted that the Irish government had entered a reservation when acceding to the United Nations Convention on the Elimination of All Forms of Discrimination Against Women in 1986 to the effect that legislation guaranteeing access to financial credit and recreational service was then under consideration. The Commission also noted that existing equality legislation was confined to matters of employment and conditions of work, and had been stimulated by directives of the European Community. Guarantees of equal access to private clubs, education, contracts and property leases were not enshrined in law. The Commission advocated an Equal Status Act, an Equality Commission with powers of investigation and enforcement, and the elimination of sexist language from legislation.

Second Commission on the Status of Women, *Report to Government* (1993)

1.3 Equal status legislation

1.3.1 NEED FOR EQUAL STATUS LEGISLATION
At present the only specific legislation providing for equality between women and men is in the area of employment or on employment related issues, such as social welfare payments and pensions.

One of the consequences of this is that the Irish government, when acceding to the United Nations Convention on the Elimination of All Forms of Discrimination Against Women at the end 1986, entered a reservation in relation to Article 13 (b) and (c) of the Convention which provides for the right of equality between women and men in the right of access to financial credit and to participate in recreational and cultural activities and sports.

The Irish reservation reads:

The question of supplementing the guarantee of equality contained in the Irish Constitution with special legislation governing access to financial credit and other services and recreational activities, where these are provided by private persons, organisations or enterprises, is under consideration. For the time being Ireland reserves the right to regard its existing law and measures in this area as appropriate for the attainment in Ireland of the objectives of the Convention.

In August 1986, the then Minister of State for Women's Affairs circulated draft legislative proposals providing for the extension of equal treatment to goods, services and facilities. The matter never got any further as there was a change of Government in February 1987 and the new Government did not pursue it.

Some matters in the equality field are covered in our law through the application of E.C. directives and statute law but again these are in the area of employment and conditions of work. The Commission has made recommendations in the Work Chapter for the amendment and extension of women's rights in this area.

Constitutional and legal issues

The Commission does not accept that the existing law and measures are appropriate to eliminate all discrimination against women. Comprehensive legal rights under the law are fundamental. These rights need to be clearly embodied in legislation and must be enforced by an effective national body.

Legislation is required dealing with discrimination on grounds of sex or marital status covering areas such as education and training, the provision of goods, facilities or services, the letting or management of premises, and in general discriminatory advertising.

1.3.2 PRIVATE CLUBS OPERATING DISCRIMINATORY MEMBERSHIP POLICIES

The Commission's recommendation in our First Statement to Government (April 1991) that public funds must not be allocated to private clubs (sporting, social or recreational) which operate discriminatory policies against women (or men) aimed at withholding from them the right to apply for full membership should be reinforced. It is ironic that prominent among the membership of these clubs are Ministers, members of the Oireachtas, judges, and top public servants, who should be the very persons to ensure that discrimination on the basis of gender is eliminated from Irish society. As the Commission sees it, membership of such clubs is incompatible with public duty.

The Commission recommends that membership of such clubs

should automatically disqualify an individual from appointment to any public office, semi-state body or top-level civil service post. This recommendation should not come into effect for two years to enable any such clubs to reconsider their attitude to full membership for women. If, at that time, there are any such clubs, the Commission recommends that any statutory advantages deriving from 'club' status should be removed. This would remove their eligibility to obtain a club liquor licence and ensure that the laws of the land do not confer a benefit on blatant sexism.

1.3.3 CONTRACT COMPLIANCE

Contract compliance would require any company, Organisation or club seeking public funding or contracts to show they do not discriminate against women, either as consumers of their services or as employees. It would require companies, organisations and clubs to examine their constitutions, rules and employment practices to ensure that they are not discriminatory and to take whatever action is necessary to remove all forms of discrimination against women.

1.3.4 EQUAL ACCESS TO, AND TREATMENT IN, EDUCATION

Equality legislation should also provide that it would be unlawful for any educational establishment in receipt of public funds to discriminate in terms of admission policy, in the way it treats individuals who apply for admission, or in the way it treats individuals after they have been admitted. Exceptions would be necessary for single sex schools (as in the case of legislation in other jurisdictions) but these exceptions should only apply to admission. Equality legislation in this area should be included in the proposed new Education Act.

1.3.5 EQUAL ACCESS TO GOODS, FACILITIES AND SERVICES

It should also become unlawful for anyone involved in the provisions of goods, facilities and services to discriminate against anyone on the grounds of sex or marital or parental status.

Discrimination in this context can include the refusal of access to goods or services, failure to provide them, or the provision of inferior quality or service. The onus of proof should be on the provider of the goods or services.

Examples of the facilities and services to which the legislation might apply are as follows:

- Access to or use of any public place
- Accommodation in a hotel, guest house, etc.
- Banking, insurance, loans, grants, credit or finance
- Entertainment, recreation or refreshment
- Education facilities
- Transport or travel facilities
- The services of any profession or trade or any public or local authority

1.3.6 LETTING OF PREMISES

The legislation would also need to make it unlawful for a person who lets premises or is involved in the management of premises, to discriminate on the basis of gender or marital status in any of the following ways: in relation to aspects of a tenancy, in rejecting or accepting applications for the premises, in his/her treatment of individuals, in relation to lists of people in need of that kind of premises. An exception would have to be made where a person is letting part of their own home.

1.3.7 OTHER ISSUES

The Commission has dealt with advertising in Chapter 8. In Chapter 3 the Commission has recommended that equal pay legislation and employment equality legislation should be codified in a consolidated Act. A number of desirable amendments to the employment equality legislation are set out in that chapter.

1.3.8 RECOMMENDATIONS

The Commission recommends that:

(a) an Equal Status Act providing for equal treatment of women and men vis-à-vis the provision of goods, facilities and services be enacted;

(b) under the proposed Equal Status legislation it should be unlawful to discriminate against any individual on the grounds of sex, marital, or parental status;

(c) the obligation of providing reasonable access to information held by the person who is alleged to have discriminated, as recommended in work related cases (see Chapter 3), should apply to all cases of alleged discrimination;

(d) membership of private clubs, sporting, social or recreational, which operate discriminatory policies against women aimed at withholding from them the right to apply for full membership, should be designated as incompatible with any public or semi-

State appointment or top level Civil Service appointment; this provision to take effect in two years;

(e) any statutory advantages deriving from 'club' status should be removed from such clubs; this provision to take effect in two years;

(f) the Government should request the Equality Commission to draw up guidelines for the introduction of contract compliance which would require any company, Organisation or club seeking public funding or contracts to show they do not discriminate against women, either as consumers of their services or as employees.

1.4 Equality Commission

1.4.1 PROPOSED EQUALITY COMMISSION

As has been stated above, the rights set out in broadly based equal status legislation must be enforced by an effective national body.

The United Nations, the Council of Europe, and the European Commission have identified four key factors governing such bodies. They are:

- the level within the government structure at which the national machinery or body operates
- its political support, authority, competence, and access to power
- its resources in terms of information, expertise, staff, finance and management
- its capacity to establish and maintain links with government departments and nongovernmental organisations.

The present equality legislation in the area of employment is enforced through the Employment Equality Agency, which also has the function of working towards the elimination of discrimination, and promoting equality of opportunity between men and women in relation to employment; keeping the employment equality legislation under review, and making proposals to the Minister for Labour (Employment Equality Act 1977, Section 35). The Employment Equality Agency constitutes an already existing, experienced Organisation dealing with equality enforcement and promotion in the field of employment. Rather than setting up an entirely new body, it would be both logical and economically desirable to extend the mandate of the Employment Equality Agency to cover all equality issues and to re-name the extended agency The Equality Commission. The Equal Opportunities Commission in Britain has this wide function covering both employment and general status.

At present, the Employment Equality Agency, although a statutory body, operates under the aegis of the Department of Labour. Members of the agency are appointed by the Minister for Labour and the agency is staffed by civil servants from the Department of Labour.

The proposed Equality Commission would have a much wider brief, no longer confined only to issues relevant to the Department of Labour. The British Equal Opportunities Commission operates under the Home Office, which is in some respects parallel to the Department of Justice, but has a wider function in respect of a number of miscellaneous bodies. The Commission feels that the Department of Justice would, like the Department of Labour, be somewhat too limited in its scope to be the relevant department for the Equality Commission.

Until the separate Department of Women's Affairs is set up (as recommended in Chapter 7) the Commission regards the Department of the Taoiseach as being the most suitable Department of State under which the Equality Commission should operate. The Department of the Taoiseach has the necessary wide scope and is the Department within which the Minister for State for Women's Affairs and the present Commission operate. Expertise on equality matters has already been created within that Department.

Membership of the Board of the Equality Commission should be broader based than that of the Employment Equality Agency in order to reflect its enlarged role, and should not be weighted, as at present, in favour of employment related bodies.

While the members of the Equality Commission should be appointed by the Taoiseach, it would be desirable that the members should, as in the case of the Employment Equality Agency, include representatives of relevant bodies such as Irish Congress of Trade Unions, the Irish Business and Employers Confederation, and the Council for the Status of Women. The number of nominating bodies should be widened.

The proposed Equality Commission should be given an independent status with regard to the recruitment of its own staff, comparable, for example, to that of the Pensions Board.

1.4.2 ENFORCEMENT OF EQUALITY LEGISLATION

In the enforcement of antidiscrimination legislation in cases which are not work related, the Commission does not propose any encroachment on the present roles of the equality officers and the

Labour Court under existing legislation. In particular it would see the equality officers being called on to investigate and make recommendations in cases which did not deal with employment. The present system has a proven track record and is functioning well in its own area of expertise. Therefore, a different method of enforcement of rights in the non-employment field would have to be set up. However, in the allocation of resources within the Equality Commission it would be important to ensure that no one aspect of discrimination should be unduly favoured. In the enforcement procedure for non-work related cases, the Commission would favour a two tier approach. First, there should be a level where complaints are dealt with on an informal basis akin to the Ombudsman, or the Mediation Service in family cases, or by a different type of equality officer. If satisfaction is not obtained at this level on a voluntary basis, there should be a right of recourse to an Equality Tribunal with power to enforce an award.

It would be important in the enforcement of rights under the proposed new legislation that the operation of the Legal Aid Scheme should be extended to include cases brought under it.

1.4.3 PROMOTION OF EQUALITY

It would also be appropriate to have a separate division in the Commission charged with the promotional aspects of eliminating discrimination. If there is not a clear demarcation within the Commission, those who are or might be respondents in an equality claim are likely to feel a constraint in working with the Commission on a voluntary basis in its promotional role. On the other hand, if there is a separate division, communications can be made on a 'without prejudice' basis so that a potential respondent will not feel compromised by any negotiations.

1.4.4 OPERATION OF THE EQUALITY COMMISSION

In summary, the proposed Equality Commission should be:

- an independent semi-state body;
- financed properly to carry out all of its functions;
- autonomous in relation to staffing and structures and with adequate finance to employ staff to carry out the range of functions laid down; with an appropriate career structure to develop and maintain expertise in the equality area, e.g. making use of the services of a mix of career public servants and fixed duration contract employees.

Its functions should include research, legal enforcement (either by itself or by means of assisting individual applicants), monitoring, and the provision of information and advice in relation to all aspects of equal rights covered by equal status legislation. It would also have a role in promoting equal opportunity policies at company and employment sector levels and in tackling barriers to women in specific sectors of employment.

The Commission would refer to the recent establishment of the Labour Relations Commission as a model for the development of the Equality Commission and its transition from the present Employment Equality Agency.

1.4.5 RECOMMENDATIONS

The Commission recommends that:

(a) the Employment Equality Agency should be reconstituted as the Equality Commission;

(b) the mandate of the Equality Commission should cover the enforcement of the proposed Equal Status Act as well as employment equality legislation;

(c) the Equality Commission should be an independent semi-state body operating under the aegis of the Department of the Taoiseach at first, and later of the Department of Women's Affairs;

(d) members of the Equality Commission should be appointed by the Taoiseach;

(e) the membership of the Equality Commission should reflect a wider spectrum than the present composition of the Employment Equality Agency;

(f) the Equality Commission should be given the power to appoint its own staff,

(g) the Equality Commission should be provided with sufficient resources to enable it to carry out its mandate in an effective way;

(h) the Equality Commission be established under the terms of the proposed Equal Status Act, not later than January 1, 1994;

    (i) the procedure for enforcement of rights under the extended equality legislation should be on a two-tier basis:

    (i) an informal conciliation procedure;

    (ii) a hearing before an Equality Tribunal whose awards would be legally enforceable.

1.10 Administration (Elimination of sexism from Acts of the Oireachtas and official forms)

1.10.1 AMENDMENT OF INTERPRETATION ACT

Section 11 (b) of the Act reads as follows:

Masculine and Feminine
Every word importing the masculine gender shall, unless the contrary intention appears, be construed as if it also imported the feminine gender. The converse of this does not apply, however. There is no provision in the Act for being able to construe the feminine gender as also importing to the masculine.

The consequence of this is that it is not possible at present to use the feminine gender in Acts or instruments of the Oireachtas which will primarily affect women.

The Commission believes that this section of the Interpretation Act as presently drafted is sexist and can contribute to stereotyped and limiting images of the respective roles of women and men.

The Commission recommends that the Interpretation Act 1937 should be redrafted with a view to:
(a) ending discriminatory and unnecessary gender-specific language in Bills, Acts and instruments of the Oireachtas, for example, by using s/he and chairperson;
(b) enabling the adoption of the feminine gender in legislative measures clearly and primarily addressed at women.

The Government responded to the recommendation on language in 1993 with the Interpretation (Amendment) Act, which requires the use in legislation both of gender-neutral language, and of the feminine gender as importing to the masculine and vice versa.

In 1994 a new government called for the creation of an all-party Joint Committee of both houses of the Oireachtas to review the Constitution (along the lines of the Committee that reported in 1967, quoted earlier in this chapter). The Joint Committee was to begin its work by examining a report on all aspects of the Constitution by a review group of experts. In the course of its discussion of Article 40.1 – with its provision that 'All citizens shall, as human persons, be held equal before the law' – the Review Group examined the question 'whether there should be a separate provision expressly guaranteeing equality between women and men'.

Constitutional Review Group, Report of the Constitutional Review Group (1996)

When women do enter paid employment they are disproportionately represented in the lower-paid and insecure areas of the labour market: 72% of all part-time workers are women and 85% of the lowest-paid part-time workers are women (see Blackwell, J. and Nolan, B., *Low Pay – The Irish Experience*, in B. Harvey and M. Daly, *Low Pay: The Irish Experience*, Dublin 1990, p. 11; EEA, op. cit, pp.. 13–14). At the other end of the employment spectrum, men occupy the senior posts in most private and public sector organisations, and, in all, 86% of employers are men (EEA, op. cit, pp 43-50; McCarthy, E., *Transitions to Equal Opportunity at Work in Ireland*, EEA, Dublin 1988; Central Statistics Office, *Labour Force Survey 1993*, Stationery Office, Dublin 1995). Men own most of the land in Ireland with 90% of farm holders being men; and women's dependency is reflected in both the tax and social welfare codes (see Second Commission on the Status Of Women: *Report to Government*, 1993).

The nature and scale of inequality between women and men are not unique to Ireland. It is a universal experience and historically has been a feature of most known societies. This fact is increasingly gaining worldwide recognition, and explicit provision has been made in the constitutions of several countries for equality between men and women (see, for example, Article 3(2) of the Basic Law of Germany). Such provisions are generally understood not only to afford protection against discrimination on the basis of sex but also to open the way for *de facto* equality between the sexes and to legitimise positive measures to accelerate the process. The advancement of the equality of the sexes has been accepted as a major goal by European states, and active consideration is currently being given by the member states of the Council of Europe to the adoption of an additional protocol to the European Convention on Human Rights whereby this equality would become an independent, justiciable human right.

Arguments for a separate provision
1. The historical and cross-cultural evidence of pervasive inequalities based on sex suggest that such inequalities need to be addressed at the constitutional level if they are to be overcome.
2. It would accelerate *de facto* equality between women and men.
3. Inequalities based on sex are increasingly being addressed in

international human rights instruments and in the constitutions of other countries.

4. It would have an important symbolic value since it would send out a message that women's continued subordination to men in so many institutions and systems is unacceptable and should be redressed.

Arguments against

1. It is invidious to include a special provision which addresses inequality on the basis of sex but not on other grounds.
2. Article 40.1 in the recommended revised form guarantees equality before the law for all individuals. This includes equality between men and women. If a separate express guarantee of equality between the sexes were included this might suggest that the general guarantee was not intended to be all-embracing and weaken its impact.

Conclusion

A majority of the Review Group does not regard it as necessary to have an express guarantee of equality between men and women having regard to the general guarantee of equality before the law and the prohibition on discrimination.

Although the Review Group recommended against the insertion into Article 40.1 of a specific reference to gender alone, it did recommend the insertion of the following clause:[5]

No person shall be unfairly discriminated against, directly or indirectly, on any ground such as sex, race, age, disability, sexual orientation, colour, language, culture, religion, political or other opinion, national, social or ethnic origin, membership of the travelling community, property, birth or other status.

This change was not made, and the issue of equal status reverted to being a matter to be addressed in ordinary legislation. In 1996 the *Second Progress Report of the Monitoring Committee on the Implementation of the Recommendations of the Second Commission on the Status of Women* indicated that 'Equal Status legislation is being prepared by the Minister for Equality and Law Reform'. The objective of the legislation was to broaden earlier anti-discrimination acts by prohibiting discrimination in non-employment areas based upon sex, marital status or sexual orientation. The Equality Act 1998 forbade all forms of discrimination and, influenced by the proposal of the Second Commission on the Status of Women for an 'Equality Commission' (quoted above), it also set up the Equality Authority, which replaced the Employment Equality Agency, to monitor and enforce the Act.

In due course the Equal Status Act 2000 amended the Employment Equality Act 1998 to extend its coverage access to all 'goods' (articles of movable property) and to a variety of services and facilities – financial, recreational and professional. In doing so the Act eliminated Ireland's reservation to Article 13(b) and (c) of the United Nations Convention on the Elimination of All Forms of Discrimination Against Women (also quoted above).

CHAPTER SIX

Violence and abuse

The agenda of women's issues was clearly expanding in the 1970s and 1980s. Topics not mentioned or not developed very extensively by the first Commission on the Status of Women (1972) were emerging as women's groups began to identify a range of policies beyond the workplace or social welfare that treated women unequally. They drew attention to the absence of laws and policies that would protect women from practices no longer considered tolerable, such as domestic violence, as well as the continuing presence of barriers that deprived women of opportunity, such as the 'glass ceiling'.

The fact that the first Commission did not mention the issues of domestic violence and rape indicates the degree to which the Commission was predominantly concerned with equality of treatment under the law. It was the appearance of rape and domestic violence on the agendas of women's movements abroad that brought the topic to the attention of the Irish women's movement. As Yvonne Galligan has noted:[1]

Violence against women emerged as an issue from 1968 onwards...Activists in this area were open to the experiences of women in other countries, particularly Britain, as contact was sustained between women working on this problem in both countries.

The law on rape in Ireland at that time was the Offences against the Person Act, passed by the British Parliament in 1861, which defined rape as 'unlawful carnal knowledge without a woman's consent' and made it punishable by life imprisonment. It also prevented the charge from being brought against the husband of a complainant, or against any boy under 14. The Criminal Law (Amendment) Act 1935 had confined the imposition of a life sentence to those convicted of the rape of a woman under 17 or of a woman who was mentally deficient. Thus the usual charge in rape cases was indecent assault, with a maximum sentence of two years.[2] The underlying assumptions were that rape was basically a sexual crime; and that the exclusion of husbands from the law implied that women were the 'property' of males and that the woman's wishes had no place in the sexual relationship.

A reform of the rape law in Britain in 1976, and the coverage of some high-profile cases of abuse in Ireland itself, prompted the Council for the Status of Women (CSW) to prepare a report, *Submission on Rape in Ireland*, which was completed in 1978. This report stated that 'the concepts which underlie the crime of Rape are outdated and no longer appropriate to the society in which we live'.[3] It called for a broadening of the definition of rape to include all forms of penetration, thus recognising the violence and brutality of rape, which was not simply conventional sexual penetration. It also called for the criminalisation of rape within marriage, thus challenging the conventional sexual notion of rape, recognising the violent character of the act and upholding a woman's right to oppose forced sexual acts even from her own husband. It sought reforms of the way in which women who alleged rape were treated; measures to ensure the complainant's anonymity; and the exclusion of evidence of her prior sexual history.[4] This report laid out what became the basic agenda for reform of the rape laws, although it would be some years before they were reflected in legislation.

It was also in 1978 that the Campaign against Rape was formed and began to lobby for changes in the law. In 1979 this group was relaunched as the Dublin Rape Crisis Centre (RCC), with the twin goals of assisting rape victims and lobbying for reform of the law on rape. In 1980 the RCC issued a report that echoed the call for reforms already made by the CSW two years earlier.

Although the governments of the day indicated their sympathy with at least some of the proposals for reform, the first official action taken on the issue was a debate on the CSW's report in the Seanad (Senate) in 1979. A private bill introduced into the Seanad by Senator Gemma Hussey in 1980 was not supported by the government of Charles Haughey. That government did, however, introduce a bill in 1980 that was intended as a modification of the Acts of 1861 and 1935. The words 'carnal knowledge' were to be changed to 'sexual intercourse'; the age and mental deficiency provisions of the 1935 Act were to be eliminated; and provisions were made for greater privacy for alleged victims in rape trials and for the exclusion of certain evidence on a woman's sexual history. However, the proposal to include other forms of penetration and other orifices was ignored, and rape within marriage was also omitted. The bill formed the basis for the Criminal Law (Rape) Act, passed in 1981. Women's groups saw the Act only as a step on the way to further reform because they were dissatisfied with the absence of the provisions mentioned above. The RCC set out to change the 1981 Act right from the start, although it took nearly a decade to get another Act passed.

The Working Party on Women's Affairs and Family Law Reform (1985) had little to say on the issue of rape, as it expected the Department of Justice to undertake a study of the issue. The RCC then made a submission to the Joint Committee on Women's Rights of the Oireachtas (Parliament), which undertook a study of all aspects of rape and issued a report, entitled *Sexual Violence*, in 1987.[5] This report stated that the main defects in the existing legislation involved failure:

(a) to define rape in its broadest sense, to include oral sex, buggery, and the use of objects such as sticks, bottles and other articles to violate a women's vagina. (b) to protect the anonymity of the victim. (c) to restrict the admissibility of irrelevant evidence as to the complainant's past sexual history. (d) to protect the complainant from feeling she is 'on trial' and that she is being 'raped' again in court. (e) to criminalise rape in marriage.

Accordingly, the Joint Committee called for a redefinition of rape to include serious sexual assault; the extension of the concept to include rape within marriage; and more sensitive administrative and judicial procedures for dealing with alleged victims.

Joint Committee on Women's Rights, *Sexual Violence* (1987)

Conclusion

In recent years women's lack of status in society has been questioned by many concerned groups and individuals and there is now a greater awareness of the need to eradicate all existing inequalities between the sexes. Nevertheless there still remains a reluctance on the part of many people to acknowledge the injustices that are still perpetrated on women in all areas of life today. This reluctance can be detected even in instances where injury and suffering has been caused to women such as by rape or other serious sexual offences. With regard to crimes of sexual assault on women one frequently hears the claim made that the responsibility for a rape rests on the woman. The actions of the assailant seem to escape severe censure. Against such a background the members of the Joint Committee realise that there is still much work to be done in educating people to acknowledge that a woman does not ask to be raped, and that every rape committed is a base and brutal violation of her person and must be punished by the rigours of the law.

The recent *Report of the Committee of Inquiry into the Penal System* (the Whitaker Report) concluded that much of the law dealing with rape and indecent assault is 'vague, and uncertain'. The members are convinced that the law as narrowly defined in existing legislation is too restrictive in its definition of rape and that serious sexual assaults such as those described in Page 8 of this *Report* [not included] should be included in a new and broadened definition of the crime. The pain, humiliation and trauma suffered as a result of assaults of this kind are no less than what is suffered as a result of rape, as defined in current legislation; indeed they can often be a lot more severe because of the unnaturalness of the practices used by an offender to achieve the domination of his victim.

The members were concerned to learn that there is an increasing number of younger males committing rape. The members have already referred to the fact that boys under fourteen years of age cannot be charged with rape and they are concerned that these boys should be made amenable to the law as otherwise they will continue, as many of them now do, to commit sexual offences in their adolescent and adult years. The members wish therefore to underline what they have said previously i.e. that boys who commit rape should receive a custodial sentence and while in detention receive the necessary professional and medical counselling to enable them to resume useful and crime free lives.

Under existing legislation the consent of a wife to intercourse with her husband is presumed always to be present. In other words there is an irrebuttable presumption that a man cannot rape his wife. Furthermore, in Ireland, for centuries, great emphasis was placed on the sacramental aspect of marriage. Women were so influenced by their religious teaching and upbringing that many of them believed it to be sinful if they refused to consent to have intercourse no matter what the prevailing domestic environment might have been.

It is the experience of those who are working with and counselling families in distress that at present many wives who are subjected to violence in the home claim that in addition to physical beatings they are frequently forced to have sex by their husbands. It is difficult to put in words what the feelings of a wife must be when a violent and perhaps drunken husband subjects her constantly to forced sexual intercourse. An act that should signify tenderness, love and unity between the couple becomes, in such circumstances, a brutal imposition of suffering on the woman. Research carried out in this particular area confirms that women raped by husbands are often traumatised at the most basic level – in their ability to trust. The violation touches a woman's basic confidence in forming relationships and trusting intimates. It can leave her feeling much more powerless and isolated than if she were raped by a stranger. (*Rape in Marriage – A Sociological View* – D. Finkelhor and K. Yello. Current Family Violence, Research Sage Ltd. 1983.)

The members of the Joint Committee are aware than many people would be reluctant to interfere in the relationship between a husband and wife. On the other hand, it would be very wrong to close one's eyes to what is known to be happening to wives who live in violent domestic surroundings. These women must be given adequate protection by the law and one of the means of doing so is by abolishing the present immunity of a husband under the existing rape legislation. If society continues to regard rape in marriage as less serious than statutory rape, it contributes to a climate where husbands feel they can indulge in sexual violence with impunity. The aim of any reform must be to ensure that a woman, on marriage, does not lose her existing protection from sexual violence.

The members have referred to the embarrassment that a woman will experience during garda investigations, which up to recent times were invariably conducted by the male members of the force, who were themselves somewhat uncomfortable in carrying out this particular duty. With the recruitment of additional women into the force and their role, where possible, in questioning the victims of rape, there are now less inhibitions on a woman to come forward and relate her experiences. The members, while acknowledging that the Gardai carry out their duties with tact and sensitivity, would nevertheless like to be reassured that the training programmes, including in-service training, for the force will always include courses dealing with the plight of rape victims so as to ensure that the gardaí are well informed on how to handle cases properly, particularly with reference to the treatment and questioning of victims. The members agreed that lectures by outside counsellors and medical personnel experienced in the field, should be a regular feature of the training programme for both recruits and commissioned officers.

It has to be recorded however that there is not sufficient training provided for doctors in dealing with cases of rape and serious sexual assault. Doctors who are at present working with victims of rape have expressed concern at the situation. It is imperative that all doctors be adequately trained in this area and the members call on the country's medical schools to provide the necessary training. At a time when the incidence of serious sexual assault is increasing, it is unsatisfactory that medical students continue to graduate, with at best, a very scanty knowledge of the treatment of rape victims. The members agreed that the medical schools should ensure that sexual assault, including rape, will become a permanent subject in the medical curriculum. Until such time as there is concerted action by the Department of Health, Health Boards and the Schools of Medicine to ensure a sufficiency of qualified medical personnel located in all areas of the country, the majority of women who are raped will have to suffer the consequences of that indignity without the support of proper medical advice and attention.

The members have referred at length to the question of child sexual abuse and they would appeal to the Government and particularly to the Minister for Health to implement their recommendations at the earliest possible date. Having regard to the serious emotional problems that sexually abused children are likely to carry into adolescence and adulthood, unless they are detected and treated at an early stage, it is imperative that properly-equipped treatment centres with all the necessary back up services be set up on a countrywide basis. The members emphasise that in their opinion expenditure incurred in providing these facilities will be instrumental in obviating the need to incur much greater expenditure in the future, if the problem is not tackled now as a matter of national priority. No single group or administration can respond in isolation to child sexual abuse. It is a community problem and must be confronted on a united basis by all the concerned agencies. Rape is a brutal and degrading crime and its serious consequences must be understood by all sections of society. Those who commit rape must be made to realise that their conduct will not be tolerated by society. The members are of the opinion that all responsible elements in the community can help in reducing the incidence of rape. They can do this by according to women the dignity and respect they are due in their own right as human beings, in every sphere of social and economic activity, and encouraging others to do likewise. Equality between the sexes has still to be achieved in this country despite the many laudable expressions of support for it one hears from time to time and the existence of equality legislation. The reality is that until such time as we have established a society where all citizens will be treated equally, men who regard themselves as the dominant sex will continue to inflict pain and humiliation on women through various forms of violence and abuse, including rape.

The debate that is now taking place regarding the crime of rape will increase an awareness of the problem among the general public. For too long society in Ireland closed its eyes to the plight of rape victims; often the woman was blamed for contributing to the rape and she was left to suffer alone with feelings of guilt and remorse. That situation is now beginning to change. The members of the Joint Committee trust that the publication of this report, the resultant debate in the Houses of the Oireachtas and the implementation by the Government of the recommendations contained therein, will:

(1) ensure a greater measure of protection and support for the victims of rape and serious sexual crimes.
(2) act as a strong deterrent to potential rapists and other sexual offenders.
(3) help in establishing a better environment in which men and women will feel safer in business, in social life and in the home itself.

The new Fianna Fáil government that took office in 1987 called for further study of the topic by the Law Reform Commission, which produced a report, *Rape and Allied Offences*, in 1988.

The preliminary version of this report had recommended that the definition of rape be left as established in the Criminal Law (Rape) Act 1981 (discussed above), engendering a strong political response from women's groups, notably at a conference in January 1988 at which two thirds of the written submissions were in favour of extending the definition.[6] The recommendations of the Commission in the published version of its report were in line with those of the CSW and the RCC, with a few added touches, such as the idea of financial compensation for the victim. in particular, the Commission recommended that the definition of rape should be expanded; that two categories of crime, 'sexual assault' and 'aggravated sexual assault', should replace the existing category of 'indecent assault'; and that increased protection should be given to the rights and privacy of complainants in court.

Law Reform Commission, *Rape and Allied Offences* (1988)

Summary of Conclusions

1. The presumption of incapacity of boys under the age of fourteen in prosecutions for offences involving sexual intercourse should be abolished.
2. The crime of rape should be defined by statute so as to include non-consensual sexual penetration of the major orifices of the body, i.e. the vagina, anus and mouth, by the penis of another person or of a person's vagina or anus by an inanimate object held or manipulated by any other person and in this form the crime should be capable of being committed against men and women.
3. Two new offences – sexual assault and aggravated sexual assault – should replace the present offence of indecent assault.
4. The new offence of aggravated sexual assault should be generally defined to cover serious forms of sexual assault, not covered by rape, attended by serious violence or the threat of serious violence or calculated seriously and substantially to humiliate, violate, injure or degrade the victim or committed while the accused has with him a firearm or weapon of offence or by a person in a relationship of authority over the victim. The offence should carry the same sentence as rape, i.e. life imprisonment. The offence should apply equally to assaults on men and women without any difference in procedure.

5. The new offence of sexual assault should encompass the less serious sexual assaults but should be undefined. It should be an indictable offence but should only be prosecutable on indictment at the election of the prosecution. The maximum penalty on indictment for sexual assault should be five years. The offence should apply equally to assaults on men and women without any difference in procedure.

6. All the procedural and evidential provisions of the Criminal Law (Rape) Act 1981 relating to trials for rape should apply equally to trials for aggravated sexual assault and sexual assault.

7. The word 'consent' in section 2 of the 1981 Act should be defined so as to make it clear that physical resistance is not a necessary element in proving absence of consent.

8. Legislation should remove the marital exemption in cases of rape.

9. Section 3 (1) of the 1981 Act (which requires an application by the accused to the court before questions can be asked concerning the previous sexual history of the complainant) should be amended so as to require an application under it in respect of questions relating to sexual experience of a complainant with the accused. Applications under section 3 (1) should normally be made at the commencement of the trial in the absence of the jury.

10. The present rules as to the anonymity of the complainant should be retained but should be extended to prosecutions for all sexual offences.

11. The protection of anonymity should not be removed from defendants.

12. Prosecutions for rape and aggravated sexual assault should be tried exclusively in the Central Criminal Court.

13. Sexual offences should not be tried in public. Five categories of persons should be admitted to the trial:
    (a) a limited number of family members and friends of the complainant as well as of the accused;
    (b) the media;
    (c) law reporters;
    (d) in particular cases, and with the leave of the court, persons carrying out research of a criminological or other scientific nature;
    (e) practising members of the legal profession, subject to such limitations as the court may impose.

14. There should be an express statutory provision enabling a judge to order the accused on conviction to pay compensation to the victim of a sexual offence in addition to any other penalty imposed.
15. There should be no time limits for prosecutions for sexual offences.
16. There should be no change in the law relating to the composition of juries for the trial of sexual offences.
17. Section 4 of the Criminal Law Amendment Act 1935 should be amended by replacing expressions such as 'idiot' and 'imbecile' with expressions more appropriate to describing the mentally handicapped and incapacitated.
18. It should no longer be mandatory for the judge in trials of sexual offences to warn the jury of the danger of convicting on the uncorroborated evidence of the complainant. Whether such a warning should be given and, if so, its terms should be left to the discretion of the judge.
19. The present law prohibiting disclosure of previous convictions of the accused should be maintained even when he has been permitted to cross-examine the complainant about his or her previous sexual history.
20. Provision should not be made for separate legal representation of the complainant.
21. Certain administrative changes should be made designed to alleviate the distress of the complainant.

General scheme of a Criminal Law (Rape) Act

1. Provide that the Act may be cited as the Criminal Law (Rape) (Amendment) Act 1988.
2. Provide that Section 2 (1) and (2) of the Criminal Law (Rape) Act 1981 be amended by:
   (a) substituting the word 'connection' for 'intercourse' and 'person' for 'man and woman';
   (b) defining 'sexual connection' as:
      (i) penetration, however slight, of the person's vagina, mouth or anus by another person's penis or of a person's vagina or anus by an inanimate object held or manipulated by any other person otherwise than for bona fide medical purposes;
      (ii) continuation of such connection.
3. Provide that a new subsection (3) be added to s. 2 defining 'consent' for the purposes of the Act as in Section 324G of the

Western Australia Criminal Code with appropriate adaptations.

4. Provide that being married to the victim at the relevant time shall not afford a defence to a charge of rape.

5. Provide that (except by special leave of the court) an application under s. 3 (2) of the Act may be made only at the beginning of the trial immediately after the arraignment of the accused, and that any evidence as to previous sexual experience of the complainant which it is proposed to adduce must be adduced at that time to the judge in the absence of the jury.

6. Provide for the amendment of s. 3 of the Act so as to require the leave of the court for the adduction of evidence or the cross-examination of the complainant as to any previous sexual experience of the complainant with the accused.

7. Provide that, notwithstanding any rule of law to the contrary, it shall not be necessary for the judge in the trial of a rape offence to warn the jury of the danger of convicting the accused on the uncorroborated evidence of the complainant.

8. Provide that, notwithstanding any rule of law to the contrary, it shall not be presumed in prosecutions of boys under the age of fourteen for offences involving sexual connection with the penis that the accused was incapable of committing the offence with which he is charged.

9. Provide that the words 'a sexual offence' be substituted for the words 'a rape offence' throughout the Act.

10. Provide that the words 'sexual offence' be defined so as to include rape, aggravated sexual assault and sexual assault and to include attempting, aiding and abetting, counselling and procuring and inciting to commit rape, aggravated sexual assault or sexual assault.

11. Provide for the abolition of the offence of indecent assault on males and females and the creation of two new statutory offences of sexual assault and aggravated sexual assault on males and females.

12. Provide for the definition of aggravated sexual assault as a sexual assault which is not rape but which is attended by serious violence or the threat of serious violence or is calculated seriously and substantially to humiliate, violate, injure or degrade the victim or is committed while the accused has with him a firearm or a weapon of offence or by a person occupying a position of authority over the victim.

13. Provide that, if warranted by the evidence given at the trial,
    (a) on a count of rape, a jury may find an accused guilty of attempted rape, of aggravated sexual assault or of sexual assault;
    (b) on a count of aggravated sexual assault, a jury may find an accused guilty of rape or of sexual assault.
14. Provide that sections 3, 4, 6, 7, 8, and 9 of the Act and section 7 of this Act shall apply to sexual assault and aggravated sexual assault in the same manner as they apply to rape.
15. Provide that if a person is convicted on indictment of any aggravated sexual assault upon a male or female he shall be liable to imprisonment for life.
16. Provide that if a person is convicted on indictment of any sexual assault upon a male or female he shall be liable to imprisonment for a term not exceeding five years.
17. Provide that the District Court shall have jurisdiction to try summarily offences of sexual assault where the Director of Public Prosecutions so elects.
18. Provide that where a person is convicted summarily of a sexual assault, he shall be liable to a fine not exceeding IR£1,000 or, at the discretion of the court, to imprisonment for a term not exceeding 12 months or to both such fine and such imprisonment.
19. Provide that rape and offences of aggravated sexual assault shall be triable on indictment only in the Central Criminal Court.
20. Provide that, where a defendant pleads guilty in the District Court to rape or aggravated sexual assault, the District Justice shall send him forward for sentence to the Central Criminal Court.
21. Provide that rape and aggravated sexual assault shall be tried otherwise than in public, but that the following categories of person shall be permitted to attend:
    (a) the immediate family and a limited number of friends of the complainant and of the accused;
    (b) accredited representatives of the press, television and radio;
    (c) members of the legal profession acting as court reporters;
    (d) such persons engaged in research as the court may permit;
    (e) practising members of the legal profession subject to such restrictions as the court may impose.
22. Provide for the payment of compensation to victims of rape, aggravated sexual assault and sexual assault.

23. Provide for the amendment of s. 4 of the Criminal Law Amendment Act 1935 by substituting for the words 'any woman or girl who is an idiot, or an imbecile, or is feeble minded' the words 'any woman or girl suffering from mental handicap' and provide for any consequential amendments of the Act.

The lobbying of the RCC and others was successful, as a bill submitted in 1988 included provisions for the elimination of the exemption for boys under 14, and for the inclusion of rape within marriage and the new categories of assault. However, the Minister for Justice preferred not to adopt the Law Reform Commission's revised recommendation on broadening the definition of rape. The final draft of the legislation finally did change the definition of rape by including two broad categories of offences, the first similar to the traditional definition of rape and the second covering other offensive acts of violence and penetration.

In 1990 the resulting legislation, the Criminal Law (Rape) (Amendment) Act, was passed by the Oireachtas. It seemed to satisfy all the constituencies concerned, even though it did not meet all the demands of any group.[7] The Act provides that failure to resist does not imply consent; spouses can be charged with rape; no irrelevant past sexual history can be included in the evidence; and the Act also provides for life sentence for rape. Two issues still remained on the agenda of women's groups: whether the complainant should have independent legal counsel, as the accused did; and what sentence was appropriate for those convicted under the Act.

In its report (1993) the Second Commission on the Status of Women made recommendations on unresolved issues, in particular on providing more legal aid to complainants, on making the sentencing of rapists more uniform and on resolving discrepancies between sentences.

Second Commission on the Status of Women, *Report to Government* (1993)

1.6.6 RAPE TRIALS

The Commission welcomes the close and effective liaison between Rape Crisis Centres, Garda Síochána and health professionals which has led to the development in recent years of sympathetic and sensitive procedures in the event of rape being reported.

The Commission also welcomes the enactment of the Criminal

Law (Rape) (Amendment) Act 1990 which, drawing on the 1988 Law Reform Commission's report, *Rape*, inter alia, extended the definition of rape, defined rape within marriage as a crime, and ensured that rape would be dealt with in the High Court.

One major unresolved issue surfacing in submissions was that the complainant (victim) in a rape case should have the right to her own legal representative. The basis for this argument is that a woman complainant may find the rape trial even more of an ordeal if she is treated merely as a means to an end, i.e. the prosecution of the accused. A woman's impression of a rape trial may be that nobody present is expressly interested in maintaining her good name.

Having considered the question of separate legal representation for the complainant, the Commission has reached the view that in an adversarial legal system such as ours, this suggestion is not feasible. In our decision the Commission shares the view of the Law Reform Commission in its report *Rape* (1988). The arguments for and against separate legal representation for the complainant are set out cogently in the Law Reform Commission's Report.

Under an amendment to the Civil Legal Aid Scheme introduced by the Minister for Justice under Ministerial Policy Directive No. 1 of 1991, where legal proceedings have commenced in respect of alleged offences of rape and aggravated sexual assault, legal advice may now be given under that scheme in connection with criminal proceedings to victims of rape and sexual assault. However, in view of the under-funding of the Legal Aid Scheme, few women are likely to benefit from this legal advice. The Commission would prefer to see a system initiated whereby separate legal advice is given as a matter of course to a complainant through the Office of the Director of Public Prosecutions (DPP) prior to the trial.

The Commission fully supports the need for sensitive and reassuring treatment of the complainant in what is bound to be a distressing experience for her. The Commission recommends that the following approach should be taken in rape trials:

(a) the Director of Public Prosecutions should separately brief a legally qualified person to attend a consultation with the complainant prior to the trial to inform and advise her of the Court procedures involved in the trial and her participation therein with a view to rendering the experience less traumatic;

(b) that immediately prior to the trial, as a matter of course, the complainant should be given a copy of her statement to the gardaí;

(c) that the Department of Justice should commission and publish a standard booklet explaining all the circumstances attending the investigation and prosecution of sexual offences, with particular emphasis on the role of the complainant as witness. The booklet should be routinely provided to the complainant.

1.6.7 SENTENCING IN RAPE CASES

In the public perception, there is a wide discrepancy on the sentencing for rape not readily explicable by the circumstances of the case as reported, as well as a perception that the rape of a man is treated as a more serious offence than the rape of a woman.

It is important that society at large and judges in particular (since it is they who pass sentence) should be conscious of the fact that rape is a crime of violence and hatred against women. It is not the result of an overwhelming sex urge and, therefore, excusable in some way. 'Date rape' and rape by a stranger are equally traumatic for a woman, and date rape should not be treated as a lesser offence.

However, public perception alone is not an adequate basis on which to formulate legal policy. It is necessary to gather statistics in regard to sentencing so that a data base is established. A brief summary of the facts and mitigating factors (if any) taken into account would also be necessary. Since all rape trials now take place in the Central Criminal Court, the gathering of such statistics should not be a difficult task. If over a reasonable period of time, the statistics disclose a continuing and unacceptable discrepancy, the Government should consider introducing a minimum mandatory sentence.

Another aspect of sentencing which requires attention is the fact that where an accused man is found guilty by a jury or pleads guilty to rape, the effect of the crime on the victim is outlined in hearsay evidence. The woman should be entitled to bring forward evidence relating to the ill effects she has suffered, if that is her wish.

Consideration should also be given to setting up regular seminars for judges, keeping them abreast current social scientific and psychological research on the significance of rape for both victim and offender. In this way it is to be hoped that sentencing would be carried out from an enlightened basis of current knowledge.

The Commission welcomes the reforms proposed in the Criminal Justice Bill 1992, as announced on 2 October 1992. In particular we welcome the measures to review unduly lenient sentences, and the obligation to be placed on courts, when determining sentences for sexual and violent offences, to take into account the effect on the victim.

The Commission recommends that:

(a) a monitoring mechanism should be set up in the Central Criminal Court to gather statistics about sentencing for rape;

(b) if the statistics disclose an unacceptable discrepancy, the Government should consider introducing a mandatory minimum sentence;

(c) before sentencing, the victim should be entitled to bring forward evidence as to the effect on her of the crime, if she so wishes;

(d) seminars should be organised on a regular basis for judges to keep them informed of up-to-date knowledge on the subject.

1.6.8 CHILD SEXUAL ABUSE

As with domestic violence generally there is likely to be considerable under-reporting of the incidence of child sexual abuse, although there has been an increased awareness of the problem and the need to respond to it in recent years. It is a feminist issue since more girls are sexually abused than boys (see 1990 Law Reform Commission Report). The Commission believes it is important to establish clear guidelines in cases of child sexual abuse or suspected abuse so that persons in positions of authority, e.g. teachers, doctors, gardai, to whom the individual case becomes known, have clear procedures to follow. To some extent the 1987 Department of Health guidelines address these issues. Mandatory reporting of suspected incidences of child sexual abuse, as recommended in the 1990 Law Reform Commission Report, is supported by the Commission.

The Commission calls for:

(a) implementation of the provisions in the Child Care Act 1990 related to protection and care of abused children;

(b) action on the recommendations of the Law Reform Commission's Report of September 1990 on Child Sexual Abuse;

(c) clear instructions and training for teachers at primary and second level on the appropriate steps to take if a suspected incidence of child sexual abuse comes to their attention;

(d) the establishment of a module on child sexual abuse in GP training;

(e) dissemination throughout the country of the Eastern Health Board's 'Stay Safe' programme, a preventive education programme for children on child sexual abuse.

The sense of dissatisfaction with the sentences in some high-profile rape cases led to the creation of a working party to investigate violence against women and children. Its report, issued in October 1996, was blunt in its conclusion: 'Essentially the non-implementation of each and every one of the recommendations contained in this report will represent a continuation of the failure of the judicial process to provide justice for women and children.'[8] The Working's Party recommendations included further refinement of the definition of rape; additional protections for complainants in the procedures of the gardaí (police) and courts; and a call for separate legal representation for the complainant. As with the Second Commission, the Working Party called for research on the sentencing patterns in rape and sexual assault cases. The last recommendation of the Working Party was for a National Commission to review the legal framework relating to sexual and other crimes against women and children.

A Task Force was set up to examine the issue of violence against women, with a special emphasis on domestic violence; it reported in 1997. At this point the emphasis in public policy was shifting away from rape and sexual violence toward the broader, interrelated issues of domestic violence and abuse of children (we shall consider these issues below.) The report of the Task Force included a section on rape and sexual assault that outlined the current status of rape law and legal procedures, and then assessed what still needed to be addressed. The report noted the small proportion of rape cases being reported to the gardaí – estimated at about one in five – and directed attention to the manner in which complainants should be treated in order to encourage victims of rape to come forward in greater numbers.

Report of the Task Force on Violence against Women (1997)

Problems with existing law and procedures

9.26 As outlined above, research has shown that women do not report cases of rape and sexual assault for fear of the way that their case is likely to be handled by the gardaí and Courts. They fear, for example, being disbelieved; humiliated and embarrassed by inappropriate questioning; re-victimised/traumatised by Gardai and the courts handling the case; and lack confidence in the willingness or ability of the gardaí to take appropriate action. While there have been real improvements in the response of the Garda in recent years, the majority of women who are raped still do not report it, despite the support and encouragement received from the Rape Crisis Centres.

9.27 Generally the member of the gardaí to whom the initial report of rape is made will not be the member in charge of the investigation. Such investigations are invariably undertaken by a team experienced in crime investigation. Having obtained all the evidence available, advice is then sought from the DPP (Director of Public Prosecutions) concerning the bringing of charges against the suspect. While it is accepted that investigations must be conducted in a thorough manner, it is of vital importance to the victim that the response of the gardaí be one of support, understanding and reassurance. Liaison should be maintained with the victim concerning the progress of the investigation. The Task Force accepts that some gardaí do liaise with the victim and it considers that this should be standard practice.

9.28 From a victim's point of view, she may feel that there is no guarantee her complaint will be properly dealt with and that all relevant evidence relating to the alleged offence will be gathered. Once the victim has made her statement to the gardaí, the victim often has difficulty in ascertaining whether the case is going to proceed. In some cases, she is not advised of a trial date; that the accused has agreed to plead guilty; is not given any advice as to what to expect in court; and is sometimes not given copies of her statement before the hearing. She has almost no opportunity to meet the solicitor or the barrister for the prosecution – for most complainants, their only contact with the prosecution is a hurried discussion shortly before the start of the trial.

9.29 In this context, the Task Force recommends that the gardaí should be given the task of liaising with the alleged victim. The complainant would be given the name of the gardaí who will be investigating the case and s/he should be available to her, at reasonable times, to advise her as to the progress in the case. She should be kept fully informed of

(i) the appropriate information contained in the book of evidence,

(ii) the reasons for any delays in progressing the case and

(iii) should have the opportunity to be present in court, even in cases where the accused proposes to plead guilty. She should be given a copy of the statement she made to the gardaí as a matter of standard procedure/practice and of any victim impact report. The complainant should also be facilitated to have consultations with prosecution counsel both before and throughout the trial such consultations should cover the nature and procedural arrangements for the proceedings.

SEPARATE LEGAL REPRESENTATION FOR VICTIMS

9.30 The question of separate legal representation for rape victims has been addressed on a number of occasions in recent years. Most recently the arguments for and against the issue were spelled out in the *Report of the Working Party on the Legal and Judicial Process for Victims of Sexual and Other Crimes of Violence against Women and Children*. The Task Force considers that the arguments put forward in support of separate legal representation for rape victims in that report are compelling but recognise that regard must also be had to the practical and constitutional implications in implementing the proposal. As has already being pointed out, the primary focus of the Task Force is on the issue of domestic violence and, therefore, it did not have the expertise available to it to come to any definitive conclusion on this matter. In the circumstances, the Task Force recommends that this matter, which is of such importance to victims of rape, should be addressed by the Department of Justice in the forthcoming *Discussion Paper on Sexual Offences*. It is understood that the Department hopes to publish the Paper in the near future.

SENTENCING POLICY

9.31 The Task Force considers that custodial sentences should be applied in all cases of rape. Only in cases of a wholly exceptional nature should non-custodial options be considered. It is also considered that sentencing policy should, in appropriate cases, include the option of a period of post-release supervision by the Probation and Welfare Service.

9.32 The Task Force recommends that it should be also practice in all cases that victims of domestic violence, rape and sexual assaults are notified by the prisons or Gardai that the unescorted release of an offender is anticipated or has taken place.

DELAYED COMPLAINT

9.33 In some rape/sexual assault cases, a woman may not make a complaint for a number of months after the incident taking place.

In circumstances where the issue of any delay that may have occurred is raised, the Task Force considers that it should be compulsory for the judge, in appropriate cases, to warn the jury that there may be valid reasons as to why she did not complain immediately following the incident.

VICTIM IMPACT REPORTS

9.34 For the purpose of determining sentencing in sex offence cases, the onus is on the judge to request Victim Impact Reports. The quality and content of such reports can vary depending on, for example, whether the complainant is receiving professional counselling or other services. The complainant can give oral evidence in relation to the impact of the offence. Such reports cannot be extracted, however, in circumstances where witnesses are unwilling or uncooperative.

9.35 On the whole, the Task Force considers that the introduction of Victim Impact Reports has been a positive development. The Task Force recommends that Victim Impact Reports be requested for trials (as happens at present) and for appeals, and that a list of suitably qualified professionals should be available to the court in cases where the victim is not attending a professional therapist. In cases where the victim disagrees with the content of the Report, this should be brought to the attention of the judge.

RAPE CRISIS CENTRES

9.36 Rape Crisis Centres provide a range of counselling and therapy, both individual and group, for women and men who are victims of rape, sexual assault and child sexual abuse. Services available can vary in different Centres. There are 15 Rape Crisis Centres located around the country. Services provided by each centre focus predominantly on counselling both by telephone and on a face-to-face basis to victims of recent or past rape, sexual assault and to victims of child sex abuse.

9.37 The Dublin Rape Crisis Centre provides a 24 hour crisis telephone service for victims of rape and sexual abuse. In 1995, a total of 6,100 calls were made to the Centre's 24-hour Crisis Line, 2,273 (37%) were repeat callers and 83% of all calls were from women.

9.38 Training for companies in the management of preventing sexual harassment within the workplace is provided. It also has a comprehensive training and education service which runs courses for professionals who come in contact with victims of sexual violence in their work.

9.39 Special counselling centres for victims of rape and sexual abuse have also been established by the Eastern Health Board in Blanchardstown, Clondalkin, Clontarf, Coolock and Tallaght.

9.40 In 1991, the Government decided that funding for Rape Crisis Centres be channelled through the Health Boards. In 1996, this funding amounted to IR£907,000. The Department of Health discussion document *Developing a Policy for Women's Health* states, 'the funding of these centres has been made as secure as the budgetary cycle of Government finances permits'.

COUNSELLING AND OTHER SUPPORT SERVICES

9.41 The Task Force considers that counselling and other support services should be made readily available to women throughout the country who have recently, or at some time in the past, been the victims of rape and sexual assault. The services available and the personnel operating within the services should be aware of the specific cultural and other needs of marginalised groups.

CONCLUSIONS

9.42 As outlined at the beginning of this chapter, the number of rape cases reported to the gardaí is relatively small as, given the nature of rape and sexual assault cases, it is inherently difficult to encourage women to come forward. Often when women do come forward, they feel like they are on trial. The recommendations of the Task Force are designed to encourage more women to report cases of sexual violence to the gardaí. The principal recommendations relate to liaising with the victim, conditions for granting of leave to cross-examine regarding a complainant's past sexual history and Gardai policy on the treatment of victims of rape, sexual assault and other sexual offences.

Recommendations

PRIORITY RECOMMENDATIONS

- The Garda Síochána should develop and publicise clear policy and practice with regard to the treatment of victims of rape, sexual assault and other sexual offences;
- once a decision is made to prosecute in a rape/sexual assault case, the task of liaising with the victim should be assigned to the investigating gardaí. Victims should also have regular consultations with counsel before and throughout the trial and should be given a copy of their statement made to the gardaí and of any Victim Impact Report, as a matter of course; and

- leave to cross-examine a complainant regarding her previous sexual history should only be granted where it is proven to the court that the evidence is substantially relevant to the facts at issue, as envisaged in the 1981 Act, as amended; the law and practice in relation to this area should be reviewed so as to ensure that the strict legal criteria, as laid down in the 1981 Act, as amended, are being adhered to.

OTHER RECOMMENDATIONS

- Expert training should be provided on a national basis to gardaí on the initial aspects of handling cases of rape, sexual assault and other sexual offences;
- it should be practice in all cases that victims of domestic violence, rape and sexual assaults are notified by the prisons or gardaí that the unescorted release of an offender is anticipated or has taken place;
- in cases of a delayed complaint, where this is raised as an issue, it should be compulsory for the judge in appropriate cases, to warn the jury that there may be valid reasons as to why she did not complain immediately following the incident;
- custodial sentences should be applied in all cases of rape. Only in cases of a wholly exceptional nature should non-custodial options be considered. Sentencing policy should include, in appropriate cases, the option of a period of post-release supervision by the Probation and Welfare Service; all rules of law or practice relating to the judge's charge to the jury as to the assessment of uncorroborated evidence of complainants in all cases of sexual assault should be abolished and the cases should be dealt with in the ordinary manner;
- information regarding counselling and support services should be made readily available to all rape and sexual assault victims;
- Victim Impact Reports should be requested for both trials and appeals and a list of suitably qualified professionals should be available to the court in cases where the victim is not attending a professional therapist; where a victim disagrees with the content of the Report, this should be made known to the judge; and
- the question of separate legal representation for rape victims should be addressed by the Department of Justice in the forthcoming *Discussion Paper on Sexual Offences.*

In their *Report* published in October 1996, the Working Group on the Legal and Judicial Process for Victims of Sexual and Other

Crimes of Violence against Women and Children made over 30 recommendations with regard to rape and sexual assault. This Task Force welcomes the fact that these recommendations are being actively considered by the Department of Justice at present and that a *Discussion Paper on Sexual Offences* is being prepared. This Paper will provide an appropriate backdrop to a further review of the adequacy of the law on sexual offences against women.

DOMESTIC VIOLENCE AGAINST WOMEN

Like rape, domestic violence was not mentioned in the report of the first Commission on the Status of Women (1972). Although the issue was widely recognised in legal circles, it was slow to come onto the national agenda. Violence against a wife was prosecutable under the Offences against the Person Act 1861, under which 'the protection was the same as that given to an individual assaulted by a stranger'.[9] However, another Victorian statute, the Married Women (Maintenance in Case of Desertion) Act 1886 was interpreted by the judiciary as meaning that when men had hurt their wives they could be treated as having deserted them and be made subject to maintenance orders.

The issue emerged little by little as women, who had long been reluctant to talk about violence in the home, began to speak out to women's groups and journalists. Women's Aid was founded in 1974 to provide refuge to battered women in Dublin. In 1976 the Family Law (Maintenance of Spouses and Children) Act was passed, making provision for the issuing of barring orders to abusive husbands preventing them from visiting their home. The patchy enforcement of the barring orders, reflecting the reluctance of the gardaí (police) to intervene in domestic disputes, served only to illustrate both the difficulty involved with controlling abusive men and how widespread the problem was. Citing the Family Law (Protection of Spouses and Children) Act 1981 as offering one of the few remedies available, the report *Irish Women: Agenda for Practical Action* (1985) addressed the issue of domestic violence and called for more training to deal with it; more awareness at all levels, from the general public to government officials; and the creation of more centres for battered women.

Working Party on Women's Affairs and Family Law Reform, *Irish Women: Agenda for Practical Action* (1985)

Violence against women not new phenomenon

4.103 Public debate on violence against women is not new. The issue of violence against wives surfaced repeatedly in the latter half of the nineteenth century in Britain, partly as a result of concern about the level of violence in working-class life generally and partly arising from publicity surrounding a number of specific cases which led to agitation for improvements in the status of women. The women's movement – then as now – saw wife assault as a crucial aspect of oppression against women, to be removed only through far-reaching changes in the rights of women generally. Until quite recent times, marriage and property laws upheld the rights of the husband over the wife who was seen as part of his property. Indeed, until very recently in this country, a husband could take action in court against any person harbouring his wife against his wishes.

Research in this area

4.105 As stated above, little research has been done on the subject of violence against women. Research done in Northern Ireland (confined to single parents) indicated that violence against women in marriage could not be dismissed as an isolated problem. Indeed it was seen as a fairly common feature of husband/wife relationships. (The author emphasised, in this regard, that the data from the Northern Ireland study was very much in line with the conclusions of the most recently published information from Britain.) The data showed that, in occupational terms, it was difficult to see any difference between violent and nonviolent males. Also, the data did not support the popular assumption that unemployment is a major cause of woman battering. With regard to 'warning' signs prior to marriage, for the overwhelming majority of battered women, the violence commenced only after the marriage. The popular stereotype of the indecisive, battered woman who cannot leave her husband and goes backwards and forwards was undermined by the data. While many women did leave and return home for many reasons, the majority of battered women had been separated for more than two years. Also, 95% of the battered women supported a democratic model of marriage rather than a model where the husband is dominant. Violent husbands, however, were nearly twice as likely as nonviolent spouses to be reported as supporting the traditional model of male dominance. In terms of frequency and nature of wife assault, battering in the majority of cases meant at least one attack every seven days. As to what provoked the attacks, the largest category of responses suggested that the violence occurred when a woman failed to do as her husband wished, questioned his actions or challenged his authority. As regards the stereotype of the 'cycle of violence' from one generation to the next, this particular survey could find no grounds for according this thesis the prominence it has in some of the literature. Finally, as to sources of support, the main pattern followed was to turn initially to the family, with over half of the women reporting that they received help from their immediate family. Friends and neighbours played a much less important role, as did clergymen, and social workers. Over half of the women had sought assistance from doctors and the majority were positive about the help received.

Legislative measures available

4.106 Turning to legislative, administrative and other measures to prevent abuses, the main existing legislative provisions are as follows:

(I) FAMILY LAW (PROTECTION OF SPOUSES AND CHILDREN) ACT 1981

The Act amends the law, as previously contained in Section 22 of the Family Law (Maintenance of Spouses and Children) Act 1976, dealing with barring orders, that is, orders excluding a spouse from the family home, usually because of violence. It enables a spouse, while awaiting the Court's decision on a barring order application, to obtain an injunction-type order, called a protection order, which directs the other spouse not to use or threaten to use violence against the applicant spouse or children or to molest them or put them in fear. Breach of a protection order, like breach of a barring order, is a criminal offence. The Act confers a power of arrest without warrant on the gardaí for breaches of barring orders and protection orders. In addition, if a person charged with breach of a barring order or protection order is given bail and then commits one or more breaches while on bail, any sentences of imprisonment imposed for the breaches will have to be served consecutively. The Act also extends the maximum duration of a barring order which can be made by the District Court from three to twelve months, and gives the court greater flexibility in dealing with the applications for barring orders.

(II) THE CRIMINAL LAW (RAPE) ACT 1981

This Act amended the law relating to rape and indecent assault on women and girls. On rape, the Act restricts the admissibility of evidence about a woman's previous sexual history and prohibits, as a general rule, the publication of the name or other identifying particulars of the rape complainant. The Act increased to ten years the maximum penalty for indecent assaults on women and girls.

(III) THE COURTS ACT 1981

The Courts Act 1981 made changes in the various jurisdictions of the Courts in family law matters, with the result that a problem which might hitherto have meant several applications to different courts, because of the diffusion of family law jurisdictions throughout the court structure, may now have all its different facets dealt with together in one application and in the lower courts.

(IV) FAMILY HOME PROTECTION ACT 1976

The main purpose of the above Act is to prevent a spouse who owns a family home from selling or otherwise disposing of it without the consent of the other spouse (unless the need for consent is dispensed with by Court order on the grounds that, in all the circumstances of the case, the refusal to consent is unreasonable).

Protective measures

4.107 Health Board Community Care Teams provide support services to all families in need. The position regarding shelters for women and children who are victims of family violence is that there are now refuges in the four main centres of population. Refuges are planned for three more towns. These refuges are run by voluntary agencies and are grant-aided by the regional Health Boards who keep the situation under constant review. They operate on diverse lines with little uniformity but all of them offer alternative accommodation to women and children who want to get away from violent homes. A range of support services is also provided in conjunction with statutory and other voluntary organisations. A Federation of Family Refuges has recently been founded. Each of the existing refuges is affiliated and links have been established with areas where residential accommodation is at a planning stage. A standard form is also being compiled for use by each of the organisations included to facilitate the collection of data at national level. There are Rape Crisis Centres, run by voluntary bodies, in the main centres of population. These provide a counselling and support service which includes legal and medical arrangements for women who have been raped or sexually assaulted. They have, in certain cases, received State grants through the Health Boards and from the budget of the Minister of State for Women's Affairs.

Concern at international level

4.108 At an international level, increasing concern is being paid to the problem of family violence. A recent United Nations Economic and Social Council resolution (1982/22) called on Member states to take immediate and energetic steps to combat the social evils associated with family violence and the UN is presently compiling a study based on the reports of member states. The last World Conference of the United Nations Decade for Women (1980) also adopted a resolution on 'battered women and violence in the family' in which states were urged to adopt measures to protect the victims of family violence and to implement programmes whose aims are to prevent abuse as well as to provide centres for the treatment, shelter and counselling of victims of violence and sexual assault and to provide other services such as alcohol and drug abuse rehabilitation, housing, employment, child care and health care.

The Council of Europe has already undertaken an initiative in relation to violence in the home.

Recommendations

4.109 The Working Party has considered the various points arising in the context of support for victims of family violence and puts forward the following recommendations:

(i) Specialist training for those involved in the administrative functions of family disputes is essential.

(ii) Public opinion should be alerted to a greater extent than at present to the extent and characteristics of violence in the family with a view to obtaining its support for measures aimed at combating family violence. Women's groups already play a role here but State Departments/Agencies play a stronger role in this respect. This would involve the dissemination of information (already done by the Department of Health in relation to non-accidental injury of children) among relevant groups concerning social and family relations, early detection of potentially conflicting situations and the settlement of inter-personal and intra-family conflicts. 'Relevant' groups should include schools. The education for relationships programme referred to earlier in the chapter would be the context in which this aspect of male/female relationships could be brought up. Adult marriage preparation courses should also cover this aspect, with couples being encouraged to see marriage as an equal partnership.

(iii)The Northern Ireland study demonstrates the crucial importance of refuges for battered women. The Women's Aid

Report supports this view, stating that 'the need for a shelter offering short-stay refuge to women will always exist'. These provide women with an opportunity to recover from their experience and help them prepare for a decision about their future. It is difficult to predict in any precise way the demand for places in these refuges. A Select Committee on Violence in Marriage in Britain recommended that there should be one family place per 10,000 population. In the context of this country's provision, it is impossible from existing data to know what the needs are. There are refuges operating throughout the country being aided largely through the Health Boards. As with other services, however, the help given will vary from one Health Board area to another resulting in an inconsistent pattern of provision. It is recommended that the Department of Health should undertake an early review of the total volume of provision and need in the country.

(iv) Many women will be forced eventually, after sustained periods of family violence, to set up home separately with their children. Local authority agencies will need, in the Working Party's view, to take greater account of the housing needs of these women in formulating their housing policies. In the Northern Ireland study, the majority of the women had eventually moved into Housing Executive property, having firstly moved in with relations or friends before getting their own accommodation. Apart from the difficulty of finding suitable housing, these women face the problem faced by single parents generally, finding employment or simply meeting the basic necessities of life. These issues are dealt with in greater detail in the chapter on single parents.

The takeover of the Dublin Women's Aid Centre by the Eastern Health Board provided a model for the creation and funding of other refuges for battered women in other parts of Ireland, with the support of the other regional health boards. A bill to provide relief for abused wives did not gain sufficient support in 1987. Meanwhile, increasing amounts of information were becoming available as pressure groups, notably AIM (Action, Information, Motivation) and Women's Aid, lobbied for changes in the Family Law (Protection of Spouses and Children) Act 1981, and studies on domestic violence, such as Maeve Casey's *Domestic Violence against Women: The Women's Perspective*,[10] revealed the depth of the problem.

In 1991 Women's Aid sought to secure the implementing of three reforms with respect to domestic violence: that the gardaí could arrest at the scene; that people cohabiting be brought within the scope of the law, in addition to married people; and that the abused spouse have access to legal aid. The report of the Second Commission on the Status of Women (1993) expressed support for the second of these proposed reforms.

Second Commission on the Status of Women, *Report to Government* (1993)

1.6 Violence against women
1.6.1 DOMESTIC VIOLENCE

Domestic violence against women is the intentional physical abuse or threat of physical abuse to a woman, in a manner that causes physical injury or pain, by the male partner with whom she lives or has lived in the recent past or by a male member of her family. It is essentially an abuse of power.

Because of its nature, it is very difficult to get an accurate assessment of the extent of domestic violence in Irish society. What can be ascertained is its reported incidence, when circumstances become so bad that the Garda Síochána are called in and/or family members seek refuge away from the family home. In 1987, the Garda Síochána reported about 500 'family row' calls a month in the Dublin Metropolitan area seeking their help. Hostels/refuges in Dublin, Cork, Limerick and Galway reported admitting 496 families leaving situations of domestic violence in 1987.

Domestic violence tends to have the following characteristics:

- men who batter are likely to come from homes where battering occurred:
- battering is stress-related, linked to such problems as financial and relationship difficulties, to unemployment etc;
- battering is linked to alcohol abuse (analysis suggests that in Ireland drink is the major factor in at least one-third of all domestic violence cases and is an element in up to half the cases presenting themselves);
- social isolation increases the risk of battering;
- spouse abuse and child abuse are inter-related.

Men who batter tend to have low self-esteem, to hold a rigid view of masculinity, and have poor impulse control.

The Commission notes that the current review of garda procedures and training in cases involving violence, including violence
against women, is expected to be completed shortly. The
Commission welcomes this initiative and generally welcomes the
dialogue and co-operation which has grown in recent years
between women's organisations providing support services to
battered women and their children, and the Garda Síochána.

1.6.2 DOMESTIC VIOLENCE: REDRESS UNDER THE LAW

Irrespective of the factors causing domestic violence, when it
emerges into the public sphere, it emerges at a time of crisis. With
regard to such situations the Family Law (Protection of Spouses and
Children) Act 1981 provides redress, mainly through barring and
protection orders which are granted by the District Court on the
application of a spouse, if the Court believes that the safety or
welfare of the spouse and any children warrants such an order. At
present protection orders are not available in their own right but are
granted ex-parte (i.e. an application by one side only) as a
preliminary step towards barring orders. The Family Law (Protection
of Spouses and Children) Act 1981 only applies within marriage. It
does not apply to violence between cohabitees, nor does it apply to
other instances of family violence, e.g. sons abusing mothers. In
those cases the battered person must apply for an injunction in the
Circuit or High Court, which is an expensive procedure,

Under the Constitution the family is the family based on
marriage. Since many households do not conform to this definition,
the Commission believes that the question of widening the
definition of family should be referred to the Law Reform
Commission to consider whether the protection afforded by the
Constitution to the marital family should be extended.

1.6.3 EFFICACY OF LEGAL REDRESS

While forms of legal redress exist for domestic violence, there is a
perception, reinforced by submissions received by the
Commission, that they are inadequate to deal with crisis situations.
When the Garda Síochána arrive at a family home in response to
a request for help, they cannot, for example, charge the assailant
with common assault unless they either witness such an assault
taking place or the victim makes a formal complaint on oath at the
station, which many are reluctant to do. Neither can they remove
the assailant from the family home if a barring or protection order
is not already in force.

This means that the woman concerned and her children can be left feeling that the law affords them no protection. At a time of her greatest vulnerability there is no practical support available to her apart from the drastic step of leaving her home. At the same time a bullying husband or partner can be reinforced in his belief that she is his property to be used and abused as he sees fit.

The Commission believes that in these kinds of crisis situations it is important to afford the battered person mental and physical relief, and peace of mind, at least temporarily. One remedy would be an amendment to the Family Law (Protection of Spouses and Children) Act 1981 so that in those crisis situations a member of the Garda Síochána could use her/his judgement to apply ex parte for a protection order and, if it is disobeyed, remove the offender from the family home. Because the incidence of domestic violence is higher at weekends and holiday periods the Commission believes it is important to have a sitting District Court on weekends and bank holidays which could process such applications. These kinds of protection orders should be available to relatives and partners who are victims of aggressors as well as to spouses.

1.6.4 RECOMMENDATIONS

The Commission recommends that the Family Law (Protection of Spouses and Children) Act 1981 should be amended to provide for the following protections:

(a) protection orders should be available as a remedy in their own right when barring orders are not available. This would provide a measure of protection for a woman cohabitee, living with a man on his property;

(b) barring orders are at present available only to married couples; they should also be available where the person seeking the order is the owner or tenant of the property; a woman who owns her own house or is a named tenant should be able to eject a violent partner;

(c) protection orders should be available as a remedy in all cases of domestic violence e.g. cohabitation, mother/son, brother/sister relationships, etc;

(d) in crisis situations the Garda Síochána should be empowered to initiate an ex-parte application for a protection order; at present it is only the spouse who can initiate such an order; this should be available for all cases of domestic violence, not just violence between spouses;

(e) there should be sittings of the District Court at weekends and bank holidays to cope with a higher incidence of domestic violence at these times.

The Commission also recommends that the question of extending the constitutional definition of the family should be referred to the Law Reform Commission for examination.

1.6.5 COUNSELLING SERVICES

Both protection orders and barring orders are essentially a response to an emergency situation – where the safety or welfare of a spouse or child is at risk because of the conduct of the other spouse. These orders may provide immediate relief from danger, but they do not resolve the problems that clearly exist in the marriage and family relationship.

The victim of continued violent behaviour needs assistance through counselling and advice. In many cases the violent spouse could also benefit from counselling to enable him to understand the roots of the violence and assist in its prevention in the future. Where alcohol is a factor, proper treatment and counselling for both perpetrators and victims is also vitally important. Participation in counselling by offenders might be taken into account by the District justice when considering the renewal of barring orders.

If the marriage has in fact irretrievably broken down, a barring order does not deal with the many other issues which will arise concerning children, maintenance and property. The couple in this position could be counselled as to the availability of mediation services, legal aid and advice, etc.

Both perpetrators and victims should be fully informed about the availability of counselling. This could well be done by District Court Clerks and Circuit Court Registrars who normally have contact with the parties or their legal advisers in these cases. Information could also be made available through Law Centres. The counselling service itself could be provided through the Probation Service, possibly with the back-up and assistance of the Community Care service of the relevant Health Board. Increased resources will need to be provided to fund a counselling service.

The Commission recommends that:
(a) counselling services should be available for both victims and offenders in domestic violence cases. Responsibility for providing counselling could rest either with the Probation Service or the Health Boards under the Community Care system;
(b) the District Court Clerk should inform offenders and victims about the availability of counselling.

In 1995 the government brought forward a bill on domestic violence that was intended to address the issues raised by the various reports and groups. This bill became the Domestic Violence Act 1996. Its provisions included: 'strengthening the powers of arrest of police authorities in domestic violence incidents; extending the law to give cohabitees protection from a violent partner and giving parents protection from violent children over 18 years of age; making safety orders available as an alternative to barring orders; and providing health boards with the powers to apply for protection orders on behalf of adult and child victims of domestic violence'.[11]

While the law was thus being strengthened, Women's Aid issued a call for a more comprehensive approach to domestic violence, aimed at prevention rather than punishment, in its publication *Making the Links* (1995).[12] One result of the ensuing debate was the creation of a task force to develop a national strategy on violence against women. Its report, issued in April 1997, focused on developing an approach based on information, education, training and intervention, as much as on the law and legal remedies.

Report of the Task Force on Violence against Women (1997): Executive Summary

Background

Responsibility for services in relation to violence against women is divided between a number of different Government Departments. Successive studies and reports such as the Federation of Refuges Policy Document on Women's Refuges, the Women's Aid study *Making the Links*, and the Report of the Working Party on the Legal and Judicial Process for Victims of Sexual and Other Crimes of Violence against Women and Children (a Working Party of the National Women's Council whose work was funded by the Department of Justice), have underlined the importance of welding the separate response of the different public agencies into a coherent national strategy.

Violence against women, in particular domestic violence, emerged as a major issue in the consultation process on the Department of Health's *Policy Document on Women's Health*. This followed on from the national survey in 1995 on domestic violence conducted for *Making the Links* which indicated the widespread incidence of violence against women, and its prevalence in all social classes and regions.

Against this background, the Government in October 1996 set up the Task Force on Violence against Women chaired by Minister of State, Eithne Fitzgerald, T.D., and asked the Office of the Tánaiste to coordinate its work. The membership of the Task Force was drawn from the relevant Government Departments and public agencies, including Garda, health board and local authority representation, as well as experts from the voluntary sector.

Focus of report
The main focus of the report is on domestic violence, as most attacks on women are in this category. This violence is a recurring problem, not once-off attacks, and it leaves its scars on children growing up in violent homes as well as on the women.

Several public and voluntary agencies are addressing separate aspects of the problem e.g. refuges provide emergency accommodation; the health boards fund refuges and provide services to children at risk; the gardaí have a pro-arrest policy in cases of domestic attack; the criminal and civil justice system apply sanctions to offenders; housing authorities provide accommodation to those who have to leave home. These different players in the public and voluntary sectors could work much more effectively if they coordinated their efforts and welded their separate responses into a coherent and coordinated approach.

In this context, the report puts forward comprehensive proposals for the development of coordinated and coherent services for women who have experienced, or have been threatened with, violence. In addition, proposals are also put forward for the development of :

- intervention programmes for perpetrators of violence; and
- preventative strategies to address the root causes of the problem.

Chapter 2: Developing a national strategy
The Task Force calls for the development of a National Strategy based on two fundamental principles:

- a total acceptance that violence against women is wrong, it is a criminal offence and there is neither an acceptable nor tolerable level of violence;
- neither society nor the judicial system should ever regard violence inflicted on a woman by a man she knows as less serious than violence inflicted by a stranger.

NATIONAL STRATEGY – KEY ELEMENTS

Seven key elements in developing a comprehensive national strategy are identified:

- the development of a comprehensive range of services for women and children which offer a safe and friendly environment in which abuse can be disclosed and tackled;
- ensuring the ready availability of accurate advice and information so that women who have experienced, or who have been threatened with, violence know the options open to them and are empowered to make informed choices;
- the adoption by service providers in the community, voluntary and statutory sectors of agreed policies, principles of good practice, written procedures, and training programmes;
- taking the needs of marginalised women always into account in the implementation of policy and practice;
- the establishment of mechanisms to enable service providers to work together to provide a gateway to specialist advice, information and practical help;
- the provision of consistent and effective responses by the judicial system that recognise the seriousness of attacks against women, promote women's confidence in the system, and make perpetrators accountable for their violent behaviour;
- putting preventative strategies in place, including the development intervention programmes for offenders and public education programmes, which challenge both the root causes of violence against women and the climate in which it can be tolerated, trivialised or even encouraged.

Chapter 3: Domestic violence – nature and extent

NATURE

Domestic violence refers to the use of physical or emotional force or threat of physical force including sexual violence, in close adult relationships. In the majority of incidences of violence or sexual assault against women the attacker is known to the woman and is likely to have or have had an intimate relationship with her. Such violence occurs in all social classes and is equally prevalent in both rural and urban Ireland.

EXTENT

The existence and extent of violence against women was until recent times, largely hidden within Irish society. In recent years however, the prevalence of violence has come more into the open.

In 1995, Women's Aid commissioned the Economic and Social Research Institute to conduct a national survey on violence against women. The results of the survey were published in its report *Making the Links*. The survey showed that:

- 7% of women had been abused in the previous year by a partner or an ex-partner;
- 18% of women had been abused at some stage of their lives;
- 10% had experienced physical violence. One third of these reported violence during pregnancy, and over a third reported attempts to strangle and choke them; multiple forms of abuse were common.

The prevalence of violence against women is also borne out by calls to various agencies:

- 8,000 calls a year to Women's Aid;
- 6,000 calls in 1996 to the Garda Domestic Violence and Sexual Assault Unit;
- 2,000 barring orders granted. 4,500 applied for [August 1994–July 1995];
- 860 arrests and 506 convictions in relation to domestic violence in 1996;
- 6,100 calls to Dublin Rape Crisis Centre in 1995 [1996 statistics not yet available].

BARRIERS TO WOMEN IN DEALING WITH VIOLENCE

The Task Force points out that women face a variety of psychological and physical barriers in trying to deal with violence in relationships. Many women also feel that existing services are incapable of responding to their needs. They feel that the legal and court systems minimise the seriousness of crimes committed against women, fail to dispense justice and make women feel at fault for what has happened.

The Task Force concluded that it is clear from the statistics available that the problem of violence against women, in particular domestic violence, is widespread and requires an effective response both in terms of service provision and preventative strategies. To determine future policy and service development there is also a need to compile more accurate and comprehensive statistics on the nature and extent of the problem.

Chapter 4: Seeking help – the options

Violence in a close adult relationship is not a once-off occurrence – it is a process. Responses, therefore, cannot be once-off but must be a continuous process of support and assistance, tailored to the needs of the woman at any point in time. Services for women and their children need to offer immediate safety from violent attack, practical advice and support to live free from violence and harassment, together with aftercare support and counselling.

Women suffering from, or threatened with, violence and abuse need both emotional and practical supports. In this context, the Task Force explored how, and to whom, a woman may disclose violence and identified the range of supports that she may need. In particular, the need to provide readily accessible information and advice, and a woman-centred approach to service delivery is stressed. This will help to ensure that women can disclose violence, know the options open to them and make informed choices about their own future and that of their children.

RECOMMENDATIONS

The current service operated by Women's Aid should become the National Freephone Helpline, operated on a 24 hour basis, 7 days a week, by trained staff, with guaranteed multiannual funding. The help line should develop a computerised Bed Bureau in conjunction with the National Federation of Refuges and other homeless services;

- Appropriate 'one stop' centres providing information and advice on the options and services available to women and children experiencing violence should be identified in each local area.
- Information regarding the National Helpline should be advertised throughout the country through the national and local press, and by posters displayed in public places such as Garda Stations, Hospitals, GP Surgeries, Community Welfare Offices, Legal Aid Centres, Health Centres, Post Offices, Supermarkets, etc.

Chapter 5: Personal safety and the role of the Garda Síochána

The Garda Síochána are often the first point of contact for women in crisis situations. The Task Force believes that the response of individual gardaí is central to an effective strategy to deal with domestic violence. The Force has a written policy on Domestic Violence Intervention, which is published as an appendix to this report [not included]. The gardaí pro-arrest policy is very important as it sends strong messages to both the abuser and the victim.

The statistics available suggest that the gardaí policy may not be implemented in a consistent manner in all Gardaí districts. In this context, the Task Force calls for an Assistant Commissioner to be given responsibility for ensuring consistency in the implementation of policy in all gardaí districts and that gardaí are given appropriate training to enable them to effectively fulfil their role in this area.

RECOMMENDATIONS

PRIORITY RECOMMENDATIONS

- The implementation of gardaí policy in relation to domestic violence, rape and sexual assault needs to be monitored to ensure consistency in implementation between individual gardaí and between various gardaí Districts; responsibility for implementing policy should be assigned to a named Assistant Commissioner at central level and named Superintendents at district level;
- Gardaí Domestic Violence and Sexual Assault Investigation Units should be established in major urban areas outside Dublin, in particular Cork, Limerick, Galway and Waterford. In all other areas, there should be a sufficient number of Gardai, accessible through the gardaí station networks throughout the country, who have been trained and given the expertise to deal with domestic violence, rape and sexual assault cases;
- The gardaí should develop strong interagency links with other statutory and voluntary/community bodies dealing with violence against women in the local area;
- Each gardaí station should have information packs available which detail local statutory and voluntary services to which women experiencing violence can be referred; information on intervention programmes for violent men should also be included.

OTHER RECOMMENDATIONS

Other recommendations are made on a number of issues including the remanding of alleged offenders in custody pending court appearance, the role of female gardaí and the collection and publication of statistics.

Chapter 6: Legal issues

The legal and judicial systems play a very important role in ensuring that victims of violence are protected to the fullest extent possible, and that offenders receive appropriate sanctions and intervention.

In this context, the Task Force believes it is particularly important that violence against women is always viewed and treated as a serious crime irrespective of whether the perpetrator is a stranger or a person known to the victim.

RECOMMENDATIONS

PRIORITY RECOMMENDATIONS

- Appropriate mechanisms should be put in place to enable the operation of the Domestic Violence Act 1996 to be monitored and kept under review in order to gauge its effectiveness in dealing with the victims of domestic violence;
- a proposal put forward by the Coolock Community Law Centre for a legal advice service for women experiencing violence to be operated in tandem with a refuge should be implemented in Coolock, in association with the local refuge, on a pilot basis and monitored as to its effectiveness;
- the setting up of regional family courts, as recommended by the Law Reform Commission, should be initiated.

OTHER RECOMMENDATIONS

A number of other recommendations are made in relation to the Domestic Violence Act, the appointment and training of the judiciary, and the operation of the Courts.

Chapter 7: Accommodation and the role of refuges

When dealing with violence the Task Force strongly advocates that women and children should be facilitated to remain in their home, or existing accommodation, whenever it is safe and practical for them to do so. The reality is however that there will be cases where this option will not be practical and a woman will be forced to seek immediate accommodation elsewhere. Crisis accommodation can be provided in a number of different ways – family/friends, hostels/shelters, private bed and breakfast and refuges. Where a woman must seek accommodation outside her circle of family and friends, the Task Force believes that refuges, properly managed and with the capacity to provide a range of supports, offer the best option at the crisis stage.

REFUGES

There is a need to increase the present level of refuge accommodation and to put the financing and funding of such accommodation on a more sound footing. The Task Force believes that the best way to develop refuges is through a partnership between the voluntary sector and the Health Boards with clear contractual obligations between both parties. The Health Boards should be responsible for grant aiding current costs as at present. The Department of the Environment also has a role in meeting capital costs of refuges under its Capital Assistance Scheme. The Task Force also highlights the importance of ensuring that refuges are sensitive to, and equipped to deal with, the needs of minority and marginalised groups in society.

TRANSITIONAL AND PERMANENT HOUSING

The availability of second-stage housing is extremely important both in terms of progressing victims back to a normal life and for easing the demand on refuge accommodation. In this regard the report recommends that transitional housing for families should be developed in parallel with refuge spaces and be funded through the Department of the Environment.

RECOMMENDATIONS

PRIORITY RECOMMENDATIONS

- Refuge accommodation should conform with minimum specified standards and provide a range of support services, including counselling for both women and children;
- outreach services should be developed both for women who have left refuge accommodation and those who cannot, or do not wish to, go to a refuge;
- the priority areas for development of new refuges should be Dublin West, South Leinster/South Midlands, West Connaught, and the North East;
- core funding of refuges should be provided, but conditional on specified criteria being met in relation to the range and quality of services provided.

OTHER RECOMMENDATIONS

There are a number of other recommendations in relation to multi-annual budgeting, standards of services and accommodation, access to schools for children living temporarily in refuges, the provision of medical and social services to women and children in refuges, the use of bed and breakfast accommodation, and the capital and current costs of providing transitional housing.

Chapter 8: Health and social services

The Task Force highlights the roles various health and social services can play in identifying the existence of domestic violence, encouraging disclosure, and providing services and support. Research has shown however that there is a large discrepancy between the numbers of women with symptoms related to living in abusive relationships who avail of health care services and the low rate of detection and intervention by medical staff. The tendency therefore is to treat the symptoms of the problem rather than its root causes. In this context, the Task Force has made a number of recommendations particularly relating to the need to train staff not only to deal with the symptoms of violence, but also to detect and intervene appropriately in such cases. It also recommends that written protocols on domestic violence be adopted by hospitals and other medical services.

RECOMMENDATIONS

PRIORITY RECOMMENDATIONS

- In a hospital setting, places should be available in an observation ward where women suspected of being victims of domestic violence can be accommodated overnight. Such a procedure would give women time and space to consider their options, rather than immediately returning to a violent environment following medical treatment;
- Health Service providers should adopt written protocols and procedures in relation to domestic violence and rape. These policies should be backed up by appropriate training for front-line staff;
- posts of Medical Social Worker should be an accepted part of the cadre of staff in the Accident and Emergency Departments of all large hospitals;
- access to accredited counselling services should be provided for women and children who have experienced domestic violence. The funding and provision of this service should form part of the development of regional service plans;
- community-based health services should have sufficient information available to them to act as a gateway for specialist services on violence against women.

OTHER RECOMMENDATIONS

There are a number of other recommendations in relation to training, medical procedures in sexual assault cases, the maintenance of proper records and the role of the social work service.

Chapter 9: Rape and sexual assault

Evidence suggests that only a small number of rape cases are ever reported to the gardaí and an even smaller number lead to criminal proceedings. Given the nature of rape and sexual assault cases, it is inherently difficult to encourage women to come forward. When they do, their experience of the criminal justice system is difficult and often traumatic. This situation is not helped by the general perception that sentencing in rape cases is sometimes both inconsistent and lenient.

The recommendations of the Task Force are designed primarily to encourage more women to report cases of sexual violence to the gardaí. In this context, the issues addressed by the Task Force include the need to liaise with victims during the period before and during the prosecution of alleged offenders; the conditions for granting leave to cross-examine regarding a complainant's past sexual history; and gardaí Policy on the treatment of victims of rape, sexual assault and other sexual offences.

RECOMMENDATIONS

PRIORITY RECOMMENDATIONS

- The Garda Síochána should develop and publicise clear policy and practice with regard to the treatment of victims of rape, sexual assault and other sexual offences;
- once a decision is made to prosecute in a rape/sexual assault case, the task of liaising with the victim should be assigned to the investigating gardaí. Victims should also have regular consultations with counsel both before and throughout the trial, and should be given a copy of their statement to the Gardai and any victim impact report, as a matter of course;
- leave to cross-examine a complainant regarding her previous sexual history should only be granted where it is proven to the court that the evidence is substantially relevant to the facts at issue, as envisaged in the Criminal Law (Rape) Act 1981, as amended; the law and practice in relation to this area should be reviewed so as to ensure that the strict legal criteria as laid down in the 1981 Act are being adhered to.

OTHER RECOMMENDATIONS

There are a number of other recommendations in relation to training of gardaí, the notification of victims about the release of an offender, separate legal representation, the availability of information, and victim impact reports.

Chapter 10: Intervention programmes for men
The Task Force examined intervention programmes for violent men and outlined the principles that should underpin such programmes. Examples of initiatives within Ireland are briefly outlined. The Task Force expresses caution about the outcomes of programmes in relation to their rehabilitative effects and the risks of giving a false sense of security which could put women's safety in jeopardy. For this reason, it is recommended that such programmes be linked to judicial sanctions and other support services for women. Research into the effectiveness of intervention programmes with sex offenders is needed, including evaluation of the clinical impact of programmes and their impact on re-offending rates.

RECOMMENDATIONS
PRIORITY RECOMMENDATIONS
- The protection, safety and security of women and children should be the paramount consideration in developing programmes;
- intervention programmes for offenders should be adequately resourced and should be available in areas where support services for women and children are already in place: the development and funding of such programmes should be the responsibility of the Department of Justice;
- existing intervention programmes with men should be subject to on-going monitoring, evaluation and review so that their effectiveness as a response to domestic violence can be gauged,
- the judiciary should have the option of referring perpetrators for assessment as regards suitability for intervention programmes in both criminal and civil cases but such programmes should never be used as an alternative to criminal or civil sanctions.

OTHER RECOMMENDATIONS
There are a number of other recommendations regarding the need for co-ordination between agencies, the role of the judicial system, post release supervision of offenders, and the expansion of the number of treatment places available in Arbour Hill.

Chapter 11: Making it happen
Services which work with abused women and their families must work together and share information both to maximise the effective use of current resources and to ensure that the best possible service

is provided. The Task Force concluded that the adoption of clear written policies in all agencies, the implementation of good practice guidelines, and the provision of effective training for personnel are essential prerequisites for the delivery of an effective service. In addition, statutory and voluntary/community bodies must co-operate and co-ordinate their services.

The Task Force proposes that a partnership approach should be developed at three levels – community, regional and national. An important part of the planning process is to ensure that all existing services, whether in the public, community or voluntary sectors, are harnessed, coordinated and utilised to their full potential. Services should be developed and brought up to the standards envisaged in this Report over the next five years.

RECOMMENDATIONS
- The establishment of Local Networks with a community based approach to the provision of services, including interagency co-ordination of services and sharing of information at a local level; as a first step in this process one local network should be piloted in each Health Board area before the end of 1997;
- Regional Planning Committees, which would have strategic focus, should be established in each Health Board Region, and include members from all relevant organisations in the public, community and voluntary sectors;
- A National Steering Committee should be established with membership drawn from all relevant sectors to advise on policy development and priorities. It should be chaired by a Minister of State with designated responsibility for the development of policies in this area.

Chapter 12: Preventative strategies
Finally, it is recommended that the proposed National Steering Committee should give priority to the development of a preventative strategy. The strategy should be aimed at both highlighting services for women and at eliminating any ambivalence or tolerance that exists in society in relation to all forms of violence against women, whether the violence occurs in the home or elsewhere. An effective preventative strategy should help to reduce both the incidence of violence and the demand for services in the longer term. There are two key components to a strategy aimed at preventing violence against women:

- a long-term strategy aimed at changing society's attitudes and values and the structures which facilitate gender inequality; and
- an improved service response, and a public awareness campaign aimed both at the prevention of violence and stopping its recurrence.

The education system and community initiatives should be developed to raise awareness, prevent and stop the recurrence of violence. It is also pointed out that in launching public campaigns against violence against women, an infrastructure of support services should be first available to respond to women and children who disclose violence as a result of the campaign.

RECOMMENDATIONS
PRIORITY RECOMMENDATIONS

- A publicly funded public awareness campaign, including TV/radio/poster, should be developed by the National Steering Committee;
- information leaflets, postcards and other material giving local information, should be displayed in places such as supermarkets, public health clinics, doctors' surgeries, churches, community centres, social welfare offices, post offices, sporting clubs e.g. GAA, soccer, rugby, golf clubs;
- special focus programmes in the education area should be introduced to provide young people with the knowledge, skills and attitudes necessary to prevent violence against women in future generations.

OTHER RECOMMENDATIONS

A number of other recommendations are made in relation to the training of teachers, gender proofing of education materials and methods, and parenting and family support programmes.

Monitoring and training
Issues around both monitoring and training are referred to in a number of chapters throughout the text. These issues are key elements in developing quality services and policies. Training is essential for all service providers to enable them to understand the dynamics of violence, and to equip them with the skills and knowledge to respond appropriately in individual cases.

TRAINING

The Task Force believes that through training people will be able to work better together and thereby enhance the quality of available services. Multidisciplinary training is of particular relevance in that:

- it facilitates the development of a common language and understanding around the issue;
- it can clarify the respective roles of service deliverers;
- it provides coherency between the various guidelines and protocols in individual agencies.

The delivery of training must cater for the different needs of personnel working in this area e.g, professional staff, volunteer staff, etc. and reflect their respective roles and levels of responsibility. The key principles underpinning training programmes should include the following:

- training should form an integral part of the planning process of all agencies;
- all training of professionals within the statutory and voluntary sectors should include models on non-discriminatory practice, and specifically deal with the issues of racism, disability and sexual orientation;
- training should reflect the differing needs of individuals;
- specific training models should be developed in partnership with relevant service deliverers;
- training programmes should reflect current good practices, research findings and changes in legislation; and
- include routine evaluation of their relevance and effectiveness.

MONITORING

References are also made throughout the Report to the importance of putting monitoring and evaluation systems in place. These systems are important from the perspectives of determining both service needs, in terms of their nature, quality and appropriateness, and policy development.

Among the recommendations made by the Task Force in this regard are:

- The gardaí should publish statistics which outline the number of calls received in relation to violence against women, the action taken and the reasons for not pursuing charges. Statistics for each district should be published annually in the Garda Annual Report;

- appropriate mechanisms should be put in place to enable the operation of the Domestic Violence Act 1996 to be monitored and kept under review in order to gauge its effectiveness in dealing with the victims of domestic violence;
- refuges should maintain records on both refuge occupancy rates and the numbers of women and children they were unable to accommodate at any point in time;
- proper records of people both suspected of being victims of domestic violence, and those who actually disclose such violence, should be maintained by all service providers in the health and social services sector.

In 1995 the government also published a discussion document *Developing a Policy for Women's Health*, which recognised the fact that incidents of violence toward women and children presented themselves initially as health matters requiring treatment. The document noted that the Kilkenny Incest Investigation had called for the provision by health boards of refuges and counselling for the victims of domestic violence, and it called for rape crisis centres to be established by each board, as well as for expanded services for victims of rape and domestic violence. Another government publication, *A Plan for Women's Health* (1997) reiterated the commitment to cooperation among agencies in responding to violence against women and children; to implementing section 6 of the Domestic Violence Act 1996, which increased the power of health officials to intervene in domestic violence situations; and to developing protocols and practices with respect to servicing victims of violence, educating medical personnel, and developing support services and counselling for victims.

SEXUAL ABUSE OF CHILDREN

The sexual abuse of children was another topic that was rarely spoken of in Ireland but was familiar to those working within the legal system. Studies have shown that, like rape, most offences of this type still go unreported. The evidence has been scanty, but 6 per cent of the adults responding to one pioneering survey indicated that they had been sexually abused as children.[13] It was also estimated that 90 per cent of the abusers were men and that 75 per cent of the abused children were girls, with an average age of 9.2 years.[14] Against this background, the issue emerged along with the question of domestic violence, as the abuse of women was often accompanied by abuse of children, including sexual abuse.

The laws in respect of sexual abuse of children was the same as for offences involving adults: the Offences against the Person Act 1861; the Criminal Law (Rape) Act 1981; the Vagrancy Act 1824; and the Criminal Law (Amendment) Act 1935. These statutes cover rape, buggery, indecent assault and indecent exposure. In addition, the Incest Act 1908 specifically made incest a criminal offence.

In 1987 the Department of Health published Child Abuse Guidelines containing advice for workers in the health and social services, and declaring it was the duty of such workers to report cases of abuse. These Guidelines were amended in 1995 to include cooperation with the gardaí: Health Boards were to notify the gardaí, and vice versa, whenever they encountered cases of abuse.

In 1989 the Law Reform Commission undertook an extensive study of the issue and suggested a series of reforms in the law, including mandatory reporting of sexual abuse by the various agencies, changes in the treatment of homosexuality as a matter for criminal law and suggestions for the taking of evidence from children.

Law Reform Commission Consultation Paper, *Child Sexual Abuse* (1989)

Chapter 10: Summary of provisional recommendations

A. THE CIVIL LAW

1. The definition of child sexual abuse proposed by the Western Australia Task Force in its 1987 Report should be adopted for child care proceedings.
2. Doctors, health workers, social workers and teachers should be under a legal obligation to report to the Director of Community Care and Medical Officer of Health (DCC/MOH) within each health board, or to the gardaí, instances of child sexual abuse in circumstances where they are aware such abuse has taken place or a reasonable person would be so aware.
3. There should be legal immunity for bona fide reports made with due care by mandated reporters. The development of the law of

negligence or breach of duty in the context of a mandatory reporting obligation should be left to the courts.

4. Failure to report should constitute a summary offence punishable by a maximum penalty of six months' imprisonment and/or a fine of IR£1,000. Prosecutions for failure to report should be instituted only with the consent of the Director of Public Prosecutions

5. A statutory duty should be placed on health boards to take at least certain minimal steps in response to a report of alleged child sexual abuse. The obligation to investigate such abuse should not be absolute. but where a decision is made not to investigate following a report of alleged abuse, the onus should be on the health board to give reasons for its failure to investigate. The law should also specify, in broad terms, the matters to be investigated.

6. The DCC/MOH should be under a general legal duty to hold a case conference in cases of suspected child sexual abuse which have not been rejected as 'unfounded'. When he or she decides not to hold a case conference, he or she should record the reasons for the decision.

7. Case conferences should have an advisory role in relation to the appropriateness of criminal proceedings.

8. Parents should, as a general rule, be invited to attend for at least part of the case conference.

9. Certain changes in practice by health boards are recommended in relation to the maintenance of child abuse lists.

PROPOSALS IN THE CHILD CARE BILL 1988

10. Section 11 provides that the maximum period for which a child may be kept in a place of safety is eight days. The DCC/MOH or a senior officer of the health board nominated by him should be enabled to apply to a District Justice for an order extending that period for a further eight days. In order to succeed in such an application, the Health Board should be required to satisfy the justice that preparations for care proceedings are advancing with all due speed, that an extension of the emergency care period is necessitated by the circumstances of the particular case and that no adequate alternative means for protecting the child are available.

11. While it is implicit in section 1l(1) of the Child Care Bill 1988 that an emergency care order should only be made where the risk to the child 'necessitates his detention in a place of safety', a more explicit rule would be preferable. The justice should be

placed under a positive obligation to consider whether other adequate means of protecting the child exist.

12. Where the level of suspicion of abuse is sufficiently high, the District Court should be given a power to authorise a health board to arrange for the medical examination and other assessment of a child. Where such an authorisation is granted, the parent should be under an obligation to present the child for examination at a given place and at a certain time or times. It should be open to the health board to apply for the order on an ex parte basis.

13. Where a place of safety order or an emergency care order is granted by the court the law should make it clear what are the minimum rights of medical examination and assessment implicit in such order and, where the health board proposes to go beyond those limits, specific authorisation from the District Court should be necessary.

14. Before making an emergency care order, the District Justice should be satisfied that the risk to the child is such as to make ex parte proceedings necessary. The health board should have to convince the justice not only that the relevant degree of risk exists, but also that the emergency nature of the situation justifies a hearing in the absence of the parents.

15. If denial of access by his or her parents to the child allegedly abused is to be the rule when a place of safety or emergency care order is made, this should be made explicit in the legislation. Consideration should be given to empowering a justice, when granting an emergency care order, having taken all the circumstances into account, to allow access by the non-abusing parent where this would not jeopardise the child's safety.

16. When dealing with an emergency situation, the District Court should have at its disposal the option of removing the alleged abuser on an ex parte basis, as an alternative to an emergency care order. The grounds for such exclusion should be the same as the grounds for an emergency care order. The right to apply for such an order should be restricted to a health board or a parent of the child. The order should be available against any member of the child's household, including siblings and perhaps against any other persons, such as babysitters, who are likely to be regularly in contact with the child.

17. A health board should be entitled to seek a protection order on an ex parte basis on the same grounds as those which at present

apply where a spouse makes the application. Any person who is a member of the household of the child against whom abuse is alleged, and any other person who is likely to have regular contact with the child, should be capable of being made subject to a protection order.

18. A positive obligation should be placed on a District Justice making the supervision order proposed in section 15(5) of the Bill in lieu of a care order to be satisfied that such order will adequately protect the child.

19. Provision should be made for the appointment by the District Justice of an independent representative for the child where, in the opinion of the justice, this appears to be necessary in the interests of the child.

20. Where, under section 17 of the Bill, the court is making or varying an order relating to access to a child who is the subject of a care order, there should be a presumption that the parents enjoy access rights unless the court otherwise decides. If a health board believes that it may be damaging to a child to see either parent while in care, or that access rights should be denied or limited in some way in the interests of the child, the onus should be on the board to convince the court of its case.

21. Where a court has determined that a child is at risk from a parent, the health board should not be permitted to return the child to his parents without a positive ruling from the court that it would not involve risk for the child.

22. Health boards should be given power to seek a barring order as an alternative to a care order in non-emergency situations. The court should be given power to grant a barring order as an alternative to a care order where the justice is satisfied that this is the most appropriate method of securing the protection of the child. Before making a barring order, the justice should be satisfied that the conditions have been met both (a) for the making of a care order, and (b) for the making of a barring order.

23. The recommendation in the Commission's Report on Illegitimacy that the right to seek a barring order should be extended to the child should be revived in the context of child sexual abuse.

24. Barring and protection orders should be available in respect of any person who is or has been a member of the abused child's household or who, while not a member of the child's household, comes into regular contact with the child.

25. A court should have power to make a barring or protection

order, as appropriate, against a person found guilty of an offence involving child sexual abuse

B. THE CRIMINAL LAW

26. Sections 61 and 62 of the Offences against the Person Act, 1861 and section 11 of the Criminal Law Amendment Act 1885, which render criminal acts of buggery and gross indecency between male persons, whether committed consensually or otherwise, should be repealed.
27. The expression 'carnal knowledge' used in the Criminal Law Amendment Act 1935 should be replaced by the expression 'sexual intercourse' as defined in Section 1(2) of the Criminal Law (Rape) Act 1981.
28. It should continue to be an offence to have sexual intercourse with a girl under the age of 17. The maximum penalty available for the offence should continue to depend on the age of the girl involved. However, consideration should be given to altering the age bands in respect of which certain maximum penalties are fixed and the penalties themselves should be re-examined.
29. The girl herself should not be made liable for the offence at (28) at any age.
30. In relation to the offence at (28), consideration should be given to the provision of a defence of reasonable mistake as to age, where the accused genuinely believed at the time of the act, on reasonable grounds, that the girl had attained the age of consent or an age attracting a less serious penalty.
31. It should be an offence to engage in anal penile penetration where one of the parties is under the age of 17 years. As with the offence at (28), the maximum penalty available should vary with the age of the person under 17. Consideration should be given to the provision of a defence to this offence similar to that suggested for consideration at (30). Consent would not be a defence.
32. Section 14 of the Criminal Law Amendment Act 1935, which provides that consent is no defence to a charge of indecent assault on a young person, should be repealed.
33. An offence of sexual exploitation should be created which would encompass the doing, procuring or inciting of an act, other than sexual intercourse or anal penile penetration, with a person below a specified age for the purpose of sexual gratification. Without prejudice to the generality of the offence as defined, specific acts could be set out as included in the definition. Consent would not be a defence.

34. It should be an offence for a person in a position of authority as defined in (35) below to engage in acts of sexual exploitation with a person who has reached the age specified for the offence at (33) but is under 17. Consent would not be a defence.

35. A person in authority should be defined as a parent, step-parent, grandparent, uncle or aunt, any guardian or person in loco parentis or any person responsible, even temporarily, for the education, supervision or welfare of a person below the age of 17.

36. Except where provision is already made for a maximum sentence of life imprisonment, there should be a greater penalty where the offences at (28), (31) and (33) above are committed by a person in authority.

C. THE LAW OF EVIDENCE

37. The court should continue to make the ultimate decision as to the competence of witnesses.

38. The oath should be replaced by a form of affirmation made after an adjudication on competence on lines similar to those suggested by the Australian Law Reform Commission, i.e. an approach which ascertains the potential witness' cognitive ability.

39. The present requirement to warn a jury before they can convict on the sworn evidence of a child and the requirement of corroboration of the unsworn evidence of a child would lapse. Were the oath to be retained as the test of competence, the warning and corroboration requirements should be abolished.

40. Expert evidence should be admissible as to competence and as to children's typical behavioural and emotional reactions to sexual abuse.

41. An exception to the Rule against Hearsay on the lines of the Washington or Florida child sexual abuse exceptions could be made on grounds of reliability where the child is available to give evidence and testifies. Where the child is not available to give evidence, it would be necessary to provide for corroboration such as the court would deem sufficient.

42. A residual exception to the hearsay rule such as is found in the Federal Rules of Evidence could be provided.

43. The presentation of evidence through a surrogate witness would represent so radical a departure from the norms of our system of criminal justice that the Commission does not think it either practical or desirable to recommend it.

44. During the prosecution and, if possible, the investigation of

these offences, the child should be questioned by disinterested but skilled child examiners who are experienced in child language and psychology, and are appointed by the court. The examiner would act as the conduit for all questions from the lawyers in the case, from the court or from the accused if he or she is representing himself or herself. The examiner's role would be to establish and maintain rapport and ease of communication with the child witness while remaining detached from the issues in the case.

45. The child complainant should be able to give her evidence behind from a screen at the trial.

46. The child complainant should be able to give evidence by means of closed circuit television at the trial.

47. Provision could be made for admitting a video-recording of the child's evidence provided the child was made available for cross-examination at the trial. A video-recording could be admissible in total substitution for the child's participation at the trial, provided a general reliability or trustworthiness requirement such as is built into the child abuse or residual hearsay exceptions in the United States was also built into this exception, or a requirement of sufficient corroboration.

48. The Commission provisionally recommends, as its preferred option for trials on indictment, that the Criminal Procedure Act 1967 should be amended to provide for the video-recording of District Court depositions in cases going forward for trial by jury, at the election of the DPP. The video-recording would be presented as the child's evidence at all trials on indictment, as the normal procedure, unless the Court decided after application by the accused that, in the interests of justice and fair procedures, the child should give evidence at the trial. In that event, the evidence could be given from behind a screen or on closed circuit television.

49. No special reform is necessary to enable anatomical dolls and other demonstrative aids to testimony to be used in court.

50. Similarly no special law reform would be necessary to enable the trial judge at his or her discretion to allow witnesses whose age or physical condition may so require to give evidence in a particular location in the court and to permit a so-called 'support person' to sit in close proximity or, in the case of very young children, to take the child on his or her lap, provided there was no communication of any sort between the witnesses and the 'support person'.

51. The Commission would not recommend the appointment of a guardian ad litem in civil or criminal proceedings to protect the interests of a child who is not a party to such proceedings. Such a proposal would be of dubious constitutionality, as it might tilt the balance of the trial unfairly against the accused and might also introduce serious and unjustifiable complications in the trial procedure.

52. Apart from provisionally recommending the video-recording of evidence as above as a means of guarding against lapses of memory on the part of the child, the Commission makes no particular recommendation relating to delay in procedure. The desirability of ensuring that trials are speedy in all cases, and not merely where children appear as witnesses, is obvious.

The reforms proposed by the Law Reform Commission were incorporated into the Child Care Act 1991, although the degree of mandatory reporting remained an open question. The Second Commission on the Status of Women (1993) called for implementation of the provisions of the 1988 Bill and for further efforts at education.

In 1996 Austin Currie, the Minister for State with special responsibility for children at the Departments of Health, Education and Justice, chaired a cabinet committee devoted to children's issues. Plans were drawn up for a National Children's Council to coordinate activities across all sectors of society. Its proposed activities were to include policy coordination, education and support.

Department of Health, *Putting Children First: Promoting and Protecting the Rights of Children (1997)*

6. Proposed initiatives
The proposed initiatives are:
(i) Designated Officers in the health boards to co-ordinate inter-agency approaches to child protection at community care level,
(ii) Regional and Local Child Protection Committees, operating at health board and community care area level, to enhance inter-agency and inter-professional approaches to child protection,
(iii) Multi-disciplinary training, under the aegis of the Regional Child Protection Committees, to increase inter-agency and inter-professional approaches to child protection,
(iv) The new Social Services Inspectorate to review the 1987 Child Abuse Guidelines and the procedure for the Notification of

Suspected Cases of Child Abuse between Health Boards and Gardai,
(v) A public information campaign to heighten public awareness of child abuse and of the system to respond to cases of child abuse,
(vi) The provision of support services by health boards for victims of past abuse,
(vii) Funding of voluntary agencies dealing with children to be conditional on procedures being in place to deal with allegations of child abuse, and
(viii)Evaluation of the impact of the above measures on the reporting of child abuse.

7. Details on proposed initiatives

(I) Designated officers in the health boards to co-ordinate the inter-agency and inter-professional response to individual cases at community care level

To ensure inter-agency and inter-professional co-operation at community care level, it is proposed that designated officers be appointed in each community care area by each health board to coordinate the response of all agencies, statutory and voluntary, to individual cases of child abuse or protection. The designated officer would be either the Child Care Manager or the Senior Social Worker.

One of the main recommendations of the Kelly Fitzgerald Report was the appointment of a Child Care Manager in each community care area. A number of health boards are already proposing to appoint Child Care Managers at community care level, to co-ordinate child protection services. It is envisaged that the Child Care Manager will act as an assistant, and report, to the General Manager in the community care area. The Child Care Manager will manage and co-ordinate services for children in a specified community care area. Among the more important tasks of the Child Care Manager will be:

• receiving all notifications of child abuse,
• taking decisions relating to the holding of Case Conferences, negotiating service agreements with voluntary service providers, ensuring inter-agency co-operation in relation to child protection and welfare, ensuring inter-professional and inter-programme co-operation in relation to child protection and welfare,
• being a budget holder for child care services, and
• supervising staff training programmes.

Child Care Manager posts have been approved for the South-

Eastern, Southern and Western Health Boards. In the development of child care services in 1997, the approval of Child Care Manager, or equivalent, posts in the other health boards will be a priority.

The Child Care Manager will have a pivotal role in convening and supporting the Local Child Protection Committee discussed below.

(II) CHILD PROTECTION COMMITTEES AT HEALTH BOARD AND COMMUNITY CARE LEVEL

There is a need for a close working relationship between social workers, the gardaí, the probation service, medical practitioners, nursing staff, teachers and other relevant professionals who have a common aim to protect children. Co-operation between the various agencies can be difficult to achieve. The establishment of Child Protection Committees, along the lines of the committees in existence in Northern Ireland, would assist in the development of inter-agency and inter-professional cooperation.

It is proposed that a Regional Child Protection Committee be established at health board level to facilitate co-ordination on a regional basis, and a Child Protection Committee in each community care area to foster co-operation locally. The proposed structure therefore allows for a regional committee, which will develop policies to improve inter-agency and inter-professional co-operation, and a more local committee to provide a forum at a local level for the sharing of knowledge and experience in relation to the protection of children.

The primary functions of the Regional Child Protection Committees will be to develop a strategic approach to child protection. Their main tasks will be to

- promote and review progress on arrangements to prevent child abuse,
- develop, monitor and review inter-agency and inter-professional child protection policies and procedures,
- monitor multi-disciplinary co-operation and bring any concerns to the local Child Protection Committees,
- identify the inter-disciplinary and inter-agency training needs and promote the development of an inter-disciplinary and inter-agency training strategy,
- keep under review ways of raising public awareness of child abuse and mechanisms to express concerns about child abuse,
- initiate research on the prevention and treatment of child abuse,
- review significant issues arising from the handling of cases and reports from inquiries,

- develop a strategy for the provision of therapeutic services to perpetrators of child abuse, and
- conduct or participate in case management reviews, as appropriate.

It is proposed that the Regional Child Protection Committee be established by a direction from the Minister for Health to Child Care Advisory Committees which have been established under Section 7 of the Child Care Act 1991. The Minister may give general directions to Child Care Advisory Committees under section 7(5) of the Child Care Act 1991. Given the highly sensitive nature of the issues which will need to be reviewed in detail before such committees, and that their primary focus will be on inter-disciplinary and inter-agency co-operation, it is envisaged that the Regional Child Protection Committees will be composed of health board management and relevant professionals. However, Regional Child Protection Committees will operate as a subcommittee of the Child Care Advisory Committees, focusing on professional and technical matters and reporting to the Child Care Advisory Committee, as appropriate, on matters of general policy.

The Regional Child Protection Committee will issue guidance on interdisciplinary and inter-agency procedures, review annually the child protection work in the region, develop a work plan for the incoming year and produce a report to go to the head of each constituent agency and the Child Care Advisory Committee.

The functions of the Local Child Protection Committee will be to:

- monitor and review the implementation at community care level of arrangements to abuse,
- implement Procedures and Policies developed by the Regional Child Protection Committees for inter-agency and inter-professional co-operation at a local level,
- review the operation of inter-agency and inter-professional cooperation at local level,
- provide a forum for a sharing of knowledge and experience by professionals on child protection at a local level,
- keep under review ways of raising Public awareness of child abuse and mechanisms to express concerns about child abuse at a local level, and
- conduct or participate in case management reviews, as appropriate.

The membership of the regional committees will consist of representatives of health board management and professional staff, educational interests, the gardai, the probation and welfare service, the Department of Social Welfare, General Practitioners and the voluntary child care sector. The membership of Child Protection Committees at community care level will mirror the membership of the Regional Committees to ensure local implementation of coordinated initiatives.

(III) MULTI-DISCIPLINARY TRAINING UNDER AEGIS OF THE REGIONAL CHILD PROTECTION COMMITTEE

The importance of the promotion of proper interdisciplinary and inter-agency training has been stressed, irrespective of the introduction of mandatory reporting, throughout the consultative process on mandatory reporting. The Regional Child Protection Committees will be given the task of developing, as a matter of priority, initiatives in relation to inter-agency and inter-professional training on the reporting of child abuse. Joint or multi-disciplinary training initiatives at local level will become the responsibility of the designated officer assigned to coordinate inter-agency responses to individual cases.

(IV) THE NEW SOCIAL SERVICES INSPECTORATE TO REVIEW THE 1987 CHILD ABUSE GUIDELINES PRODUCED BY THE DEPARTMENT OF HEALTH AND THE PROCEDURE FOR THE NOTIFICATION OF SUSPECTED CASES OF CHILD ABUSE BETWEEN THE HEALTH BOARDS AND GARDAI

The procedures to be followed in the management of cases of suspected child abuse are in accordance with the Department of Health's 1987 Child Abuse Guidelines. These guidelines were amended in 1995 by the Guidelines for the 'Notification of Suspected Cases of Child Abuse between Health Boards and Gardai' in relation to the circumstances in which the Health Boards and the gardai are to notify suspected cases of child abuse to each other and in relation to the consultation that should take place between both agencies following such a notification.

It is proposed that the new Social Services Inspectorate, to be established in the Department of Health, will review the content and workings of the Child Abuse Guidelines and the Health Board/gardai notification procedures to take account of the issues raised in relation to child protection during the consultative process on mandatory reporting. These issues include the reporting of cases of pregnant girls under the age of seventeen and the position of health board counselling services providing therapeutic support to victims of abuse.

One of the central recommendations of the Report of the Kilkenny Incest Investigation Team concerned the need for inter-programme collaboration between hospital and community care staff members concerning the identification, notification and follow-up of child abuse. Health boards have improved arrangements for the assessment and management of child abuse cases. with particular importance being attached to cooperation and coordination between their hospital and community care programmes.

A number of health boards have formulated regional guidelines for the investigation and management of cases of suspected child abuse based on the Department's guidelines. These guidelines protect vulnerable children by ensuring that staff have guidance on the investigation and management of situations where children are at risk of abuse or neglect.

Any review of the Department's guidelines and procedures would serve as a basis for regional guidelines by the remaining health boards and assist those boards already with guidelines in any reviews which may be undertaken.

Consideration will be given, in the review by the Social Services Inspectorate, of the value of giving procedures outlined in the Child Abuse Guidelines a statutory basis in regulations.

(v) PUBLIC AWARENESS CAMPAIGN TO CREATE AN INCREASED AWARENESS OF CHILD ABUSE

A common understanding and approach to the problem of child abuse will also serve as a basis for a properly coordinated public awareness campaign to inform opinion on child abuse prevention strategies and, when abuse has occurred, on how to react to, and the services available for, families and victims. The need for a campaign to heighten public awareness received much support at the consultative forum. It is important that the issue of reporting child abuse should not be perceived as an issue of concern exclusively for professionals. The role of the public in combating child abuse is of vital importance. Public awareness of child abuse has been heightened by a series of tragic cases such as the Kilkenny Incest Case and the death of Kelly Fitzgerald. However, a systematic and planned approach is required to the fostering of public awareness of child abuse.

One of the arguments in favour of mandatory reporting was that it could change attitudes to child abuse and raise the general awareness of society to what is a difficult issue to confront. A national publicity campaign could achieve the same aim. It has been argued that the secretive nature of Irish society in the past in dealing with difficult issues fostered an environment which allowed child abuse to take place. A public awareness campaign would allow for more open and frank discussion of the realities of child abuse. It would heighten public awareness of the support services available to vulnerable children and to families which may be in difficulty. It would create a climate which would allow victims to come forward in the clear knowledge of the support and understanding available from the health services. AIDS awareness campaigns have fostered an environment which allows for more open and frank discussion of issues of sexual behaviour. A carefully constructed national public awareness campaign on child abuse may achieve a similar result in relation to child abuse.

A campaign to raise awareness of child abuse without resulting in a flood of unsubstantiated child abuse reports from members of the public will need to be very carefully constructed. It is important that careful consideration is given to the message to be conveyed on such a complex issue. Such a campaign would not only be directed at the personal behaviour of people, as in public health campaigns on smoking, alcohol and AIDS, but also at raising an awareness and understanding of the varied and complex nature of child abuse itself and of the many support services available to victims and families at risk. The Minister of State will engage media consultants and professionals involved in the care and protection of children to assist in the production of a public campaign to increase awareness of child abuse.

The Regional and Local Child Protection Committees will also have a role in promoting regional and local initiatives on raising awareness of child abuse.

(VI) HELPLINE FOR VICTIMS OF PAST ABUSE, OPERATED BY HEALTH BOARDS
A heightened public awareness of child abuse and neglect, following some of the recent child abuse scandals, has brought to light new revelations of incidents of child abuse and neglect alleged to have occurred some twenty, thirty or even forty years ago. The Chief Executive Officers of the Health Boards have accepted that they have a responsibility to respond to the needs of the victims of past abuse and have established a steering group to develop a counselling service for adult victims of past abuse. It is proposed to establish a counselling service in each health board for such victims. On 6 June 1996 the Minister of State gave a commitment in response to a Parliamentary Question that such a service would be established in the near future.

A full counselling and therapeutic service will be provided by the boards in response to the needs of those who have been abused in the past. The service will be provided by the adult health care service and will respond to the problems which may emerge, such as depression, guilt, addiction, personality disorder and relationship problems. The proposed service will fall under the ambit of the health board's mental health services.

The service will fulfil a dual role –

A listening and counselling service: The person manning the service will have the necessary experience and training to enable them to offer a sympathetic and patient ear. This in itself can prove therapeutic for some. The staff will have the training and expertise usually associated with the caring professions of social work, nursing and psychology. It is estimated that in the great majority of contacts, this service will be all that is required.

An information and referral service: The service provider will act as a link for clients who require further services. They will help clarify what additional services a client requires and arrange a consultation, where necessary.

Legal difficulties which have emerged in the drawing up of guidelines for the development of this service are being resolved as a matter of priority with the assistance of the Attorney General's Office. As soon as these difficulties have been addressed, the service for past victims of abuse will be established.

(VII) FUNDING OF VOLUNTARY AGENCIES DEALING WITH CHILDREN TO BE CONDITIONAL ON PROCEDURES BEING IN PLACE TO DEAL WITH ALLEGATIONS OF CHILD ABUSE

The Minister of State is concerned to ensure that all agencies dealing with children have clear procedures in place to deal with allegations of child abuse. Regional and Local Child Protection Committees will ensure more effective inter-agency and inter-disciplinary co-operation. Many voluntary organisations with responsibility for children have well developed procedures in place in relation to allegations of child abuse and work closely with health boards when such allegations arise. However, in order to ensure that all voluntary agencies develop effective mechanisms to respond to allegations of child abuse, each voluntary agency dealing with children will be asked, as a pre-condition of public funding by the health board or the Department of Health, to put in place procedures to deal with allegations of child abuse which are consistent with national guidelines and approved by the appropriate Health Board.

(VIII) EVALUATION OF THE IMPACT OF THE ABOVE MEASURES ON THE REPORTING OF CHILD ABUSE

The Minister of State will commission research to evaluate the impact of the initiatives outlined above over the next three years. The outcome of that evaluation will influence future decisions on arrangements to ensure the effectiveness of the response to children who have been abused. If at that stage it is clear that the introduction of mandatory reporting would be in the best interests of children, or that some other form of statutory basis to ensure co-operation between agencies is required, the necessary legislation will be introduced.

CONCLUSION

Issues raised in previous chapters dealt mainly with women's economic and legal security. The materials in this chapter have brought to light even more fundamental considerations: women's personal and physical security and safety against such crimes as rape, domestic violence, and the sexual abuse of children.

We have seen that women's economic and legal progress required the enactment of antidiscriminatory legislation. It appears on the face of it, however, that laws protecting women's personal well-being were already in place in the 1960s. The Offences against the Person Act 1861 and the Criminal Law (Amendment) Act 1935 both provided criminal penalties for rape. The 1861 Act and the Married Women (Maintenance in Case of Desertion) Act 1886 offered protection against domestic violence. In the case of child abuse, once again the 1861 Act was the central statute, being supplemented in this instance by the Vagrancy Act 1824, the Criminal Law (Amendment) Act 1935 and the Incest Act 1908.

The fact that the first Commission on the Status of Women did not consider these matters does not mean that women believed that these existing legal protections were adequate. Indeed, their shortcomings had become a centrepiece of discussion and reports from the mid-1970s onwards. Some of the major flaws in the 1861 and 1935 Acts were removed with the passage of the Criminal Law (Rape) Act 1981 and the Criminal Law (Rape) (Amendment) Act 1990. Nonetheless, in the mid- to late 1990s several official and unofficial reports expressed dissatisfaction, both with the small number of rape cases reported – estimated at about one in five – and with the procedures followed by the Garda and the courts.

As major policy issues, rape and sexual violence were joined in the 1980s by concerns over domestic violence, as well as the physical and sexual abuse of children. However, the provisions of the Family Law (Protection of Spouses and Children) Act 1981 applied only within marriage for fifteen years after it was enacted. Then its scope was broadened by the Domestic Violence Act 1996. A complementary strategy of prevention was urged by the Task Force on Violence Against Women in 1997.

Finally, measures were taken in the 1980s to strengthen protections against child abuse. The Child Care Act 1991 incorporated a number of institutional and procedural reforms, while the National Children's Council, established in 1996, acted to coordinate activities related to protection of the rights of children.

CHAPTER SEVEN

Women and education

BARRIERS TO EQUAL OPPORTUNITY IN THE 1970s

By 1972, when the first Commission on the Status of Women was preparing its report, sweeping changes were already in progress in Irish education. An influential report, *Investment in Education* (1965) had emphasised the link between educational excellence and economic progress, and in 1966 the government had decided to provide free second-level education (also known as secondary education or post-primary schooling). This led to a large increase in the demand for places. Changes in the Irish economy brought with them a heightened demand for a well-educated and skilled work force, triggering a dramatic expansion of capital investment in Irish universities to accommodate the increase in student numbers.

The first Commission on the Status of Women focused on equality of opportunity for girls and women at all levels and in all types of educational institution. This was partly a conscious response to Ireland's vote in favour of the United Nations Declaration on the Elimination of Discrimination Against Women of 1967. It also reflected the Commission's belief that equality of educational opportunity for girls was a necessary condition for women attaining equality of opportunity with men in all areas.

Commission on the Status of Women, *Report to Minister for Finance* (1972)

519. Equality of access to schooling does not, of course, exclude the possible qualitative differences in education referred to by the International Labour Organisation. Several of the submissions made

to us concerning the education of girls have referred to the preponderance of single-sex schools and have contended that, for instance, the facilities for teaching science subjects in girls' schools is often inadequate and inferior to that available in boys' schools. The tenor of these submissions has been that segregated education has a built-in tendency to be unequal education and that a greater degree of co-education would ensure for girls the same encouragement and opportunity as for boys.

520. Connected also with the question of co-education is the subject of sex-role development of children, particularly in the early years, and their occupational aspirations. Experience in the home and in society outside school has, no doubt, a much greater influence on the sex-role development of children than any experience in school. In the average Irish household the mother does not work outside the home and accordingly girls are to a large extent conditioned to visualise themselves in a housekeeping role. These early attitudes to sex roles may, however, be reinforced in the normal education process by, for instance, depicting girls and women in school textbooks as always engaging in traditional pursuits. We have examined a number of primary school textbooks and there is some evidence that the interests and activities of girls depicted in them do tend to follow this pattern. We consider that care should be taken to ensure that the profile of the typical girl or woman in school textbooks should show her in active occupations and pursuits as well as in the 'traditional' female image. It has been suggested to us also that the social attitudes which condition thinking in relation to the allotting of different roles to the sexes derive to some extent from the fact that large numbers of girls are educated by members of female religious orders, who up to recent years may have tended to follow traditional lines of approach to women's role in society, without any emphasis on the idea of equality of status of men and women and who may have discouraged what might be called 'career mindedness'. If this effect has occurred, it is likely to diminish greatly in the future as there is a very clear change in outlook among the religious orders and a much greater involvement in outside activities.

521. It is sometimes argued that investment in the education of girls is, in comparison with the education of boys, largely a wasted investment because girls normally provide a return on the investment only for relatively few years between leaving school and getting married and that the older the age to which the girl remains in full-time education the less is the return on the

investment. We cannot accept that this argument has any validity. The benefits of an extended education are, if the woman chooses to be a full-time housewife rather than continue in employment, merely deflected from her previous occupation to her equally important new occupation and manifest themselves in a different way. In addition, she is better able to deal with the various problems that may arise in marriage and if she decides later in life, or if necessity obliges her, to re-enter employment – for instance, on becoming widowed or due to desertion – she is better qualified to meet this challenge. In this connection, it is interesting to note that there is a strong tendency for longer education for girls to lead to greater labour force participation by them over a period of years. The figures in Table 27 [designated Table 8.1 in this book], taken from the Census of Population 1966, show that the higher the educational level attained by a woman the greater is the probability that she will be gainfully occupied.

Table 8.1

Females who ceased full-time education, distinguishing gainfully occupied and non-gainfully occupied (1966 census)

Highest type of educational establishment attended full-time	Total	Gainfully occupied	Non-gainfully occupied
Primary	565,265	130,383 (23.1%)	434,882 (76.9%)
Secondary	183,548	70,408 (38.4%)	113,140 (61.6%)
Vocational	76,638	33,786 (44.1%)	42,852 (55.9%)
Secondary and Vocational	56,185	27,887 (49.6%)	28,298 (50.4%)
University	29,750	17,649 (59.3%)	12,101 (40.7%)

522. More recent figures on the participation of women in the labour force by educational level than those shown in Table 27 [Table 8.1, above] were obtained in the survey referred to in paragraph 11 [not included] and these confirm the tendency for labour force participation rates of women to rise with increasing educational attainment. Approximately half the married women in the sample who had attended university or who had other professional or technical qualifications were in employment as compared with approximately one in ten of those who had not gone beyond primary school. In addition, those with higher educational attainments were more likely to be working full-time than those with lower levels. The surveys of women graduates referred to in paragraph 16 also showed a very high labour force

participation level among graduates. In the survey of UCD graduates, for instance, 96 (77%) of the 125 graduates who returned questionnaires were working. The surveys were, however, more successful in contacting more recent graduates than older graduates and this would be likely to have the effect of increasing the percentage working. Also, a large proportion of the respondents were located in the teaching profession where it is not unusual for married women to remain employed after marriage.

523. A subject that has been brought to our attention many times as being of importance in relation to equality of educational and employment opportunity for girls is that of career guidance. Girls have in the past tended to study subjects and courses without any clearly defined career in view or else they have aimed at careers in already overcrowded occupations. Effective career guidance at an early stage in a girl's career could do a great deal to remedy this position and to encourage girls to adopt a less conservative attitude towards career patterns. It could also help to alter the educational consequences for girls of the sex-typing of many occupations by encouraging them to aim at careers which may in the past have been regarded as 'men-only' preserves. Of course the career guidance offered to girls must be realistic and take account of their potential, trends in employment and the likelihood of access to the proposed employment. Career guidance also has an important part to play in influencing a girl to look ahead of the immediate pattern of her career on leaving full-time education. There may be a tendency for some girls to feel that difficult course options at post-primary level are not worth taking as they expect to be in employment for only a short period of time before marriage. Good counselling at the appropriate time can encourage such girls to anticipate the possibility, and indeed the increasing probability, of a second phase of employment at some stage after marriage and to plan their educational courses accordingly. The Department of Education has stated its recognition of the importance of student guidance programmes which would commence as soon as a student, whether a boy or a girl, first enters the post-primary school and would continue up to the time he or she leaves school, in order that serious career planning mistakes may be avoided. A psychological service has been established in the Department of Education in order to help schools set up a student guidance service and to provide expert advice on special problems. A teacher training programme in career guidance commenced in 1968 and by 1972, 73 male teachers and 38 female teachers had participated in it. About

25% of the 850 post-primary schools have a guidance service in operation and it is hoped that some guidance will be available in most schools within the space of a few years.

535. A further criticism that has been levelled at the education of girls at the secondary level is that there is a very noticeable tendency for them to concentrate on 'arts' subjects rather than on Mathematics or Science subjects. This criticism seems to be borne out by an investigation of the numbers examined and the numbers taking honours papers and pass papers in a recent Leaving Certificate examination. The figures in Table 31 [not included] show a very great tendency on the part of girls taking the examination to enter in large numbers for honours papers in subjects such as Home Economics, Biology and Art, to the detriment of subjects such as Mathematics, Physics and Chemistry.

University Education

543. The figures in Table 34 [designated Table 8.2 in this book] show that the approximate equality of participation in full-time education that exists between boys and girls up to the age at which university education commences, that is about 18 years, changes rapidly after that age in favour of boys. The Table shows the total number of full-time students, male and female, in the National University of Ireland and in the University of Dublin combined, in each academic year in the five year period from 1964–65 to 1968–69 (the latest year for which university statistics are available to the Central Statistics Office).

Table 8.2
Number of full-time students in the National University of Ireland and the
University of Dublin 1964–65 to 1968–69

Year	Men	Women	% Women
1964–65	8,966	4,040	31.1
1965–66	9,789	4,358	30.8
1966–67	10,646	4,632	30.8
1967–68	10,730	5,108	32.3
1968–69	11,246	5,662	33.5

The proportion of women attending full-time university courses over this period remained fairly constant although there was a tendency towards a slight increase from 1966–67. The proportion of women attending university has in fact fluctuated for many years between 25% and 34%. For instance, the percentage in 1930–31 was 33%, in 1938–39, 25%, in 1948–49, 28% and in 1958–59, 26%. There is no reason to suppose that the upward trend in recent years will not continue and indeed with the extension of the university grants scheme it may gain a greater momentum. At present, however, the position is, roughly, that for every two boys who continue fulltime education at university level, only one girl will do so.

544. Women who do go to university tend to congregate, much more than men, in a narrow range of faculties. Table 35 [designated Table 8.3 in this book] shows, for the National University of Ireland and the University of Dublin combined, the number of males and females in each faculty in 1968–69.

In that year, almost 7 out of 10 women were pursuing Arts or Social Science courses as compared with less than 4 out of 10 men. As against this, women comprised only about 1% of students in the faculty of Engineering. In the Science faculty, men outnumbered women by almost 3 to 1, but even this level of participation by women in the faculty is surprisingly high in view of the relatively small number of girls taking honours papers in Mathematics and Science subjects at Leaving Certificate level. The only explanation that offers itself for this is that a much larger proportion of girls who do take honours courses in Mathematics and Science at secondary level have a science career (or possibly teaching) in mind than is the case with boys. Apart from Arts and Social Science, the faculties with the highest concentration of women were Science, Medicine and Commerce; women accounted for over one-quarter of students in each of these faculties and the proportion of women students in the universities pursuing such courses was not very much different from the proportion of men – 10.2% as compared with 12.6% in the case of Science, 9.2% as compared with 11.8% in Medicine, and 5.2% as against 7.6% in Commerce. Dairy Science was the only faculty in which women were not represented and, as far as we are aware, no woman pursued a degree course in this faculty prior to 1968–69. We understand that the faculty is open to women but that they are not availing of it.

The very high proportion of women in the Arts faculty is reflected in the subsequent employment pattern adopted by women graduates, with a very high proportion of them entering the teaching profession. Of the 215 graduates from whom replies were received in the survey referred to in paragraph 16 [not included], 122, or 56.7%, were employed as teachers.

Table 8.3

Full-time students in various faculties in the National University of Ireland and the University of Dublin (combined) in 1968–69

Faculty	Men	Women	% Women in Faculty	Men/Women in Faculty as % of total men/women	
				Men	Women
Architecture	160	35	17.9	1.4	0.6
Agriculture and Forestry	553	10	1.8	4.9	0.2
Veterinary Medicine	350	13	3.6	3.1	0.2
Arts and Social Science	4,025	3,907	49.3	35.8	69.0
Commerce	850	295	25.8	7.6	5.2
Dairy Science	137	–	–	1.2	–
Business Studies	322	17	5.0	2.8	0.3
Dentistry	172	27	13.6	1.5	0.5
Engineering	1,210	14	1.1	10.8	0.2
Law	325	69	17.5	2.8	1.2
Medicine	1,329	523	28.2	11.8	9.2
Pre-Medicine, Pre-Dental	378	175	31.6	3.4	3.1
Science	1,418	577	28.9	12.6	10.2
Total	11,229	5,662			

545. In general, the results obtained by women in primary degree examinations are not as good as the results obtained by men. In the period from 1964–65 to 1968–69, honours primary degrees conferred, as a percentage of total primary degrees conferred, ranged from 31.7 to 32.8 for men and from 23.6 to 31.1 for women. In Arts and Social Science over the same period, the percentage of women gaining honours degrees ranged from 24.0 to 27.9 and the percentage of men from 26.9 to 33.6. In the other faculties in which there is a substantial proportion of women – Science, Medicine and Commerce – the same kind of pattern emerges. In Medicine, during the period mentioned, the percentages of men graduating with honours ranged from 6.6 to 20.2 and those for women from 2.5 to 10.2; in Science, the percentage ranges were from 54 to 60 for men and from 32 to 52 for women. Women did somewhat better in Commerce where the percentage gaining honours degrees ranged from 12.8 to 32.9 as compared with 15.9 to 21.6 for men.

Table 8.4

Honours primary degrees conferred by the National University of Ireland and the University of Dublin as a percentage of total primary degrees conferred on men and women (separately) in each year from 1964–65 to 1968–69

	Men	Women
1964–65	32.5	27.8
1965–66	31.7	27.4
1966–67	32.8	23.6
1967–68	31.8	26.8
1968–69	32.2	31.1

547. In general, the main disability affecting women as a whole in relation to university education is that their participation in education at this level is much lower than that of men. The reasons for this position are difficult to identify, particularly as girls are participating equally with boys in secondary level education and are obtaining as good results as boys in the Leaving Certificate examination. In addition, there are no formal barriers placed by the universities on the entry of girls. It is probable that decisions by parents in this matter have reflected general attitudes of society and that many parents may have been inclined to invest in university education for boys in preference to girls. As stated above, the extension of the university grants scheme can be expected to bring about an improvement in the position. Also, removal of the marriage bar on a general basis and the growing acceptance of the fact that marriage need not be the end of a woman's career in employment will, we feel, operate very strongly to redress the present imbalance.

Having surveyed the situation of women in education, the Commission then made a number of recommendations for action to improve their status and opportunities at all levels. These proposals were presented in a usefully concise form in the 'Summary of Recommendations' at the end of the report, from which the following list of the Commission's proposals on education is excerpted.

Commission on the Status of Women, *Report to Minister for Finance* (1972)

(45) Primary education (paragraphs 526 and 527)
    (i) Opportunities which may arise in future to introduce co-education in specific instances should be availed of to the

fullest extent and the joint training of male and female teachers should be introduced where this is possible. (Paragraph 526)

(ii) Schools should be encouraged by the Department of Education to provide instruction in subjects which go beyond the traditionally accepted range of interests of either sex. (Paragraph 527)

(46) Post-primary education (Paragraphs 537 and 541)

(i) The Department of Education should investigate means by which the number of girls taking Mathematics and Science subjects to Leaving Certificate level could be significantly increased and it should initiate a definite programme designed to achieve this result. (Paragraph 537)

(ii) As a basis for effective career guidance in Vocational Schools, the Department of Education, the Vocational Education Authorities and the Department of Labour should cooperate to initiate studies with a view to identifying areas of technical and skilled employment in which job opportunities for girls are likely to expand and girls should be encouraged to pursue the course options relevant to such employment. (Paragraph 541)

In 1978 the Women's Representative Committee, in its *Second Progress Report on the Implementation of The Recommendations in the Report of the Commission on the Status of Women*, noted some positive developments. The Committee cited the growing demand for coeducation as well as the fact that all teacher training was now mixed. It was also true that education policy was now aimed at increasing the numbers of girls taking mathematics and science courses. Career guidance, particularly in vocational schools, had been expanded and upgraded. Nevertheless, the Committee emphasised that many of these efforts required a long-term commitment and sustained scrutiny if the goal of equal opportunities in education was to be accomplished. The Committee declared its belief that:

a great deal of inequality of educational opportunity in general education still exists, despite recent developments in education, and...the curricula followed by girls in post-primary schools is a contributory factor to the streaming of girls into typically female occupations and to the lack of representation of women in senior positions. The Committee realised at a very early stage the importance of educational opportunity for girls and believed that equality in employment is unlikely to be achieved for women unless our educational system is accessible to each person regardless of sex.

POLICIES FOR CHANGE IN THE 1980S

Whereas, in the 1970s, gender-based discrimination in employment and welfare was amenable to legislative remedies on the principle of the 'equality contract' (see Chapters 1 and 2 of this book), there were no formal legal or administrative barriers to Irish girls or women in education. This actually made it more difficult to effect any changes: distinctions between 'men's pay' and 'women's pay', or between 'men's jobs' and 'women's jobs', proved easier to eliminate than the entrenched, often unspoken or unpublicised perceptions that there were 'girl's subjects' and 'boy's subjects'. Since 1970 many, if not most, of the recommendations of the various bodies established to examine the participation of women in education have centred on taking down such 'invisible barriers' to equal opportunities. The persistence of such concerns is evidenced by their extensive treatment in a series of documents: *Irish Women: Agenda for Practical Action* (1985) by the Working Party on Women's Affairs and Family Law Reform; *The Report to Government* of the Second Commission on the Status of Women (1993); and the *Second Progress Report of the Monitoring Committee on the Implementation of the Recommendations of the Second Commission on the Status of Women* (1996). While the first Commission on the Status of Women had offered just four recommendations on education (see above) and there were only three in *Irish Women: Agenda for Practical Action*, the Second Commission, however, made some forty recommendations.

Notwithstanding the first Commission's reference to an 'absence of barriers', both the Women's Representative Committee and the Working Party on Women's Affairs and Family Law Reform noted that up to 1977–78 there were 'administrative rules and regulations which discriminated against girls and women teachers'. These barriers were deleted from the Department of Education's rule books in the late 1970s. Colleges of education, which trained students for careers in teaching, became co-educational at the same time.

Yet these welcome developments were seen to be insufficient, as the Working Party put it, 'to eliminate sexism or change the education system in a fundamental way'.

By the early 1980s educational policy-makers had recognised the need for a comprehensive plan for attaining equality in education. The Employment Equality Agency and the Department of Education commissioned the Economic and Social Research Institute (ESRI) to prepare a report on the education system. The ESRI's report, *Sex Differences in Subject Provision and Student Choice in Post-primary Schools* (1983), also known as the Hannon Report, demonstrated the existence of sexism in the school system and the need for measures to eliminate it. The report and the Employment Equality Agency's response resulted in the formation of a Department of Education Working Party, which in turn developed a *Programme for Action in Education 1984–1987*, published in 1984. This offered several general guidelines for action and then moved on to consider the issue of sexism. Paragraph 2.12 of the document called for discussion with publishers on the issue of sexism in textbooks used in national schools. As a result, in May 1984 the Department of Education published *Guidelines for Publishers on Sexism and Sex-stereotyping in Primary School Textbooks.* Only textbooks that comply with the guidelines are now added to the approved list, although textbooks published before May 1984 can remain on the approved list even if they contain material judged to be sexist.

The Working Party on Women's Affairs and Family Law Reform provided details of these developments in its *Agenda* (1985). It also reiterated the ESRI's emphasis on adult education.

Working Party on Women's Affairs and Family Law Reform, *Irish Women: Agenda for Practical Action* (1985)

Programme for Action in Education
3.15 The Programme for Action in Education contains the first ever positive commitment by Government to develop a strategy to eliminate sexism in education. The Minister outlines how she will develop this strategy as follows:

- a programme will be organised to raise the level of awareness amongst educators, parents and pupils so that a concentrated effort will be made to break down traditional barriers and provide better preparation for all young people for adulthood and the world of work;

- the nomination of women to the selection boards for principals of national schools will be encouraged;
- in the course of the proposed review of teacher training programmes, the need to make teachers more aware of their role in eliminating sexism in education will be emphasised;
- regional seminars will be held to make school managers and teachers aware of all aspects of sex differentiations within the school situation and, in particular, in relation to curricular provision;
- discussions will be initiated with publishers concerning the question of sexism/sex-stereotyping in school textbooks;
- the extent to which sexism/sex-stereotyping is reflected in the school curriculum will be the responsibility of the National Board for Curriculum and Examinations which has a specific remit in this regard.

The implementation of the Programme for Action in Education
3.16 A Coordinating Committee has been set up within the Department of Education to coordinate the implementation of the measures referred to in paragraph 3.15 above and to date the following initiatives have been taken:

SEX-STEREOTYPING
(i) Discussions have taken place with the principal educational publishers and agreement has been reached on guidelines, based on the standards set out by the International Reading Association, which will be applied to all new textbooks and to existing books as they are revised. These standards will also be applied to the Department's examination papers. These guidelines define stereotyping as 'a commonly held view of the characteristics of groups, beliefs and institutions, often simplified and rigid'. No allowance is made for individual differences. The process of stereotyping related to sexes often concentrates on characteristics which are specific to biological sex differences. Most instances of sex-stereotyping appear to relate to the female sex, but the full and accurate meaning of the term includes stereotyping 'whereby males or females are arbitrarily assigned to roles determined and limited by their sex'. Sexism is described as 'discrimination against (another) sex'. This is usually perceived as being against the female sex, portraying too restrictive a view of their

roles and rights. The term has the implications of bias and of premeditated distortion. These definitions are those adopted world-wide and have been devised by the International Reading Association whose guidelines for evaluating sex-stereotyping in reading materials is incorporated in the document agreed with the publishers.

EEA CODE OF PRACTICE
(ii) Special measures are being taken to ensure that women are appointed to the selection boards for teachers and that the code of practice of the Employment Equality Agency in regard to interview procedures be put into practice. Insofar as second-level school appointments are concerned, the Department of Education has drawn the attention of school management authorities to the code and indicated the Minister's support for it. The principal patrons of national schools have agreed to a request from the Minister to have a woman nominated to the selection boards for teachers. The Rules of Procedure for Boards of Management have been revised so as to ensure that the Employment Equality Agency's code of practice in relation to interview boards and appointment procedures is followed in all cases.

MEASURES TO TACKLE SEXISM
(iii) A series of regional seminars for Principals of second-level schools was held in 1984. The inspectors organised seminars for Principals of national schools and part of the time was devoted to an examination of school policy, ethos, tradition and teaching materials in the light of the Minister's commitment to eliminate sexism and sex-stereotyping. Courses in education management being organised by the Department for second-level Principals will also deal with this matter. Furthermore, the inspectors are encouraging managerial authorities of mixed schools to offer all the subject provision equally to boys and girls and, in particular, to offer girls the opportunity and actively encourage them to take technical subjects.

Subject choice and take-up
3.17 One of the principal criticisms made in recent years has been the small number of girls taking higher-level mathematics in second-level schools. While there is still room for further improvement, it should be recognised that the numbers have increased by 365% over the period 1973–83. Table 1, at the back of the Chapter [not included], sets out the growth in the numbers of pupils taking higher-level programmes in mathematics in post-primary schools in that period. The Minister has appealed to school authorities to offer all optional subjects equally

to both boys and girls and, in particular, to offer and encourage girls to take up Physics, Chemistry and Technical Subjects and boys to take up Home Economics. Schools which do not have the full facilities for Science or Home Economics teaching or the specialist teachers required are being encouraged to share facilities locally, especially amongst small neighbouring schools.

The educational guidance service

3.18 It is recognised that school guidance counsellors have a special role to play in raising the level of awareness of girls of the educational opportunities available, the importance of subject choice for further education and careers. School authorities will be encouraged to have a school guidance programme so as to involve all the school staff in the establishment of school objectives and the provision of the best possible service to all pupils.

Principles of guidance service

3.19 The quality of the guidance service available to girls will determine the pace of change which must be brought about to eliminate sexism in the education system and broaden the educational and vocational opportunities available to girls. The criteria which should underline the service, in relation to equal opportunities, will include the following:

Guidance programmes for girls

- must assist them in learning basic skills necessary for optimum vocational decision-making;
- must expand the occupational horizons which currently exercise constraints on their decision-making;
- must counteract the psychological pressures which operate to inhibit the range of women's occupational choice and the massive stereotyping of occupations by sex to which girls are exposed;
- must cater for the interaction of the roles of marriage, motherhood and occupation;
- must assist the development of behaviours which enhance sound vocational decision-making as well as sound decision-making and coping behaviours in other spheres of life.

Amongst the methods used to develop such skills effectively would be exposure to role models of adult women who have followed different combinations of marriage, parenthood and career patterns.

Counselling programmes

3.20 Counselling programmes for girls must include a variety of approaches to expose them to a wide range of occupational opportunities as well as helping them to focus on their perception of their future roles, so that women will not only be able to choose and develop in a wider range of occupations, but will be able to combine a successful career with marriage, parenthood, and homemaking in a world in which sex roles will become more equalised.

THE CURRICULUM AND EXAMINATIONS BOARD AND CURRICULUM DEVELOPMENT

3.21 This Board was set up on an interim basis on 23 January, 1984 and will be established on a statutory basis in 1986. The Board will be concerned with the structure and content of curricula at first and second level and it has been given a specific remit to take account of the recent research carried out in relation to sex differences in subject provision and student choices in Irish Post-Primary Schools and of the Department's evaluation and proposals in regard to this research. In its first published policy document, the Board states inter alia:

> The Board welcomes intervention strategies to reduce sex-stereo-typing in education. It also welcomes initiatives to create a favourable climate for change, especially through teacher development: a highly professional teaching force is of central importance.

Curriculum development

3.22 Three major curriculum projects, located in the Curriculum Centres in Shannon and Dublin and the Town of Galway VEC, were initiated in 1983. The projects have the broad aim of promoting active links between schools and the local community in order to provide young people with a better social and vocational preparation for adult life. The projects are co-funded by the Department of Education and the Commission of the European Communities and form part of a Community-wide programme of projects aimed at improving the preparation of young people for adult and working life.

Details of curriculum development projects

3.23 The Shannon Project focuses primarily on the development of alternative programmes within the educational system and the main thrust will be towards the development of alternative senior cycle programmes leading to national certification, which will link in with the work of the Curriculum and Examinations Board in this area. The Dublin Project is concerned principally with the social and vocational preparation of young people in the inner city with poor prospects of employment, and the ethos of the project will be to broaden the educational experience of participants to include activities which emphasise the link between the world of the school and the world of adult responsibility. The Galway Project emphasises the development of the skills and aptitudes of the student as well as the value of continuing inservice development of teachers and the need for the promotion of attitude changes on the part of pupils, parents, teachers and the community at large in the area of subject and career choice.

RELEVANCE OF PROJECTS TO GIRLS

3.24 All three projects pay particular attention to the problems facing girls and young women in finding and entering suitable employment. While they all share the goal of attitude change, which is the particular concern of the Galway project, both Shannon and Dublin are undertaking specific interventions directed at girls and young women. Shannon has developed a familiarisation course on non-traditional occupations for girls at school, involving the use of a variety of materials and experiences. Dublin is developing a programme for young women who have left school to develop confidence and competence in their lives and thereby strengthen their self-image.

Sex categories of schools

3.25 It has been stated in the Programme for Action in Education that educating children of both sexes together is more in keeping with the concept of equality between the sexes and provides a better basis for developing cooperative but equal roles of men and women in adult life. Tables 2 and 3 [not included] show the position with regard to co-education, at primary and post-primary level, between 1975/76 and 1982/83, with a trend towards co-education growing in both sectors. The Programme for Action provides that proposals for new primary schools on a co-educational basis will be encouraged and the reorganisation of school provision on such a basis will be facilitated. Any reorganisation will have to take into account the total provision of primary education within an area.

Primary schools

3.26 Insofar as primary schools are concerned, the rural schools have generally been mixed while the larger schools in the urban areas have catered separately for boys and girls. To some extent this was due to the involvement of the religious orders but it is also due to the desire to allow women to become principals of large schools, because up to 1975 the rules for national schools required a male principal to be appointed to schools which catered for boys.

Secondary schools

3.27 Secondary schools were traditionally separate boys' and girls' schools, mainly due to the involvement of the religious orders. There has been a movement towards co-educational schools and, where local circumstances permit, schools are facilitated in this regard. The new types of Community and Comprehensive schools (with two exceptions for local reasons) are all co-educational. Vocational and Technical schools, with few exceptions, have been co-institutional in the past but in recent years many of these schools function on a co-educational basis, a trend which will be encouraged and will continue where school facilities are suitable for such arrangements.

Participation of women in higher education

3.28 As in other areas of education, legislative arrangements ensure equality of access to the institutions of higher education. Conditioning and the concept of the traditional role of women has been and is (although to a diminishing extent) reflected both in the numbers of women who seek places in higher education, and in the course area to which they seek admission. Those women who have moved into third-level education tended, and still tend, to apply for courses in areas traditionally associated with women undergraduates and workers – the humanities, business, languages, social sciences, and to move to careers in these areas, particularly teaching.

UNDERLYING REASONS FOR SEX-STEREOTYPING

3.29 A number of factors have contributed to this situation e.g.

(1) *constraints* in pupil's choice of subject at second level; these are imposed by structural arrangements within the second-level system, by imbalances in the range of subjects offered and by subject packages within the curriculum; in many schools, students of both sexes still find it difficult to opt for subject packages which are non-traditional for their sex for both practical and psychological reasons;

(2) *attitudinal factors* such as

• sex-stereotyped influences within the formal and informal educational environment;

- sex-linked behaviour (caused by traditional structures rather than current attitudes);
- attitudes (parental, school, society generally).

Applications procedure

3.30 There is no discrimination in the selection process for admission to higher education courses. For the majority of higher education institutions, application is through the Central Admissions Office, and based on performance in the Leaving Certificate or Matriculation examinations. In their applications for admission to courses women still show a marked preference for those professions traditionally associated with women and the numbers of women applying for courses in areas such as engineering and agricultural science is still disproportionately small. Table 4 [not included] shows the gradually improving participation of women in higher education from 1972/73.

ADULT EDUCATION

3.31 In the course of the examination of the findings of the ESRI Report on Sex and Schooling it was recognised that the adult education agencies have an important part to play in educating parents to break down the traditional barriers and prejudices which some parents may have in aspirations for sons and daughters. In July, 1984, the Minister for Education asked all the organisations and agencies involved in adult education to do everything possible to improve the awareness of parents in this regard.

Report of Commission on Adult Education

3.32 The Report of the Commission on Adult Education on Lifelong Learning recognises the changing position of women in Irish society and the important role adult education can play in releasing the potential of women as contributors to all aspects of Irish life, including the economy. It also recognised that adult education should promote awareness of women's rights and of the necessity to persevere in securing them.

IMPORTANCE OF ADULT EDUCATION TO WOMEN

3.33 Women have particular needs in the area of adult education. For instance, many women wish to re-enter working life outside the home after their children are reared. This emphasises the need for 'continuing' education for them during their time in the home in order to keep in touch with current educational developments, and to provide them with specific skills and aptitudes for a future working life. In addition, adult education fulfils a need for social and human development. It can, by increasing people's awareness of their worth and of the contribution they can make to society, do much to help the individual and thereby the community. Adult education can be particularly helpful to mothers who, despite the rapid pace of social change in society, continue to have a key role in the family. The present pace of life changes so quickly that the generations must be able to continue communicating with one another in a wide range of areas. The complexities of career choice for children, the consequences of employment not being available, new behavioural patterns among the youth, the drug culture etc. impose many strains on modern parents. By assisting parents, and particularly mothers, to cope with this phenomenon, adult education can act as an important stabilising influence in society.

Adult education agencies

3.34 The range of adult educational opportunities which are open to women is both broad and diverse. The Vocational Education Committees have supported and promoted adult education for many years and are the largest single provider of adult education ranging from leisure courses to third-level degrees. At present, around 120,000 people take part in their courses, and in the general non-certificate courses, the ratio of women to men is in the order of 2:1. In addition, the country's community and comprehensive schools – now more than fifty in number – have begun to constitute a significant part of the adult education service. In the Deed of Trust for Community Schools, it is specified that these schools 'would provide adult education facilities in the area and ... would make facilities available to voluntary organisations and to the adult community generally'. Many of these schools have developed into community learning centres which attract large numbers of adults, and are the focus of many formal and non-formal educational activities. Other adult education outlets include voluntary secondary schools, ANCO, the universities, the NIHEs, the trade unions and a number of other voluntary agencies

RECOMMENDATION

3.35 There are, however, certain constraints in the way of many women wishing to undertake adult education. Many women find it difficult to meet the fees required to attend classes. In the case of third-level education, there is a time limit on the taking up of higher education grants, which militates against 'mature' students. Finally, where day classes are involved, the absence of adequate creche facilities is a real barrier for mothers with young children. As regards the first point, the removal of the existing fees for adult education classes would, however, be difficult to justify for one category, such as women working at home. A wider criterion of need would have to be established. Equally, in the case of the higher education grants scheme, opening it up to mature students generally would have significant cost implications at the present time. The removal of existing financial barriers for those who are not in a position to fund further education courses – the bulk of whom would be women – is in principle desirable and it is recommended that specific proposals to remove these barriers should be pursued. As regards the provision of creche facilities this is an area which women themselves could, in consultation with the new adult education advisors being appointed by the VECS, pursue with school authorities. The cooperation of the authorities in this development will be essential, if women with family responsibilities are to be given the opportunity to pursue adult education courses.

FURTHER DEVELOPMENTS IN THE 1990s

Several documents bearing upon gender issues in education appeared in the eight years between the publication of the *Agenda* and the issuing of the report of the Second Commission on the Status of Women in 1993. They provide data on the changing patterns in Irish education.

An official policy paper, *Department of Education – Gender Equality* (1990), reaffirmed that 'it is the policy of the Department of Education to promote gender equality in education and to eliminate sexism and sex stereotyping'. A Green Paper in 1992 and a White Paper in 1993 both restated the same commitment, while the White Paper also included responses to several recommendations made by the Second Commission.

Finally, the Working Group on the Elimination of Sexism and Sex-stereotyping in Textbooks and Teaching Materials in National Schools issued its report in 1992. To a large extent, the Working Group expressed disappointment at the slow pace of change. It concluded that 'sexism and stereotypical presentation remains [sic] in school textbooks and teaching materials, often to a degree unrepresentative of the present reality in society'. While the Working Group believed that this finding applied to all the areas it examined, it appeared to be especially applicable to the Cúrsaí Cómhrá – (Ghaeilge) ('Conversational Course – Irish') series, a study of which had uncovered sexist language and images. The Working Group made fourteen recommendations

Working Group on the Elimination of Sexism and Sex-stereotyping in Textbooks and Teaching Materials in National Schools, Report (1992)

Chapter 7: Recommendations
Number 1: The Working Group recommends that all text books approved for use in National Schools should be examined using the checklist recommended in this report, and that those textbooks identified as sexist should be withdrawn on a phased basis within five years of the date of such identification.

Number 2: The Working Group recommends that the 1984 *Guidelines for Publishers on Sexism and Sex-stereotyping in Primary School Textbooks* be replaced by the revised document contained in this report, *Regulations for Publishers on Sexism and Sex-stereotyping in Primary School Textbooks*, and that, in future, only books that comply with the regulations should be approved for use in National Schools. An award scheme should be initiated for new publications that best promote gender equality.

Number 3: The Working Group recommends that Rule 66 of the *Rules for National Schools* should be extended in scope so as to encompass in addition to textbooks all workbooks, illustrations and other teaching materials. Any changes or additions to the list should be notified to schools annually.

Number 4: The Working Group considers that the Cúrsaí Cómhrá – (Ghaeilge) series should be phased out over two years and that work should commence immediately on a new conversational Irish series which would rigidly adhere to the Regulations. In the interim, the Working Group recommends that the Department advise schools and Colleges of Education of the gender imbalance in the series which has been highlighted in the study, and advise the use of discretion by teachers in using the series, pending the issue of a new programme.

Number 5: The Primary Curriculum Review Body Report (1990) recommended revised subject guidelines across a range of subjects.

The Working Group recommends that all such guidelines should include direct reference to equal opportunity for boys and girls, and further recommends that the *Teachers' Handbook* of 1971 be revised as necessary so as to remove all sexist references, particularly in the following subject areas: Art and Crafts, Mathematics, Music and Physical Education.

Number 6: The Working Group recommends that a further examination should be conducted into other aspects of the Curriculum to establish the extent of omission of women from the Curriculum textbooks, and from related workbooks, and to recommend remedies.

Number 7: The Working Group recommends that the Gender Module in preservice education be reviewed to ensure that due emphasis is given to the topic and to ensure that the role of the teacher in promoting equal opportunity in the classroom is adequately highlighted.

Number 8: The Working Group recommends that in-service education on the topic of Gender Equality in Primary Education should be planned to ensure that all teachers and inspectors are given an adequate programme of in-service training on the topic within the next five years. It is recommended that at least one day's training should be provided for every teacher and inspector.

Number 9: The Working Group recommends that the practice of registering boys and girls separately in all official records should be discontinued.

Number 10: The Working Group recommends that a campaign should be initiated which would make parents more aware of the major role they play in relation to the non-stereotypical development of their children.

Number 11: The Working Group recommends that an information pack which could be made available to schools and Parents' Associations should be produced in order to increase awareness of the issue. This pack should include a copy of the *Regulations for Publishers* and checklist, an example of a completed checklist, and some background information on the research on this issue.

Number 12: The Working Group recommends that a positive action programme be initiated in a number of National Schools to redress gender bias in textbooks and teaching materials and to develop a programme for general use in National Schools.

Number 13: The Working Group felt that changes in textbooks and teaching materials should be supported in the promotion of gender equality by attention to school Organisation procedures such as those raised in the *E.C. Action Handbook* (Sections 2.1 and 3.2), and recommends that schools be requested to have regard to such equality matters when drawing up *pleananna scoile* [school plans].

Number 14 :While the Department of Education is not involved in the approval of religious education textbooks and teaching materials, the Working Group recommends that the authorities who sanction such books should be made aware of the *Regulations for Publishers* and the checklist contained in this report, and be requested to comply with these,

The Third Oireachtas Joint Committee on Women's Rights published a lengthy report in March 1992, entitled *Gender Equality in Education in the Republic of Ireland (1984–1991)*. This is a wide-ranging survey of developments in such areas as co-education, teacher training, the curriculum and adult education. That the Joint Committee offered thirty-nine recommendations suggests that, despite the progress that had been made, there was much yet to be done. The Joint Committee advocated more vigorous action to identify and remove from use textbooks containing sexist material. Here, too, the revision of the Irish language curriculum and materials was seen as a matter of urgency.

The Joint Committee also expressed concern about the lower performance of girls in mathematics at the age of 13 compared to their performance at the age of 9, as well as their performance in higher-level mathematics, chemistry and physics. On a general level, it suggested that 'whole school' reviews be undertaken, with an emphasis on preparation for life and gender equity. It also recommended a review of admission requirements in those departments of third-level institutions 'where young women are seriously under-represented'. Finally, there were a number of recommendations dealing with such administrative matters as funding for in-service training, promotion criteria, and interviewing and hiring procedures.

The report of the Second Commission on the Status of Women (1993) contained a lengthy chapter on education that explored gender equity and opportunities for girls and women, from pre-schooling through third-level institutions to 'second chance' education. The Report first of all called for general equality legislation that would extend protection against discrimination to the field of education. There followed a host of specific recommendations covering a wide variety of educational practices and procedures. Many were aimed at modifying traditional views on gender roles in education as these views affected students, teachers and administrators. In the light of this exploration the Second Commission put forward forty-one recommendations. These covered such matters as combating sexual stereotyping in staff attitudes and in textbooks; the provision of guidelines and training for teachers; and the need for equity in the appointment of school inspectors and administrators. The Commission also emphasised the need for curriculum review and development at both the second level (secondary or post-primary schools) and the third level (institutions devoted to higher and further education). Finally there were recommendations for expanding adult and 'second chance' education.

Second Commission on the Status of Women, *Report to Government* (1993)

Complete list of recommendations
- tackling, in line with the Council of Europe recommendation cited at 8.8.2 [not included], sex discrimination and stereotyped thinking in organisational structures;
- equitably funding women's sports organisations and activities, including facilities and services such as child care;
- ensuring that all sports stadia should have adequate toilet facilities for women and men.

19. COSPOIR (PARAGRAPH 8.8.4)
The Commission recommends that:
(a) Cospoir be reconstituted as a matter of urgency;
(b) it be given the task of implementing the National Sports Policy outlined in paragraph 8.6.3 above [not included];
(c) its membership should be selected in line with the 40%/60% gender balance set out in our First Statement to Government.

20. SPORTS FUNDING (PARAGRAPH 8.8.5)
The Commission recommends that adoption and implementation of a proposed Code of Conduct for equal opportunities in sport should be a criterion for deciding on eligibility for National Lottery and other public funding.

Education

1. LEGISLATION FOR EQUALITY IN EDUCATION (PARAGRAPH 9.1.2)
The Commission recommends that:
(a) legislation be enacted to provide for equality of opportunity

between girls and boys in terms of access and subject choice;
(b) a gender equity provision should be incorporated in the proposed Education Act;
(c) the Minister for Women's Affairs together with the Equality Commission, as proposed by this Commission (see Chapters 1 and 7), should have a monitoring function in the implementation of equality policy in education.

2. PROMOTION AND MONITORING OF GENDER EQUALITY POLICY (PARAGRAPH 9.1.3)

The Commission recommends that:
(a) a designated officer at Assistant Secretary level in the Department of Education should be assigned responsibility for the promotion and implementation of gender equity policy in all areas of the education system; the promotion and implementation of this policy should not await the formal enactment of legislation providing for equality in education as recommended in 9.1.2;
(b) under the supervision of the designated officer, responsibility for the promotion and implementation of gender equity policy in all areas of the education system should be the sole concern of a full-time Principal Officer or equivalent with an appropriate support staff.

3. CO-EDUCATION (PARAGRAPH 9.1.4)

The Commission recommends that in co-educational schools, proper monitoring and review procedures be put in place at individual school and departmental level, and accompanied by sympathetic policies such as outlined in 9.1.5(e) below, to ensure that girls in co-educational schools are not disadvantaged academically or socially vis-á-vis boys.

4. EQUALITY POLICY IN CO-EDUCATIONAL SCHOOLS (PARAGRAPH 9.1.5)

The Commission recommends the development by the Department of Education of an equality policy to be implemented by all co-educational schools. Implementation should be reviewed and monitored by the Department of Education. This policy should have the following key features:
(a) equal access to all subjects for both genders;
(b) advice on timetabling to ensure that when choices are provided 'girls' subjects' are not set directly against 'boys' subjects' with an attendant pre-programmed choice;

(c) in-service training for teachers to develop an awareness of sexism, with particular emphasis on the teacher's own attitudes, on classroom management, and on peer-group pressures on pupils;

(d) the selection of non-sexist teaching materials;

(e) as an interim measure, it may be helpful to use single sex groupings in some subject options, particularly in non-traditional subject areas for girls, as a method of developing the self-confidence of girls;

(f) positive interventions to influence the attitudes of students and parents; in particular, to make the connection for students and parents of the significance of subject choice for eventual career and earning power;

(g) integrating both genders in the management structures and organisation of the school; men should be included in caring roles and women should be assigned positions of authority.

5. EQUALITY POLICY IN SINGLE-SEX SCHOOLS (PARAGRAPH 9.1.6)

The Commission recommends that:

(a) the Department of Education should actively promote co-education, particularly in primary schools, and should introduce an incentive scheme to encourage the amalgamation of single-sex schools;

(b) with the exception of points 9.1.5(b) and 9.1.5(e) all the other features outlined in 9.1.5 above should be implemented in single sex schools.

6. SCHOOL INSPECTORATE (PARAGRAPH 9.1.7)

The Commission recommends that:

(a) the Department of Education should review the recruitment, deployment, and working procedures of primary and post-primary school inspectors with the aim of increasing the number of women inspectors;

(b) when the Department next advertises for inspectors, it should emphasise that it is an equal opportunities employer and encourage women to apply for posts; and

(c) all school inspectors, those already serving and those to be appointed in the future, should participate in in-service training on gender equity issues.

7. IN-SERVICE COURSES AND PRE-SERVICE TRAINING (PARAGRAPH 9.1.8)

The Commission recommends that:

(a) the Department of Education should initiate a programme of in-service training designed to raise teachers' awareness of gender equity issues;

(b) there should be a target of having all existing teachers complete such training within a 5 year period with priority being given to teachers in schools which are going co-educational as a result of amalgamation;

(c) such in-service courses should be of at least one day's duration;

(d) the best format for these courses be researched, drawing inter alia on the experience of teachers;

(e) gender equity should be a module in all in-service courses, i.e. in specific subjects. This module should take account of any specific research emerging on the Irish experience of education;

(f) all incoming teachers should be educated in gender equity issues as part of their training whether in teacher training colleges or the Education Departments of Universities;

(g) with regard to Primary Schools, the gender module in pre-service education should be revised to ensure that the role of teachers in promoting equal opportunity in the classroom is highlighted, as recommended by the Working Group on the Elimination of Sexism and Sex-stereotyping in Textbooks and Teaching Materials in National Schools (see paragraph 9.1.9).

8. SEXISM AND SEX-STEREOTYPING IN BOOKS AND MATERIALS (PARAGRAPH 9.1.9)

The Commission recommends that:

(a) the recommendations in the report of the Working Group on the Elimination of Sexism and Sex-stereotyping in Textbooks and Teaching Materials in National Schools be implemented;

(b) the Working Party on the Elimination of Sexism in Textbooks, Teaching Materials and Curricula in Post-primary Schools be re-established with a definite timescale to complete its work and report to the Department of Education;

(c) the Department of Education should implement the recommendations of the Post-primary Working Party once it has finished its task;

(d) the Department of Education should direct the National Council for Curriculum and Assessment to draw up lists of gender-fair reading books and reading material for use in the different subjects; and to increase the representation of women in the various syllabi. The NCCA should in due course take account of any proposals emerging from the Post-primary Working Party referred to at (b) above;

(e) Department aided or approved curriculum development projects should require that the texts and materials produced are free from stereotypes and have a positive approach to promoting gender equity.

(f) the Department of Education should ensure that examination questions are free of sexism.

9. GUIDELINES FOR TEACHERS ON NON-SEXIST BEHAVIOUR (PARAGRAPH 9.1.10)

The Commission recommends that:

(a) guidelines for teachers for non-sexist behaviour in the classroom be established by the Department of Education in consultation with the teachers' unions and the Employment Equality Agency;

(b) these guidelines should be linked into the proposed in-service training module for existing teachers and into the proposed gender equity module for trainee teachers (see Recommendation 9.1.7).

10. HIDDEN CURRICULUM (PARAGRAPH 9.11)

The Commission recommends that:

(a) schools should examine their organisation, practices, policies and allocation of resources to ensure that a gender equity policy and programme of action to redress imbalances can be put in place;

(b) if necessary, school boards of management should be required to adopt a gender equity policy and action programme for day-to-day implementation by the school principal and staff;

(c) the gender equity action programme should be composed of 3 elements designed to ensure equality (i) for pupils, (ii) for staff and (iii) in administrative practices.

11. ROLE OF PARENTS (PARAGRAPH 9.1.12)

The Commission recommends that:

(a) the Minister for Education should develop a policy to enable parents to take a greater role in the education of their children;

(b) accordingly, the Minister for Education should allocate resources to the National Parents' Councils (Primary and Post-primary) in order to facilitate the establishment of Parents' Committees as an organised representative structure to liaise with School Boards of Management;

(c) information be targeted at parents on how Boards of Management are organised and what their respective rights and duties are;

(d) school managements should have an onus to advise parents on the importance of the rationale for gender equity policies;

(e) the Department of Education should prepare a leaflet for parents on the implications of subject choice for long-term career prospects;

(f) school administration and organisation should take account of the time commitments of both parents and their need to plan ahead, e.g. through providing parents at the beginning of each term with a list of days when the school will be closed.

12. APPOINTMENT OF SCHOOL PRINCIPALS (PARAGRAPH 9.1.13)

The Commission recommends that:

(a) appointments to the interview board for the position of school principal should be made from a panel whose members have attended a training course on selection and appointment procedures and criteria;

(b) these courses should include sensitivity to and awareness of gender equity issues;

(c) the Department of Education should introduce attendance at such courses and placement on these panels as a requirement for eligibility to serve on an interview board;

(d) persons serving on interview boards should, as a matter of routine, be provided with a copy of the EEA's Code of Practice on Interviews.

13. CHILD ABUSE PREVENTION PROGRAMME (PARAGRAPH 9.1.14)

The Commission recommends that:

(a) the Stay Safe Child Abuse Prevention Programme should be implemented nationwide during the academic year 1993/94;

(b) an appropriate programme on sexual abuse for Post-primary schools should be devised and implemented with a view to extending it nationwide by the academic year 1995/96;

(c) for the purpose of training teachers on the implementation of the programme, the Department of Education should grant a special training day to all schools;

(d) sufficient funds should be provided by the Health Promotion Unit and/or National Lottery to fund the implementation of the programme (teaching materials, office facilities, training etc.);

(e) all schools and their teachers should be required to participate in the programme and to organise parent meetings to facilitate greater awareness of child sexual abuse and ways of dealing with it.

14. EDUCATION FOR LIFE, RELATIONSHIPS AND PARENTING (PARAGRAPH 9.1.15)

The Commission recommends that:

(a) education for life, relationships, and parenting should be introduced at primary school level and taught as a core subject right through post-primary level;

(b) a module on the importance of equality in the lives of women and men and the injustice of inequality be included in all 'education for life' programmes;

(c) the subject of education for life, relationships and parenting should incorporate a module on prejudice against Travellers and persons who experience discrimination due to race or religious belief; the module should, at post-primary level, also deal with homophobia;

(d) a sex education programme should be developed by the Department of Education which will give young people, male and female, a sense of personal autonomy and responsibility in relationships; it should be introduced in primary schools and continued in all second-level schools at a level appropriate to each age group (see Chapter 5).

15. PHYSICAL EDUCATION AND SPORT (PARAGRAPH 9.1.16)

The Commission recommends:

(a) the development and implementation of a national policy for school sport; a basic requirement of this policy should be the provision of sports facilities for all schools and of trained physical education teachers for Post-primary schools. Smaller schools could share teachers and facilities;

(b) that a key objective in the development of a national school sports policy should be the equitable treatment of boys and girls with regard to the allocation of facilities, transport, time and expertise, particularly in the context of team sports;

(c) that when community sports facilities are being developed, they should be built where they are accessible to schools;

(d) that teaching approaches should reflect an acceptance of all body types in the context of physical activity and that physical education generally should promote more positive body images in all pupils and among girls in particular;

(e) that as physical education programmes are drawn up by the Department of Education and at individual school level, they should reflect the desirability of providing opportunities for both boys and girls to participate in a range of activities, including those which have traditionally been strongly identified with one sex, e.g. football, dancing, as well as those which are gender-neutral, e.g. swimming;

(f) that the practice of having same-sex physical education teachers and pupils should be examined in the context of the development of a school sports policy as it reinforces the segregation of boys and girls;

(g) that as part of their training all physical education teachers should be taught to be aware of, and avoid, sex-stereotyping in carrying out their work.

16. YOUTH ORGANISATIONS (PARAGRAPH 9.1.17)

The Commission recommends that:

(a) youth organisations should develop equal opportunity programmes with specific targets;

(b) grants should be provided by the Department of Education to youth service providers which operate equal opportunity programmes;

(c) mixed units should be introduced in hitherto single sex youth organisations;

(d) more female voluntary youth leaders should be encouraged, through the provision of specific training.

17. STATISTICS (PARAGRAPH 9.1.18)

The Commission recommends that the Minister for Education should have her/his Department implement a policy on statistics, whereby a range of information broken down on a gender basis would be collected and made available routinely in order to monitor effectively the implementation of equality policy.

18. PROVISION OF PRE-SCHOOL EDUCATION (PARAGRAPH 9.2.1)

The Commission recommends that:

(a) community-based pre-school education be adopted by the Government as a policy aim;

(b) the Departments of Health, Education and the Environment should work together to draw up a plan of implementation with children coming from situations of disadvantage getting immediate priority;

(c) a regional child care coordinator should be appointed in each Health Board area (see Chapter 4);

(d) as a first step, the waiting list for places for disadvantaged children should be eliminated.

19. IMPLEMENTATION OF CHILD CARE ACT (PARAGRAPH 9.2.2)

The Commission recommends that the Government should implement immediately the section of the Child Care Act dealing with regulations for the purpose of health, safety, welfare, and development of children attending pre-school services (see Chapter 4).

20. GUIDELINES FOR PRE-SCHOOL EDUCATION (PARAGRAPH 9.2.3)

The Commission recommends that the Department of Education should develop guidelines on the recommended activities and aims of pre-school education. These aims and activities should incorporate a positive gender equality dimension.

21. RECOGNISED STANDARDS FOR TEACHERS AND PRE-SCHOOL ASSISTANTS (PARAGRAPH 9.2.4)

The Commission recommends that the Department of Education should establish a common, recognised standard or range of standards for pre-school teachers and assistants, having regard to the nature of the work involved and the existing range of qualifications.

22. PRIMARY TEACHERS' HANDBOOK (PARAGRAPH 9.3.1)

The Commission recommends that the NCCA should prioritise the elimination of sex stereotyping and promote equality for boys and girls when drawing up all aspects of the Primary School Curriculum, i.e. when developing a statement of philosophy, teacher guidelines, curriculum handbooks, teaching materials and textbooks, and new science and technology subjects.

23. BOARDS OF MANAGEMENT (PARAGRAPH 9.3.2)

The Commission recommends that:

(a) the Department of Education should revise the Rules of Boards of Management of Primary Schools so that the Chairperson is elected by all the members of the Board of Management instead of being appointed by the patron;

(b) the Minister should require 50% – or as near as possible to that percentage – of the patron's nominees to the Board of Management to be women.

24. SUBJECT CHOICE (PARAGRAPH 9.4.1)
The Commission recommends that:
(a) first-year pupils in post-primary education should be allowed to sample a wide range of subjects so they can make the choice of a course of study and of eventual career based on their aptitudes;
(b) the widest possible curriculum should be available in all schools;
(c) to help facilitate this policy, gender equity issues should be taken into account when schools are amalgamated, to ensure that the accommodation and facilities can meet this need;
(d) the results of pilot projects should be made public so that the efficacy of such initiatives can be established. If positive conclusions have been drawn from these pilot projects, these can then inform policy making for equality.

25. NEW TECHNOLOGICAL SUBJECTS (PARAGRAPH 9.4.2)
The Commission recommends that:
(a) in providing technology on the school curriculum, schools should ensure that girls as well as boys have equal access to the full range of technology subjects to Leaving Certificate level;
(b) sampling/taster opportunities in non-traditional and new technology areas should be provided for pupils throughout second-level education (see Chapter 10).

26. POSITIVE ACTION PROGRAMME ON SUBJECT CHOICE (PARAGRAPH 9.4.3)
The Commission recommends that:
(a) the Department of Education should set in train a positive action programme designed to promote the choice of non-traditional subjects by girls, in view of the fact that subject choice has such an impact on careers; key elements of this programme would include:
  • increased provision of career guidance and counselling at junior and senior cycles for all pupils;
  • the agreement of targets between the Department of Education, school management and teacher unions for the provision of choice in non-traditional subjects in a fixed number of schools by a particular date with a view to introducing them into all schools within an agreed timetable;
(b) the Department of Education should prepare a leaflet for parents on the implications of subject choice for long-term career options; this could be complemented by seminars held by second-level schools for parents of incoming pupils;
(c) at individual school level the School Board of Management

should work closely with the school career guidance counsellor to ensure that there is actually a strategy on subject and career choice in place in each school (see Chapter 10).

27. LEAVING CERTIFICATE VOCATIONAL PROGRAMME (PARAGRAPH 9.4.4)
The Commission recommends that:
(a) pupils who wish to undertake the Leaving Certificate Vocational Programme should be allowed to choose from a wider range of subjects and that the list of approved subjects should be broadened to include, for example, the subjects of home economics, art and agricultural science;
(b) in the medium term, the Department of Education should ensure that non-traditional subjects which are to be added to the approved list are actually made available to all pupils who choose them;
(c) there should be close liaison between State training agencies and the Department of Education in relation to subject choice, training and career opportunities for young women (see Chapter 10).

28. BOARDS OF MANAGEMENT (PARAGRAPH 9.4.5)
The Commission recommends that:
(a) there should be at least 40% representation of either sex on post-primary school Boards of Management and that the Chairperson of the Board should be elected by members of the Board;
(b) training should be provided for Board members in relation to their responsibilities as Board members, and particularly with regard to gender equality.

29. APPOINTMENT AND PROMOTION OF TEACHERS (PARAGRAPH 9.4.6)
The Commission recommends that:
(a) boards charged with the recruitment of teachers be required by the Department of Education to adopt a Code of Practice based on that of the Employment Equality Agency to ensure gender equity in appointment and promotion procedures;
(b) the Green Paper proposal with regard to a minimum representation of both sexes on selection Committees be included in the Education Act;
(c) selection committees should receive training on the avoidance of discrimination based on sex and marital status;
(d) the Department of Education should draw up a recruitment guide which sets out gender-fair procedures for recruitment, including shortlisting.

30. DISADVANTAGED AREAS (PARAGRAPH 9.4.7)

The Commission recommends that more resources should be made available in the Department of Education budget for compensatory programmes and home liaison schemes for schools in disadvantaged areas (see Chapter 5).

31. NON-TRADITIONAL CHOICE AT THIRD LEVEL (PARAGRAPH 9.5.2)

The Commission recommends that positive intervention measures to encourage more women to take up non-traditional courses of study at third level should be implemented in order to overcome the cultural bias which militates against women making an informed choice based on their own aptitudes. Such measures should include:

- active encouragement of young women into non-traditional areas, e.g. technology, agricultural science. The promotional literature produced by colleges should convey positive images of women and overt encouragement into new and non-traditional subjects;
- open days to be held by third-level colleges specifically for girls' schools at which the advantages of choosing a non-traditional subject and the career options it would open up could be stressed. The best stage for reaching girls would be at junior cycle, second-level, so that they are then in a position to choose the right mix of subjects in their Leaving Certificate;
- the making and distribution of videos by colleges as aids to recruitment. Colleges could make videos which show women successful in a range of traditional and non-traditional courses of study;
- development and expansion of the FÁS series of leaflets on different career options and the education and abilities required in each case. FÁS's career vision series which sets out career options on video could be expanded to reinforce the 'normality' of women and men pursuing non-traditional occupations. These leaflets and videos should be distributed routinely to schools for use by parents;
- the revision of textbooks which are sex-stereotyped, and textbooks which may not feature girls and women at all. This requires specific initiatives lead by the Department of Education, implemented at college level, and underwritten by funding;
- the positive use of role models. A policy needs to be developed whereby young women who are successful in non-traditional disciplines and careers could visit schools to encourage more girls to choose beyond the stereotypes.

32. Equal opportunity issues (paragraph 9.5.3)

The Commission recommends that:

(a) all third-level colleges should be required to develop and implement equal opportunities policies and action programmes and a policy on sexual harassment for students and employees;

(b) there should be transparency in the appointment and promotions procedures in colleges with the inclusion of women on all interview boards in line with the Employment Equality Agency's Code of Practice on Equality of Opportunity in Employment;

(c) staff recruitment policy should also consider the importance of recruiting women to areas where they are under-represented, and in colleges where there is serious under-representation of women, e.g. specific Departments in the University of Limerick, Dublin Institute of Technology, and most Regional Technical Colleges;

(d) Equal Opportunities Officers should be budgeted for in each third-level college.

33. Access by adult students (paragraph 9.5.4)

The Commission recommends that:

(a) access by adult women to the general third-level grants scheme should be monitored to see if additional measures are required;

(b) the eligibility of older women for ESF-funded courses should be publicised;

(c) for adults over 25 years of age, it should be possible to aggregate the grades from Leaving Certificate subjects obtained over a number of years in order to qualify for a grant under the existing grants scheme;

(d) for adults seeking entry to third-level education, a system of credits, which can be built up in modular form in order to reach the appropriate educational standard for colleges, should be developed;

(e) as an alternative to (d) above, colleges should open up a proportion of places to older students who may lack the qualifications criteria required. Entry to these places – a small proportion of the overall places available – should be decided by interview or on the basis of performance in a foundation course;

(f) more evening courses should be provided.

34. Child care facilities (paragraph 9.5.5)

The Commission recommends that women students and staff have access to child care facilities (see Chapter 4).

35. REPORT OF COMMITTEE ON WOMEN ACADEMICS (PARAGRAPH 9.5.6)
The Commission recommends that:
(a) the Minister for Education should direct the HEA to adopt and implement the recommendations in the report of the Committee on the Position of Women Academics in Third-level Education (1987) forthwith;
(b) the Minister should direct the NCCA to adopt a similar set of recommendations for the colleges under its aegis.

36. ADULT EDUCATION AGENDAS OF WOMEN (PARAGRAPH 9.6.2)
The Commission recommends that the Government should develop a coherent strategy of adult education that responds to the actual and diverse needs of adult women returning to education, i.e. by providing opportunities for self-development, preparing women for returning to or establishing a career, and enabling women to assist in their children's education.

37. ADULT EDUCATION AT PRESENT (PARAGRAPH 9.6.3)
The Commission recommends that
(a) adequate financial provision be made to realise the adult education strategy proposed in paragraph 9.6.2;
(b) specifically, the self-financing principle for adult education courses provided under the aegis of the VECs should be ended or restricted to recreational activities;
(c) the provision of daytime adult education courses should be increased and extended to rural areas.

38. SELF-HELP INITIATIVES (PARAGRAPH 9.6.4)
The Commission recommends that:
(a) funding should be made available to self-help adult education groups on the basis of clear criteria as part of an overall adult education policy;
(b) the Department of Education should require VECs to furnish public information, via local press etc., on the size of each VEC's Adult Education and Community Literacy Budgets in order that women's self-help groups can seek financial support on an informed basis;
(c) in order for self-help women's groups to prosper it is also essential that there should be: (i) a supportive adult education officer in each region; (ii) guaranteed premises; and (iii) child care facilities during course hours.
(d) the Department of Education should carry out a feasibility study

into the development of an additional short-stay, State-funded or part State-funded residential college providing adult education and self-development courses.

39. SUPPORT MECHANISMS FOR WOMEN (PARAGRAPH 9.6.5)

The Commission recommends that regional women's education officers should be appointed to act as facilitators for women's self-help education groups and to respond to their needs. These officers might come under the aegis of AONTAS, VECs or the Department of Education, as the Minister deems most appropriate and effective.

40. PESP COMMITMENT (PARAGRAPH 9.6.6)

The Commission recommends that action on the proposed initiatives on adult education as set out in Section IV paragraph 69(0) of the PESP be implemented and, in particular, that local women's self-help groups should be represented on the proposed consultative group to advise on development needs in adult training and education.

41. LINKING ADULT EDUCATION AND TRAINING (PARAGRAPH 9.6.7)

The Commission recommends that an adult education strategy should be linked in to training opportunities in order that women (and men) can build on skills they may have acquired and aptitudes developed.

The *Second Progress Report of the Monitoring Committee on the Implementation of the Recommendations of the Second Commission on the Status of Women* (1996) outlined its view of the outcomes of the Second Commission's work, in education as in other fields. For the most part, the Monitoring Committee felt that it had positive results to report. First of all, it cited the government's affirmation, in the White Paper on Education published in 1993, of the principle of equality as the 'cornerstone of national educational policy'. Legislation to combat discrimination was about to be introduced by the Minister of Equality and Law Reform. This ultimately became the Equality Act 1998.

The Monitoring Committee's report then described recent changes in educational practices and procedures calculated to promote gender equality. At the administrative level, the task of supervising the changes had been assigned to an Assistant Secretary of Education. There had been changes in recruitment policies for the position of school inspector and in the composition of the boards of management of primary schools.

There had been a number of initiatives affecting teachers at the primary and secondary levels, notably in relation to in-service training, and new guidelines, including a *European Union Handbook*, now offered practical advice on gender equality issues. Although the Second Commission had recommended the active promotion of co-education, discussion of its implications for girls continued. Research was under way examining practices in both single-sex and co-educational schools. The formulation of an equality policy for all coeducational schools was in process, emphasising equal access of all students to all subjects, including 'non-traditional' courses. Steps were being taken to increase parental involvement in school matters.

Inevitably the school curriculum, textbooks and instructional material came under scrutiny in the context of gender equality. The task remained to eliminate gender stereotyping in these categories and to help teachers deal with the more subtle forms of gender 'tracking'. In addition, new courses offering wider choices were being introduced. Some were also anti-discriminatory, in the sense that they addressed prejudices against Travellers and people of other races and religions. At the post-primary level there was a programme called 'Relationships and Sexuality' that included the subject of homophobia. Extracurricular activities were being examined for gender bias and a review of the physical education curriculum was under way to ensure equitable treatment of boys and girls.

Third-level and adult education were also addressed by the Monitoring Committee. In the former case, the Higher Education Authority had assumed responsibility for monitoring gender equality measures. These included efforts to advise young women on careers, and in particular to encourage women to explore non-traditional courses of study such as technology or agricultural science. In addition to the monitoring initiatives, the Higher Education Authority had directed third-level institutions under its aegis to develop policies to promote gender equality in hiring and promotion of both academic and administrative staff. This was particularly needed, according to the Monitoring Committee, in colleges and in areas where women were under-represented. Third-level institutions were required to formulate policies and procedures for preventing sexual harrassment of students and employees.

In 1993 the Second Commission on the Status of Women had called for a 'coherent strategy of adult education' suited to the needs of women returning to education. The Monitoring Committee noted that a Further Education Authority was to be established to provide for that purpose. It was to seek to balance the 'level, type and variety of programmes to meet student and community needs, including the appropriate location of courses'.

CHAPTER EIGHT

Women's health

The report of the first Commission on the Status of Women (1972) did not contain a separate chapter on women's health. It made only a few references to such health-related issues as family planning and maternity leave, and noted the expansion in home help services under the Health Act 1970, which had also established the eight regional health boards.

In contrast, by 1985, when the Working Party on Women's Affairs and Family Law Reform published its *Irish Women: Agenda for Practical Action*, it felt it necessary to devote an entire chapter to health services, with particular emphasis on those services that it considered to be most relevant to women.

Working Party on Women's Affairs and Family Law Reform, *Irish Women: Agenda for Practical Action* (1985)

Relevant issues

4.1 In discussing issues relating to the provision of health services, it is difficult to be very precise about differentiating between services targeted to all groups within the population and those of particular relevance to women. The issues which the Working Party felt had the most bearing on women's health were the following:

(1) The development of the maternity and child welfare services (including the role of public health nurses).
(2) The location, planning and organisation of maternity hospitals.
(3) The issue of dental, optical and treatment benefit for the spouses of insured workers.
(4) Health education.
(5) Services for the prevention and treatment of specifically female

illnesses, or illnesses which have a disproportionate effect on
women (e.g. alcoholism).
(6) The provision of grants by the Health Boards etc. to organisations providing services for women.
(7) The home help service.
(8) Miscellaneous.

Day care provision for children is also a major issue which falls
under the Department of Health. However, in view of the wide
number of aspects involved, it is being dealt with in a separate
chapter.

Health indicators
4.2 It is worth looking briefly at some of the indicators of health,
morbidity, etc., differentiating men and women. As already indicated,
women's life expectancy is greater than men's. During the present
century, women's life expectancy has risen more rapidly than men's.
According to Central Statistics Office figures it has risen by as much as
3.1 years between 1961 and 1979, during which time men's life
expectancy rose only by 1.4 years. Female mortality rates from various
causes show striking differences to male rates. For instance, more
males die from heart disease, lung cancer, birth injuries, and diseases
of early infancy and motor vehicle accidents than females.

4.3 It would not be feasible to go into all the factors such as class,
occupational status, women's childbearing and housewife role etc.
which have a bearing on women's health. These are discussed in a
broad way in a report prepared for the Health Education Bureau on
issues relating to women's health. This study points to the close
interaction between all the various factors influencing health, but
nonetheless underlines the traditional differences between men and
women's health and life expectancy, as well as the differences
between women themselves, depending on their employment
status, social class, educational achievement etc. In terms of policy,
the limited research available on all these areas would make it
difficult if not impracticable to consider differential health provision
related to gender, but nonetheless policy makers should be aware
of the existing data available with a view to better informing policy
decisions. This is particularly true in the case of promotional health
programmes and the geographical location of particular medical
services. For instance, there is now considerable evidence of
differences in health status between social classes. The Black Report
carried out in Britain pointed to differences in availability and in the
quality of care available in different localities. Also, it found that the

structuring of health institutions in accordance with the values of the middle-class consumer had implications for the provisions of services to the less well-off, who suffered from lack of command over resources such as the ability to express themselves, time and money. Relating the various factors to women particularly, the Black Report showed that social class had a particularly detrimental effect on women in the case of circulatory disease, endocrine, nutritional and metabolic diseases of the digestive system.

Poverty and mental health
4.4 There is also some evidence of a link between poverty and women's mental health. A recent study found that among women with children at home, working-class women were four times more likely to suffer from a definite psychiatric disorder. Research of this type in Ireland, while limited, points to a similar pattern.

4.5 As already indicated, the implications of the various factors affecting women's health are impossible to determine precisely but it is nonetheless useful to highlight them, in order to set the various proposals being made in a particular context.

Health Education
4.46 The importance of health education is now well recognised and accepted throughout the community. A recent commentator in the field of health care recently stated: 'I am secure in saying that each added pound of expenditure in appropriate categories of prevention can yield greater benefits in this country, in the form of health and life, than equal added expenditure in medicine.' He went on to state that: 'a system which tolerates a dangerous and unhealthy environment and lifestyle, whether in the name of economic growth, human freedom, or saving money, and then spends millions to treat the resulting illnesses, is worse than merely inequitable and inefficient'.

ESTABLISHMENT OF HEALTH EDUCATION BUREAU
4.47 It was in recognition of the need to carry out preventative and educational programmes in the health care area that Governments in many countries established agencies to promote the idea of education for better health. In Ireland, in 1975, the Health Education Bureau (HEB) was established, with the functions of drawing up and executing programmes of health education, evaluating health education activities and acting as a national centre of expertise and knowledge in all aspects of health education.

MEASURING EFFECTIVENESS OF HEALTH EDUCATION
4.48 Before going on to elaborate on the work of the Bureau, it is worth stating that the link between 'persuasion' or information programmes on changes in human behaviour is difficult to measure. Even though considerable resources can be spent on a particular programme, the effect on the 'target' group may be minimal, (e.g. heavy cigarette consumers, the overweight). However, the effectiveness of these programmes on non-target groups may in fact be quite high, thus leading to a social environment where non-healthy living is discouraged.

THE WORK OF THE BUREAU
4.49 The Health Education Bureau to date has involved itself in a variety of projects, including nationwide campaigns aimed at the reduction of cigarette consumption, excessive alcohol consumption, the encouragement of physical exercise and vaccination programmes for children.

LIFE CYCLE APPROACH
4.50 The Bureau is at present employing a life cycle model in framing its programme format in an effort to identify key issues, phases and needs in health and illness throughout the life cycle. Even if programmes change from year to year continuing emphasis is given by the Bureau to key areas, such as the establishment of programmes on a co-operative basis with statutory and other national bodies with similar objectives; the making of programmes accessible and meaningful to the poor and the poorly informed; and the direction of programmes at women where women are more advantageously placed to influence the health of society as a whole. Current programmes of the Bureau include the following: work with voluntary bodies, community health education, pregnancy education and education for parenthood, infant welfare, childhood and adolescence, mid-life, later life, essential services, positive health promotion, and public visibility.

AMOUNT SPENT ON PROGRAMMES DIRECTLY AFFECTING WOMEN
4.51 The two programmes most directly affecting women's welfare – those dealing with pregnancy education and infant welfare – accounted for IR£160,000 in 1983 out of a total Budget of IR£1.25m (over 12% of the total Budget). The position in 1984 was that IR£423,000 was projected by the Bureau to be spent in the area of maternity and child health (over one-third of their total budget).

Most of the other programmes will also of course indirectly affect women's welfare.

RECOMMENDATION
4.52 In a context of limited resources, the Health Education Bureau has to decide each year within its annual budgetary allocation what its priorities should be. These will clearly change from year to year. The Working Party feels that a continuous component of the work of the Bureau will always have to be a programme geared to pregnancy, parenthood, and child welfare. The need for relevant information in this field will be an ongoing one for the foreseeable future, with a continuing high birth rate and a high number of women in the population in the childbearing age group. Particular categories of women need specialised advice such as older women, women who have given birth to a disabled child and women who have particular obstetrical difficulties. There is a need also for regular information about vaccination of infants, infant and childhood illness and early infant and childhood diet.

HEALTH EDUCATION AND SCHOOLS
4.53 Since its origin in 1975, the HEB has supported programmes and initiated developments which aimed to promote greater awareness and responsibility for health among pupils and training in various forms of communication skills for teachers. In addition, the HEB promotes and gives support to developmental groupwork projects being carried out in schools and through national youth organisations. Also, the Bureau and individual health boards are involved in a variety of projects in health board areas. Examples of some projects are teacher training and the provision of materials to pupils in the Lifeskills Programme (North Western Health Board), developmental groupwork with teachers and pupils, including the provision of materials (Western Health Board), the Ogra Chorcai Project which offers training to teachers and group leaders with similar general aims and the Education for Living Programme being carried out by North Tipperary Vocational Education Committee (Mid-Western Health Board).

POSITION IN SCHOOLS
4.54 In Primary schools, health education is included in the Physical Education Section of the New Curriculum. Its child-centred and experiential approach provides the basic ingredients for developing

attitudes and values conducive to good health behaviour. However, the implementation of a specific health education programme such as that referred to above, seems to be dependent on particular school policies and the initiatives taken by individual teachers. Within post-primary schools, health education is not a specific subject area.

RECOMMENDATION

4.55 The Working Party believes that in view of the need to inculcate at an early age the desirability of a healthy lifestyle, primary teachers should be given at least an elementary knowledge of health education in the Colleges of Education and that basic health education should be a regular feature of the school Curriculum in all primary schools. The Working Party welcomes the provision in the Programme of Action in Education in relation to health education in second-level schools (recommendation 2.4 [not included]) and underlines the need for the new Curriculum and Examinations Board to pay particular attention to devising a framework whereby a programme of health education, including education for relationships and marriage, will be part of the curriculum of all post-primary schools. The Board should consult with the Health Education Bureau in this process.

Services for the prevention and treatment of specifically female illnesses, or illnesses which have a disproportionate effect on women

ISSUES FOR DISCUSSION

4.56 Under this heading, the issues which seem most relevant for consideration are services for cancer patients and for those suffering from alcoholism and mental illness. The effects of smoking, and occupational health are also discussed.

DIFFERENTIAL IMPACT OF ILLNESSES ON MEN AND WOMEN

4.57 As pointed out earlier in the chapter, there are some differences in the type of diseases which affect men and women. It is often argued that differences in life expectancy between men and women should decline as women increasingly adopt the 'lifestyles' of men. However, a recent study suggests that on the basis of trends in countries where there is a much greater proportion of women in paid employment, this cannot be assumed, as the same types of differences in life expectancies are observable. An indication of the differences in the types of illnesses which men and women suffer from is given by the Table [not included] which shows the number of discharges and average duration of stay in hospital by diagnostic category in 1980.

DATA ON SPECIFIC ILLNESSES AND DEATH RATES

4.58 The differences are most marked for accidents, poisonings and violence, diseases of the respiratory system, diseases of the circulatory system, 'special admissions and consultations', congenital abnormalities and diseases of the blood, in all of which males predominate. The areas where females outnumbered males, and in all but two areas very slightly, were diseases of the genitourinary system (17,687 females as against 10,003 males), neoplasms, diseases of the musculo-skeletal system and connective tissues, endocrine, nutritional and metabolic diseases, and 'miscellaneous' (17,367 females as against 2,772 males). The total number of males involved was 189,200 as against 183,699 females. The average duration of stay however was longer for females (10.7 days as against 9.7). Table 2 [not included] shows the deaths registered during the year 1983 classified by cause. It is notable that there are seven areas where females outnumbered males slightly (excluding 9 deaths due to obstetric): these are diabetes mellitus (52.9% female), anaemia (52.8% female), meningitis (52.6% female) pneumonia (53.8% female), influenza (64.3% female), congenital anomalies (51.2% female) and signs, symptoms and ill-defined conditions (52.9% female). (Some of these illnesses may be related to the fact that the proportion of women among the elderly is higher than that of men.) Looking at cancers specifically, Table 3 [not included] shows the death rate in Ireland from all cancers from 1961 to 1980 for males and females aged 55–64 per 100,000 corresponding population. Table 4 [not included] shows the number of deaths caused by cancer of the trachea, bronchus and lung in Irish males and females from 1961 to 1980. The fairly sharp increases for both sexes throughout the 1970s is notable. Setting the data on illness and death in a wider comparative context, Table 5 [not included] shows the death rates by cause for the four countries of the U.K. and for Ireland in 1978. This data shows that Ireland has relatively low death rates from heart disease, cancer, pneumonia and bronchitis. The rates of death for cerebro-vascular diseases, congenital abnormalities, infective diseases and motor accidents are all relatively high.

DATA ON FEMALE CANCERS

4.59 A much discussed health problem for women today is cancer. Female cancers such as breast cancer and cervical cancer seem to be on the increase in Western countries generally. In Ireland, there is, unfortunately, not a great deal of available data on the incidence of these cancers. The following table gives information on mortality from these cancers. In addition, the Medico-Social Research Board drew the Working Party's attention to work being carried out in the Department of Social Medicine in University College, Cork, where a detailed tumour register is being kept. From this it is possible to note that for women the highest risk for cancer is cancer of the breast at 1 in 15.

Table 9.1
Mortality from two forms of cancer among Irish women, 1978–83

	Cervical	Breast
1978	49	546
1979	60	499
1980	53	582
1981	61*	491*
1982	57*	577*
1983	57*	540*

* Provisional figures

SERVICES FOR FEMALE CANCER PATIENTS

4.60 Apart from hospital and medical services available generally, specific services for female cancers include twenty-nine cervical smear test clinics being held throughout the country in health centres, thirteen of which are supported by the Irish Cancer Society's Information Services. Breast self-examination instruction clinics are being undertaken in local Health Centres and in Industry, by public health nurses from the Eastern Health Board. Various voluntary organisations exist in the community which give support to people and their families who are affected by cancer. The Irish Cancer Society itself provides a support, information and education service to the community in this field. The Society provides a Reach to Recovery Programme giving rehabilitative support to women who have had breast surgery, which is designed to meet women's physical, emotional and cosmetic needs.

MEDICAL TECHNOLOGY

4.61 In the area of health services, medical technology has been developing rapidly. A particularly important field, but one associated with very high costs, is diagnostic imaging. X-rays, the elementary form of diagnostic imaging, are now being supplemented by CAT (Computer-assisted) scanning. Laser technology, specifically, is now being used as a method of treatment for cervical cancer. As an indication of the cost of the equipment, a recent 'Carbon Dioxide Laser' which was presented to the Galway Regional Hospital, cost IR£45,000 raised by means of voluntary contributions. Similar equipment is available in the National Maternity Hospital, Dublin. A small number of hospitals in this country have facilities for mammography, which can be used to detect breast cancer.

ADEQUACY OF SERVICE

4.62 In the case of cervical smears, as stated, only 29 health centres throughout the country carry out these tests. There are several hundred health centres throughout the country, however, who do not cater for this need. In particular no service is provided in Cork, Kerry, Cavan, Monaghan, Sligo or Wicklow. Also, for persons outside the General Medical Service scheme, there is a charge for these tests which can vary widely, depending on where the test is carried out (varying from health centre, to maternity hospital, to general practitioner). In some cases, a person has to pay a double fee – the doctor's fee and the hospital's fee – for carrying out the test. A further drawback of the existing service is the long delay involved in processing the tests.

RECOMMENDATION

4.63 In a wider national context, the Working Party would not be in a position to estimate the needs from the point of view of medical equipment such as mammography, laser equipment, or indeed the availability of facilities both in health centres and hospitals around the country. Because of the extremely high costs involved in new forms of medical technology, there is a need for greatly improved evaluation of the medical, economic and social implications of decisions to purchase this equipment. There is a growing body of work internationally on the evaluation of the new technologies and their cost effectiveness, which can be drawn upon. In view of the particular needs of women in the area of cancer prevention, the Working Party recommends the carrying out, as a priority, of a cost benefit type analysis of the needs in this area, which would identify, on the basis of organisational, geographical, economic and social criteria, the range of facilities which should be aimed for – both in terms of medical equipment and services – to help reduce the risks associated with these specific cancers and provide higher rates of cure. (In particular it is regrettable that sizeable areas of the country do not have access through the health centres to cervical smear testing services. While it is up to each Health Board to decide their own priorities it would, in our view, be desirable, if at all possible, to have this service available throughout the country.)

Alcoholism
CHANGE IN ALCOHOL CONSUMPTION AMONG WOMEN
4.64 Drinking, heavy drinking and alcoholism have long been considered male characteristics. However, changing social roles have awakened interest in the drinking patterns of women. Alcohol is now a hazard which affects an increasing number of women and among women of childbearing age it has been identified – after smoking – as the second most common environmental cause of problems in an unborn baby's development.

CHARACTERISTICS OF WOMEN ALCOHOLICS
4.65 As regards the characteristics of women alcoholics, studies based on American research tend to indicate that the average woman alcoholic drinks at home alone. Women alcoholics have, therefore, a relatively low rate of social problems related to alcoholism and are rarely seen in bars. Comparisons of men and women alcoholics have yielded many results, such as that women are less likely than men to be arrested for drinking; men have higher rates of auto accidents in relationship to drinking; male alcoholics tend to have a poorer work history. There are also differences in relation to frequency and amount of intake, specific drink imbibed, and time of day during which drinking occurs. Women, particularly those of upper socioeconomic status, tend to telescope their stages of alcoholism into much shorter periods of time. In terms of social class, it appears that lower-status alcoholic women have drinking patterns and problems quite similar to those reported for the average alcoholic male.

THEORIES OF CAUSATION AMONG WOMEN
4.66 As regards theories on causation, numerous authors contend that the causes for male and female alcoholism differ. One of the stresses unique to women is hormonal. Hormonal difficulties leading to depression can, it appears, in turn lead to heavy drinking. Furthermore, the menopause is often linked with 'problem' drinking, as is sometimes giving birth. Sex-role confusion has also been identified as a causal factor, as has marital

disruption, with rates of divorce, separation and desertion higher among women alcoholics.

FOETAL ALCOHOL SYNDROME

4.67 One of the most detrimental aspects of female alcoholism is in relation to the effect on the developing foetus. While alcohol and pregnancy have been known to have a long history of incompatibility, it is only in the last decade that systematic research has led to the identification of the particular syndrome known as 'foetal alcohol syndrome'. The characteristics associated with this include the following:

(i) pre-natal growth deficiency, characterised by short birth length and low birth weight;

(ii) post-natal growth deficiency, characterised by continuing failure to thrive;

(iii) skull and facial abnormalities;

(iv) joint and limb abnormalities;

(v) cardiac defects, mental deficiency and delayed mental development.

Even in the absence of the above mainly-physical manifestations, researchers are only very recently recognising that these children are, in addition, exposed to a range of learning and behavioural handicaps. Also, while research has concentrated largely on alcoholic mothers, there are gaps in our knowledge of the extent to which the offspring of moderate drinkers may be at risk.

DATA ON ALCOHOLISM IN IRELAND

4.68 Looking at the data for Ireland on female alcoholism, it is known that the number of persons resident in Irish psychiatric hospitals and units for alcohol-related conditions has risen from 392 to 688 from 1971 to 1981, in keeping with the increase in admissions for this condition over the same period. In 1981, alcoholism and alcoholic psychosis accounted for more admissions than any other individual disorder . Alcoholism accounted for over one quarter of all admissions. (It should be noted, however, that for females, alcoholism came fourth in the list of disorders accounting for all admissions and third in the list for first admissions.) Table 7(a) [not included] shows all and first admissions to psychiatric hospitals and units, sex and diagnosis, numbers and rates per 100,000 population in 1981, and Table 7(b) [not included] gives details of the Irish Psychiatric Hospital Census for 1981, sex and diagnosis, numbers (with rates per 100,000 population). It is notable from Table 7(a) [not included] that males outnumber females by over 4 to 1 for both all admissions and first admissions for alcoholism and alcoholic psychosis. This may reflect the fact that the disease expectancy rate for men and women is different, as shown in Table 8 [not included]. For 1980, for example, the data show that out of every 100 men and every 100 women surviving to 65, 10.12 men and 2.71 women will require to be treated at least once in their lifetime.

DATA DOES [*SIC*] NOT REFLECT SCALE OF PROBLEM

4.69 It must be borne in mind that the figures quoted do not represent the total casualties from alcoholism. Some alcoholics do not present anywhere and some are treated privately by family doctors, or in general hospitals or private nursing homes. On the basis of a World Health Organisation formula, which estimates that as many as 5 or 6 out of every 100 drinkers may develop a dependency on alcohol, the Irish National Council for Alcoholism (INCA) estimate that about 75,000 of an estimated 1.5m drinkers in Ireland will go on to develop alcoholism at some point in their lives. The INCA also estimate that female alcoholism, while not as high as for males, is increasing (see, for example, data for one clinic at Table 9 [not included]) and they note that the death rate for cirrhosis of the liver – considered to be an important index of alcoholism – shows that the increase in female cirrhosis is very much greater than the increase in the male rate. The INCA also point to the changing age structure for alcoholism. Table 10 [not included] shows data for 1965, 1979 and 1981 (not broken down in terms of sex). This indicates a clear shift towards younger age groups, with a drop in both first and all admissions in the age group from 45 upwards. Data concerning drink-related offences is set out in Table 11 [not included]. It is notable that while the percentage of female convictions is still small, the trend is upwards.

FUTURE TRENDS GENERALLY

4.70 Looking towards the future, existing trends throughout Western countries suggest, firstly, a continuation in the rise in consumption of alcohol, with a consequent increase in heavy drinking. Secondly, it is expected that there will be a convergence of patterns of consumption for alcoholic beverages, with patterns of drinking for men and women and adolescents and adults becoming less and less distinguishable.

TRENDS FOR WOMEN

4.71 Looking at the position of women in particular, it is expected that as women's roles continue to change, to come nearer to those of men, which imply similar opportunities for alcohol use, women will tend to consume in a similar way to men. Concurrently there will be a rise in alcohol-related problems, such as crime, car accidents and in terms of disease, cirrhosis of the liver and diseases affected by alcohol such as several types of cancer, heart disease, pneumonia, ulcers, hypertension. Women are known to be at a greater disadvantage than men for several liver diseases, pneumonia and some other diseases, which implies a disproportionate effect for women with a rise in consumption. Finally, there is increasing concern about the long-range effect of drinking – in terms of mutation – in the case of women of child-bearing years.

RECOMMENDATIONS

4.72 In view of the bleak picture presented in relation to female alcoholism, the Working Party considers that it is a matter deserving considerably more research and analysis in an Irish context. A first stage in any attempt to meet the problem is at the educational level. It is recommended therefore, that:

(i) schools should be encouraged to procure and use the alcohol education pack prepared by the Health Education Bureau and to create opportunities for alcohol education within the school curriculum;

(ii) the Department of Health should seek the full co-operation of the medical profession in advising women of the potential risk to the foetus which may be associated with maternal consumption of alcohol. This is particularly important, as no 'safe' level or pattern of drinking during pregnancy has yet been established. Ideally, it should become standard practice at pre-natal visits to enquire and advise in relation to alcohol consumption. Education in this area should also be part of the training of public health nurses, who visit mothers post-natally (at which time also alcohol consumption can become a problem).

(iii) the need for more research in this area is clear as there are still many unanswered questions in the area, such as the 'safe' level of drinking, relationship to social class, educational level, existing psychiatric disturbance, etc...In view of the considerable economic and social ill effects to the community as a whole caused by alcohol-related illnesses, research and educational establishments funded by the State should be encouraged to devote more attention to the area.

Women and mental illness

SEX DIFFERENCES AND MENTAL HEALTH

4.73 Research in this field suggests that there is considerable evidence to indicate that women have higher mental illness rates than men. A medical explanation for this would suggest differences based, for example, in the female reproductive cycle. A sociological explanation would look at women's role in society which might predispose her to a greater extent to mental illness (see, for example, discussion in later part of chapter on 'occupational health' [not included]). Other approaches refer to the fact that sex differences appear to be specific to certain illness types, e.g. identifying women with depressive illness and men with mental illness involving anti-social behaviour.

DATA IN IRELAND

4.74 Data for Ireland show, on the basis of census data, consistently excess male rates for persons resident in psychiatric hospitals and units. This contrasts with the situation in England, where, for similar periods, the overall male resident rates were lower and the female rate higher. 'All admission' rates to hospitals for Ireland show the same male excess rate. Finally, if one examines data relating to 'persons in receipt of all forms of psychiatric care, both within hospital and in the community', there is a male excess rate. These findings are contrary to the findings in other countries.

EXPLANATIONS FOR IRISH DATA

4.75 Suggestions as to why this situation exists include:
(i) demographic factors: the high proportion of elderly, single, male farmers in this country;
(ii) the strong historical trend towards institutionalised treatment for mental illness;
(iii) the tendency for males to suffer to a greater extent than females from schizophrenia, alcoholism and personality disorders, implying an increased likelihood of hospitalisation.

Lower than expected female depression rates in this country account for the lower female treatment rates. The latter may, however, reflect an inadequately developed community-based service in rural Ireland, in particular. In the Carlow area, for example, there is an excess female rate for persons contacting all forms of care, reflecting perhaps the fairly well-developed out-patient psychiatric services there. The Medico-Social Research Board paper referred to concludes, in fact, that the shortfall in women's rates for depression is primarily a rural phenomenon and is in part a function of the limited availability of alternative services to hospitalisation and the lesser willingness on the part of rural women to express their feelings or seek support. The most recent evidence suggests, however, that this may be changing and that as features of rural culture change, e.g. decline in family size, rising expectation of women about careers etc. these women may become more aware of feelings of dissatisfaction and show greater willingness to express these feelings. The Paper emphasises, however, that medical help may not always be what is needed in response to women's depression; greater flexibility in working life such as availability of part-time work, child-minding facilities, and women's support groups could make an important contribution to alleviating the problem (these issues are dealt with in other chapters in this Report).

RECOMMENDATION

4.76 A specific form of depression affecting women is Post-natal depression. This can be a crippling problem, causing considerable distress not only for the mother but for the family also. In the Report on 'Women in the Home' carried out by the Council for the Status of Women, which was based on meetings of women around the country, several groups drew attention to the lack of appreciation of this problem and the absence of treatment generally. This has implications, in our view, for the training of personnel involved in the maternity and child welfare services. Public health nurses in particular, who play key roles in the community in this field, should be particularly alert to the nature of this illness so that it can be more readily identified and treated. Greater attention is needed to treatment of this condition also. In this context, health centres could play a wider role. In any implementation of change in the maternity services scheme (as referred to earlier in the chapter) the Working Party believes that services for Post-natal depression should be improved.

Smoking

DATA ON SMOKING

4.77 In developed countries, smoking became established as primarily a male habit and women started to smoke at a much later stage. In

Ireland, since 1972 there has been a clear-cut reduction in the percentage of male smokers, with a later and less sharp decline for female smokers. The estimated cigarette consumption of women of childbearing age particularly has increased greatly during the past two decades. There are also strong links with social class, with the Irish data reflecting international trends. Higher socioeconomic groups have lowered their smoking rates rapidly in recent times while those in the lower socioeconomic groups have continued to smoke heavily.

HEALTH CONSEQUENCES OF SMOKING

4.78 The health consequences of smoking are well-documented. It is now generally accepted that smokers develop diseases of the heart and blood vessels, lung disease and cancer of other organs more frequently and at a younger age than do non-smokers. The birthweight of babies born to mothers who smoke during pregnancy is significantly lower than babies born to non-smoking mothers.

DEATHS FROM SMOKING-RELATED CANCERS

4.79 Cancer has increased in importance as a cause of death in recent years. Table 14 [not included] shows the number of all tumour deaths in Ireland at all ages in 1961, 1977 and 1982 together with the number and percentage of such deaths which were caused by all smoking-related cancers, and specifically by cancers of the trachea, bronchus and lung. It is notable that the smoking-related cancers increased both in terms of actual numbers of deaths and as a percentage of all tumour deaths, both for males and females. Also, the cancers of the trachea, bronchus and lung have more than doubled in the period for females, as a percentage of all tumour deaths.

SMOKING AND PREGNANCY

4.80 Turning to smoking and pregnancy, most of the original research confirming the deleterious effects of maternal smoking on foetal growth was carried out in the Coombe Hospital in Dublin. One study revealed a gradual decrease in baby weight as maternal cigarette consumption increased up to 20 cigarettes per day. In general, there was a significant association between baby weight and number of cigarettes, and maternal age or parity had little effect on this correlation. A further study revealed that with maternal smoking there was an increase in the proportion of abortions, stillbirths and neonatal deaths. A study in Britain looked at the subsequent development of children of both smokers and non-smokers and it was shown that at age 11 the children of smokers (in this study mothers smoking more than 10 cigarettes per day) were shorter in height and less advanced in reading, mathematics and general ability compared with the non-smokers' offspring.

ANTISMOKING MEASURES

4.81 A range of antismoking measures have already been adopted in this country, such as the 1978 legislation which led to controls on advertising, sponsorship and sales promotion, taxation measures and restrictions in the sale of tobacco to minors. The Government have recently announced a range of new measures to help combat the health hazards of smoking. The new legislation which will shortly be introduced will provide for a health education levy on the tobacco companies of 2 per cent of their advertising and sponsorship budgets. The revenue will go to the Health Education Bureau to intensify its antismoking campaign. (The Health Education Bureau has spent the following amounts on antismoking campaigns: 1979 – IR£38,792, 1981 – IR£174,000, 1984 – IR£250,000.) The legislation will also provide for the banning of smoking in certain areas and facilities used by the public. These will include school classrooms, public transport, hospital wards and public offices. Finally, amendments to the 1979 Tobacco Products (Control of Advertising, Sponsorship and Sales Promotion) Regulations to provide for stronger controls in relation to health warnings on tobacco product packages and advertisements are also due to be introduced.

RECOMMENDATION

4.82 Continuous campaigns by the Health Education Bureau are, in the Working Party's view, justified, in view of the high cost to the community of smoking in terms of the resulting ill health. We would stress the need for health care professionals to continue to intervene in this area in terms of advising and seeking to influence their patients to give up smoking. It is generally accepted that women in societies such as ours have a greater concern about health issues. They arrange for those services and act as role models for their children. This provides an obvious avenue for intervention by health care providers. However, research from the US, where antismoking programmes are at an advanced stage of development, indicates that a majority of smokers claim not to have received advice about smoking from doctors. Nurses spend more time directly with patients and nurses in the same research survey generally believed it was their responsibility to convince people to stop smoking. Given the important role-modelling effect of nurses, the need for adequate training and counselling in this area is clear. Finally, lay groups have been found to play an important role in helping women to give up smoking, particularly women of lower socioeconomic status who tend to be influenced less by media campaigns and education programmes. In the Irish context, we believe that all the women's organisations and in particular the 'national' ones such as the Council for the Status of Women and the Irish Countrywomen's Association should, as part of their informational role, use their influence to draw attention to the hazards of smoking. The Working Party believes that the proposed new legislation on smoking will make an important contribution in this area. Maternity hospitals should be included in any restrictions being imposed on smoking in designated areas. At the moment, while there are 'no smoking' signs in certain areas in these hospitals, the experience is that these tend to be ignored, as hospitals are not in a position to enforce what are non-binding measures. In any restrictions being imposed, smoking by staff and visitors should be prohibited and smoking by patients should be restricted, perhaps to certain areas or times in the hospital.

PROPOSALS FOR IMPROVING HEALTH SERVICES

The Second Commission on the Status of Women also provided extensive coverage of health issues in its *Report to Government* (1993). At the outset it called for a review of health services, and for the development and implementation of a national plan for women's health based on a review of findings. The Commission offered a number of recommendations on such topics as patients' rights, women's employment at various levels of the health care industry, health education, mental illness and the new concerns about HIV/AIDS.

Second Commission on the Status of Women, *Report to Government* (1993)

Health

1.NATIONAL PLAN FOR WOMEN'S HEALTH

The Commission recommends that:

(a) the Department of Health should review the present health services and their delivery to examine how they can best meet the needs of women. This review should be carried out in consultation with women's groups, Health Boards, medical representatives and social partners. The review should be carried out by end-1993 and its findings should be incorporated into a national plan for women's health which is then brought to Government for decision and implementation;

(b) the differential effects of policy decisions on women and men should be assessed by the Department of Health when policy changes are being proposed, with a routine Ministerial requirement that all health proposals are examined for their gender-related implications.

2. ACCESS TO MEDICAL RECORDS
The Commission recommends that appropriate legislation be enacted to establish the right of access by individuals to all their hospital records.

3. WOMEN MEDICAL PERSONNEL
The Commission recommends that:

(a) The Department of Health, Health Boards, and hospitals should be obliged to adopt equal opportunity programmes with specific targets and strategies;

(b) Health Boards and hospitals should be required by the Department of Health to provide a certain number of job-sharing posts, to include training posts;

(c) Health Boards and hospitals should also be required by the Department of Health to pursue a more flexible approach to part-time work to facilitate the management of domestic and occupational commitments;

(d) women should constitute at least 40% of interview boards for medical and nursing posts;

(e) professional bodies should promote similar equal opportunity policies for their members.

4. ADVERSE WORKING CONDITIONS
In conjunction with the equal opportunities strategies outlined at paragraph 11.2.4 [not included] the Commission recommends that the Department of Health, Health Boards, hospitals and professional bodies should review within one year:

(a) the present system of short-term contracts for non-consultant hospital doctors;

(b) the exceptionally long working hours frequently required of junior hospital doctors.

5. PATIENTS' CHARTER

The Commission recommends that:

(a) a patients' charter should be drawn up by the Department of Health which deals specifically with women's health issues, particularly with the right to gynaecological services and female sterilisation. One approach worth considering would be to broaden the scope of the proposed Charter for expectant mothers to deal with all women's health issues;

(b) an amplified charter of patients' rights setting out clearly defined conditions regarding eligibility for community health services should be drawn up and clearly displayed in GP and hospital waiting rooms.

6. CARER'S ALLOWANCE

The Commission recommends that:

(a) the carer's allowance should not be means-tested on the income of the carer;

(b) if the carer's allowance has to be means-tested, it should be means-tested on the means of the person being cared for;

(c) medical eligibility for care should be decided on the basis of diagnosis by the Director of Community Care, Area Medical Officer, consultant geriatrician or other appropriate consultant specialist.

7. INTEGRATION OF CARERS IN COMMUNITY CARE SYSTEM

The Commission recommends that:

(a) a network of registered and trained carers be established and employed by the local health authorities under the community care system, or provided by voluntary bodies in association with these authorities;

(b) as a first step towards achieving a comprehensive network, a number of pilot projects should be initiated in 1993/94 with a view to developing an effective policy in this area;

(c) entitlement to the services of community carers should be determined on the basis of an assessment of the means and needs of persons requesting the service, who have already been diagnosed by a consultant geriatrician or other appropriate consultant specialist.

8. RESPITE CARE

The Commission recommends that a system of back-up services for carers in the home, including respite care, advisory services and day care centres, should be established in each Health Board area as an integral part of community care policy.

9. HOME HELPS

The Commission recommends that:

(a) in order to implement a policy of community care/home help, the categories of people eligible to receive the service should be extended to take account of the needs of groups such as mothers with handicapped children or other disadvantaged categories;

(b) Health Boards should be obliged as well as empowered to provide a comprehensive home help service;

(c) policy on the categories to be assisted under the home help scheme should be decided at national level by the Minister for Health and implemented by each Health Board;

(d) costs of provision of the service should incorporate an element of means-testing so that a fee would be charged, according to means, to non-medical card holders. This would open up access to the scheme to a wider group of people in need of such service;

(e) information on the scheme should be freely available from, and actively promoted by, the Department of Health.

10. RATES OF PAY OF HOME HELPS

The Commission recommends that all home helps be paid a national realistic hourly rate.

11. MENTAL HANDICAP PLACES

The Commission recommends that, as a priority, residential and day places should be provided for mentally handicapped people who need them, but who currently have to be cared for at home.

12. COMMUNITY CARE AND THE ELDERLY

The Commission recommends that provision for the elderly within the community care system should take the form of locally based sheltered housing providing low-level care.

13. RAPE CRISIS CENTRES

The Commission recommends that:

(a) existing Rape Crisis Centres be given secure multi-annual funding on a contractual basis such as Health Boards already provide to voluntary bodies for some community and planning functions;

(b) where a regional Rape Crisis Centre does not exist, the Health Boards in question establish one, staffed by persons with appropriate expertise;

(c) all Rape Crisis Centres and Health Boards should maintain regular close liaison with a view to implementing the most appropriate and sympathetic policies for the victim of sexual assault; it is also important that Rape Crisis Centres should network with each other.

14. WOMEN VICTIMS OF DOMESTIC VIOLENCE

The Commission recommends that:

(a) where a regional domestic violence shelter does not exist, the Health Boards in question should establish one, or should support women's groups already active in the field; such refuges should be staffed by persons with appropriate expertise;

(b) where there are existing shelters which are functioning effectively, they should be given secure multi-annual funding on a contractual basis such as Health Boards already provide to voluntary bodies for some community and family planning functions;

(c) all domestic violence shelters and Health Boards should maintain a regular close liaison;

(d) each Health Board should maintain a list of confidential addresses for women in emergency domestic violence situations;

(e) an emergency 24-hour telephone service should be established in each Health Board area for victims of domestic abuse occurring at weekends and holiday periods.

15. FAMILY CENTRES

The Commission recommends that drop in family centres should be established in each Health Board area for stressed parents, mothers in particular.

16. POST-ABORTION REHABILITATIVE CARE

The Commission recommends that the Department of Health should set in train a study on the long-term implications for the wellbeing of women who have had abortions, with a view to drawing up a public health policy within the constraints of the law which would try to meet the needs to be determined.

17. APPOINTMENTS SYSTEM

The Commission recommends that the Department of Health should put in place a mechanism for monitoring hospital practices in relation to outpatient appointments to ensure that the Patients' Charter commitment is realised and that out-patients do, in practice, receive individual appointment times.

18. PARENTAL ACCOMMODATION IN HOSPITALS

The Commission recommends that hospitals should make provision for overnight accommodation and facilities for parents of children in hospital, especially those parents who must commute long distances.

19. WOMEN ON HEALTH BOARDS AND HOSPITAL BOARDS

In order to counteract the deficit of women at decision-making level, and specifically to represent the women consumers who fund and use hospital services, the Commission recommends that:

(a) as a priority the Minister of Health in making appointments to Health Boards should establish gender balance and that at least 40% of the members of all Hospital Boards appointed by the Minister for Health should be women;

(b) the professional bodies which elect members of Health Boards should achieve gender balance in their nominations, if necessary by rotation;

(c) that as a condition of funding the Minister for Health should have the right to appoint at least two women to the Boards of all publicly funded voluntary hospitals to represent women users of the service.

20. CONSULTATION WITH WOMEN'S GROUPS

The Commission recommends that all hospitals should seek to establish consultative links with women's groups concerned with health issues in order to inform their policies and the delivery of their services to women.

21. DENTAL BENEFIT SCHEME

The Commission recommends that the Health Promotion Unit should launch a publicity campaign to encourage eligible spouses of PRSI workers to avail of their entitlement to low-cost dental treatment.

22. DENTAL SERVICES FOR MEDICAL CARD HOLDERS

The Commission recommends that more funds should be made available for public dental treatment services.

23. TREATMENT OF LIFE-THREATENING CONDITIONS DURING PREGNANCY

The Commission recommends that legislation be enacted which ensures that pregnant women have the right to prompt and appropriate medical intervention including palliative care in the case of life-threatening conditions.

24. CHILDBIRTH

The Commission recommends that:

(a) all maternity hospitals and units should provide single delivery units, and should be responsive to the needs of mothers with regard to birthing positions;

(b) women should be allowed to choose any companion or none, as they wish, to stay with them during delivery;

(c) the attendance of student doctors and midwives at gynaecological examination or birth should be a matter for the woman concerned and her permission should be specifically requested;

(d) epidurals should be available on the basis of choice by the woman, following consultation with her gynaecologist, and all maternity hospitals and units should provide an adequate epidural service;

(e) maternity hospitals and units should adopt a flexible approach to visiting times, especially for immediate family members including children, within reasonable limits;

(f) maternity hospitals and units should ensure that their practices do not militate against the wishes of women who wish to breastfeed their babies. Information and advice on breastfeeding should be provided by trained staff to women who choose to breastfeed. The hospitals might cooperate with La Leche League to devise a suitable supportive programme for breastfeeding mothers;

(g) maternity hospitals and units should establish consultative links with groups such as the Association for the Improvement of Maternity Services and La Leche League in order that the experiences of women can be taken account of in organising and developing maternity hospital practices and mothers can avail of peer group support and advice;

(h) the Department of Health should put in place a mechanism to monitor the implementation of recommendations (a) to (g) above.

25. MISCARRIAGE AND STILLBIRTH

The Commission recommends that:

(a) separate accommodation should be provided in maternity hospitals for women who have had miscarriages or stillbirths;

(b) appropriate follow-up counselling for the woman and her partner should be offered;
(c) the Births and Deaths Registration Act 1863 should be amended in order to set up a separate State register for stillbirths and to issue certificates to the parents of stillborn children;
(d) until this State register is established, that maternity hospitals should set up and maintain their own register of stillborn children in order that parents are given recognition of the stillbirth of their child.

26. ALLOWABLE MEDICAL EXPENSES FOR MATERNITY

The Commission recommends that routine medical maternity expenses should be allowable against income tax, as is currently the situation with all other routine medical expenses.

27. REIMBURSING STERILISATION EXPENSES

Since the Minister for Health is the sole shareholder in the Voluntary Health Insurance Board, the Commission recommends that the Minister for Health should direct the VHI to change the policy of excluding sterilisation from reimbursement.

28. PARENTING AND BABY CARE PROGRAMMES

The Commission recommends that all maternity hospitals and units should organise and publicise programmes to teach practical aspects of parenting and baby care to first-time parents.

29. FAMILY PLANNING RECOMMENDATIONS

The Commission recommends that:
(a) the Department of Health should ensure that there is public access to all legal forms of family planning, and that sufficient funds be provided to ensure such access is effective in practice;
(b) medical card holders should be offered a full range of family planning services;
(c) where family planning agencies are in receipt of public funds, these agencies should be required to provide information and services on all legal forms of family planning;
(d) the Department of Health and its Health Promotion Unit should be responsible for producing and widely disseminating leaflets, videos, etc. on all legal methods of family planning, either through their own structures or by contracting this responsibility out to approved family planning agencies;

(e) the family planning services on offer in each area should be comprehensive, including:
- information on all legal forms of family planning, medical and non-medical;
- advice on appropriate forms of family planning for the individual concerned;
- prescription, fitting, or sale of family planning devices and measures;
- information on male vasectomy and female sterilisation (tubal ligation);
- counselling, where an individual is interested in vasectomy or tubal ligation;
- vasectomies and tubal ligation.
(f) maternity hospitals, as a condition of public funding, should incorporate a family planning service advising on all legal methods of family planning as part of post-maternity care;
(g) general practitioners should display a notice in their surgeries that they offer information on family planning.

30. FEMALE STERILISATION

The Commission recommends that:
(a) publicly funded hospitals should, as a condition of funding, provide sterilisation in line with expressed demand; a decision on sterilisation should be made by the woman in consultation with her doctor;
(b) the woman's partner should be routinely consulted about the operation, but his consent should not be necessary for an operation to proceed;
(c) advice on sterilisation and appropriate counselling should be provided in the context of the family planning services as recommended in paragraph 11.8.7 [not included].

31. MALE STERILISATION

The Commission recommends that:
(a) current practice on vasectomies should continue; as with female sterilisation, appropriate counselling for the operation should be provided; the man's partner should be consulted, but her consent to the operation should not be essential;
(b) the Health Promotion Unit of the Department of Health should prepare and widely disseminate information on vasectomy as a fertility control option.

32. EDUCATION FOR LIFE, RELATIONSHIPS AND PARENTING

The Commission recommends that:

(a) a sex education programme should be developed by the Department of Education which will give young people, male and female, a sense of personal autonomy and responsibility in relationships. The programme should be introduced in primary schools and continued in all second-level schools at a level appropriate to each age group (see Chapter 9, Education [not included]);

(b) in a targeted Health Promotion Unit campaign girls should be given an appreciation of the opportunities foregone through early unplanned pregnancy, and boys should be informed of the responsibilities of parenthood and the need to share responsibility for contraception.

33. RELATIONSHIP EDUCATION FOR EARLY SCHOOL LEAVERS

The Commission recommends that:

(a) the Health Boards in association with the Health Promotion Unit should develop strategies through their community care programmes designed to contact and provide early school leavers with support and advice on sex education, relationships and parenting;

(b) training and resources should be provided for community care workers working in this area;

(c) the community care system should assist support groups for young mothers with babies, and facilitate young mothers to obtain advice on family planning methods.

34. ROLE OF VOLUNTARY ORGANISATIONS

The Commission recommends that, as a general policy, Health Boards and authorities should enter into funding arrangements with voluntary organisations for the provision of agreed services on a multi-annual basis; with accepted standards of accountability applying, e.g. annual reports, audited accounts etc.

35. MENTAL HEALTH STRATEGY FOR WOMEN

The Commission recommends that the Minister for Health should adopt and implement a specific mental health strategy geared to the monitoring, prevention and treatment of mental health problems as they affect women. The strategy should be implemented within the overall context of psychiatric policies and services. The first phase of this strategy should entail an appropriate research project to be carried out within an urgent time limit.

36. PREVENTIVE HEALTH
The Commission recommends a health education programme which disseminates information on a targeted basis as well as raising awareness generally. We believe this strategy should be integrated, with its message and objectives being driven home in the community, in schools and in the workplace.

37. ROLE OF HEALTH PROMOTION UNIT
The Commission recommends that:
(a) Health Promotion Unit publications and videos should be widely available for use by schools, employers, voluntary organisations, local groups, etc;
(b) lists of publications and videos should be widely publicised; the lists should be regularly updated and made available, in particular, to all schools;
(c) there should be regular formal liaison between the Health Promotion Unit and the Directors of Community Care in each Health Board in order to devise strategies and campaigns for preventive health programmes at local/regional level, with particular reference to disadvantaged groups.

38. CERVICAL SCREENING
The Commission recommends that:
(a) there should be a national campaign to publicise the importance and availability of cervical smear tests;
(b) cervical smear tests should be available for screening as well as diagnostic purposes to medical card holders under the General Medical Services Scheme;
(c) the interval between the taking of a smear test and the issue of a result should not exceed one month; women whose smear tests have been found to be abnormal should be entitled to a second test to confirm/refute the findings of the first test.

39. BREAST CANCER
The Commission recommends that the health services should immediately build up diagnostic services for breast cancer screening; in the medium term there should be a national breast cancer screening programme aimed at enabling women in the high-risk group to have access to mammography for screening purposes.

40. GENETIC COUNSELLING
The Commission recommends that a national genetic counselling

service should be developed, in particular so that it is available in a general hospital and is not subject to an Ethics Committee. It is essential that such counselling be given before any decision is made to become pregnant so that an informed decision can be made.

41. HIV/AIDS AND OTHER STDS
The Commission recommends:
(a) the formulation and implementation of a preventive health policy on the HIV virus and AIDS specifically targeted at women, explicitly drawing attention to the particular risks they face; such a health policy could either be run directly by the Health Promotion Unit of the Department of Health or could be contracted out to a suitable organisation or group;
(b) that in schools, an age-appropriate education strategy for AIDS prevention should be taught, set within a programme of sex and relationship education;
(c) amendment of family planning legislation to provide for the sale of condoms through vending machines;
(d) the development of strategies to assist and support the children of HIV-positive mothers, including fostering and adoption;
(e) that the Health Promotion Unit of the Department of Health should prepare and widely disseminate a leaflet on sexually transmitted diseases other than HIV/AIDS and how they affect women.

DEVELOPING A PLAN FOR WOMEN'S HEALTH

The *Second Progress Report of the Monitoring Committee on the Implementation of the Recommendations of the Second Commission on the Status of Women* (1996) pointed to action taken on a number of the Commission's specific recommendations. A Charter of Rights for hospital patients was in place and a Freedom of Information Bill had been submitted to the Oireachtas in 1995. To enhance equality of opportunity in employment, a review of the personnel policies of health care agencies was under way. Home help services for older people were being strengthened, as were facilities and services for mentally handicapped people cared for at home.

In other findings, the Monitoring Committee noted that the

Health Insurance Act 1994 did not require insurers to cover treatments associated with 'male or female birth control, infertility and any form of assisted reproduction'. There was, however, increased funding for rape crisis centres and women's refuges, and provision was being made for family counselling centres and post-abortion counselling.

The Second Commission had recommended a number of specific changes for maternity hospitals and units. These included changes in delivery room practices and procedures, support from hospital staff for women who wanted to breastfeed, and special accommodation and counselling for women who had had miscarriages or still births.

Many of the concerns raised by the Second Commission were addressed in the Minister for Health's *Discussion Document on Women's Health* (1995) and were formalised into a series of recommendations in the Department of Health's *A Plan for Women's Health*, from which the following excerpt is taken.

Department of Health, *A Plan for Women's Health 1997–1999*

This Plan for Women's Health, 1997, has been developed in response to a growing concern that women's health needs were not always being met by the health services. In 1993, the Second Commission on the Status of Women recommended that the Department of Health should respond to this concern by publishing a policy document on women's health and engage in extensive consultation with women prior to preparing a plan for women's health.

The first part of the recommendation was implemented with the publication of the *Discussion Document – Developing a Policy for Women's Health* in June 1995. The Discussion Document looked at the health services from a woman's point of view. It analysed the health status of Irish women and pinpointed the main causes of mortality and morbidity among women. Following the principles of the *Health Strategy – Shaping a Healthier Future*, the Document identified the scope for preventing premature mortality and increasing health and social gain. The Document provided a detailed analysis of most of the health issues of concern to women and suggested priorities to be addressed in a plan for women's health. The priorities suggested in the Discussion Document for improving the health of Irish women were:

- a reduction in smoking;
- the introduction of national screening programmes for breast and cervical cancer;
- improvements in the maternity services;
- better services for victims of domestic violence and rape;
- better access by Traveller women to health services;
- increased representation of women in the health services;
- increased research on many aspects of women's health.

The Discussion Document suggested that assisting the improvement of women's health in the developing world should also be a priority of a women's health policy.

The process of consultation began at national level with a conference on women's health on 30 June, 1995. Consultation at regional and local level was organised by the health boards, building on the experience of two boards which had already invited women to comment on their health needs and the health services available to them. The process was greatly strengthened by the involvement of the National Women's Council which has 156 affiliated organisations representing over 300,000 women throughout the country. The Council agreed to be a partner with the Department and the health boards in organising the consultation process. This partnership stimulated an extensive and innovative process of consultation with women.

The Council, with funding from the Department, appointed a coordinator to liaise with the statutory side in structuring the consultation. In each health board region, the Council appointed 'counterparts' to work closely with health boards in organising the consultative process. Each health board in turn appointed a women's health coordinator to carry the consultation forward.

Consultation with women on health issues took many forms. Conferences, workshops, exhibitions and seminars were held on the full range of topics in the Discussion Document or on specific topics. Every effort was made to provide child care facilities and sign interpreters at venues and to ensure that they were accessible to disabled women. Some boards organised listening meetings with an open invitation to women to discuss any health issue of concern to them. Written submissions were also invited from a large number of organisations with an interest in women's health. Over 50 were received in the Department alone. There was considerable media coverage of the Discussion Document and of the consultation. The first debate in the Dáil on women's health began on 9 November, 1995.

The overall thrust of the consultative process was positive.

Women welcomed the opportunity to give their views on health issues. The quality of the responses showed how deeply many women had reflected on health issues and how important these issues were to them. On the whole, women were appreciative of our health services, even if they were critical of certain elements. Women endorsed the analysis in the Discussion Document of women's health issues and of the need for a plan for women's health. They did, however, highlight shortcomings in the Discussion Document and issues which had been inadequately covered.

Major deficits in the health services in relation to women which were identified in the consultative process were the difficulty women experienced in accessing information on health and health services, the lack of a structured counselling and complementary health service, and the fact that the health services are not woman-friendly. These are issues which were hardly touched upon in the Discussion Document and they demonstrate how essential it was to consult women before embarking on a plan to improve their health. Women, during the consultative process, endorsed the need identified in the Discussion Document to improve services for women who are victims of violence or who are caring for a dependent family member. They asked for enhanced family planning and maternity services, and more support for breastfeeding and new mothers in general. They would like more counselling services available in non-medical settings to help women in stressful situations. There was strong support for the development of screening programmes for breast and cervical cancer and for the removal of the barriers which make it difficult for disadvantaged, Traveller and disabled women to access services.

There was a strong view among the women consulted that there should be greater representation of women at all levels of the health services. They felt strongly that the kind of consultation with women which took place on the Discussion Document should find a permanent expression in the health services, at national, regional and local level.

At the conclusion of the period of consultation, a report was prepared in each health board on the organisation and outcome of the process. Some of these reports were prepared in consultation with representatives of the National Women's Council. A national seminar was held in March 1996 to reflect on the outcome of the consultative process and identify priorities to be addressed in this *Plan for Women's Health*. Health boards have already begun to respond to the issues which arose in relation to the organisation and delivery of their services.

This *Plan for Women's Health* responds to the issues raised during the consultative process and builds on the analysis in the Discussion Document. This *Plan* is action-oriented. It specifies the action which will be taken at national level by the Department of Health to improve women's health. It identifies the action to be taken by health boards in regional plans for women's health to improve health services for women. There is a commitment in this Plan that women will be consulted more at all levels in the health services. The commitment to consultation is expressed most fully in the decision to establish a Council for Women's Health. The Council will be a centre of expertise on women's health issues, foster research into women's health, evaluate the success of this *Plan* in improving women's health and advise the Minister for Health on women's health issues generally.

This *Plan* has four main objectives for the health services in relation to women. These are:

- to maximise the health and social gain of Irish women;
- to create a woman-friendly health service;
- to increase consultation and representation of women in the health services;
- to enhance the contribution of the health services to promoting women's health in the developing world.

This *Plan* will provide a coherent framework for the improvement of women's health and health services for women to the beginning of the next century. It will succeed to the extent that the gap between the health indicators for Irish women and women in the EU reduces, health issues that are important to women are addressed and women consider that they have access to the information they need about health and that the health services are more user-friendly.

The success of this *Plan* in achieving its objectives in relation to women's health will be measured in a number of ways. A narrowing of the gap in health indicators for Irish women and women in the EU will be an important source of information for evaluation. The extent to which there is increased representation of, and consultation with, women in the health services can also be measured against current practice. Women's experiences of the health service and the extent to which they consider it to be more woman-friendly than now will be evaluated on an on-going basis.

Action: The Department of Health will work with health boards and women's organisations to pilot innovative approaches to informing women about health services and to disseminate good practice. Actions in this area will take cognisance of the outcome of the Consumer Health Information Research Project currently underway. Surveys will be undertaken to examine the extent to which women are better informed about health services as a result of these initiatives.

Action: The Department of Health and the health boards will work with women's organisations and other agencies at national, regional and local level to develop and enhance consultation and co-operation for health promotion.

Action: The Minister for Health has identified an improvement in cancer services as a priority for health service development. He has recently published a strategy for the development of cancer services – *Cancer Services in Ireland: A National Strategy* in November 1996 – which outlines measures to prevent cancer and to improve the effectiveness of services for those with the disease. The Minister announced a major action plan in March 1997 which detailed how the National Cancer Strategy would be implemented. The Department of Health will work with the health boards, voluntary organisations in the cancer area and women's organisations to implement the strategy. Specific action in relation to lung, breast, cervical and skin cancer is discussed in the following sections.

Action: The Department of Health will work at national level to inform women of the link between smoking and lung cancer and of the scope for preventing mortality from this disease. Health boards, in implementing their women's health plans, will work with women's organisations to increase awareness of the benefits of a smoke-free lifestyle and support women in their efforts to refrain from smoking. The Department will act on initiatives in the National Cancer Strategy in relation to training of general practitioners in counselling techniques for smoking cessation and will press for an EU-wide approach to banning advertising of tobacco products.

Action: As part of the implementation of the National Cancer Strategy the Department of Health will ensure that arrangements are in place for the first phase of a breast cancer screening programme in 1997 and that a national screening programme for breast cancer will be in place before the end of 1999.

Action: A national screening programme for cervical cancer will be established in 1999 or earlier, if resources permit. An expert advisory committee, which includes a representative of the National

Women's Council, will be set up to oversee the establishment, implementation and monitoring of the screening programme. The Mid-Western Health Board area will be the pilot site for the first stage of the programme. Pending the establishment of a national screening programme, the Minister has allocated IR£5 million to improve current arrangements for the taking and investigation of cervical smears.

Action: The Department of Health and the health boards will work to increase awareness among women of the dangers of excessive exposure to sunlight and of the importance of consulting a doctor early about changes in the skin.

Action: The Department of Health will monitor the performance of the Dental Treatment Services Scheme and the impact it is having on the oral health needs of particular groups in the population, including women.

Action: The Department of Health is committed to the implementation of the National Breastfeeding Policy for Ireland. It will work closely with women's organisations and other statutory agencies at national level to create a more supportive environment for breastfeeding.

Action: The Department of Health will review the implementation of the *Guidelines on Family Planning* issued in 1995 to ensure that services are being provided as recommended. Health boards, in their plans for women's health, will outline the steps which they are taking to develop family planning services which promote women's overall health and well-being. These steps will include information on fertility, sexuality and the way in which the needs of particular categories of women will be met. Funding will be made available for innovative proposals.

Action: The Department of Health will develop an effective and properly targeted educational programme in relation to crisis pregnancy based on the conclusions and recommendations of the abortion research study.

Action: The Department of Health is currently considering how best to encourage and inform the necessary public debate on human assisted reproduction.

Action: Health boards will, in the context of their women's health plans, review the provision of services related to the menopause. They will seek to ensure that this aspect of women's health is dealt with by sensitive and informed professionals, whether through the general practitioner service, through women's clinics in association with gynaecology services or by contract with other agencies.

Health boards will provide a comprehensive service to deal with urinary and faecal incontinence among women. This service will be based on a team approach involving gynaecologists, urologists, physiotherapists and nurses.

Action: In relation to violence against women, the Department of Health will:

- play a full role in relation to the coordination of Government policy by the Office of the Tánaiste and encourage a coordinated response within the health and personal social services to women who are victims of violence;
- ensure the implementation of section 6 of the Domestic Violence Act 1996 which gives health boards new powers to intervene to protect women against violent spouses;
- work closely with health boards, voluntary hospitals and the Irish College of General Practitioners to develop protocols in relation to the recognition of violence against women and good practice in relation to referral of such women;
- work closely with the training and education bodies in the health and personal social services to increase the awareness of professionals of violence toward women. The Health Boards as part of their women's health plans will: develop support services for women and children who are victims of violence; provide counselling and specialist investigation and treatment services for victims of rape and sexual abuse.

Action: The health services will be more proactive in relation to promoting mental health among women. The following action will be taken with a view to developing the capacity of the health services to promote mental health over the lifetime of this Plan:

- the Department of Health will commission research on the factors which undermine women's mental health;
- new mental health legislation will be passed as soon as possible which will give health boards an explicit statutory remit to promote mental health. The legislation will also bring procedures for the treatment of mentally disordered patients into conformity with the requirements of the European Convention on Human Rights;
- the Department of Health, in implementing the Health Promotion Strategy, will work closely with the National Women's Council to promote and protect the mental health of women;
- the health boards, in the implementation of their plans for

women's health, will promote women's mental health through providing greater access to counselling, information, support for self-help groups and liaison between primary health and the mental health services.

Action: The health care requirements and other needs of those who have been diagnosed as positive for Hepatitis C virus/antibodies will be monitored and re-assessed on an on-going basis to ensure that the necessary support services are provided to meet their needs. The Consultative Council on Hepatitis C will play a major role in this process.

Action: The Department of Health and the health boards in the implementation of the plans for women's health at national, regional and local levels will ensure that a high priority is given to improving the health of women who are socially and economically disadvantaged.

Action: The Department of Health will continue to work with the Department of Education to ensure the development of programmes to promote the personal and social development of young women. Health boards as part of their plans for women's health will develop programmes to reduce the rate of unplanned pregnancy among teenage girls, recognising the particular pressures such women face. In developing the maternity services they will also provide greater support to young single mothers and their children. Funding will be made available for innovative projects which foster inter-agency cooperation and develop good practice.

Action: The Community Mothers Scheme will be extended to all health boards. Projects similar to the Homestart Programme will be introduced in each health board area. The issue of parenting programmes for older children is being considered by the Commission on the Family which has been established by the Minister for Social Welfare. The Minister for Health will take cognisance of the recommendations of the Commission on the matter.

Action: The Department of Health is committed to the implementation of the health provisions of the programme in favour of Travellers recommended in the *Report of the Task Force on the Traveller Community*. Health boards will improve Travellers' access to health services and ensure that these services are delivered in a culturally appropriate way.

Action: The Department of Health is committed to the expansion of services for people with disabilities. Health boards in their women's health plans will review the extent to which their services are accessible to women with disabilities, in consultation with such women. They will also review the need for disability awareness training for their staff. Health boards will use their role as funders of voluntary organisations and other service providers, to ensure that all projects they fund become open and welcoming to women with disabilities and deal with them fairly and equally. Funding will be made available for innovative projects and the sharing of successful approaches to improving services to women with disabilities.

Action: The Minister will continue to give priority to the development of services for disabled and dependent people, including respite and home support services for carers. Health boards will consult with carers about the services they need, foster self-help groups for carers and fund voluntary organisations supporting carers.

Action: The Minister is committed to promoting healthy ageing and to ensuring that the targets of the Health strategy in relation to dependent elderly people, the majority of whom are women, are achieved. A Social Services Inspectorate will be established in the Department of Health which will develop an expertise in promoting high standards of care for the dependent elderly. Health boards will review the standards of care of dependent elderly patients in voluntary and private nursing homes and in their own hospitals and homes, in line with their statutory responsibility and in the context of their plans for women's health.

Action: Health boards will be asked to ensure that health professionals are informed about lesbian health issues and that staff respect the sexual orientation of lesbian women.

Action: The Department of Health and the relevant health boards will work closely with the prison authorities to develop programmes for drug-addicted women prisoners, to improve the mental health services available to women prisoners and to ensure close co-operation in relation to maternity and child care services.

Health boards will improve the provision of liaison psychiatric services for women in prison and will, in cooperation with the prison authorities, structure posts of consultant psychiatrist and professional support staff with a significant commitment of their time to the prisons.

Action: The Department of Health will support health boards in the provision of health services, including screening and treatment, for women working in prostitution. Information on maintaining health and on the availability of services will be designed specifically for these women.

Action: Health boards will continue to support drug misuse

prevention activities through a range of health education and treatment initiatives. Special attention will be paid to women drug misusers, both in prison and in the community. Rehabilitation projects such as the 'SAOU' Project will be extended. Regional and local drug teams will coordinate voluntary and State activities.

Health boards, in their health education programmes for young people, will place greater emphasis on the particular dangers to which women are exposed in relation to HIV.

Action: The Department of Health will work with the Department of Foreign Affairs and the Agency for Personal Services Overseas to develop a strategy to increase the contribution of the health services to promoting women's health in the developing world.

Ireland will continue to support the work of the World Health Organisation in the developing world and, in particular, in the Newly Independent States of the former Soviet Union.

Action: Each health board will establish an advisory committee on women's health, with at least two representatives of the National Women's Council. Representation of the National Women's Council on the health board advisory committee will not preclude representation of other specific groups which have a mandate for a particular and relevant women's interest.

Action: The Department of Health is developing an Equal Opportunities Policy for the Health Services and a programme of action to implement the policy. The Department will also promote the principle of gender balance in the membership of health boards, committees and working groups throughout the health services. The Office for Health Management will promote equal opportunities in management development.

Action: Each health board will prepare a regional plan for women's health to implement the commitments of the national Plan and the issues identified during the consultative process over the period 1997–1999. Health boards will review their staff development and training programmes to include sensitivity training in relation to attitudes to women clients and patients.

In *Ireland's Combined Second and Third Reports under the UN Convention on the Elimination of All Forms of Discrimination Against Women* (Dublin: Stationery Office, February 1997), the Irish government alluded to various items in the forthcoming Plan for Women's Health. These were offered as evidence that Ireland had addressed health care issues of particular significance to women.

CHAPTER NINE

Women's participation in politics and public life

LOW LEVELS OF PARTICIPATION

The highly visible activities of Constance Markievicz in the early years of the twentieth century – as a participant in the Easter Rising, the First Dáil Éireann and the Anglo-Irish War, and as the first woman ever to be elected to the British Parliament or to serve as a cabinet minister anywhere in western Europe – might convey the impression that women have been playing a critical role in Irish politics ever since the founding of the Free State in 1922, and even earlier. The election of Mary Robinson as President of Ireland in 1990, followed by the election of Mary McAleese as her successor in 1997, might seem to reinforce the impression that women now, as in the 1920s, are playing a major role in Irish politics and the administration of the Irish Republic. However, no woman other than Constance Markievicz held a cabinet position during the fifty years up to 1972, and during the same period the average number of women in the Dáil was four, or about 3 per cent of the total. The record in the Seanad (Senate), whether in its first form (1922–36) or after its reform under the Constitution of 1937, was no better; nor was that of the various elected local authorities. The number of women appointed to statutory and other bodies up to the 1970s was minuscule and the role of women in the political parties was essentially clerical.

Numerous causes for women's historically low level of political inactivity (not only in Ireland, of course) have been identified, including the widely held attitude that a woman's place is in the home, the sheer difficulty of engaging in political activity and the role of political parties as gatekeepers in promoting, or failing to promote, the activity and candidacies of women.[1] The first Commission on the Status of Women

(1972) took up this theme. It noted the low level of participation by women in all forms of politics and administration, and concluded that it was due, not to any legal provisions, but to cultural and practical barriers, along with expectations on the part of men and of women themselves.

Commission on the Status of Women, *Report to Minister for Finance* (1972)

Women in politics and public life

481. Representations concerning the participation of women in politics have been made to us by only a very small number of the organisations and individuals from whom we received submissions. We have, however, sought, and obtained, the cooperation of the three main political parties represented in Dáil Éireann, in discussing the extent to which women do, in fact, participate in political activity, the problems which confront them and the type of action which would be necessary to improve the present situation.

482. There are no constitutional or legal provisions in Ireland restricting the participation of women in politics and we have not, in our examination of this matter, found evidence of any other formal discrimination against them. Ireland has ratified the United Nations Convention on the Political Rights of Women (1952) which provides that women shall, on equal terms with men and without any discrimination, be entitled to vote in all elections, be eligible for election to all publicly elected bodies established by national law, and be entitled to hold public office and to exercise all public functions established by national law. Apart, however, from the exercise of the franchise, women do not engage in politics, at any level, on anything like the same scale as men do. It appears to be the case that there is a certain amount of prejudice against them doing so, not only by men but by women themselves, and that there are serious practical and cultural difficulties in the way of their more complete involvement in political activity.

483. There are many different levels of political participation. At the lower end of the scale, a person may exercise the right to vote and be moderately interested in political news and events. At the other extreme, the person may be an active member of a political party devoting a large amount of time to political activities, be seeking or holding office at one level or another in the party or be an elected representative. Any distinctions that exist between the political involvement of men and women at the lower end of

the scale are not very serious, but as one progresses towards the centre of political power it is very obvious that women play a rapidly decreasing part. This pattern is not, however, confined to political organisation – it is reflected in most other spheres of national life.

484. Although there are no official figures available, there is no evidence to indicate that the percentage of women voters actually voting in elections is any different from the percentage of men doing so and the general impression seems to be that the percentages are probably very similar to each other. This pattern is common to most European countries. In a survey covering Belgium, France, Greece, Italy, the Netherlands, Norway, Spain, Sweden and the United Kingdom, in 1968, the Council of Europe found that the percentage of persons voting is about the same for men and women, and, in fact, women sometimes are in the majority.

485. The only information of a general nature that has come to our notice concerning Irish women's interest in politics is that obtained in an opinion poll carried out by Social Surveys (Gallup Poll) in April, 1970, covering a sample of over 2,000 respondents throughout the country. The results of the survey were published in the October, 1969, December, 1969, and the April, 1970, issues of *Nusight* magazine. The questions in that survey included one enquiring how interested the respondent was in the outcome of the next (June, 1969) general election. The survey found that there was a notable difference between the attitudes of men and women to politics as disclosed by the answer to this question and by the answer to certain other questions in the survey. The proportion of women 'only a little interested' or 'not interested' was much higher than in the case of men – 35% as against 47% – and only 25% of women as against 33% of men described themselves as 'very interested'. In reply to a question to persons not in membership of a political party as to whether they would join a party if they agreed with most of its aims, there was again a significant difference between men and women. Amongst the women respondents only 11% said they would join as against 18% of the men. Only 3% of the women surveyed were already in membership of a party, as compared with 9% of men. Those interviewed were also asked whether they had heard of any party publishing new policies recently. Overall, 23% of women had heard of party policies as compared with 38% of men.

486. As there are approximately equal numbers of men and

women in the population, the figures quoted in paragraph 485 concerning membership of political parties suggest that women account for approximately one-quarter of the total membership. In order to get some idea as to whether women are playing an active part once they have joined the parties and whether they are attaining positions of responsibility, we asked the three main parties for information concerning the proportion of women with officer status (Chairman, Secretary, etc.) in their organisations and we are obliged to them for the information supplied. In order to avoid identifying the position in any one party we refer here only to percentages based on aggregated figures. In general, the proportion of women with officer status is well below what would be expected having regard to the proportion in membership. Overall, only about 6% of officer posts are filled by women and the great majority of the posts held by them are as Secretary or Treasurer of a local branch. Only about 8% of women who have obtained officerships are in a position of Chairman or Vice Chairman. At National Executive level of the three parties, only 3 out of a total of 123 members – 2.4% – are women.

487. The representatives of all three political parties with whom we had discussions have emphasised that not only is there no discrimination against women becoming party members but that the parties welcome them as members. They do admit, however, that historical and social attitudes have tended to represent political activity as being more appropriate for men than for women and that this probably has the effect of discouraging women from becoming members of local branches. It must also be remembered that women, and particularly married women with young children, have, in general, less free time to devote to pursuits of this nature due to domestic responsibilities. In addition to these factors, it is also the case that many women are members of voluntary organisations which do not discuss political matters, at least on a party level, and this may lead to a certain reluctance on the part of a number of able women to engage in other areas of activity which may be directly concerned with party policies.

488. The number of women candidates and the number of successful women candidates, as compared with the corresponding figures for men, at each of the Dáil elections since 1957 are shown in Table 20 [designated Table 10.1 in this book].

Table 10.1
Women candidates in elections to Dáil Éireann, 1957–69

Election	Candidates		Elected (Percentage of total elected shown in brackets)	
	Men	Women	Men	Women
16th Dáil (1957)	278	11	141 (96%)	6 (4%)
17th Dáil (1961)	292	9	141 (98%)	3 (2%)
18th Dáil (1965)	273	8	139 (97%)	5 (3%)
19th Dáil (1969)	263	11	141 (98%)	3 (2%)

We are grateful to the students of the School of Public Administration for researching these figures and those quoted in paragraphs 491 and 492.

Two women were elected in by-elections to the 16th Dáil (out of 3 women candidates) and 3 in by-elections to the 17th Dáil (out of 3 women candidates). All of these successful women candidates in by-elections were the widows of the Deputies whose deaths gave rise to the by-elections. There were 2 unsuccessful women candidates in by-elections to the 18th Dáil but neither were widows of deceased deputies. Only 9 individual women were involved in the 22 successful candidatures in the four Dáil elections and by-elections referred to above; of these, 8 were the widows of former Dáil Deputies.

489. The figures in paragraph 488 show that the low level of participation of women in politics at branch level is very much accentuated in the area of public representation. This problem is found in other countries also. In Britain, for instance, only 4.1% of the members of the House of Commons (26 out of a total of 630) elected in 1966 and 1970 were women. In France, approximately 1.6% of the Chamber of Deputies are women and in the United States none of the 100 members of the Senate and only 3.3% of the House of Representatives are women.

Women who do become members of a local branch of a political party seem content to stay at that level and not to push themselves forward for public office. Here again the question of family responsibilities is probably an important factor, especially in view of the very large amount of time which must be devoted to canvassing support by an election candidate. The common method of entry to political representation for women in Ireland is by marriage or family relationship with a former Dáil Deputy. This is understandable to the extent that most wives of Deputies will be very much involved with their husband's work while he is alive and will be interested in continuing that work if he dies. The parties have also made it clear to us that the decision to support a candidate for election is done in the expectation that the candidate will have a good chance of success. A candidate's name must be well-known in the constituency and in this respect the widow of a deceased Deputy has an advantage over other women candidates. Also, there is an element of what is referred to as a 'sympathy' vote involved. The parties consider, however, that this sympathy element does not last beyond the woman's first election and that at subsequent elections the woman Deputy has to stand on her record. A woman (other than the widow of a deceased Deputy who starts with this very strong initial advantage) who does come into political prominence, does so against very great odds and is usually a woman of very strong character and ambition. Once elected to the Dáil, there is no indication that a woman engages in work which is different from her male counterparts or that she confines herself to what are commonly regarded as 'women's questions'. Neither is there any evidence that she is discriminated against in any way in Dáil activities, for instance, in involvement in Dáil committees and so forth.

The Council of Europe report referred to in paragraph 484 points out that very much the same general picture in relation to women standing for election is also true of many other countries. The report states that the situation everywhere is a most disappointing one, that very few women stand for election and, as a rule, very few get elected, even in countries where women have long been taking an active part in political life.

The proportion of women members in the national parliaments of a number of other countries is shown in Table 21 [designated Table 10.2 in this book]. There has not been any tendency in these countries for the percentage of women in parliament to increase. The general trend has been, rather, for the percentage to decrease after the first elections in which women have the vote and to become more or less stabilised at a very low level.

Table 10.2

Representation of women in national parliaments in Ireland and certain other countries*

		Men	Women	Percentage Women
Ireland	Dáil Éireann	141	3	2.0
	Seanad Éireann	55	5	8.3
Britain	House of Commons	604	26	4.1
France	Chamber of Deputies	479	8	1.6
	Senate	279	4	1.4
Federal Republic of Germany	Bundestag	493	32	6.1
Italy	Lower House	614	19	3.0
	Upper House	310	5	1.6
Belgium	Chamber of Deputies	206	6	2.8
	Senate	172	6	3.4
Netherlands	Lower House	137	13	8.7
	Upper House	73	2	2.7
Luxembourg	One House	56	2	4.3
Norway	Lower House	102	10	8.9
	Upper House	33	5	13.2
Denmark	One House	149	30	16.8
United States	House of Representatives	421	14	3.3
	Senate	100	–	–
Canada	House of Commons	259	5	1.9
	Senate (Non-elective)	102	4	3.8
Japan	House of Representatives	478	8	1.7
	House of Councillors	237	13	5.6
Sweden	Riksdag	305	45	13.0

*Figures relate to current assemblies. We are indebted to the Embassies in Ireland of various countries and to the Department of Foreign Affairs for the information.

490. It has been suggested that the list system of proportional representation, which operates in Austria, Belgium, Denmark, Finland, Greece, Iceland, Italy, Luxembourg, the Netherlands, Norway, Sweden, Switzerland and the Federal Republic of Germany, would be a more effective electoral system for ensuring a larger proportion of women members in Parliament. Under this system, a voter chooses not between individual candidates but between lists of candidates sponsored by parties or other organisations. The seats given to each party are, as a general rule, filled by taking names from each party's list of candidates in the order in which they have been placed on it by the party. The parties and organisations involved would, accordingly, have a greater chance to ensure a fairer

representation by women by including an equitable proportion of women on the lists. There is little evidence, however, that this has happened and the proportion of women members of Parliament in those countries with the list system remains at a very low level.

491. In panel elections to the Seanad since 1957, there have been 16 women candidates (as compared with 398 men) and of these, 7 have been elected (as compared with 165 men). A total of 8 women have been nominated to the Seanad by the Taoiseach during this period in comparison with 36 men. Of the 4 women candidates on the Universities panel over the period, only one was elected. The corresponding figures for men were 57 candidates and 23 elected.

The number of men and women candidates, the number elected and the Taoiseach's nominations to each Seanad since 1957 are shown in Table 22 [designated Table 10.3 in this book].

Table 10.3
Seanad Éireann, 1957–1969

Candidates	*Nominated		Elected	
	Men	Women	Men	Women
Taoiseach's nominations				
1957	9	2		
1961	9	2		
1965	8	3		
1969	10	1		
Universities				
1957	9	2	6	
1961	16	6		
1965	15	1	6	
1969	17	1	5	1
Panels				
1957	105	6	41	2
1961	96	5	42	1
1965	99	2	42	1
1969	98	3	40	3
TOTAL	455	20	224	16

*Of the 60 members of An Seanad, 11 are nominated by the Taoiseach and the remainder are elected.

492. In the most recent local elections (1967), there were 118 women candidates (out of a total candidature of 3,142) and of these, 54 were elected. Of those women who stood for election, the highest percentage of women elected was to County Councils (69%) and the lowest percentage was to County Borough Councils (18%). Our attention has been drawn in discussions on this area to the fact that

the best course for a person, whether male or female, who aspires to political representation on a national level is to commence by becoming a member of a local authority. Although the number of women candidates who contested the local elections in 1967 was very small, in comparison with the number of men candidates, the proportion of successful women candidates was relatively high. If a greater number of women candidates were to contest the local elections it seems likely that there would be a considerable increase in the number of women sufficiently experienced and well-known to be suitable for selection as candidates for Dáil elections.

493. The type of result which can be achieved by women's organisations making a concerted effort to get more women elected has been demonstrated in the Norwegian municipal elections in 1971. The Norwegian National Council for Women (an umbrella organisation for 23 nationwide women's organisations and 35 Local Women's Councils) launched an intensive campaign aimed at getting more women elected to the Municipal Councils. Mainly as a result of this campaign, the overall percentage of women in the Municipal Councils rose from 9.5% to 14.8%, an increase of almost 60%, and in many cases the number of women was doubled.

Table 10.4
Local elections 1967

	Number of seats	Number of candidates		Elected (% of total elected		Success Rates*	
		Men	Women	Men	Women	Men	Women
County Councils	687	1,373	29	667	20	49%	69%
				(97%)	(3%)	36	18%
County Borough Councils	108	287	34	102	(94%)	(6%)	
Borough and Urban District Councils	537	1,060	41	517 (96%)	20 (4%)	49%	49%
Town Commissioners	207	304	14	199 (96%)	8 (4%)	65%	57%

*(Number elected shown in brackets as a percentage of the number of candidates of each sex separately)

494. In general, then, the picture presented of women's involvement in politics is one of relatively small participation at local level, with a progressive decline of involvement at the higher levels. This, of course, is true of women's participation in many

other areas where the promotion of women comes up against serious obstacles and traditional attitudes. It is true also of practically all countries abroad. The exceptional cases where women have come into political prominence – for instance in India, Ceylon and Israel, where the Prime Ministers are women – only serve to highlight the general absence of women from positions of political responsibility. There is a strong indication that women are themselves in a certain measure to blame for this situation by displaying a considerable degree of apathy. It has also been suggested that women's educational background is at fault and that even with equality of access to education the present large degree of segregated education operates to preserve a traditional division of interests between the sexes. In politics, this manifests itself in the orientation of women to believe that political power and activity is primarily for men. There is clearly a great need for really impressing on girls that they have a part to play in political life and that the general failure of women to participate more fully in political activity can only operate to their disadvantage. The United Nations Commission on the Status of Women has drawn attention to the part that education must play in this matter and has referred to the necessity for an intensive programme of civic and political training to ensure that women realise the full extent of their rights, obligations and abilities, that young people be encouraged to participate in political activity and that civic education be available at all educational levels, including adult educational institutes.

495. In this connection it is, we feel, a very welcome development that the extra-mural courses run by the Universities now include citizenship courses with wide and interesting curricula and we would suggest that the women's organisations should encourage their members to participate in these. We note also that the Institute of Public Administration have established a Working Party which will examine the contribution of the educational system to the development of community life; we hope that the working party will consider how girls may, throughout their education, be influenced towards a more active interest in politics, so long regarded as a reserved role for men.

496. In relation to the participation of women in political life at local level, we feel that the changing social climate, and the increasing role which women are playing in the social and economic life of the country, will operate very positively to increase their political involvement. There can be no doubt, however, having regard to the experience of other countries, that this process, on its

own, will have visible results only very gradually. The immediate problem is, we feel, to bring about an increased awareness by women that politics is not meant to be a male preserve, that they should interest and involve themselves in this area and that it is only by doing so that they can have a really effective say in formulating the social and economic policies which affect their everyday lives. As we have indicated, the growth of this political awareness can be stimulated by placing a much greater emphasis in schools and institutes for adult education on the teaching of civics and on the political role of women and their responsibilities in public life. Attention was drawn by many of the bodies making submissions to the National Adult Education Survey to the lack of adequate provision for instruction in civics and leadership at the level of adult education and a widespread improvement in this respect could certainly be expected to result in an increase in the active involvement of both men and women in politics. We urge the Department of Education to use every available means to encourage and guide the teaching of civics at all levels of education under its control. In addition, the political parties themselves should make greater efforts to attract women members and to let it be seen that they welcome them. Once they become members, they should be treated equally with men and should be given posts of responsibility in the organisation on merit. Progress of women within the parties will be clearly related to their willingness to work hard and to perform uncongenial tasks where necessary. The women's organisations, also, have a part to play in providing training in public speaking and civics and encouraging a greater political and social awareness among their members even if the organisations themselves are non party political.

497. It is only by an intensive programme of civic and political education at all levels as outlined in paragraph 496 that we can see any prospect of a significant increase in the proportion of women actively involved in politics.

Involvement of women in voluntary non-party-political organisations
498. In practically every country, women's interest in civic problems and their commitment in the area of social responsibility tend to manifest themselves in involvement in voluntary non-party-political organisations rather than in organised political activity. Ireland is no exception to this and the variety of women's organisations is shown in Appendix A [not included] which lists the organisations from which we

have received submissions. The work of these organisations covers a wide range of activity. Some, for instance, are organised principally as pressure groups to improve the position of a particular category of women; others, for example, may have a greater emphasis on consumer protection or on educational, social, cultural or recreational activities.

499. The Council of Europe survey referred to in paragraph 484 revealed that in many countries a consultative role is given to the women's associations by the Government. The most advanced country in this respect is Sweden where draft legislation is circulated, to, inter alia, the women's organisations for their comments and in this way these organisations are given the opportunity of expressing their opinion on legislation regarding social security, training, the education of consumers, school questions, adult education and so on. The Swedish women's associations receive substantial grants from the State under the budget appropriations for adult education to allow them to comply with this task, and to allow a more comprehensive discussion of the problems. Apart, however, from such direct consultative arrangements, it is clear from the report of the survey that women's associations in every country perform a very useful function in fostering a greater consciousness among their members of social problems and in advancing adult education. The report notes that all countries were in agreement that the women's associations represent a major factor, perhaps even the main factor, in adult education, even those associations which have such a strong political flavour that they form an adjunct to a political party. It is noted also that it is in the countries where the educational movements are the most highly developed that the most active and influential women's associations are found.

500. The various women's organisations in Ireland are playing a very important role in educating and training women to participate more fully in various aspects of community life and they have, we believe, the potential to develop and greatly increase this role. We have already referred (paragraph 496) to the desirability of such organisations fostering a greater political consciousness among their members with a view to remedying the present low level of active participation by women in politics. Apart from this type of educational activity, the associations also have an increasingly important part to play in acting as pressure groups to ensure that existing discriminations against women are remedied as speedily as possible. In this connection we feel that many of the recommendations made in this report can be more quickly implemented if there is serious and continued pressure for action on them by the various women's associations. We urge that

individual associations should concentrate on specific problems and see them through to a satisfactory conclusion rather than disperse their energies over too wide a range of activities. In addition, we consider that the growth of a greater degree of cooperation and exchange of ideas between women's organisations and men's organisations would be a most welcome development.

501. We consider also that there should be greater liaison between Government Departments and women's organisations under which specific problems would be referred to the organisations for comment before action is taken on them and that the organisations should press for consultation of this nature. Such consultation can, we feel, operate to improve standards of voluntary organisations and to bring a greater degree of discipline to the manner in which problems are approached.

502. It would clearly be impossible for Government Departments to consult individually with a large number of different organisations and it would be advisable, in the interests of women, that the various associations should form a single representative body which would undertake responsibility for acting as a liaison body between Departments and the individual organisations and for the preparation of submissions on matters relating to the implementation of this report or on any other legislative proposals of particular concern to women. This body might be an extension of the Ad Hoc Committee of Women's Organisations on the Status of Women whose representations were largely responsible for the setting up of this Commission, with suitable additions from any other interested groups and might act for an experimental period of, say, 5 years. We note from press reports that there have been some recent moves in this direction and that a coordinating council of women's organisations has been formed.

503. We recommend that some financial assistance be made available by the State to a body recognised by the Government as being representative of women's interests to assist in defraying secretarial expenses, to engage expert advice on complicated technical matters and to help meet the cost of sending persons on short training courses or to seminars dealing with matters being considered or likely to be considered by the body.

Women appointed to statutory and other bodies

504. The various Ministers of State have responsibility in many instances for the appointment of persons to statutory Bodies and to non-statutory advisory Commissions, Councils and Boards. In

a number of cases, local authorities, trade unions and employer and professional organisations can also nominate persons to these Bodies. An examination of such appointments shows that, in general, women are very poorly represented and frequently there is no woman at all included. The proportion of women serving on a number of such Bodies is shown in Table 24 [designated Table 10.5 in this book].

Out of a total of 59 Board members (other than Chairmen) at present serving on the Boards of ten of the major semi-State Bodies, only one is a woman. There is no woman Chairman of the Board of any of these Bodies.

505. The proportion of women on advisory bodies, such as the Food Advisory Committee, the Prison and Reformatories Visiting Committees, the Factories Advisory Council and the Advisory Council on Itinerancy, is somewhat higher but is still quite small. In these bodies, only 11 of the 84 members are women. The Radio Telefís Éireann Review Body has 2 women members out of a total of 14. There are 3 women out of a total of 27 on the Consultative Council on General Medical Practice.

506. The Civil Service Commissioners, whose main function is the selection of staff for appointment to positions in the civil service, and the Local Appointments Commissioners, who perform the same function in relation to local authority staff, are appointed by the Government. Traditionally, the Ceann Comhairle is appointed to both Commissions. None of the other 5 Commissioners is a woman. The two Commissions have a joint staff of which only two officers above the level of Executive Officer are women out of a total of 17 staff members above that level.

507. In the labour relations field, where nominations are made by employer and trade union organisations, the position is equally discriminatory. There is no woman member of the Labour Court, there is only one woman on the employer and trade union panels of the Redundancy Appeals Tribunal and there is no woman Rights Commissioner. The Employer/Labour Conference which is comprised of 25 employer members (of whom 5 are nominated by the State in its capacity as employer and 20 are nominated by the Irish Employers' Confederation and State Bodies) and 25 labour members (nominated by the Irish Congress of Trade Unions), has only one woman member – a trade union member.

Table 10.5

Examples of women serving on a selection of statutory and other bodies

	Total Chairmen/ Directors/Members	Number of of Women
Electricity Supply Board	5	Nil
Córas Iompair Éireann	7	Nil
Aer Lingus	7	Nil
Radio Telefís Éireann	7	Nil
Bord Fáilte	9	1
Comhlucht Siuicre Éireann	7	Nil
Córas Tráchtála	7	Nil
Industrial Development Authority	9	Nil
Shannon Free Airport Development Co.	6	Nil
Voluntary Health Insurance Board	5	Nil
Food Advisory Committee	9	Nil
Prison and Reformatories Visiting Committees	51	6
Factories Advisory Council	9	1
Advisory Council on Itinerancy	15	4
Radio Telefís Éireann Review Body	14	2
Consultative Council on General Medical Practice	27	3
Civil Service Commission and Local Appointments Commission	6	Nil
Labour Court	5	Nil
Redundancy Appeals Tribunal	16	1
Rights Commissioners	2	Nil
Health Boards	243	15
Metric Board	18	5
Advisory Committee on Value-Added Tax	24	5
National Prices Commission	6	1
Working Party to consider proposals for the establishment of a Central Consumer Consultative Council	10	6

508. Although 26 out of 795 persons elected to County Councils and County Borough Councils at the last local elections were women, there are only 2 women among the 129 persons appointed by such authorities to the recently formed Health Boards. In the case of representatives of the professional groups appointed to these Boards, 8 out of 90, or approximately 9% are women, but the woman representative is in each case a representative of the

practically all-female general nursing profession. One of the highest proportions of Ministerial appointments to statutory Bodies is to be found in this area as 25% (6 out of 24) of the persons appointed to the Health Boards by the Minister for Health are women.

509. Three recently appointed groups have a higher than usual proportion of women members. These are the Metric Board on which there are 5 women out of a total of 18 members, the Advisory Committee on Value-Added Tax on which there are 5 women out of a total of 24, and the working party considering proposals for the establishment of a central consumer consultative organisation which has 10 members, of whom 6 are women. While it was probably considered desirable to have consumer organisations represented on these Bodies, the improvement was no doubt due in part to pressure by the women's organisations to have a say in the formulation of measures of such importance to their members. These organisations had previously voiced strong criticism of the complete absence of women from the ten-strong membership of the Decimal Currency Board.

510. There is little doubt that the present general subordinate position of women in employment, their very limited representation at responsible levels in trade unions and employer organisations, and their domestic commitments all operate to restrict the area of choice among women when appointments of this kind are being made. We cannot accept, however, that these factors are completely responsible for the extremely low proportion of women included in such appointments and the figures quoted must, we feel, lead to the conclusion that a substantial amount of prejudice and discrimination, either deliberate or otherwise, exists.

511. We are opposed to the idea that any quota arrangement should be applied to the apportionment of these appointments between men and women and we consider that women should only be appointed where they are suitably qualified. Nevertheless, we believe that the Government, the professional associations and trade union and employer organisations have a responsibility to bear in mind the desirability of selecting a fair proportion of suitable women for nominations or appointments under their control and we recommend that greater efforts should be made by these various Bodies to identify and approach such women when future appointments are being made. The women's organisations can play an important part in improving the present position by exerting pressure on the appointing agencies and by submitting to them lists of women with appropriate qualifications and experience who are willing to serve on committees and commissions and they

should continue to pursue such a policy actively.

512. We are particularly concerned at the absence of women from the Labour Court in view of the importance of this Body in ensuring equality of status for women in relation to their treatment in employment. We do not suggest that the absence of women from the Court has resulted in discriminatory treatment of women but we do feel that this is an area where steps should be taken to avoid any possible accusation of discrimination and we consider that the achievement of this objective could be greatly assisted by the appointment of at least one woman member to the Court. The Industrial Relations Act 1969 provides that the Labour Court shall consist of a Chairman and either, as the Minister for Labour may from time to time in his discretion determine, four or six ordinary members of whom equal numbers shall be workers' members and employers' members. Provision is also made for the appointment of a Deputy Chairman of the Court. The Court as at present constituted (December, 1972) consists of a Chairman, Deputy Chairman and 4 members (2 workers' and 2 employers' members).

We recommend, accordingly, that if the Minister for Labour should determine to avail of the power conferred in the Industrial Relations Act 1969 to expand the Labour Court by the appointment of a further two members, he should try to ensure that at least one of the new appointees is a suitably qualified woman.

513. The number of persons that may be appointed Civil Service Commissioners or Local Appointments Commissioners is fixed by law at 3 Commissioners in each case. The Ceann Comhairle is, as mentioned in paragraph 506, normally appointed to both Commissions and the remaining members are usually civil servants at the level of Department Secretary (that is, Head of Department) or a level of seniority close to this. As stated in the footnote to Table 16 on Page 101 [not included] there were, as at 1 January, 1972, only two women at Principal level and none at a higher level. There appears to be little immediate prospect therefore of a woman being appointed to either Commission. In relation to the staff of the Commissions, we feel that there should be a greater representation of women at more senior levels and we recommend that steps be taken to achieve this.

WOMEN ON BOARDS OF STATE-SPONSORED BODIES

As with education, the difficulty in attempting to remedy the gender imbalance in political and administrative participation was that it was not so susceptible to changes in the law as were, for example, employment or social welfare. The first Commission 'welcomed developments' and offered exhortations to the universities, the Department of Education and women's groups, but the actual recommendations of the Commission – to increase funding for a yet to be formed women's umbrella organisation, to urge statutory bodies to approach women about appointment to their boards and to give one of the two places on an expanded Labour Court to a woman – were thin gruel indeed.

However, in the 1970s and early 1980s the amount of political activity by women increased. The three main political parties all moved, to some extent, in the direction of making conscious efforts to recruit more women candidates for posts within their own organisations and on elected public bodies. In 1972 only 2.4 per cent of all the members of the three parties' national executives were women. Thirteen years later the proportions were 11.1 per cent for Fianna Fáil, 12.5 per cent for Fine Gael and 13.8 per cent for Labour. In 1979 a woman was appointed to a cabinet position, the first in Ireland since Constance Markievicz; and the number of women in the Dáil had risen from 3 deputies out of 144 (as of 1972) to 14 out of 166 by the time that the Working Party on Women's Affairs and Family Law Reform published its *Irish Women: Agenda for Practical Action* in 1985. The number of women appointed to boards of state-sponsored bodies was only slightly higher in 1985 than it had been in 1972, with women accounting for about 12 per cent of the membership of 124 such bodies.

Interestingly, when the Working Party came to consider the issue of women's participation in public life, it focused exclusively on the composition of these boards. It recommended an increase in the number of women appointed, on the grounds that the imbalance in gender 'no longer represents the reality of women's contribution to economic and social life'.

Working Party on Women's Affairs and Family Law Reform, Irish Women: *Agenda for Practical Action* (1985)

Appointment of women to the boards of state-sponsored bodies

POSITION REGARDING REPRESENTATION OF WOMEN ON STATE BOARDS

11.1 The report of the Commission on the Status of Women (December, 1972) stated a belief that the Government, the Professional Associations, Trade Unions and Employees'

Organisations have a responsibility to bear in mind the desirability of selecting a fair proportion of suitable women for nominations or appointments to bodies under their aegis. A recent survey of the membership of some 124 state bodies with appointed Boards showed that women accounted for only some 12% of total Board membership. It is evident, therefore, that the talents and contributions which women can make in decision-making processes have not been fully exploited.

VIEWS OF COUNCIL FOR THE STATUS OF WOMEN AND EMPLOYMENT EQUALITY AGENCY

11.2 The Council for the Status of Women have produced two reports entitled *Who Makes the Decisions?* identifying the extent of participation by women on the boards of State-sponsored bodies. The reports call on the Government, which have primary responsibility in nominating persons to State-sponsored bodies, to take steps to ensure the appropriate representation of women on these bodies. The reports recommend that the Government embark upon a serious process of seeking out women who are suitable for appointment to boards. The point is made in the Council reports that women should not be excluded from important areas of community life. They represent half the population, and are equally affected by the decisions of state bodies. The Employment Equality Agency in its Annual Report for 1978 also expressed the view that the appointment of a greater number of women to such boards and commissions would not only enable society to benefit from their contribution but would help to break down prejudices, thus fostering the concept of equality. In its report of 1979, it concludes that the absence of women from high levels of policy and planning and from decision-making areas where policies become effective, deprives society of the skills of well qualified women. Society is also denied the opportunity of advice from women whose expertise has been gained from hitherto unrepresented areas of experience.

NATIONAL REGISTERS

11.3 A National Women's Talent Bank was set up by the National Federation of Business and Professional Women's Clubs and the Women's Political Association in 1970. The rationale behind its establishment was to compile and maintain a register of women willing and competent to serve on boards, committees, commissions and to help correct the imbalance of female/male representation. The Bank, which is now operated through the

Council for the Status of Women, comprises women with professional qualifications, specialised skills or with a record of voluntary work in any area. In addition, the Office of the Minister of State for Women's Affairs has been building up a register of women available for appointment to boards etc. Both of these Registers can be of considerable practical use to Ministers when vacancies arise on boards under their aegis.

SITUATION ELSEWHERE

11.4 The under-representation of women on State boards and agencies and in decision-making areas generally, has also been of concern to women's organisations elsewhere. A recent study in Canada carried out by the Canadian Advisory Council on the Status of Women indicated concern that only around 15% of appointments to federal organisations were filled by women. The study noted that appointments are a well-known source of political patronage, but that women who are active in political organisations are not receiving their 'due rewards'. In Britain a recent Employment Opportunities Commission (EOC) Report considered ways in which the number of women appointed to public bodies could be increased. The Report concluded that the small number of female appointments did indicate a bias against women and that suitably qualified and experienced female candidates could be found 'if positive action were taken to seek out appropriate women for appointment and the criteria for selection were broadened'. The report looked at the operation of the Public Appointment Unit of the Management and Personnel Office which was established in 1975 to make more open the system of drawing up a list of men and women able and willing to serve on public bodies. This list is available for Government Ministers to consult when they make appointments. Nominations for the list are by (a) personal recommendation (b) nomination by a representative organisation or (c) self-nomination. The Report suggested that women would not fare well under (a) which in their view was dependent on the 'old boy network'. In the case of (b), as women are not frequently holding executive positions in the nominating organisations, they were unlikely to fare well through that process. Under (c) there was the suspicion that selectors are less impressed by self-nomination than by nomination through other channels. The Working Party also examined the criteria by which persons are judged suitable for public life and felt that they may not give due recognition to the various ways by which women gain qualifications and experience, for example through their membership of women's organisations and active participation in voluntary work. Through the latter pursuits, considerable administrative experience can be gained along with skills in public speaking and knowledge of committee procedure.

The position of women in decision-making areas was one of the topics considered by the European Parliament Committee of Enquiry into the situation of women in Europe. The Committee noted that on the basis of an analysis of figures indicating the percentage of women in top jobs in the Member States, there had been progress compared with the past. However, progress varied widely according to the sectors analysed and the countries examined, and in general women continued to remain in a minority in decision-making areas, to the point where in some instances there is a total absence of women.

RATIONALE FOR APPOINTMENT OF WOMEN TO BOARDS ETC.

11.5 Since State boards and agencies recommend and enforce Government policies which have a direct impact on the lives of men and women, it is vital that women be adequately represented when appointments are being made. As more active consumers than men, women use public services to a greater degree than men and can have a richer experience of various public authorities and their work. While a specialist expertise may be essential for a proportion of the membership of some bodies, a consumer or lay view is often useful and desirable. The involvement of women in key decision-making areas can also help to break down prejudice against women and so advance their position in society. The Council for the Status of Women, in their second report dealing with women on the boards of State-sponsored bodies, consider in this context that appointments of women to State boards is a key indicator of the seriousness with which the Government take the question of overcoming or redressing the imbalance which has heretofore existed in relation to the involvement of women in public life. While acknowledging that, due to historical and social circumstances, a greater number of men than women will have obtained professional and other qualifications in areas of relevance to particular State boards, the Council point out that possession of these qualifications does not represent the totality of human experience nor do they have exclusive relevance for even those bodies with a narrow technical remit.

RECOMMENDATIONS

11.6 In recent times in this country, political parties have recognised, in their election manifestos for example, the need to include more women on boards and in decision-making areas generally, and Governments have identified this area as one of their policy objectives. While more and more women are being appointed to State bodies etc., as already pointed out, the overall percentage has remained largely unchanged. Part of the reason for this is that a large number of appointments run for a period of some years (e.g. five years) so that women are being considered only for the appointments arising in any one year. It would take some time, therefore, before a sizeable impact could be made on the overall percentage even under the most favourable conditions. To achieve such an impact, however, a strengthened approach to the appointment of women to boards and agencies will be necessary. Many of the recommendations already made by the Working Party would, if implemented, be helpful in enabling more women to become available and willing to serve on boards etc., such as those relating to more flexibility in employment, positive action programmes, child care facilities. In addition the Working Party recommends the following:

(i)   As a start, Ministers should be exhorted to seek out and appoint at least one and preferably more women to boards under their aegis. Each Minister should set a target for an increased proportion of women to be appointed to the public bodies for which they are responsible. A large number of State boards have no women on them at present. While accepting that there are many occupational areas where women in general are found in small numbers, they nonetheless exist in almost every sphere of economic and social activity. The, present situation of imbalance, with all male boards the norm in sectors such as industry and agriculture, no longer represents the reality of women's contribution to economic and social life.

(ii)   The Public Appointments Unit which exists in the British system is worthy of consideration. It would provide a wide list of possible candidates for appointments. While it does not necessarily follow that women would automatically fare better through this system, its existence would create greater opportunity for women to be at least considered. If a Unit of this nature were in operation, the criteria by which names would be put forward should be broad enough to include the range of experience which many women are likely to have to a greater extent than men. For instance, weight should be given to experience gained in voluntary organisations or in informal community activity.

(iii) Nominating bodies should continue – as at present in many cases – to be encouraged by Ministers to include women nominees. As these organisations are important spring-boards for entry into public life, they should pursue more vigorously ways in which women could be more positively encouraged to participate in the branch, the local affairs of the organisation and in public life generally.

PROPOSALS FOR QUOTAS AND TARGETS

Between 1985, when the Working Party published its *Agenda*, and 1993, when the Second Commission on the Status of Women issued its report, there was a further increase in women's participation both in elected bodies and on state boards. Nevertheless, starting from such a low base, progress remained distinctly limited.

The number of women who were victorious in the general (national) and local elections in 1991 represented just 11 per cent of the total number of election winners, which was nonetheless an increase from 8 per cent in 1985. By 1993 there were 20 women among the 166 members of the Dáil and eight women among the 60 Senators. The number of women in the Dáil had thus increased sevenfold since 1972, but it was still only 12 per cent of the total, while the number of women Senators, though it had doubled since 1972, was just 13 per cent of the total. Meanwhile, the proportion of women among the membership of boards of state-sponsored bodies had increased, but only from 12 per cent to 14 per cent, in the eight years between the publication of the Working Party's *Agenda* and the appearance of the Second Commission's report. Accordingly, the Second Commission addressed virtually every dimension of women's participation in politics and policy-making, from women's attitudes to politics to cabinet-level concern for women's affairs, and produced the most far-reaching proposals for remedying gender imbalance.

Second Commission on the Status of Women, *Report to Government* (1993)

7.1 Introduction

This chapter deals with the participation by women in political and economic life. In particular, we make a number of recommendations to political parties as to how they might facilitate a higher level of representation by women in the Oireachtas. We also recommend, to both political parties and social partners, how they might increase the numbers of women in senior representative and decision-making positions. We examine the means whereby women's concerns and perspectives can be taken into account in policy-making, and to that end, we recommend the establishment of a fully fledged Department of Women's Affairs, headed by a Minister of Cabinet rank.

7.2 Participation

7.2.1 1990 EUROPEAN VALUES STUDY

The 1990 European Values Study, which is carried out across the EC countries, provides interesting data on the relative participation of women and men in political and other organisational activities in Ireland. Table 7.1 [designated Table 10.6 in this book] shows that the number of people who are members of political parties is extremely small. The figure has changed over time but men remain almost twice as likely as women to be active in political parties.

Table 10.6

Membership of a political party by sex and period, 1981 and 1990

1981		1990	
Women	Men	Women	Men
%	%	%	%
3	7	3	5

Table 7.2 [designated Table 10.7 in this book] illustrates that men consider themselves more interested in politics than are women. The percentage of people who express least interest in politics has declined substantially over time; for men, between 1981 and 1990 the figure drops from thirty five per cent to twenty one per cent; while for women, the corresponding figures are fifty four per cent and thirty six per cent.

Table 10.7
Extent of interest in politics by sex by period, 1981 and 1990

| | 1981 | | 1990 | |
	Women	Men	Women	Men
	%	%	%	%
Very interested	3	6	4	13
Somewhat interested	19	26	26	32
Not very interested	24	32	34	34
Not at all interested	54	35	36	21

An interest in politics does not necessarily translate into discussion of politics. Social norms may deem that such discussion is inappropriate in certain situations or less appropriate for some social groups than others. The evidence presented in Table 7.3 [designated Table 10.8 in this book] does show that at both points in time women were considerably less likely than men to engage in discussion of politics. However, the probability of women engaging in such activity increased significantly. In 1981, five per cent of women discussed politics frequently but by 1990 this figure had risen to nine per cent. Correspondingly, while at the earlier date over six out of ten women indicated that they never discussed politics, by 1990 the figure had dropped to five out of ten.

Table 10.8
Frequency of discussion of politics by sex by period, 1981 and 1990

| | 1981 | | 1990 | |
	Women	Men	Women	Men
	%	%	%	%
Frequently	5	12	9	15
Occasionally	34	52	41	53
Never	62	36	50	32

It is interesting to contrast the scale of women's participation in politics with their participation in voluntary activities generally. Women are more likely than men to be members of social welfare, religious, educational or cultural organisations. They are about equally likely to be members of local community organisations or professional organisations. However, they are substantially less likely to be members of youth work organisations, sports or recreational clubs, and trade unions, see Table 7.4 [designated Table 10.9 in this book].

Table 10.9
Membership of voluntary organisations by sex

		Women %	Men %
(i)	Social welfare	9	5
(ii)	Religious	16	12
(iii)	Education and culture	12	8
(iv)	Trade unions	5	13
(v)	Local community action	4	3
(vi)	Professional associations	5	5
(vii)	Youth work	6	11
(viii)	Sports or recreation	16	33
(ix)	Women's groups	9	–

Women believe themselves less interested in politics than men are, although this interest is growing; men are twice as likely as women to be members of a political party; and there is no big difference between the participation of women and men in voluntary organisations, although there is a very significant difference in the types of organisations to which they are likely to belong.

Reinforcing the survey evidence, popular impression would suggest that in Ireland women make up the backbone of parent/teacher associations, caring organisations, and self-help groups. Complex educational and poverty issues are dealt with by these kinds of organisations; issues which shape the society we live in. Yet women identify themselves as less interested in politics than men, and are less likely to be members of political parties. The paradox is that the dearth of women in political life is not due to lack of interest in issues, and is certainly not due to women's lack of commitment of time and energy in organisations and groups set up with the intention of furthering the common good.

The Commission believes that there are compelling structural and attitudinal reasons why women are not involved full-time in political life and why the campaigning and organisational experience they show in other areas of activity is not translated into politics. These reasons include: limiting cultural and social values; the difficulties in devoting themselves simultaneously to family life, paid employment and political tasks; and the ongoing reluctance of political parties to select women candidates. It has to be said that, measured by results, political parties as currently constituted in their structures and practices are not friendly towards women. The Commission believes that it is not healthy for democracy or good for women that women make up such a small proportion of our elected representatives. It is essential that women's perspectives are well-represented in the most important representative forum in our society.

The whole point of a representative political system is to work within that system to bring about positive change and development. The consequences of our present imbalanced representation is that women's interests often have to be lobbied for from outside the Oireachtas and that issues of central concern to society, such as child care, community care, and flexibility in working life are compartmentalised as 'women's issues' and made marginal to the main political agenda of the day. Women are effectively outside the arena where social and economic policies are initiated, or changed. In our view this is unlikely to change until a critical mass of women representatives has been attained. The Commission, therefore, seeks to encourage more participation at grassroots level by women in politics and more active (and rewarding) participation in the sense of office-seeking at each level of party organisation by women already in and women entering political life. To that end, we address our recommendations not only to the Government but also to the individual political parties in the Oireachtas.

7.2.3 EDUCATING FOR POLITICAL PARTICIPATION

In order to encourage a greater level of participation by women the Commission believes that the function and importance of politics needs to be taught in schools, at primary and second level. Because of the structural barriers they face it is particularly important to facilitate the development in girls of a political consciousness. Girls should be encouraged to use their cognitive and presentational skills in public speaking and drama. Debating and sports contests are also helpful in developing assertiveness, competitive spirit, and resilience, useful skills they will need as women in political life.

The Commission recommends that:

(a) politics and governance should be included as a module in the post-primary subject of social and environmental studies, the curriculum for which is currently being devised by the National Council for Curriculum and Assessment (NCCA);

(b) teachers should encourage the development of a political consciousness in their pupils;

(c) girls should be encouraged by both teachers and parents to join organisations – all kinds of organisations – in order to develop meeting and presentational skills and an acquaintance with how organisations work and take decisions.

7.2.4 WOMEN'S GROUPS

Local women's groups are often the most dynamic change agents in communities, and local community groups and women's organisations can act as a gateway for women to enter party politics. In Chapter 2 [not included] the Commission makes a number of recommendations as to how the Department of Social Welfare's scheme of grants for locally based women's groups might be improved. Such groups and organisations have an important role to play in encouraging women to become members of the political party of their choice, to seek election to local Government, and to participate actively in the most important forums of public life. To some extent this is being done at a macro level, e.g., by the support of the Council for the Status of Women and the Women's Political Association for women election candidates.

The Commission recommends that women's organisations should adopt a policy of encouraging their members to become involved in the formal political structure and to provide back-up and encouragement for women who choose to do so.

7.2.5 SENIOR LEVEL OF RESPONSIBILITY IN SOCIAL PARTNER ORGANISATIONS

The social partners, representative of employers, trade unions and farming organisations, play a very significant role in setting the agenda nationally for debate on economic and social issues. This is particularly the case in the context of the Programme for Economic and Social Progress (PESP) where a consensus programme has been agreed by the Government with all parties involved and where a forum, the Central Review Committee, exists in which problems can be aired and resolved and implementation of the agreed provisions in the programme monitored. While the structures of the social partner organisations are perhaps not directly comparable they all share a common feature in that women are poorly represented at senior levels of responsibility.

For example, while women comprise approximately 33% of all organised labour, their representation on executive and other decision making committees is not commensurate with their numerical strength. Only three trade unions have women represented on their executives in proportion to or greater than their women membership.

This underrepresentation of women at senior level is mirrored in employer and farming organisations. The employer organisations have a low number of women among their membership and at executive level. In farming organisations, while in principle membership may be on the basis of the family with women participating as much as men, this is in practice not the case and women have minimal representation at executive level.

In commenting on the representation of women in the trade union movement, it is important to note that the movement has seen considerable progress since the introduction of an equality programme in 1982. One concrete sign of this is that in the Central Review Committee of the PESP, the trade union representatives include a woman. More recently one of the employer organisations, the CIF, is also represented by a woman.

The Government are also party to these negotiating bodies and are represented on these committees by the various relevant Government Departments. Women are also grossly underrepresented on the Government side.

Overall, women are grossly underrepresented on the social partnership negotiating teams and on the Central Review Committee of the PESP. Strategies should be put in place to ensure that women are represented equitably on such negotiating bodies by all parties to the structures.

The Commission recommends that:

(a) all social partner organisations should establish definite programmes and timetables to achieve proportional representation of women in their decision making bodies by the year 2000;

(b) specifically, as a temporary positive action measure, reserved seats or places for women should be introduced on executive committees or decision-making forums.

7.3 Politics

7.3.1 BARRIERS TO PARTICIPATION

The question confronting us as a society is how women may be enabled to participate in politics and public life to a greater extent. Let us look at the existing reality. Submissions to the Commission indicate that political culture in Ireland is predicated upon the notion of 'the serviced male', i.e., a man who has a full-time spouse looking after him, caring for children and home, and acting as an additional secretary or administrative assistant. For a woman to enter politics and seek office when this model applies would, in many cases, require her to fulfil three roles, as a breadwinner, as a primary carer/domestic manager, and as a politician. How, then, can this situation be changed to make entry into political life more possible for women? Firstly, we are calling for some behavioural modification from male partners to help women become active in politics and to help women currently active in politics to realise their potential. In so doing we are not calling for women politicians to be facilitated to become a mirror image of the stereotyped male politician. We are simply calling for a better, mutually agreed apportionment of domestic responsibilities between male and female partners.

7.3.2 ABOLITION OF DUAL MANDATE

Secondly, the Commission is calling on political parties to eliminate the practice of dual mandate, i.e., simultaneous representation by an individual in the Oireachtas and County Council, or in the Oireachtas and European Parliament.

At first sight the practice of a dual mandate may not seem like a gender issue. In the view of the Commission a dual mandate, spanning Dáil and European Parliament, or much more prevalently, spanning Dáil/Seanad and local authorities, is too demanding in terms of the time commitment and workload required from any individual and presupposes the input of a subordinate spouse.

Abolition of dual mandates would enable more individuals, including more women, to participate as political representatives – surely a healthy development for democracy. Entry to local politics is significant, not only in itself, but also as a proving ground for national politics. In our view a policy of ending the dual mandate could be incorporated into an overall local Government reform package and could be linked to a Department of the Environment information programme designed to explain the respective roles of County Councils, Government, and EC. Upon election to the Dáil or European Parliament, the Commission recommends that a politician's membership of a local authority should automatically cease, the vacancy to be filled by cooption. Upon election to the Oireachtas or European Parliament we recommend that her/his existing membership of the other assembly should cease, with the seat being filled by usual procedures.

The Commission recommends that the Government and all political parties in the Oireachtas should eliminate the practice of dual mandate, i.e. simultaneous representation in Oireachtas and County Council or in Oireachtas and European Parliament. This should come into force at the next election.

7.3.3 POSITIVE ACTION PROGRAMME TO INCREASE REPRESENTATION BY WOMEN IN POLITICS

The Commission believes that it is necessary that all political parties, if they are serious about giving women equitable representation, should adopt a positive action programme incorporating the measures we set out in the remainder of this section. The specific measures making up the programme should be reinforced by an overall strategy to promote non-sexist language and behaviour among party members and representatives.

7.3.4 QUOTAS

The introduction of a quota system by political parties is a key strategy for increasing political participation by women. Essentially, a quota is a minimum mandatory percentage of women and men candidates set as an objective by political parties. There is an argument that because quotas introduce preferential treatment for women, the principle of a participation quota constitutes an infringement of the principle of equality. In the opinion of the Commission, this is not the case. Quotas are not intended to operate in isolation but as one important element of a strategy to remedy the deep-seated causes of under-representation of women. Other important elements in this strategy would include financing, training, and selection procedures.

The Commission would like to stress that we see quotas as a temporary compensatory measure of the kind provided for in the United Nations Convention on the Elimination of All Forms of Discrimination against Women, to which Ireland is party. Ideally, parties should seek a gender mix of candidates as they seek a gender mix of members. A fixed-term commitment to a quota could be incorporated in party constitutions to bring this aim about.

Because the question of quotas or devising the basis for a quota is quite complicated, we are attaching at Appendix 7.1 [not included] an outline of quotas currently applied in a number of Council of Europe countries. France is the only country that attempted to introduce a law on quotas. This would have prevented more than 75% of people on the lists of candidates for local elections being of the same sex. The proposed legislation was found to be unconstitutional and in breach of the principle of the equality of all citizens before the law. However, in many European democracies, such as France, Sweden, Norway, Denmark, Austria and Germany, several of the political parties have voluntarily adopted internal quota systems for positions of responsibility within their parties and for candidates standing in local and national elections. This has significantly increased the number of women in parliament and in the higher echelons of political parties in many of these countries.

7.3.5 REPRESENTATION ON NATIONAL EXECUTIVE AND OTHER PARTY COMMITTEES

The practice of reserving a number of seats for women on the National Executive/Executive Committee has already been established by a number of parties in Ireland. We believe that this practice should be followed by all our political parties as a temporary compensatory measure with a view to bringing more of a gender balance to important positions in political parties. This practice could be a very effective strategy in bringing women to prominence and in giving them a strong base from which to build their political profile. The strong representation of women on the Front Bench of the British Labour Party, for example, is, we believe, indicative of the effectiveness of this positive action strategy as in Britain it follows on from the practice of securing a higher representation of women on the National Executive. The Commission, therefore, calls on all the political parties in the Oireachtas to adopt this practice.

The principle of this kind of positive action in politics is not new, as many parties have reserved seats for youth members on the national executive and other party committees. In the view of the Commission, women are at least as under-represented as young people and political parties should treat women in a similar manner in order to allow their voices to be heard and to support their emergence as candidates for political office.

7.3.6 WOMEN'S OFFICERS IN POLITICAL PARTIES

At present, political parties which have reached the representative threshold of seven seats in Dáil Éireann have Youth Officers part-funded by the Exchequer, through the Vote of the Department of Education (Minister of State's subhead). In 1991 this amounted to a subsidy of IR£7,000 per political party. The Commission believes that there is a strong case for a similar level of funding for Women's Officers in political parties. The role of Women's Officers would be to encourage greater participation by women at all levels of political activity by examining barriers to participation, reviewing structures, etc., in order to heighten an awareness in political parties of issues that are important to women or that impact specifically on women, and to consider all issues from a woman-centred perspective. Funding at the level provided for

Youth could constitute a subsidy for a full-time Women's Officer or payment for a part-time Women's Officer, as best suited to the needs of the particular political party

7.3.7 MAKING THE PRACTICE OF POLITICS WOMAN-FRIENDLY
We have already referred in paragraph 7.3.1 above to the societal constraints that make it more difficult for the average woman to participate in politics than the average man. The practices of political parties and of the Oireachtas reflect in microcosm the same outdated organisational view that, by and large, negatively affects women. The Commission is, therefore, calling on political parties to review such factors as the time and place of their meetings, the availability of creche facilities at larger meetings, and the sitting hours of Dáil and Seanad with the twin aims of encouraging greater participation by women and of recognising the family commitments of both men and women.

7.3.8 POSITIONS OF AUTHORITY IN POLITICAL PARTIES
In order that women should be equally represented in the higher echelons of political parties, it is important that they should be enabled to play a role in party nomination procedures; i.e., be elected as officials at party branch level and at all higher decision-making levels. To that end, the Commission recommends that male and female officers should be elected in all party branches and higher organisational tiers on the basis of a minimum 40% representation for either sex within each branch, and that party constitutions should be amended where necessary to make this practice possible among all the Oireachtas political parties.

7.3.9 LOCAL AND GENERAL ELECTIONS
At both local and national level, Irish political parties have been slow to select women candidates to run for election. In the 1991 Local Elections, for example, many incumbent women councillors decided not to run, while some prospective candidates failed to get selected. This calls into question both the selection procedures adopted by political parties and the way the political system currently operates, which may discourage potential women candidates from entering or re-entering political life. Even when they have been selected as candidates by their parties, women are less likely than men to win a seat e.g. in the 1991 election women made up 15% of party candidates, but won

only 11% of the seats contested (see Table 7.5 [designated Table 10.10 in this book]). This low proportion of women councillors contrasts with the pattern in many other European countries, where in local government, women's representation far exceeds that of their national parliamentary visibility. Nevertheless, the Commission welcomes the fact that, at 11%, the proportion of women representatives at a local level has risen from 8% in 1985 and just 6.8% in 1979.

In the November 1992 General Election, all the parties, except the two largest, selected more women to contest the election than they had done in the 1991 local elections (see Table 7.6 [designated Table 10.11 in this book]). The Commission is pleased to note that this general election proved the most successful for women candidates in the history of the State, with a record 20 women being elected to the Dáil (see Table 7.7 [designated Table 10.12 in this book]). It is interesting to note that all but one of the new women deputies had previous local government experience. The other woman elected had considerable experience in the public sphere as a leader of a national women's organisation.

Table 10.10

Women as a percentage of candidates elected through party affiliation, local elections, June 1991

Party	Candidates			Elected		
	Total	Women	%	Total	Women	%
Fianna Fáil	643	71	11	358	22	6.14
Fine Gael	472	70	15	270	31	11.48
Progressive Democrats	122	25	20	37	12	32.43
Labour	200	29	15	90	14	15.55
Workers Party	80	20	25	24	4	16.6
Green Party	59	19	31	13	5	38.46
Total	1,576	234	15	792	88	11.11

Note 1: No female Sinn Féin, Republican Sinn Féin or Christian Principles Party candidates were elected.

Note 2: This chart does not include independent candidates.

(Compiled by the Council for the Status of Women)

Table 10.11
General election, 1992: candidates

Party	Total Candidates	Male	Female	% Male	% Female
Fianna Fáil	122	110	12	91.20	8.80
Fine Gael	91	78	13	85.70	14.30
Labour	42	34	8	80.06	19.94
Progressive Democrats	20	11	9	57.15	42.85
Democratic Left	20	14	6	70.00	30.00
Workers Party	19	13	6	68.20	31.80
Green Party	18	11	7	36.40	63.60
Sinn Féin	41	35	6	86.05	13.95
Others	107	86	21	75.60	24.40
Total	480	392	88	81.67	18.33

Source: Dr Frances Gardiner, Trinity College, Dublin

Table 10.12
General election, 1992: deputies

Party	Total	Male	Female	% Male	% Female
Fianna Fáil	68	63	5	92.6	7.4
Fine Gael	45	40	5	88.9	11.1
Labour	33	28	5	84.8	15.2
Progressive Democrats	10	6	4	60.0	40.0
Democratic Left	4	3	1	75.0	25.0
Others	6	6	0	100.0	0.0
Total	166	146	20	88.0	12.0

Source: Dr Frances Gardiner, Trinity College, Dublin

This reinforces our point that, by and large, candidates need a strong local base in order to be successful in general elections. There is little point in political parties engaging in a hurried selection of women candidates immediately prior to elections simply in order to enhance their gender profile. It may result in short-term media attention, but is not a serious strategy to increase participation by women.

The Commission therefore wishes to emphasise that the establishment of quotas and targets for women should be carried out over time as a medium-term strategy. In particular, it is important that the political parties should encourage and select women to run for election at a local level, so that they build up a base of experienced women councillors to contest general elections.

In conclusion, it is generally the smaller parties who have been to the fore in nominating women candidates to contest elections. The Commission is therefore calling on the larger two parties in particular to rethink their strategies. Women who fail at selection conventions or feel disillusion with party politics, may be tempted to go it alone. However in view of the fact that only 6 Independent councillors are women and no woman Independent has ever been elected to the Dáil, the most viable option for women at present is to get involved in political parties. Their support for women as part of a well thought-out long- and medium-term strategy is therefore essential.

7.3.10 RECOMMENDATIONS

The Commission recommends that all political parties should immediately adopt a positive action programme to encourage increased participation generally by women in politics and increased representation by women. The positive action programme should include the following elements:

(a) minimum party quotas for women candidates;
(b) a strategy promoting non-sexist language and behaviour among party members and representatives;
(c) reserved seats for women on National Executives/Executive Committees of political parties;
(d) making political party practices more accepting of family responsibilities of both women and men through such practices as revising sitting hours of Dáil and Seanad, and providing creche facilities at meetings;
(e) office posts in party branches and higher tiers should be elected on the basis of a minimum 40% representation of either sex;
(f) selecting women candidates considerably in advance of elections to allow them develop profiles as serious candidates.

The Commission also recommends the part-funding by the exchequer of a Women's Officer for each Dáil political party having reached the threshold of seven seats (on same basis as Exchequer currently part funds Youth Officers i.e. IR£7,000 per youth officer per year).

7.3.11 INCREASED REPRESENTATION OF WOMEN IN SEANAD ÉIREANN

The Commission is of the view that it is possible to increase the number of women in Seanad Éireann dramatically without having to amend the Constitution.

At present, Seanad Éireann has 60 members. Of these, 43 are elected by members of the Oireachtas and members of county and county borough councils; six are elected by NUI and Dublin University graduates; and the remaining eleven are nominated by the Taoiseach.

The 43 Senators elected by members of the Oireachtas, county and county borough councillors, are elected to five different panels, each of which has between eleven and five seats. Within each panel a certain quota of members elected has to come from each of two sub-panels. Candidates for each of the panels are either on the 'nominating bodies' or 'Oireachtas' sub-panels. As originally conceived, the 'nominating bodies' sub-panel was intended to represent vocational and other interests. In practice the elected candidates on both sub-panels are invariably political party members.

The changed format which the Commission recommends is that the Government should replace the existing sub-panels by a 'Women's sub-panel' (comprised entirely of women) and a 'Men's sub-panel' (comprised entirely of men). The quota of candidates to be elected from each subpanel would remain unchanged, i.e., sixteen from each sub-panel. The existing bodies with nominating rights could retain them, as would the Oireachtas, and the electorate would remain unchanged.

This would guarantee a minimum of sixteen women and sixteen men elected on the five panels, with the gender composition of the remaining eleven (out of forty-three) being decided by the Seanad electorate of incoming TDs, outgoing senators and councillors.

With regard to the six University members, the Constitution was changed in 1979 to allow for the inclusion among this electorate of graduates from other Institutions of Higher Education. In introducing legislation to give this force, the Government could establish sub-panels to bring about the election of three women and three men.

Finally, the Taoiseach nominates eleven members to the Seanad. These could be comprised of men and women in proportions opposite to those of the eleven ex-quota candidates elected to the panel seats.

This would result in a Seanad Éireann comprised of 50% women and 50% men. The implementation of this proposal would have the inestimable benefit of bringing about equal representation in the Second House without requiring a referendum or being significantly more complicated than the current procedures for election to Seanad Éireann.

The Commission recommends that the Government implement a proposal as outlined to bring about equal representation by women and men in Seanad Éireann. The Commission also recommends that all the political parties in the Oireachtas should support the proposal and accordingly nominate equal numbers of women and men candidates for the panel seats.

7.3.12 INCREASED REPRESENTATION OF WOMEN IN DÁIL ÉIREANN

The Commission has set out at paragraphs 7.3.3 to 7.3.11 the measures which it believes the Government and individual political parties should undertake in order to facilitate the increased participation of women in politics and a fairer representation of women in the Oireachtas. The objective of these initiatives would be to establish a significantly large number of women in political life (at least 30% membership of the Dáil), so that the concerns of women are mainstreamed and their views heard. We would hope that the initiatives we have spelt out would result in many more women in Dáil Éireann. It is important that developments in the level of representation by women should be kept under review so that further initiatives can be taken, if necessary.

The Commission recommends that the Minister for Women's Affairs should keep the level of representation by women in Dáil Éireann under review so that if, ten years after publication of the Commission's Report there is still not a sufficient number of women TDs, the Minister can bring forward legislative proposals for gender quotas.

7.4 Policies

7.4.1 NOMINATING WOMEN TO THE BOARDS OF STATE-SPONSORED BODIES

In our First Statement to Government (April 1991) the Commission recommended that:

(a) in the current lifetime of the Boards of all State-sponsored bodies women should be appointed to all casual vacancies to be filled by direct Government appointment, unless there are objective criteria for appointing a man;

(b) as the Boards of State-sponsored bodies are reconstituted or set up, Government policy should guarantee a minimum of 40% of both men and women among the direct Government nominees.

The Government has accepted this recommendation and committed itself to work towards these guidelines. There are approximately 2,400 seats on the boards of State-sponsored bodies, with two-thirds of these being filled on the basis of direct appointment by Government. The remaining one-third of places are filled by individuals who, while appointed by the Government, are actually nominated by a range of nominating bodies who enjoy nominating rights or courtesies. The representation of women among those nominees is even lower, at 15%, than the number of direct women appointees, at 17% (1992 appointments).

The Commission recommends that the Government should require nominating bodies to practise a gender balance policy similar to that applied by the Government. In cases where nominating bodies only nominate one individual they could alternate terms of service between men and women.

7.4.2 WOMEN AND THE MANAGEMENT CULTURE

The low level of women represented on the Boards of State-sponsored bodies is indicative of a general culture which largely excludes women. In April 1992, Network, the organisation for women in business, industry, the professions and the arts, published research on the difficulties women face in access to senior management/board positions and the typical attributes of a board member.

The research suggested that one major reason for the dearth of women on boards of management was the fact that directors are almost invariably chosen from a small pool of personal business acquaintances of existing board members, particularly people whom board members have served with in the past, or are currently serving with on other boards. The selection of a candidate, as with other board decisions, is generally made by consensus agreement rather than a majority decision. These factors contribute to a very conservative process for the selection of new board members, making it very difficult for women, even when they have the necessary business experience, to break into the selection process. Board members tend to be wary of anybody who might disrupt the existing atmosphere of the board, and 'anybody', regrettably, often includes women. This finding underlines the importance of the Government's acceptance of the recommendation of the Commission's First Statement (April 1991) that there should be a gender balance among appointees to State Boards, and of the recommendation at 7.3.1 above. The Commission believes that the increased presence of women on State boards should over time lead to a widening of the pool from which directors are appointed in the private sector.

7.4.3 CONSULTATION AND REPRESENTATION OF WOMEN

Until such time as women are equally represented at a local, national and European level in politics, administration and decision-making, women's views and perspectives are unlikely to be taken fully into consideration by policy makers. The Commission, therefore, recommends that consultation with women's groups on a local and national basis should form an integral part of policy making. At the moment, women's interests and national women's organisations are treated much less seriously than youth organisations in terms of consultation and funding. Contrast the National Youth Council (NYCI) funding of IR£205,000 with the Council for the Status of Women's funding of IR£114,000 (1991 figures). Similarly, one youth organisation, the NYCI, is represented on the National Economic and Social Council; in the PESP, another youth organisation, Macra na Feirme, takes part as a component body in the Government's dialogue with the social partners.

The Commission recommends that women should be recognised as a factor in the social partner equation. In particular, we recommend that women's interests should be represented on the NESC and that there should be 40% representation of women on Bord Pleanala and on the boards of bodies with responsibility for education and training, such as VECs, Eolas, Teagasc, FÁS and CERT.

7.4.4 WOMEN ON THE SOCIAL PARTNER AGENDA

In principle, in their dialogue with Government, the designated social partners represent the women members of their respective interest groups. In practice, these discussions take place almost exclusively among men because such is the composition of the Central Review Committee, the PESP's primary forum for discussion and decision-taking (see paragraph 7.2.5). Decisions taken in the context of the PESP impact on the income and quality of life of everyone in the community. Indeed, it is probably the most important economic and social forum in the State outside the Oireachtas. The fact is that women working in the home, 49% of adult women, are not specifically included among parties to the PESP.

The question arising is how can women, and agendas set by women, be brought fully into the social partner equation in the context of all future programmes similar to the PESP?

The Commission recommends that the following strategy should be set in place:

(A) PRE-PROGRAMME CONSULTATION

A consultation process should be carried out by the Programme secretariat and management team on a systematic and planned basis to assist in formulating the programme agenda (a certain amount of such consultation already took place in drawing up the PESP). The purpose of this consultation process is to provide a focus and context which complements the negotiations of the social partners.

For women's interests, we believe that the appropriate body to fill this consultative role is the Council for the Status of Women.

(B) ADVISORY COMMITTEE

The second stage of the process should be that an Advisory Committee drawn from consultative groups such as the Council for the Status of Women should link in to the Programme's Central Review Committee via the programme secretariat and management team in order to monitor progress of the programme. One of the main functions of this committee would be to keep items of concern active on the Programme agenda.

7.4.5 LEVEL OF FUNDING OF COUNCIL FOR THE STATUS OF WOMEN

At paragraph 7.4.2 above, we have referred to the fact that the State recognises the role of the Council for the Status of Women as representative of women's interests and concerns. We have also commented on the Council's under-funding. The Council for the Status of Women (CSW) provides women's organisations at local, regional and national level with a forum in which women's views, opinions, experience and perspectives can be shared and developed.

Through its work at national level the CSW brings such views and perspectives to bear on policy and decision-making, while at the same time encouraging and supporting the work of its affiliates and other women's groups to work locally and regionally.

The CSW's development of training for women (as exemplified by the NOW programme) and the development of leadership and developmental programmes for women's groups around the country should be supported and promoted.

The Commission recommends that the annual grant to the Council for the Status of Women should be doubled at least.

7.5 Women's affairs: policy-making
7.5.1 PRESENT SITUATION

As of November 1992, the situation as regards policy issues is that the Taoiseach has assigned specific responsibilities for women's affairs to all members of the Government, each in his/her area of responsibility.

In addition, the Taoiseach has appointed a Minister of State with responsibility for Women's Affairs. The Commission welcomes the appointment of a Minister of State with responsibility for functions of a monitoring and coordinating nature.

We note, however, that of necessity, this responsibility is of a part-time and reactive nature: among other factors the Minister of State also holds the demanding portfolio of European Affairs.

7.5.2 CABINET MINISTER FOR WOMEN'S AFFAIRS

In the view of the Commission, the situation as outlined in paragraph 7.5.1 is unsatisfactory as an organisational response to the concerns and needs of women. We believe that the organisation of Ministerial portfolios should ensure that there is a Government Minister at the Cabinet table able to comment – from women's perspectives and taking account of women's needs – on items brought before Government for decision.

The Commission has already sought to tackle this issue by the recommendation in our First Statement to Government that every Memorandum for Government should set out the probable impact on women of the proposed policy change. The Government accepted this recommendation and its implementation should, in our view, bring about, over time, a greater appreciation of and attention to the fact that policy decisions can impact differently on men and women.

Implementation of that recommendation, while important in itself, needs to be complemented by the appointment of an advocate for women's interests at the primary decision-making body in the State: the Cabinet table.

The Commission believes that the Minister for Women's Affairs should be appointed with a mandate of
- progressing equality and equal opportunities;
- assisting women's support and development organisations.

It should be possible to staff this Department by redeployment of existing civil servants.

The Commission recommends the establishment of a Department of Women's Affairs, headed by a Minister of Cabinet rank, with its own budget, staff and policy areas.

7.5.3 DEPARTMENT OF WOMEN'S AFFAIRS – POLICY FUNCTIONS

The Commission envisages the Department of Women's Affairs as being trans-sectoral in terms of the issues it deals with, i.e., issues of concern to it could arise in all Government Departments. In this way its role would be similar to the Department of Finance or Department of Foreign Affairs rather than to a line Department such as Health or Agriculture and Food.

The particular operational mechanisms for monitoring implementation of equality and equal opportunities across the range of Government policy, such as an interdepartmental committee, would be one of the most important first decisions of this Department.

The Commission recommends the following as constituting the main responsibilities of the Department of Women's Affairs within the overall policy aims set out at paragraph 7.5.2:

- monitoring implementation of the recommendations of the Commission; the development of policy initiatives;
- serving as national focal point for periodic national reports required under United Nations Convention on the Elimination of All Forms of Discrimination against Women;
- participating in appropriate forums of EC, OECD, Council of Europe, etc., with regard to policy-making on issues of concern to women.

THE RESPONSE OF THE GOVERNMENT AND THE PARTIES

In 1979 women accounted for 9.6 per cent of the membership of the boards of state-sponsored bodies. The proportion was not much higher by 1993, when the National Women's Council of Ireland (NWCI) successfully urged the Second Commission to recommend quotas; or by 1997, when the NWCI published *Who Makes the Decisions in 1997?*, the fourth in its series of reports on the issue, in which it pointed out that 'If that rate of progress was maintained, at around two percentage points increase every four years, . . . it would take 80 years to achieve balanced participation'.[2]

It is not perhaps very surprising, then, that the Second Commission, having seen the membership of women on state boards increase from about 9 per cent in 1972 to 15 per cent in 1992, called for the establishment of a 40 per cent quota for women on these boards and for the selection of women only to fill vacancies in the lifetime of then current boards.

In 1991 the Government adopted a policy of seeking to achieve increased gender representation on boards, as the

Commission urged even before it issued its report. The proportion of women appointed increased to the extent that by 1996 it was 26 per cent and by 1998 it was 29 per cent. The Department of Education made gender representation a requirement for university and other boards, but other departments relied on persuasion.[3] By 1998 some 31 per cent of the 224 state-sponsored bodies had exceeded their quota of 40 per cent, but the NWCI was calling attention to the fact that, as of 1997, of the 211 nationally appointed boards, 172 had male chairpersons and only 39 had women chairs. The non-binding policy was less persuasive to the non-governmental organisations that made nominations to these boards, and they still nominated proportionately fewer women than government departments did. The 'social partners' which in Ireland means the trade unions, business associations and agricultural organisations, were also slow to respond to the drive for quotas.

The Second Commission also called for the creation of a Department of Women's Affairs, headed by a cabinet minister, to promote equality between the sexes, opportunities for women, and the interests and activities of women's organisations. Such a department has not yet been created. The political parties adopted different policies in response to increased pressure for greater participation by women in their organisations and as candidates in elections. Women had joined parties in greater numbers during the 1980s and 1990s, in response to the general increase in women's public activity. By 1998 women represented about 33 per cent of the memberships of both Fianna Fáil and Fine Gael, 40 per cent in the Labour Party and about 50 per cent in the Progressive Democrats (a relatively new party that had broken away from Fianna Fáil). On the national executives of the parties in 1998 the proportions were 30 per cent for Fianna Fáil, 21.4 per cent for Fine Gael, 26.3 per cent for Labour and 46.6 per cent for the Progressive Democrats. When compared to the figures for 1972 (given above), it is clear that there had been significant gains in women's representation within the leadership of the four main parties.

Each party had in fact approached the issue in its own way. Fianna Fáil, the party that had been the largest in the Dáil ever since the 1930s, had attracted Constance Markievicz and other outstanding women to its ranks when it was founded in the 1920s, but it had marginalised women from leadership positions, both at the local and the national level, by the time it entered government. In 1977 the party leader, Jack Lynch, had added women to the list of Fianna Fáil candidates in the general election for the Dáil, bringing the number to ten, which at that time represented 40 per cent of the 25 women candidates from all parties, or 6.6 per cent of the 376 candidates standing. In 1981 the party established a Women's Consultative Committee. Its name was changed to the National Women's Committee in 1985 and then it was transformed in 1996 into the Fianna Fáil National Women's Forum. An annual women's conference was initiated and women's coordinators were appointed in the constituencies to increase party membership and give voice to women's issues.[4] However, Fianna Fáil rejected the use of quotas, relying instead on the exhortation and encouragement of women. In their study of gender and Irish party politics, Yvonne Galligan and Rick Wilford argue that the strategy 'was slow to take effect' and that only modest progress was made in the 1990s, with the notable exception of Fianna Fáil's decision to nominate Mary McAleese for the presidency in 1997.

By the middle of the 1990s Fianna Fáil's position on achieving equality and greater opportunities for women included policies on women's health, economic independence and the divorce referendum. Only in 1997 did the party begin to move closer to the recommendations of the Second Commission on issues such as extension of social insurance to part-time workers and legal representation for women alleging rape and sexual assault. A shift in the party's position on moving more women into decision-making positions became evident in its manifesto commitment, also in 1997, to introducing 'quotas and targets for women as a medium-term strategy'.[5] Galligan and Wilford note that this shift in Fianna Fáil's position with respect to women was geared to appeal to working women, while its manifesto's references to women as mothers and homemakers were intended to appeal to women working in the home. In line with its ideological heritage as the party founded, and led for decades, by Eamon de Valera, the social conservative who wrote the Irish Constitution, Fianna Fáil's approach to women's issues is thus not aimed at changing the traditional role of women, or the gendered division of labour, but rather at easing the pressures of changing conditions impinging on traditional women's roles.

Fine Gael, sharing both its origins and the orientation toward women with Fianna Fáil, did not welcome women into its leadership stratum in the early years of the state. Governments formed by Cumann na nGaedheal, as Fine Gael was initially known, enacted measures such as the Civil Service Act, which forbade women civil servants from working after marriage. The conservative base of the party shared the broader social beliefs that a woman's place was as mother and homemaker. However, under the leadership of Garret FitzGerald in the 1980s there was an increase in the proportion of women in leadership positions and a greater interest in raising issues of concern to women. A Women's Group was established within the party in 1985. In the 1990s the party's efforts to increase the number of women in senior leadership positions led to their holding positions in proportion to their membership in the party, at 33 per cent; a women's officer was also appointed. Nevertheless, Fine Gael was not committed to introducing quotas for women and its manifesto for the general election in 1997, entitled *Securing a Safer Society*, did not particularly emphasise women's issues as such, but rather folded them into general policies on crime and other issues.[6] Fine Gael nominated Mary Banotti for the presidency in 1997, a move that reflected its reaction to the election of Mary Robinson in 1990 and the weak performance of its own candidate, Austin Currie, in the presidential election that Ms Robinson won.

The Labour Party was historically no more receptive to notions of equality for women than the other major parties were, and its ability to strike out in new directions has always been limited by its third-party status (which has led it into several coalitions with Fine Gael and one brief alliance with Fianna Fáil). From the 1960s onwards, however, Labour broadened its agenda and recognised that, while the formal ideology of the party was participatory and inclusive, its practices were not. A National Women's Committee, founded in 1971, sought to raise the issues of participation and woman-friendly policy, but it was not incorporated into the Labour Party's structures until 1979. It later changed its name to the Labour Women's National Council. In 1981 Labour reserved two seats for women on its National Executive. It adopted a quota system in 1991, mandating 20 per cent representation of women in its constituency organisations and among its candidates in elections. By 1995 the quotas had risen to 25 per cent, and the party promised an eventual rise to 40 per cent. The fact that Mary Robinson, Ireland's first woman President, had been Labour's nominee for the office in 1990 proved symbolically significant for the party, which in 1997 nominated another woman, Adi Roche, for the presidency, in an election in which all the candidates were women. The Labour Party's manifesto for the general election in 1997, *Making the Vital Difference*, incorporated an extensive agenda of policy proposals with respect to women in the areas of equality, workplace rights, education and representation. Labour appeared to be more committed than the other three main parties to recognising and reinforcing the changing role of women in Irish society.

The Progressive Democrats have consistently had a high level of participation by women in their constituency organisations and they were the first Irish party to be led by a woman. Mary Harney, who had been a co-founder of the party in 1985, assumed the leadership in 1993. Her high visibility had the effect of drawing women to the party, which, being smaller than the other three main parties and a relatively newer party, offered a higher degree of access and mobility for women. Although the Progressive Democrats had no official policy favouring quotas for women, it also lacked the ingrained habits and attitudes that still tended to hamper or exclude women's participation in the older parties. The party does not have a separate women's group and its approach to policy is gender-neutral in that the commitment to women's equality is taken as given. Thus its manifesto for the general election in 1997, *A New Deal*, had no extended articulation of policy toward women. Galligan and Wilford suggest that this represents a rather sterile, 'technocratic' approach to women's issues and does not convey any sensitivity to the complex religious, social and biological norms that condition the place of women in Irish society.[7]

Finally, two minor parties, the Green Party and Democratic Left, entered the Oireachtas only after women's participation had become a major issue. The former had originated as a pressure group, the Green Alliance, that was already committed to gender equality, and it maintained this position after winning a seat in the Dáil for the first time in 1989. The latter was founded in 1992 as the final vehicle for a group of socialists who had broken away from Sinn Féin in 1970 (it has since merged with the Labour Party). It was therefore predictable that both these parties would rapidly and enthusiastically adopt quotas of 40 per cent for representation of women within their organisations and among their candidates. Thus, by 1997 all the parties represented in the Oireachtas had at last accepted that it was their duty to promote women's interests.

Conclusion

Margaret Ward gave the title *The Missing Sex: Putting Women into Irish History* to her book on the absence of women from Irish historiography (Dublin: Attic Press, 1991). In the policy domain covered by this book, the period from 1922 to 1972 could be seen as the period of 'the missing sex', while the period from 1972 to 1997 could be seen as one of 'putting women into Irish public policy'. If the first fifty years of the Irish state excluded women, then the next twenty years were concerned with treating women equally. The 1990s could be seen as the period in which women began to be treated justly.

As we stated in the Introduction, the *Report to Minister for Finance* submitted by the first Commission on the Status of Women in 1972 remains the watershed document in a story that reflects, not a only a shift in the content of policy, but also a shift in attitudes toward women in the political culture. With few exceptions, the policies applied between 1922 and 1972 were reflective of a traditional culture in which the status of women was not essentially different, except for the right to vote, from what it had been before the granting of autonomy to Ireland in 1922. The dominant idea of individual rights excluded women, and was confined to males with power and property. The claims of the first stage of the women's suffragist movement at the turn of the century, on such issues as the workplace, the legal system, child abuse or domestic violence, were not to be realised in the Free State. The fight for women's suffrage was the first effort to reinforce the idea that, in the shift of power from London to the Irish people, the people should include all those living in the new state, not just men.

The quest for the rights of women in Ireland can, then, be construed as having four stages, only two of which are covered in depth in this book. The first was the initial movement for the right to vote, and the extension of the claims on rights made by women, through the women's suffrage movement. That movement had been played out before 1922.

In Ireland the second stage lasted from the granting of autonomy from Britain in 1922 until 1972. The status of women in this period, characterised by cultural and religious elevation coupled with political and economic exclusion, was not unlike their status in other nation states in Europe at the time, but it was infused with a particular image of the place of women in the Catholic Church's view of the family. Ireland remained untouched by the changes that occurred after 1957 in the other European states that formed what is now the European Union. The third stage could be called the 'equality contract', as the 1970s witnessed a series a changes in the law and policy, calling for the equal treatment of women in the realm of employment and state services. This stage was focused on issues of formal equality and the rectification of discrimination, and thus there was an emphasis on the idea that women should be treated in the same ways as men.

The fourth stage shifted the agenda to issues in which formal equality had always pretty much existed, such as the illegality of violence, access to education or treatment for health problems, but effectively spotlighted the practices that made them discriminatory towards women. In this stage emphasis was placed on the fact that women should not be treated exactly like men because that would be punitive or exclusionary. Discussion of the issues of rape and domestic violence reflected the double standard that existed, and suggested that women should be treated differently under certain circumstances. Informal exclusion from educational opportunities was shown to be as damaging to the future of young women as explicitly discriminatory wage rates. The fact that women have different health issues was shown to lead to their exclusion whenever health policy did not take that difference into account. The agenda thus shifted from being a domestically driven, and increasingly long, list of specific policy complaints – as reflected in the report of the Second Commission on the Status of Women, with its fifty-one pages of recommendations – to an international agenda of women's rights, marked by claims of fundamental equality, to be recognised by such legislation as the Equality Act 1998, which excludes all forms of discrimination on any invidious basis.

While the women's movement in Ireland was still in its earliest stages in the late 1960s, Ireland's entry into the European Economic Community (now the European Union) in 1973 was a driving force behind the changes that occurred in the second stage of equality in employment and state services. The effects of membership of the European Union cannot be overstated in the realm of equality legislation, for European directives have been as important as the domestic political environment. Although the original Treaty of Rome of 1956 called for equal pay for women, and subsequent directives called for equality in pay among member states by 1964, neither goal had been achieved. Thus the report of the first Commission on the Status of Women helped to mobilise women in Ireland behind the European directives against discrimination and compelled the Irish government to respond with legislation on equal pay and, later, employment, social security and pensions.

The women's movement and the various organisations reflecting the different ideologies of feminism also came to play an increasingly important role in the shift from the third stage, of formal equality, to the fourth stage of equality, which recognised and valued gender difference within law and policy. Feminism as a movement immediately generates favourable and unfavourable responses, and, further, raises the question of what particular feminist lens one uses to focus on power and change. As M. McIntosh has put it, 'There is never an entirely acceptable stance for outsiders toward a movement of liberation.'[1] However, this book is content to identify the women's movement as a stimulus to the pressure group activity that helped to effect the policy changes noted in the various chapters. Feminism was also very important in changing the consciousness that prevailed in Irish culture. The pressure from the formal organisations not only kept the treatment of women at the forefront of debate, but also pointed out the assumptions and values that undergirded the policies of the second stage of women's rights in Ireland. Triggering the opposition to proposals on abortion and divorce, the women's movement in effect demanded that practices and values that had long been taken for granted would now have to be either justified or abandoned. In doing so the women's movement addressed questions of religious values, pluralism, individualism and the very sexist texture of Irish society.

We should not minimise the impact of European directives on the fourth stage of women's rights in Ireland. Directives on sexual harassment (1990), maternity leave (1992), child care (also 1992) and parental leave (1996) have been important stimulants to change in Irish legislation. Finally, during the 1990s the European Union also produced directives on mainstreaming gender issues, requiring gender impact statements and gender proofing in all legislation in 1996.

The convergence of European directives with the rise of the Irish women's movement contributed to the expansion of the movement's own agenda, from pressing for equal opportunity to raising the much wider issue of the place of women in Irish society. The way in which the feminist movement effected the degree and rapidity of the changes is charted in detail in works such as Linda Connolly, *The Irish Women's Movement: From Revolution to Devolution* (New York: Palgrave, 2002) and Yvonne Galligan, *Women and Politics in Contemporary Ireland* (London: Pinter, 1998).

We can conclude with three observations. The first is that the agenda of women's rights in Ireland is far from having been fully achieved. The treatment of more marginalised women became clear in the increasing awareness of women and the work of the Council for the Status of Women. The poor, the rural, the elderly, prisoners and Travellers are hardly in commanding positions when it comes to access to resources and claims on the rights to have them. The policies that have been announced and formally implemented still need to be fully executed, as for example, on the question of equal pay for equal work, which is far from being in place throughout the Irish economy. The paternal culture will not disappear overnight. Second, the women's movement has been, and will doubtless continue to be, an umbrella that covers a range of different and even incompatible views about the status of women in Ireland. They range from claims for equal treatment and a gender-blind society to assaults on male domination, sexism and patriarchy. Third, opposition to the women's movement has been mobilised and is engaged in what Tom Garvin has called 'the politics of denial and cultural defence', invoking an imaginary past and then sanctifying it by rejecting all change since the period of the imagined ideal.[2] With respect to women, this ideal sanctifies the family model, within which women ought to remain at home. Claims that the family ideal is being eroded through excessive individualism and materialism will continue to be part of the value landscape that confronts all attempts to make changes in policy.

The fourth stage in the quest for women's rights in Ireland is now in process, and it has been only partially excavated in this book. The policies that emerged in health and education in the 1990s, the quest for political participation, and the demand that modern Ireland be freed from covert or overt sexism in textbooks and advertisements, and elsewhere, will continue. The fight will be dealing with more elusive attitudes and practices than the more obvious laws and policies of the past. Just as the United States has found that dealing with racist attitudes is more difficult than dealing with formalised discrimination, so Ireland will find that dealing with sexism is more difficult than dealing with the kind of discrimination that can be combated by legal means alone.

List of Stationery Office Publications excerpted:

The Committee on the Constitution, *Report of the Committee on the Constitution*, 1967

Commission on the Status of Women, *Report to the Minister for Finance*, 1972

The Task Force on Violence Toward Women, *The Report of the Task Force on Violence Toward Women*, 1977

Working Party on Women's Affairs and Family Law Reform, *Irish Women: Agenda for Practical Action*, 1985

Joint Committee on Marriage Breakdown, *The Report of the Committee on Marriage Breakdown*, 1985

Oireachtas Joint Committee on Women's Rights, *Report on Sexual Violence*, 1987

Social Welfare Commission, *Report of the Social Welfare Commission*, 1988

Law Reform Commission, *Rape and Allied Offences*, 1988

Law Reform Commission, *Child Sexual Abuse*, 1989

Working Group on the Elimination of Sexism and Sex Stereotyping in Textbooks and Teaching Materials in the National Schools, *Report of the Working Group on the Elimination of Sexism and Sex Stereotyping in Textbooks and Teaching Materials in the National Schools*, 1992

Second Commission on the Status of Women, *Report to Government*, 1993

The Monitoring Committee on the Implementation of the Recommendations of the Second Commission on the Status of Women: *Second progress Report of The Monitoring Committee on the Implementation of the Recommendations of the Second Commission on the Status of Women*, 1996

Constitutional Review Group, *Report of the Constitutional Review Group*, 1996

Department of Health, *Putting Children First: Promoting and Protecting the Rights of Children*, 1997

Department of Health, *A Plan for Women's Health 1997–1999*, 1997

Bibliography

Barry, Bernadette, *Women at Home: A Report on Nationwide Get-togethers* (Dublin: Council for the Status of Women, 1983)

Barry, Ursula, 'The Contemporary Women's Movement in the Republic of Ireland', in Ailbhe Smyth (ed.), *Feminism in Ireland: Women's Studies International Forum*, 11:4 (New York: Pergamon, 1988), pp.317–22

Barry, Ursula, 'Movement, Change and Reaction: The Struggle over Reproductive Rights in Ireland', in Ailbhe Smyth (ed.), *The Abortion Papers, Ireland* (Dublin: Attic Press, 1992)

Beale, J., *Women in Ireland: Voices of Change* (Dublin: Gill and Macmillan, 1986)

Beaumont, Catriona, 'Women and the Politics of Equality: The Irish Women's Movement, 1930–1943', in Maryann Gialanella Valiulis and Mary O'Dowd (eds), *Women and Irish History* (Dublin: Wolfhound, 1997), pp.185–205

Beaumont, Catriona, 'Gender, Citizenship and the State in Ireland, 1922–1990', in Scott Brewster, Virginia Crossman, Fiona Becket and David Alderson (eds), *Ireland in Proximity: History, Gender, Space* (London and New York: Routledge, 1999), pp.94–108

Blackwell, John, *Women in the Labour Force* (Dublin: Employment Equality Agency, 1986)

Blackwell, John, *Women in the Labour Force* (Dublin: Employment Equality Agency and University College Dublin Resource and Environmental Policy Centre, 1989)

Bradley, Anthony and Maryann Gialanella Valiulis (eds), *Gender and Sexuality in Modern Ireland* (MA: University of Massachusetts Press, 1997)

Breen, Richard, Damian F. Hannan, David B. Rottman and Christopher T. Whelan (eds), *Understanding Contemporary Ireland: State, Class and Development in the Republic of Ireland* (Dublin: Macmillan, 1990)

Brown, Alice and Yvonne Galligan, 'Views from the Periphery: Changing the Political Agenda for Women in the Republic of Ireland and Scotland', *West European Politics,* 16, 2 (1993), pp.165–89

Callan, Tim and Brian Farrell, *Women's Participation in the Irish Labour*

Market (Dublin: National Economic and Social Council, PI. 84491, 1991)

Carabine, J., 'Constructing Women, Sexuality and Social Policy', *Critical Social Policy*, 34 (1992), pp.23–37

Carney, C., E. Fitzgerald, G. Keely and P. Quinn, *The Cost of a Child: Report On the Financial Cost of Child-rearing in Ireland* (Dublin: Combat Poverty Agency, 1994)

Casey, Maeve, *Domestic Violence Against Women: The Women's Perspective* (Dublin: Federation of Women's Refuges, 1987)

Clancy, Mary, 'Aspects of Women's Contribution to the Oireachtas Debate in the Irish Free State, 1922–37', in Maria Luddy and Cliona Murphy (eds), *Women Surviving: Studies in Irish Women's History in the 19th and 20th Centuries* (Dublin: Poolbeg, 1990), pp.206–32

Connolly, Alpha (ed.), *Gender and the Law in Ireland* (Dublin: Oak Tree Press, 1993)

Connolly, Brid and Anne B. Ryan (eds), *Gender and Education in Ireland*, vols I and II (Maynooth: MACE, 1999)

Connolly, Eileen, 'The Republic of Ireland's Equality Contract: Women and Public Policy', in Yvonne Galligan, Eilis Ward and Rick Wilford (eds), *Contesting Politics: Women in Ireland North and South* (Boulder, CO: Westview Press, 1999), pp.75–89

Connolly, Linda, *The Irish Women's Movement: From Revolution to Devolution* (New York: Palgrave, 2002)

Conroy Jackson, Pauline, 'Women's Movement and Abortion: The criminalization of Irish Women', in Drude Dahlerup (ed.), *The New Women's Movement: Feminism and Political Power in Europe and the USA* (London: Sage, 1987), pp.48–63

Cook, G. and A. McCashin, 'Male Breadwinner: A Case Study of Gender and Social Security in the Republic of Ireland', in A. Byrne and M. Leonard (eds), *Women and Irish Society: A Sociological Reader* (Belfast: Beyond the Pale, 1997), pp.167–80

Coogan, Tim Pat, *Disillusioned Decades: Ireland 1966–1987* (Dublin: Gill and Macmillan, 1987)

Coulter, Carol, *The Hidden Tradition: Feminism, Women and Nationalism in Ireland* (Cork: Mercier Press, 1993)

Council for Social Welfare, *A Statement on Family Law Reform* (Dublin: Council for Social Welfare, 1974)

Council for the Status of Women, *Submission on Rape in Ireland* (Dublin: Council for the Status of Women, 1978)

Council for the Status of Women, *Who Makes the Decisions?* (Dublin: Council for the Status of Women, 1985)

Council for the Status of Women, *Submission to the Commission on the Status of Women* (Dublin: Council for the Status of Women, 1991)

Cousins, M., *Social Welfare and the Law in Ireland* (Dublin: Gill and Macmillan, 1995)

Cullen-Owens, Rosemary, *Smashing Times: A History of the Irish Women's*

Suffrage Movement 1889–1922 (Dublin: Attic Press, 1984)

Curtin, Chris, Pauline Jackson and Barbara O'Connor (eds), *Gender in Irish Society* (Galway: Galway University Press, 1987)

Daly, Mary E., 'Women in the Irish Workforce from Pre-industrial to Modern Times', *Saothar*, 7 (1981), pp.74–82

Daly, Mary E., *Women and Poverty* (Dublin: Attic Press, 1989)

Daly, Mary E., 'Women in the Irish Free State, 1922–1939: The Interaction between Economics and Ideology', in Joan Hoff and Maureen Coulter (eds), *Irish Women's Voices Past and Present* (Indiana: Indiana University Press, 1995), pp.99–116

Daly, Mary E., '"Oh, Kathleen Ni Houlihan, Your Way's a Thorny Way!": The Condition of Women in Twentieth-Century Ireland', in Maryann Gialanella Valiulis and Anthony Bradley (eds), *Gender and Sexuality in Modem Ireland* (MA: University of Massachusetts Press, 1997), pp.102–26

Daly, Mary E., 'Women and Work in Ireland', *Studies in Irish Economic and Social History*, 7 (1997)

Department of Health, *Cancer Services in Ireland: A National Strategy* (Department of Health, 1996).

Donnelly, Aileen, 'Social Welfare Law', in Alpha Connolly (ed.), *Gender and the Law in Ireland* (Dublin: Oak Tree Press, 1993), pp.90–108

Doyle, Anne, 'Employment Equality Since Accession to the European Union', in G. Kiely, Anne O'Donnell, Patricia Kennedy and Suzanne Quinn (eds), *Irish Social Policy in Context* (Dublin: University College Dublin Press, 1999), pp.114–38

Drudy, Sheelagh and Kathleen Lynch, *Schools and Society in Ireland* (Dublin: Gill and Macmillan, 1994)

Dublin Rape Crisis Centre, *First Report* (Dublin: Dublin Rape Crisis Centre, 1979)

Duncan, William, *The Case for Divorce in the Irish Republic* (Dublin: Irish Council for Civil Liberties, 1979)

Eager, Clare, 'Splitting Images – Women and the Irish Civil Service', *Seirbhís Phoibli*, 12, 1 (1991), pp.15–23

Employment Equality Agency, *Women in the Labour Force* (Dublin: Employment Equality Agency, 1995)

Evans, Mary (ed.), *The Woman Question* (London: Sage, 1994)

Fahey, Tony and Christopher Whelan, 'Marriage and the Family', in Christopher T. Whelan (ed.), *Values and Social Change in Ireland* (Dublin: Gill and Macmillan, 1994), pp.45–81.

Fennell, Nuala and Mavis Arnold, *Irish Women: Agenda for Practical Action: A Fair Deal for Women, December 1982–1987, Four Years of Achievement* (Dublin: The Stationery Office for the Department of Women's Affairs and Family Law Reform, 1987)

Ferriter, Diarmaid, *Mothers, Maidens and Myth: A History of the Irish Countrywomen's Association* (Dublin: Irish Countrywomen's Association, 1994)

Finlay, Fergus, *Mary Robinson: A President with a Purpose* (Dublin: O'Brien Press, 1990)

Finnegan, Richard, *Ireland: The Challenge of Conflict and Change* (Boulder, CO: Westview Press, 1983)

Finnegan, Richard and James L. Wiles, *Aspirations and Realities: A Documentary History of Economic Development Policy in Ireland Since 1922* (Wesport, CO: Greenwood Press, 1993)

Finnegan, Richard and James L. Wiles, *A Guide to Irish Government Publications: 1972–1992* (Dublin: Irish Academic Press, 1995)

Finnegan, Richard and Edward McCarron, *Ireland: Historical Echoes, Contemporary Politics* (Boulder, CO: Westview Press, 2002)

Finnegan, Richard and James L. Wiles, *A Comprehensive Guide to Irish Government Publications: 1922–2000* (Dublin: Irish Academic Press, 2004)

Fitzsimons, Yvonne, 'Women's Interest Representation in the Republic of Ireland: The Council for the Status of Women', *Irish Political Studies*, 6 (1991), pp.37–52

Flanagan N., *Women and Poverty in the European Community: Issues in the Current Debate* (Dublin: University College Dublin Department of Social Policy and Social Work, 1993)

Flanagan, N. and V. Richardson, *Unmarried Mothers: A Sociological Profile* (Dublin: National Maternity Hospital Department of Social Policy and Social Work/Social Work Research Unit, 1992)

Galligan, Yvonne, 'Party Politics and Gender in the Republic of Ireland', in Joni Lovenduski and Pippa Norris (eds), *Gender and Party Politics* (London: Sage, 1993), pp.147–67

Galligan, Yvonne, *Women and Politics in Contemporary Ireland: From the Margins to the Mainstream* (London: Pinter, 1998)

Galligan, Yvonne, Eilis Ward and Rick Wilford (eds), *Contesting Politics: Women in Ireland, North and South* (Boulder CO: Westview Press/Political Studies Association of Ireland, 1999)

Galligan, Yvonne, 'Women in Politics', in John Coakley and Michael Gallagher (eds), *Politics in the Republic of Ireland* (London: Routledge, 1999), pp.294–319

Gardiner, Frances, 'Political interest and Participation of Irish Women, 1922–1992: The Unfinished Revolution', *Canadian Journal of Irish Studies*, 18, 1 (1992), pp.15–39

Gardiner, Frances, 'The Impact of EU Equality Legislation on Irish Women', in Yvonne Galligan, Eilis Ward and Rick Wilford (eds), *Contesting Politics: Women in Ireland, North and South* (Boulder CO: Westview Press/Political Studies Association of Ireland, 1999), pp.38–54

Garvin, Tom, 'The Politics of Denial and Cultural Defence: the Referenda of 1983 and 1986 in Context', *The Irish Review*, 3 (1988), pp.1–7

Gervin, Brian, 'The Divorce Referendum in the Republic, June 1986', *Irish Political Studies*, 2 (1987), pp.93–8

Gervin, Brian, 'Ireland and the European Union: The Impact of Integration and Social Change on Abortion Policy', in Marianne Githens and Dorothy McBride Stetson (eds), *Abortion Politics: Public Policy in Cross Cultural Perspective* (New York and London: Routledge, 1996), pp.165–88

Gray, Jane, 'Gender Politics and Ireland', in Joan Hoff and Maureen Coulter (eds), *Irish Women's Voices: Past and Present* (Indiana: Indiana University Press, 1995), pp.240–9

Hayes, Liz, 'Working for Change: A Study of Three Women's Community Groups', *Report Research Series* 8 (Dublin: Combat Poverty Agency, 1990)

Hesketh, Tom, *The Second Partitioning of Ireland: The Abortion Referendum of 1983* (Dublin: Brandsma Books, 1990)

Hussey, Gemma, *The Cutting Edge: Cabinet Diaries 1982–87* (Dublin: Gill and Macmillan, 1990)

Inglis, Tom, *Moral Monopoly. The Rise and Fall of the Catholic Church in Modem Ireland*, 2nd edn (Dublin: UCD Press, 1998)

Jackson, Nuala, 'Family Law: Economic Security', in Alpha Connelly (ed.), *Gender and the Law in Ireland* (Dublin: Oak Tree Press, 1993), pp.109–29

Jackson, Nuala, 'Family Law: Fertility and Parenthood', in Alpha Connelly (ed.), *Gender and the Law in Ireland* (Dublin: Oak Tree Press, 1993), pp.130–50

Jackson, Pauline, 'The Women's Movement and Abortion: The Criminalisation of Irish Women', in Drude Dahlerup (ed.), *The New Women's Movement. Feminism and Political Power in Europe and the US* (London: Sage, 1986), pp.48–63

Jackson, Pauline, 'Outside the Jurisdiction: Irish Women Seeking Abortion', in Chris Curtin, Pauline Jackson and Barbara O'Connor (eds), *Gender in Irish Society* (Galway: Galway University Press, 1987), pp.203–23

Joint Committee of the Oireachtas on Women's Rights, *Sexual Violence* (1987)

Joint Committee of the Oireachtas on Women's Rights, *Changing Attitudes to the Role of Women in Ireland: Attitudes Towards the Role and Status of Women 1975–1986* (PI. 5609, May 1988)

Joint Committee of the Oireachtas on Women's Rights, *Motherhood, Work and Equal Opportunity – A Case Study of Irish Civil Servants* (PI. 8249, July 1991)

Kelleher Associates and Monica O'Connor, *Making the Links: Towards an Integrated Strategy for the Elimination of Violence against Women in Intimate Relationships with Men* (Dublin: Women's Aid, 1995)

Kennedy, Finola, 'The Family in Transition', in Kieran A. Kennedy (ed.), *Ireland in Transition: Economic and Social Change Since 1960* (Cork: Mercier Press, 1986), pp.91–100

Kennedy, Patricia, 'Women and Social Policy', in G. Kiely, Anne O'Donnell, Patricia Kennedy and Suzanne Quinn (eds) *Irish Social*

Policy in Context (Dublin: University College Dublin Press, 1999), pp.231–53

Keogh, Dermot, *Twentieth Century Ireland: Nation and State* (Dublin: Gill and Macmillan, 1994)

King, Deborah, *Women at Work* (Dublin: An Gum, 1976)

Kingston, J., A. Whelan and I. Bacik, *Abortion and the Law* (Dublin: Round Hall Press, 1997)

Law Reform Commission, *Rape and Allied Offences* (Dublin: Law Reform Commission, LRC24–19881, 1988)

Lee, J.J., 'Women and the Church Since the Famine', in Margaret MacCurtain and Donnachadh O'Corrain (eds), *Women in Irish Society: The Historical Dimension* (Dublin: Arlen Press, 1978), pp.37–45

Lee, J.J., *Ireland 1912–1985: Politics and Society* (Cambridge: Cambridge University Press, 1989)

Lentin, Ronit, '"Irishness": The 1937 Constitution and Citizenship: A Gender and Ethnicity View', *Irish Journal of Sociology*, 8 (1998), pp.5–24

Lewis, J. (ed.), *Women and Social Policies in Europe: Work, Family and the State* (New York: Edward Elgar, 1993)

Luddy, Maria, *Women in Ireland 1800–1918: A Documentary History* (Cork: Cork University Press, 1995)

Luddy, Maria and Cliona Murphy (eds), *Women Surviving: Studies in Irish Women's History in the 19th and 20th Centuries* (Dublin: Poolbeg, 1990)

Lynch, Irene, 'Labour Law', in Alpha Connelly (ed.), *Gender and the Law in Ireland* (Dublin: Oak Tree Press, 1993), pp.47–89

McCashin, Anthony, *Lone Parents in the Republic of Ireland: Enumeration, Descriptions and Implications for Social Security*, Broadsheet Series, Paper No. 29 (Dublin: Economic and Social Research Institute, 1993)

McCashin, Anthony, *Lone Mothers in Ireland: A Local Study* (Dublin: Oak Tree Press, 1996)

MacCurtain, Margaret, 'Women, the Vote and Revolution', in Margaret MacCurtain and Donnachadh O'Corrain (eds), *Women in Irish Society: The Historical Dimension* (Dublin: Arlen Press, 1978), pp.46–57.

MacCurtain, Margaret and Donnachadh O'Corrain (eds), *Women in Irish Society: The Historical Dimension* (Dublin: Arlen Press, 1978)

Maher, Mary, 'Five Reasons Against a Referendum', in Mavis Arnold and Peader Kirby (eds), *The Abortion Referendum: The Case Against* (Dublin: Anti-Amendment Campaign, 1982), pp.9–12

Mahon, Evelyn, 'From Democracy to Femocracy: The Women's Movement in the Republic of Ireland', in Patrick Clancy, Sheelagh Drudy, Kathleen Lynch and Liam O'Dowd (eds), *Irish Society: Sociological Perspectives* (Dublin: Institute of Public Administration, 1995), pp.675–708

Mahon, Evelyn, Catherine Conlon and Lucy Dillon, *Women and Crisis Pregnancy: A Report Presented to the Department of Health and Children* (Dublin: The Stationery Office, 1998)

Mahon, Evelyn, 'State Feminism in Ireland', in Yvonne Galligan, Eilis Ward and Rick Wilford (eds), *Contesting Politics: Women in Ireland, North and South* (Boulder, CO: Westview Press, 1999), pp.55–73

Manning, Maurice, 'Women in Irish National and Local Politics 1922–77', in Margaret MacCurtain and Donnachadh O'Corrain (eds), *Women in Irish Society: The Historical Dimension* (Dublin: Arlen Press, 1978), pp.92–102

Manning, Maurice, 'Women and the Elections', in Howard R. Penniman and Brian Farrell (eds), *Ireland at the Polls 1981, 1982 and 1987 – A Study of Four General Elections* (Durham, NC: Duke University Press, 1988), pp.156–66

Millar, I., S. Leeper and C. Davies, *Lone Parents, Poverty and Public Policy* (Dublin: Combat Poverty Agency, 1992)

Mulvey, Cris, *Changing the View: Summary of the Evaluation Report on the Allen Lane Foundation's Programme for Women's Groups in Ireland 1989–1991* (Dublin: Allen Lane Foundation, 1992)

Murphy, Cliona, *The Women Suffrage Movement and Irish Society in the Early Twentieth Century* (London: Harvester, 1989)

National Economic and Social Forum, *Jobs: Potential of Job Sharing* (Dublin: National Economic and Social Forum, 1996)

National Women's Council of Ireland, *Report of the Working Party on the Legal and Judicial Process for Victims of Sexual and Other Crimes of Violence Against Women and Children* (Dublin: National Women's Council of Ireland, 1996)

Nolan, Brian and Dorothy Watson, *Women and Poverty in Ireland* (Dublin: Combat Poverty Agency, 1999)

O'Carroll, J.P., 'Bishops, Knights and Pawns? Traditional Thought and the Irish Abortion Referendum Debate of 1983', *Irish Political Studies*, 6 (1991), pp.53–71

O'Connor, Paul A., *Issues in Irish Family Law* (Dublin: Round Hall Press, 1988)

O'Connor, P., *Emerging Voices: Women in Contemporary Irish Society* (Dublin: Institute of Public Administration, 1998)

O'Dowd, Mary and Sabine Wichert (eds), *Chattel, Servant or Citizen: Women's Status in Church, State and Society* (Belfast: Institute of Irish Studies, 1995)

O'Leary, Cornelius and Tom Hesketh, 'The Irish Abortion and Divorce Referendum Campaigns', *Irish Political Studies*, 3 (1988), pp.43–62

O'Neill, Cathleen, *Telling It Like It Is* (Dublin: Combat Poverty Agency, 1992)

Randall, Vicky and Ailbhe Smyth, 'Bishops and Bailiwicks: Obstacles to Women's Political Participation in Ireland', *Economic and Social Review*, 18, 3 (1987), pp.189–214

Reid, Madeline, *The Impact of Community Law on the Irish Constitution* (Dublin: Irish Centre for European Law, 1988)

Riordan, Patrick, 'Abortion: The Aftermath of the Supreme Court's Decision', *Studies*, 81, 323 (1992), pp.293–302

Robinson, Mary, 'Women and the Law in Ireland', in Ailbhe Smyth (ed.), *Feminism in Ireland: Women's Studies International Forum*, 11, 4 (New York: Pergamon, 1988), pp.351–5

Rose, Catherine, *The Female Experience: The Story of the Woman's Movement in Ireland* (Galway: Arlen House, 1975)

Rose, Kieran, *Diverse Communities: The Evolution of Lesbian and Gay Politics in Ireland* (Cork: Cork University Press, 1994)

Rothman, D.B., *Income Distribution within Irish Households: Allocating Resources within Ireland*, Research Report Series No. 18 (Dublin: Combat Poverty Agency, 1994)

Rowley, Rosemary, 'Women and the Constitution', *Administration*, 37, 1 (1989), pp.42–62

Ryan, Louise (ed.), *Irish Feminism and the Vote: An Anthology of the* Irish Citizen *Newspaper 1912–1920* (Dublin: Folens, 1996)

Ryan, Louise, 'A Question of Loyalty: War, Nation and Feminism in Early Twentieth Century Ireland', *Women's Studies International Forum*, 20, 1 (1997), pp.21–32

Scannell, Yvonne, 'The Constitution and the Role of Women', in Brian Farrell (ed.), *De Valera's Constitution and Ours* (Dublin: Gill and Macmillan, 1988), pp.123–36

Shorthall, Sally, 'The Dearth of Data on Irish Farm Wives: A Critical Review of the Literature', *Economic and Social Review*, 22, 4 (1991), pp.311–32

Smyth, Ailbhe, 'Women and Power in Ireland: Problems, Progress, Practice', *Women's Studies International Forum*, 8, 4 (1985), pp.255–62

Smyth, Ailbhe (ed.), *Feminism in Ireland: Women's Studies International Forum*, 11, 4 (New York: Pergamon, 1988)

Smyth, Ailbhe (ed.), *The Abortion Papers: Ireland* (Dublin: Attic Press, 1992)

Smyth, Ailbhe (ed.), *Irish Women's Studies Reader* (Dublin: Attic Press, 1993)

Smyth, E., 'Labour Market Structures and Women's Employment in the Republic of Ireland', in A. Byrne and M. Leonard (eds), *Women and Irish Society: A Sociological Reader* (Belfast: Beyond the Pale, 1997), pp.63–80

Stationery Office, *Green Paper on Abortion* (Dublin: Government Publications Office, 1999)

Tansey, Jean, *Women in Ireland: A Compilation of Relevant Data* (Dublin: Council for the Status of Women, 1984)

Taylor, George (ed.), *Issues in Irish Public Policy* (Dublin: Irish Academic Press, 2002)

Townshend, Charles, *Ireland in The 20th Century* (London: Arnold, 1999)

Tweedy, Hilda, *A Link in the Chain: The Story of the Irish Housewives Association 1942–1992* (Dublin: Attic Press, 1992)

Valiulis, Maryann Gialanella and Mary O'Dowd (eds), *Women and Irish History* (Dublin: Wolfhound, 1997)

Walsh, Mary Ena, *Women in Rural Ireland* (Dublin: Council for the Status of Women, 1983)

Ward, Eilis and Orla O'Donovan, 'Networks of Women's Groups and Politics: What (Some) Women Think', *UCG Women's Studies Review* 4 (1996), pp.1–20

Ward, Margaret, *The Missing Sex: Putting Women into Irish History* (Dublin: Attic Press, 1991)

Wiley, M. and B. Merriman, *Women and Health Care in Ireland: Knowledge, Attitudes and Behaviour* (Dublin: Oak Tree Press in association with the Economic and Social Research Institute, 1996)

Yeates, N., 'Gender and the Development of the Irish Social Welfare System', in A. Byrne and M. Leonard (eds), *Women and Irish Society: A Sociological Reader* (Belfast: Beyond the Pale, 1997), pp.145–66

Notes

Introduction

1 See Linda Connolly, *The Irish Women's Movement* (New York: Palgrave 2002).
2 See Yvonne Galligan, *Women and Politics in Contemporary Ireland* (London: Pinter 1998).

Chapter 1

1 *Report of the Royal Commission on the Status of Women in Canada* (Ottawa: Information Canada, 1970).
2 Government Social Survey, *A Survey of Women's Employment* by Audrey Hunt, Vol. 1. SS 379.
3 Eileen Connolly, 'The Republic of Ireland's Equality Contract', in Yvonne Galligan et al. (eds), *Contesting Politics* (Boulder, CO: Westview Press, 1999), pp. 74–89.

Chapter 3

1 Aileen Donnelly, 'Social Welfare Law', in Alpha Connelly (ed.), *Gender and the Law in Ireland* (Dublin: Oak Tree Press, 1993), p. 90.
2 Social Welfare Commission, *Report of the Social Welfare Commission* (Dublin: Stationery Office, 1988), p. 25.
3 Donnelly, 'Social Welfare Law', p. 94.
4 Ibid.
5 Pat O'Connor, *Emerging Voices: Women in Contemporary Irish Society* (Dublin: IPA, 1998), p. 178.
6 Monitoring Committee on the Implementation of the Recommendations of the Second Commission on the Status of Women, *Second Progress Report* (Dublin: Government Publications, 1996), p. 58.
7 See Brian Nolan and Dorothy Watson, *Women and Poverty in Ireland* (Dublin: Combat Poverty Agency, 1999).
8 National Women's Council of Ireland, *Towards Women's Full Equality in the New Millennium* (Dublin: National Women's Council of Ireland, 1999), pp. 10–11.

Chapter 4

1   See Nuala Jackson, Chapter 6, 'Family Law: Economic Security', and Chapter 7, 'Family Law: Fertility and Parenthood', in Alpha Connelly (ed.), *Gender and the Law in Ireland* (Dublin: Oak Tree Press, 1993).
2   Information in this paragraph on community of property has been drawn from the British Law Commission Working Paper No. 42 referred to in the footnote on Page 175 [not included]. The difficulties and advantages of community systems are dealt with in detail in Part 5 of the Paper.
3   This section draws upon Jackson, 'Family Law: Fertility and Parenthood', pp. 136–43.

Chapter 5

1   B. Gervin, 'The Divorce Referendum in the Republic, June 1986', *Irish Political Studies*, 2 (1987), p. 98.
2   Third Report of the Second Joint Committee on Women's Rights, *Changing Attitudes to the Role of Women in Ireland: Attitudes towards Moral Issues in Relation to Voting Behaviour in Recent Referenda* (Dublin: Stationery Office, 1988), p. 2324.
3   D. Keogh, *Twentieth Century Ireland: Nation and State* (Dublin: Gill and Macmillan, 1994), pp. 333–37.
4   See Tom Hesketh, *The Second Partitioning of Ireland: The Abortion Referendum of 1983* (Dublin: Brandsma Books, 1990).
5   Constitutional Review Group, *Report of the Constitutional Review Group* (Dublin: Stationery Office, 1996), p. 230.

Chapter 6

1   Yvonne Galligan, *Women and Politics in Contemporary Ireland* (London: Pinter, 1998), p.113.
2   Ibid.
3   Council for the Status of Women, *Submission on Rape in Ireland* (Dublin: Council for the Status of Women, 1978).
4   Galligan, *Women*, p. 114.
5   Fourth Report of the Joint Committee on Women's Rights, *Sexual Violence* (Dublin: The Stationery Office, 1987), pp. 8–9.
6   Galligan, *Women*, p. 121.
7   In a close analysis of verdicts and sentences in rape cases Caroline Fennell has found that the language of the law on rape, including the reforms of 1990, still reflects a male image of rape and male language concerning the idea of rape as a sexual act and/or as a violent act, and finds that judges, while recognising the violence inherent in the act of rape itself, are inclined to be more severe in sentencing when the act is accompanied by other forms of violence towards the victim. See Caroline Fennell, 'Criminal Law and the Criminal Justice System: Women as Victim', in Alpha Connelly (ed.), *Gender and the Law in Ireland* (Dublin: Oak Tree Press, 1993), pp. 151–70.
8   *Report of the Working Party on the Legal and Judicial Process for the Victims of Sexual and Other Crimes of Violence Against Women and Children* (Dublin: Stationery Office, 1996). p. 120.

9   Galligan, *Women*, p. 2.
10 See Maeve Casey, *Domestic Violence Against Women: The Women's Perspective* (Dublin: Federation of Women's Refuges, 1987).
11 Galligan, *Women*, p. 134.
12 Kelleher Associates and Monica O'Connor, *Making the Links: Toward an Integrated Strategy for the Elimination of Violence Against Women in Intimate Relationships with Men* (Dublin: Women's Aid, 1995).
13 Law Reform Commission Consultation Paper: *Child Sexual Abuse* (Dublin: Law Reform Commission, 1989), quoting a pilot survey 'Child Sexual Abuse in Dublin', p. 6.
14 Pat O'Connor, *Emerging Voices: Women in Irish Society* (Dublin: Institute for Public Administration, 1998), pp. 117–18.

Chapter 9

1   Yvonne Galligan, 'Women in Politics', in John Coakley and Michael Gallagher (eds), *Politics in the Republic of Ireland* (third edition, London: Routledge, 1999), pp. 294–319; and Yvonne Galligan and Rick Wilford, 'Women's Political Representation in Ireland', in Yvonne Galligan, Eilis Ward and Rick Wilford (eds), *Contesting Politics: Women in Ireland, North and South* (Boulder, CO: Westview Press/Political Studies association of Ireland, 1999), pp. 140–45.
2   National Women's Council of Ireland, *Who Makes the Decisions in 1997?* (Dublin: National Women's Council of Ireland, 1997), p. ii.
3   Galligan and Wilford, 'Women's Political Representation', pp. 139–40.
4   Yvonne Galligan and Rick Wilford, 'Gender and Party Politics in the Republic of Ireland,' in Galligan, Ward and Wilford (eds), *Contesting Politics*, pp. 154–7.
5   Ibid., p. 157, quoting Fianna Fáil, *People Before Politics*, Manifesto (Dublin, 1997).
6   Ibid., p. 159.
7   Ibid., p. 161.

Conclusion

1   M. McIntosh, 'Feminism and Social Policy', in D. Taylor (ed.), *Critical Social Policy* (London: Sage, 1996), pp. 13–26.
2   Tom Garvin, 'The Politics of Denial and Cultural Defence: the Referenda of 1983 and 1986 in Context', *The Irish Review*, 3 (1988), pp. 1–7.